Fodor's

NAPA AND
SONOMA

WELCOME TO NAPA AND SONOMA

California's premier wine region, the pleasures of eating and drinking are celebrated daily. It's easy to join in at famous wineries and rising newcomers off country roads, or at trendy in-town tasting rooms. Chefs transform local ingredients into feasts, and gourmet groceries sell perfect picnic fare. Yountville, Healdsburg, and St. Helena have small-town charm as well as luxurious inns, hotels, and spas, yet the natural setting is equally sublime, whether experienced from a canoe on the Russian River or the deck of a winery overlooking endless rows of vines.

TOP REASONS TO GO

★ **Fine Wine:** Rutherford Cabernets, Carneros Chardonnays, Russian River Pinots.

★ **Spectacular Food:** Marquee Napa chefs, farmers' markets, Sonoma cheese shops.

★ **Cool Towns:** From chic Healdsburg to laid-back Calistoga, a place to suit every mood.

★ **Spas:** Mud baths, herbal wraps, couples' massages, and more in soothing settings.

★ **Winery Architecture:** Stone classics like Buena Vista, all-glass dazzlers like Hall.

★ **Outdoor Fun:** Biking past bright-green vineyards, hot-air ballooning over golden hills.

Fodor's NAPA AND SONOMA

Editorial: Douglas Stallings, *Editorial Director*; Salwa Jabado and Margaret Kelly, *Senior Editors*; Alexis Kelly, Jacinta O'Halloran, and Amanda Sadlowski, *Editors*; Teddy Minford, *Associate Editor*; Rachael Roth, *Content Manager*

Design: Tina Malaney, *Associate Art Director*

Photography: Jennifer Arnow, *Senior Photo Editor*

Maps: Rebecca Baer, *Senior Map Editor*; David Lindroth, Mark Stroud (Moon Street Cartography), *Cartographers*

Production: Jennifer DePrima, *Editorial Production Manager*; Carrie Parker, *Senior Production Editor*; Elyse Rozelle, *Production Editor*; David Satz, *Director of Content Production*

Business & Operations: Chuck Hoover, *Chief Marketing Officer*; Joy Lai, *Vice President and General Manager*; Stephen Horowitz, *Head of Business Development and Partnerships*

Public Relations: Joe Ewaskiw, *Manager*

Writer: Daniel Mangin

Editors: Margaret Kelly (lead editor); Alexis Kelly, Jacinta O'Halloran (editors)

Production Editor: Jennifer DePrima

Production Design: Liliana Guia

2nd Edition

ISBN 978-0-14-754686-9

ISSN 2375–9453

All details in this book are based on information supplied to us at press time. Always confirm information when it matters, especially if you're making a detour to visit a specific place. Fodor's expressly disclaims any liability, loss, or risk, personal or otherwise, that is incurred as a consequence of the use of any of the contents of this book.

PRINTED IN THE UNITED STATES OF AMERICA

10 9 8 7 6 5 4 3 2 1

CONTENTS

DID YOU KNOW?

The Dry Creek Valley north of Healdsburg is known for Zinfandel grapes, but Chardonnay, Sauvignon Blanc, Cabernet Sauvignon, and varietals from France's Rhône region are also grown here.

ABOUT THIS GUIDE

Fodor's Recommendations

Everything in this guide is worth doing—we don't cover what isn't—but exceptional sights, hotels, and restaurants are recognized with additional accolades. Fodor's Choice ★ indicates our top recommendations. Care to nominate a new place? Visit Fodors.com/contact-us.

Trip Costs

We list prices wherever possible to help you budget well. Hotel and restaurant price categories from **$** to **$$$$** are noted alongside each recommendation. For hotels, we include the lowest cost of a standard double room in high season. For restaurants, we cite the average price of a main course at dinner or, if dinner isn't served, at lunch. For attractions, we always list adult admission fees; discounts are usually available for children, students, and senior citizens.

Hotels

Our local writers vet every hotel to recommend the best overnights in each price category, from budget to expensive. Unless otherwise specified, you can expect private bath, phone, and TV in your room. For expanded hotel reviews, facilities, and deals visit Fodors.com.

Top Picks

★ Fodor's Choice

Listings

- ✉ Address
- ✉ Branch address
- ☎ Telephone
- 📠 Fax
- 🌐 Website
- ✉ E-mail
- 🎟 Admission fee
- 🕒 Open/closed times
- [M] Subway
- ✥ Directions or Map coordinates

Hotels & Restaurants

- 🏨 Hotel
- 🛏 Number of rooms
- 🍴 Meal plans
- W Restaurant
- ✍ Reservations
- 👔 Dress code
- 💳 No credit cards
- [$] Price

Other

- ⇨ See also
- ☞ Take note
- ⛳ Golf facilities

Restaurants

Unless we state otherwise, restaurants are open for lunch and dinner daily. We mention dress code only when there's a specific requirement and reservations only when they're essential or not accepted.

Credit Cards

The hotels and restaurants in this guide typically accept credit cards. If not, we'll say so.

EUGENE FODOR

Hungarian-born Eugene Fodor (1905–91) began his travel career as an interpreter on a French cruise ship. The experience inspired him to write *On the Continent* (1936), the first guidebook to receive annual updates and discuss a country's way of life as well as its sights. Fodor later joined the U.S. Army and worked for the OSS in World War II. After the war, he kept up his intelligence work while expanding his guidebook series. During the Cold War, many guides were written by fellow agents who understood the value of insider information. Today's guides continue Fodor's legacy by providing travelers with timely coverage, insider tips, and cultural context.

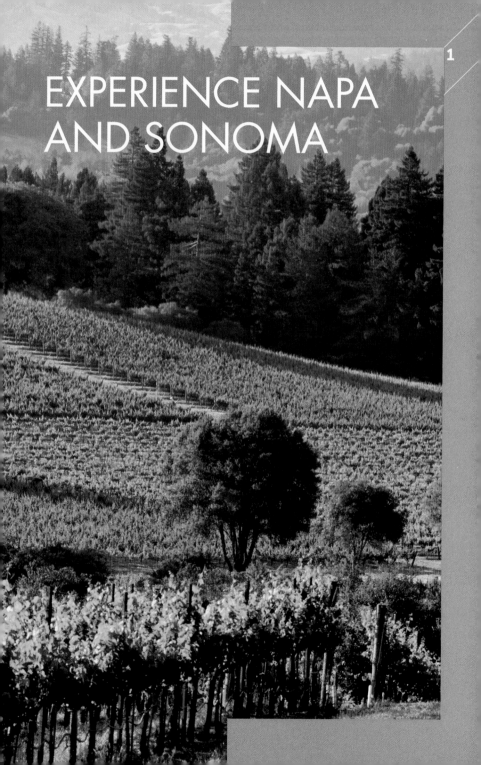

EXPERIENCE NAPA AND SONOMA

WHAT'S WHERE

The following numbers refer to chapters.

3 Napa Valley. By far the best known of the California wine regions, Napa is home to some of the biggest names in wine, many of which still produce the same bottles of Cabernet Sauvignon that first put the valley on the map. Densely populated with winery after winery, especially along Highway 29 and the Silverado Trail, it's also home to luxury accommodations, some of the country's best restaurants, and spas with deluxe treatments, some incorporating grape seeds and other wine-making by-products.

4 Sonoma Valley. Centered on the historic town of Sonoma, the Sonoma Valley goes easier on the glitz but contains sophisticated wineries and excellent restaurants. Key moments in California and wine-industry history took place here. Part of the Carneros District viticultural area lies within the southern Sonoma Valley. Those who venture into the Carneros will discover wineries specializing in Pinot Noir and Chardonnay. Both grapes thrive in the comparatively cool climate. Farther north, Cabernet Sauvignon and other warm-weather varietals are grown.

5 Northern Sonoma, Russian River, and West County. Ritzy Healdsburg is a popular base for exploring three important grape-growing areas, the Russian River, Dry Creek, and Alexander valleys. Everything from Chardonnay and Pinot Noir to Cabernet Sauvignon, Zinfandel, and Petite Sirah grows here. In the county's western parts lie the Sonoma Coast wineries, beloved by connoisseurs for European-style wines from cool-climate grapes.

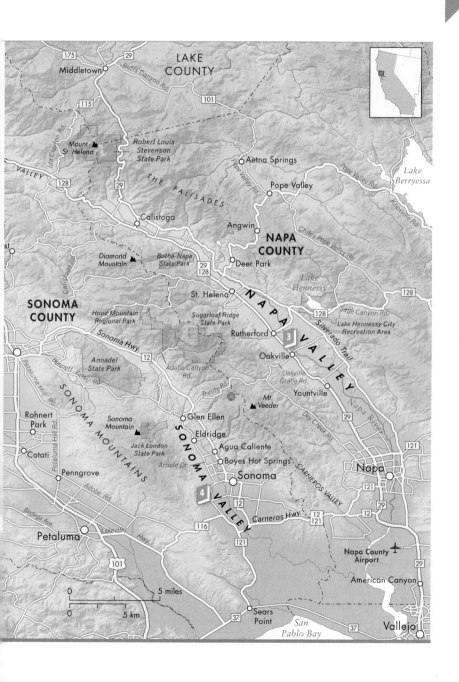

Middletown

LAKE
COUNTY

175

29

Butts Canyon Rd.

101

115

Ida Clayton Rd.

Mount
St. Helena

Robert Louis
Stevenson
State Park

Aetna Springs

Pope Valley

Pope Valley Rd.

Lake
Berryessa

VALLEY

128

THE PALISADES

29

Pope Valley Rd.

Knoxville Rd.

Calistoga

Angwin

NAPA
COUNTY

Chiles Pope Valley Rd.

Calistoga Rd.

Diamond
Mountain

Botha-Napa
State Park

29
128

Deer Park

Lake
Hennessy

SONOMA
COUNTY

Hood Mountain
Regional Park

St. Helena

128

NAPA

Sage Canyon Rd.

Lake Hennessy City
Recreation Area

Sonoma Hwy.

Sugarloaf Ridge
State Park

128

Rutherford

3

Silverado Trail

VALLEY

128

12

Annadel
State Park

Adobe Canyon
Rd.

Oakville

Oakville
Grade Rd.

Napa River

Bennett Valley Rd.

Trinity Rd.

Yountville

Rohnert
Park

SONOMA MOUNTAINS

Sonoma
Mountain

Glen Ellen

Mt.
Veeder

Dry Creek Rd.

29

Cotati

Jack London
State Park

Eldridge

Agua Caliente

Boyes Hot Springs

CARNEROS VALLEY

121

Penngrove

Arnold Dr.

SONOMA VALLEY

Sonoma

Napa

Adobe Rd.

4

12

121

Petaluma

Petaluma Hill Rd.

Lakeville Hwy.

116

Carneros Hwy.

12
121

12
29

Bodega Ave.

121

Napa County
Airport

29

101

0   5 miles

0   5 km

Sears
Point

37

San
Pablo Bay

American Canyon

37

Vallejo

NAPA AND SONOMA PLANNER

About the Restaurants

Farm-to-table modern American cuisine is the prevalent style in the Napa Valley and Sonoma County, but this encompasses both the delicate preparations of Yountville's Thomas Keller, whose restaurants include The French Laundry, and the upscale comfort food served throughout the Wine Country. The quality (and hype) often means high prices, but you can find appealing, inexpensive eateries, especially in Napa, Calistoga, Sonoma, and Santa Rosa. *For details and price-category information, see the charts in each regional chapter.*

About the Hotels

The fanciest accommodations are concentrated in the Napa Valley towns of Yountville, Rutherford, St. Helena, and Calistoga; Sonoma County's poshest lodgings are in Healdsburg. The spas, amenities, and exclusivity of high-end properties attract travelers with the means and desire for luxury living. The cities of Napa and Santa Rosa are the best bets for budget hotels and inns. *For details and price-category information, see the charts in each regional chapter.*

Getting Here and Around

San Francisco is the main gateway to Napa and Sonoma, which lie due north of the city. Driving is the best way to explore this region. The easiest route to southern Napa and Sonoma counties is to head north across the Golden Gate Bridge on U.S. 101 and east on Highway 37 to Highway 121. Follow signs for the towns of Sonoma (45 miles from San Francisco) and Napa (about 52 miles). Remain on U.S. 101 if your destination is Santa Rosa (55 miles) or Healdsburg (70 miles). Several roads lead from U.S. 101 into western Sonoma County.

By car. Roads are well maintained here, and distances between towns are fairly short: you can drive from one end to the other of either valley in less than an hour if there's no traffic. The Mayacamas Mountains divide Napa and Sonoma, though, and only a few winding roads traverse the middle sections, so the drive between valleys can be slow. The quicker connector is Highway 121, which runs east–west between southern Napa and Sonoma counties. The far-northern route—from Highway 128 just north of Calistoga, take Petrified Forest Road and Calistoga Road to Highway 12—has a few curves but rewards with great vistas.

By public transportation. Visitors without cars can take van, bus, or limo tours from San Francisco. Taking public transit to Sonoma, Napa, Santa Rosa, and Healdsburg can be time-consuming, but once you arrive at your destination, you can take advantage of taxis and other options. If you're determined not to drive, an enjoyable option from San Francisco is to board the San Francisco Bay Ferry bound for Vallejo. In Vallejo you can transfer to VINE Bus 29, whose stops include the transit hub in downtown Napa. *For more information about public transportation, see Getting Here and Around in the Travel Smart chapter. For more information about local bus service, see the Bus Travel sections for the individual towns.*

Planning Your Time

Many first-time visitors to the Wine Country pack as many wineries as possible into a short vacation. Besides being exhausting, this approach goes against the area's laid-back ethos. So you can experience the region without running yourself ragged, we've put together a few strategies for maximizing your winetasting fun.

Avoid driving during rush hour. From roughly 4 to 6 pm on weekdays the cars of tourists are joined by those of commuters, resulting in traffic jams. The worst bottlenecks occur on Highway 29 in both directions around St. Helena and southbound between Rutherford and northern Napa.

Get an early start. Tasting rooms are often deserted before 11 am. On the flip side, they're usually busiest between 3 and closing.

Slip off the beaten track. When Napa Valley's tasting rooms along Highway 29 and the Silverado Trail are jammed, those on Spring Mountain or in far northern Calistoga might be relatively uncrowded. If you're based in Healdsburg, you might find the wineries in the Russian River Valley packed, whereas the ones in the Alexander Valley are comparatively quiet.

Think quality, not quantity. Spend most of your time at a few wineries each day, focusing on your interests. Perhaps you'd like to sample wines from a particular type of grape, or are curious about the different varietals offered by a certain vineyard. Wine-and-food seminars are also a good idea.

Visit on a weekday. From May through October, roads and wineries are less crowded on weekdays. Year-round, tasting rooms are usually the least busy on Tuesday and Wednesday.

Reservations

Book hotels well in advance. Hotel reservations, always advisable, are generally necessary from late spring through October and on many weekends. To be on the safe side, book smaller hotels and inns at least a month ahead. Many of these have two-night minimums on weekends, three nights if Monday is a holiday.

Call restaurants ahead. Reserving a table, or asking your hotel to reserve one for you, can save you time waiting at the door.

Reserve at wineries, too. If you're keen to taste at a specific winery, double-check hours and tour times and, if possible, make a reservation. You can often make reservations for tastings, tours, seminars, and other events. Keep in mind that visits to many wineries are by appointment only, either because their permits require it or because they want to control the flow of visitors to provide a better experience.

NAPA AND SONOMA TOP ATTRACTIONS

Winery Visits

(A) Tasting wines and touring wineries are favorite Wine Country pastimes. Some places enhance the experience with art galleries, high design, stunning views, or a little razzle-dazzle; others are content to let their wines and gracious hospitality do the talking. Superb wines and amiable guides make Rutherford's Frog's Leap Vineyards an ideal stop.

Luxurious Spa Treatments

Pleasure palaces like the Fairmont's Willow Stream Spa in Sonoma, with its natural thermal pools and luxurious massage and other treatments, deliver the ultimate in self-indulgence. The spa's signature bathing ritual includes exfoliating showers, an herbal steam bath, and a sauna.

Olive Oil Tasting

(B) At classy Round Pond Estate's olive oil tasting in Rutherford, you can dispense with swirling wines and learn to swish the aromatic oils in your mouth

like a pro. Tours begin with a walk past olive trees and into the state-of-the-art mill, then proceed to the tasting, which includes red-wine vinegars.

A Meal at The French Laundry

(C) Chef Thomas Keller's Yountville restaurant is considered one of the country's best, and with good reason: the mastery of flavors and attention to detail are subtly remarkable, and the master sommelier's wine pairings elevate Keller's soaring cuisine all the more.

Art Tours at di Rosa

If you've ever wondered what it would be like to buy every piece of art that tickled your fancy, tour the galleries and grounds of the di Rosa arts center, whose discerning founder did precisely that. His passion was Northern California art from the 1960s to the present.

Blending Seminars

At Joseph Phelps, Raymond, and elsewhere you can try your hand at fashioning a Bordeaux-style blend from Cabernet Sauvignon and other grapes. In addition to having a fun and educational time, you'll gain a deeper appreciation of the skill and knowledge crafting fine wines requires.

Food and Wine Pairings

St. Francis and Ram's Gate are among the Sonoma County wineries whose tastings pair fine wines and small gourmet plates. Tastings over at Jordan are part of an estate tour with stops at the organic garden that supplies the ingredients and a hilltop vista point with 360-degree views of the 1,200-acre property.

Hot-Air Ballooning

(D) Few experiences in the world are as exhilarating (and yet marvelously serene) as an early-morning balloon ride above the vineyards—a bucket-list staple and deservedly so. Most begin at dawn and end in late morning with brunch and sparkling wine.

Cooking Demos at the CIA

(E) Instructors and guest chefs beguile students and visitors during one-hour cooking demonstrations at the Culinary Institute of America's St. Helena and Napa campuses. Recipes reflect what's in season at the time, and a glass of wine often accompanies the dish that's prepared.

Cycling Through the Vineyards

(F) Gentle hills and vineyard-laced farmland make Napa and Sonoma perfect for combining leisurely back-roads cycling with winery stops. Napa Valley Bike Tours and the affiliated Sonoma Valley Bike Tours conduct guided rides that include picnic lunches among the grapevines.

TOP NAPA WINERIES

Far Niente

(A) You can tour the 1885 stone winery and view gleaming classic cars before sitting down to taste Far Niente's famed Cabernet Sauvignon blend and Chardonnay. The small size of the tour groups, the beauty of the grounds, and the quality of the wines make expensive Far Niente worth the splurge.

Artesa Vineyards & Winery

(B) The modern, minimalist layout of this winery blends harmoniously with the surrounding Napa landscape, yet Artesa makes a vivid impression with its outdoor sculptures and fountains. You can savor the wines—and the vineyard views—from tasting bars, indoor seating areas, or outdoor terraces.

Stony Hill Vineyard

The longtime winemaker at this winery on Spring Mountain's eastern slope crafts Old World–style, mostly white wines in a low-tech cellar that looks like something out of

The Hobbit. The dense woods on the drive up to the winery and the steeply banked vineyards surrounding it reinforce the sense of timeless perfection each bottle expresses.

Domaine Carneros

(C) The main building of this Napa winery was modeled after an 18th-century French château owned by the Champagne-making Taittinger family, one of whose members selected the site Domaine Carneros now occupies. On a sunny day, the experience of sipping a crisp sparkling wine on the outdoor terrace feels noble indeed.

Inglenook

History buffs won't want to miss Inglenook, which was founded in the 19th century by a Finnish sea captain and rejuvenated over the past several decades by filmmaker Francis Ford Coppola. You can learn all about this fabled property on a tour or while tasting in an opulent salon, or just sip peacefully at a wine bar with a picturesque courtyard.

1

Schramsberg
(D) The 19th-century cellars at sparkling-wine producer Schramsberg hold millions of bottles. After you learn how the bubblies at this Calistoga mainstay are made using the *méthode traditionelle,* and how the bottles are "riddled" (turned every few days) by hand, you can enjoy generous pours.

Joseph Phelps Vineyards
(E) In good weather, there are few more glorious tasting spots in the Napa Valley than the terrace at this St. Helena winery. Phelps is known for its Cabernet Sauvignons and Insignia, a Bordeaux blend. The wine-related seminars here are smart and entertaining.

The Hess Collection
(F) Before heading to this Napa winery's tasting room to sip excellent Cabernet Sauvignons and Chardonnays, take the time to wander through owner Donald Hess's personal art collection, full of works by important 20th-century artists such as Robert Rauschenberg and Francis Bacon.

Silver Oak
This winery produces one wine a year, a Bordeaux-style Cabernet Sauvignon blend, at its Oakville location. It's poured at tastings along with the Cabernet-dominant blend made at Silver Oak's other winery, in Sonoma County's Alexander Valley. Tastings also include older vintages for comparison.

Venge Vineyards
Kirk Venge consults on the blending of several exclusive wineries' Cabernets and other wines, but his own winery is delightfully casual, and the cost of both tastings and bottles is reasonable given the quality. With its vineyard views, the ranch-house tasting room's porch is a magical perch. Book ahead to visit here.

TOP SONOMA WINERIES

Lasseter Family Winery

Pixar executive producer John Lasseter and his wife opened this secluded Glen Ellen winery specializing in Bordeaux- and Rhône-style wines made from organically grown grapes. As might be expected of a master storyteller, the winery's tale is well told on tours that precede tastings in a room with mountain and vineyard views.

Merry Edwards Winery

(A) Serious Pinot Noir lovers make pilgrimages to this spot in Sebastopol to experience wines that celebrate the singular characteristics of the Russian River Valley appellation. Tastings are offered several times daily.

Iron Horse Vineyards

(B) Proof that tasting sparkling wine doesn't have to be stuffy, this winery on the outskirts of Sebastopol pours its selections outdoors, with tremendous views of vine-covered hills that make the top-notch bubblies (and a few still wines) taste even better.

Copain Wines

(C) The emphasis at this hillside winery outside Healdsburg is on European-style Pinot Noirs whose grapes come from vineyards north of Napa and Sonoma in Mendocino County. Winemaker Wells Guthrie, a master at crafting complex wines from cool-climate grapes, also makes Chardonnays and Syrahs.

Three Sticks Wines

The chance to make Pinots and Chardonnays from Three Sticks's prized Durell and Gap's Crown vineyards lured Bob Cabral from his longtime post at an exclusive Sonoma County winery. Guests taste Cabral's gems at the lavishly restored Adobe, west of Sonoma Plaza.

Ridge Vineyards
(D) Oenophiles will be familiar with Ridge, which produces some of California's best Cabernet Sauvignon, Chardonnay, and Zinfandel. You can taste wines made from grapes grown here at Ridge's Healdsburg vineyards, and some from its neighbors, along with wines made at its older Santa Cruz Mountains winery.

Ram's Gate Winery
(E) Ultramodern yet rustic Ram's Gate perches grandly on a windswept hill in southern Sonoma, a mere 30 miles northeast of the Golden Gate Bridge. If traffic's light, you can leave San Francisco and be sipping Chardonnay or Pinot Noir in less than an hour.

Matanzas Creek Winery
(F) A sprawling field of lavender makes the grounds of Matanzas Creek especially beautiful in May and June, when the plants are in bloom. But the Santa Rosa winery's Asian-inspired aesthetic makes it delightful year-round, especially if you're a fan of Sauvignon Blanc, Chardonnay, or Merlot.

Patz & Hall
This winery is known for single-vineyard Chardonnays and Pinot Noirs made by James Hall, who consistently surpasses peers who have access to the same high-quality fruit. At Salon Tastings in a stylish ranch house a few miles south of Sonoma Plaza, the wines are paired with gourmet bites.

Scribe
Two sons of California walnut growers established this winery on land in Sonoma first planted to grapes in the late 1850s by a German immigrant. Their food-friendly wines include Riesling, Sylvaner, Chardonnay, Pinot Noir, Syrah, and Cabernet Sauvignon.

IF YOU LIKE

Shopping

Fine wine attracts fine everything else— dining, lodging, and spas—and shopping is no exception. The five towns below stand out for quality, selection, and their walkable downtowns.

Healdsburg. Hands-down the Wine Country's best shopping town, Healdsburg supports stores and galleries selling one-of-a-kind artworks, housewares, and clothing. One not to miss: Gallery Lulo, for its jewelry, small sculptures, and objets d'art.

Napa. A good place to start is the Oxbow Public Market, where stands selling teas, spices, honey, and chef's tools do business alongside upscale eateries. To the west along Main Street, the best shopping is between 1st Street and 5th Street, where the chocolate-covered wine bottles at Vintage Sweet Shoppe, in the Napa River Inn, make great gifts.

St. Helena. Galleries, housewares, and clothing and other boutiques are packed into Main Street's 1200 and 1300 blocks. Of note for ladies are Pearl Wonderful Clothing, where celebrities and regular folk pick up the latest fashions, and Footcandy, known for drool-worthy heels.

Sonoma. Shops and galleries ring historic Sonoma Plaza and fill adjacent arcades and side streets. Head south of town to Cornerstone Sonoma for its groovy but tasteful furniture and housewares shops.

Yountville. The town's one-stop retail spot is V Marketplace, right on Washington Street. Its two floors of shops include Knickers and Pearls (lingerie), Montecristi Panama Hats, and Kollar Chocolates. You'll find additional stylish shopping along Washington Street between Mulberry and Madison.

Spas

Spa choices abound, and—with ornate treatments involving brown sugar, Cabernet, and other ingredients—the only real question is how much pampering can your wallet withstand. The facilities below stand out among other worthy contenders in Napa and Sonoma.

Spa at Bardessono, Yountville. The spa at the Hotel Bardessono brings treatments to guests in their rooms, which are equipped with concealed massage tables, but in the main facility guests and nonguests alike can enjoy massages, body scrubs, facials, and other relaxing and rejuvenating regimens.

Spa at Kenwood Inn, Kenwood. The experience at the Kenwood Inn's small spa is marvelously ethereal. Signature treatments employ the French line Caudalíe's wine-based Vinothérapie treatments, among them the Honey & Wine Wrap and the Crushed Cabernet Scrub.

Spa Dolce, Healdsburg. This popular day spa just off Healdsburg Plaza specializes in skin and body care for men and women and waxing and facials for women. Spa Dolce's signature body-scrub treatment combines brown sugar with scented oil.

Spa Solage, Calistoga. The experts at Solage Calistoga's tranquil spa developed the "Mudslide," a kinder, gentler version of the ooey-gooey traditional Calistoga mud bath. Instead of immersing yourself in volcanic ash, you slather on fine mud mixed with French clay in a private heated lounge, then take a power nap in a sound-vibration chair. In addition to enjoying spa treatments, you can take fitness and yoga classes here.

Outdoor Activities

Driving from winery to winery, you may find yourself captivated by the incredible landscape. To experience it up close, you can ride in a balloon, hop on a bike, paddle a canoe or a kayak, or hike a trail.

Bicycling. The Wine Country's mostly gentle terrain and pleasant daytime climate make a two-wheeled spin past vineyards a memorable event. Full packages at outfitters may include bikes, lodging, winery tours, and a guide—or you can just rent a bike and head off on your own.

Canoeing and kayaking. The Napa and Russian Rivers provide serene settings for canoe and kayaking trips past trees, meadows, vineyards, and small towns. Half- and full-day self-guided trips are the norm. You can float with the current to a pickup spot, from which you'll be whisked by van back to your starting point.

Hiking. Of many worthy hiking spots, two associated with literary luminaries have unforgettable views, and a third winds through scenic redwoods. A 10-mile hike (a bit steep in spots) in Calistoga's Robert Louis Stevenson State Park leads up Mt. St. Helena, and 20 miles of trails traverse Glen Ellen's Jack London State Historic Park. Over in Guerneville, redwoods tower over trails both easy and strenuous at Armstrong Woods State Natural Reserve. In spring and fall you can hike through the grapevines at Healdsburg's Alexander Valley Vineyards.

History

History buffs often head to Sonoma to view its mission, near Sonoma Plaza. Winery stops east of the plaza provide insights into the origins of California wine making. Visits to Charles Krug and Beringer in St. Helena reveal the Napa Valley side of the story.

Buena Vista, Gundlach Bundschu, and Scribe, Sonoma. These sites occupy land farmed in the late 1850s by three wine-making pioneers. Count Agoston Haraszthy of Buena Vista receives all due credit for his viticultural and promotional accomplishments, although Jacob Gundlach (of what's now Gundlach Bundschu) and Emil Dresel, who grew grapes on the current Scribe site, appear to have been wiser businessmen.

Charles Krug and Beringer, St. Helena. The Napa Valley's oldest winery opened in 1861 after Agoston Haraszthy lent Charles Krug a small cider press. Beringer Vineyards, founded in 1876 by brothers Frederick and Jacob Beringer, is the valley's oldest continuously operating property. Tours at both wineries focus on early Napa Valley wine making; for more 19th-century history, take the tour at Inglenook in Rutherford.

Sonoma Plaza, Sonoma. The last of 21 California missions established by Franciscan friars sits northeast of Sonoma Plaza. You can tour the mission, its barracks, and a small museum. A tall sculpture in the plaza marks the spot where in 1846 American settlers raised a crudely drawn flag depicting a bear and declared independence from Mexico. The "Bear Republic" lasted only a month, but within five years California had achieved statehood.

THE JOYS OF EATING LOCAL

The concept "eat local, think global" has long been established doctrine in the Wine Country, home to many artisanal food producers, family farmers, and small ranchers. The catalyst for this culinary and agricultural revolution occurred in nearby Berkeley with the 1971 debut of Chez Panisse, run by food pioneer Alice Waters. Initially called California cuisine, her cooking style showcased local, seasonal ingredients in fresh preparations. It also introduced American chefs to international ingredients and techniques. As the movement spread, it became known as new American cooking and these days often falls under the heading of modern American.

In the early 1980s, John Ash began focusing on food's relationship to wine. His eponymous Santa Rosa restaurant helped set the standard for the variant later dubbed Wine Country cuisine. Ash credits Waters with inspiring him and other chefs to seek out "wholesome and unusual ingredients." Today's appeals to reduce the nation's carbon footprint added another wrinkle to the culinary maxim's "think global" component, prompting further emphasis on supporting local agriculture and food production. Much of the back-to-the-earth movement's R&D takes place at Napa and Sonoma's farms and enclaves of artisanal production.

Farms and Gardens

A good way to experience the Wine Country's agricultural bounty and the uses to which chefs put fruits, herbs, vegetables, and other ingredients is to visit one of the local farms and gardens that supply produce to top restaurants (some of which have their own gardens as well). In summer and early fall you can visit Jacobsen Orchards as part of a Secret Garden Tour and wine tasting booked through Yountville's Hill Family Estate Winery. The 1.3-acre Jacobsen farm, a five-minute drive from downtown, grows figs, peaches, pears, apricots, heirloom tomatoes, green beans, and culinary flowers—even snails—which appear on plates at chef Thomas Keller's The French Laundry and elsewhere. If you're dining at Keller's restaurant you'll appreciate your meal all the more after tasting, for instance, the difference between fresh basil leaves and flowers and learning that Keller's chefs sometimes use herbs' flowers rather than their leaves to impart more delicate flavors. Over in Santa Rosa, you can tour the 3-acre culinary garden outside the Kendall-Jackson tasting room, which supplies produce for the winery's wine and food pairings and top restaurants in the Wine Country and beyond.

Farmers' Markets

Farmers, of course, sell their goods to local high-end grocers, but a more entertaining way to sample the goodies is to browse the same outdoor farmers' markets that local chefs do. The two biggest ones, both in Sonoma County, are the year-round market in the town of Sonoma and the Healdsburg market, held from May through November. Many a Sonoma chef and even a few from Napa can be spotted at either of these popular markets. Two high-profile Napa Valley markets, one in Crane Park in St. Helena on Friday morning, the other next to Napa's Oxbow Public Market on Tuesday and Saturday morning, operate from May through October. All of these markets are perfect places to assemble items for a picnic, by the way.

Fruit

The Wine Country's diverse climate makes it an ideal place to grow many types of fruit. Healdsburg's Dry Creek Peach & Produce, for instance, grows more than 30 varieties of white and yellow peaches, along with nectarines, plums, figs, persimmons, and other fruit. Rare fruit varieties grown in Napa and Sonoma include prickly pears, loquats, and pluots, a plum-apricot hybrid. The pluot, a fairly recent creation, involved the reverse engineering of the plumcot, a hybrid developed in Sonoma County by horticulturist Luther Burbank. Another fruit that fares well in these parts is the Meyer lemon.

Vegetables

Some chefs give top billing to their produce purveyors. One recent menu touted a salad containing heirloom tomatoes from Big Ranch Farms of Napa and Solano counties. Over in the Sonoma Valley, another restaurant described the main ingredients in a mushroom salad as all locally grown, in some cases in the wild. There's no equivalent of an appellation for vegetables, but that didn't stop a St. Helena restaurant from informing diners that its Swiss chard came from Mt. Veeder—what's good for Cabernet Sauvignon is apparently also good for leafy greens. Other local vegetables gracing Wine Country menus include artichokes, multihue beets and carrots, and heirloom varieties of butternut squash, beans, and even radishes.

Meat

Family-owned ranches and farms are prominent in the region, with many raising organic or "humane-certified" beef, pork, lamb, and poultry. Upscale restaurants are fervent about recognizing their high-quality protein producers. A well-known St. Helena restaurant, for example, credits Bryan Flannery for various beef cuts on its menu, and you'll see the name Green Star Farm (of Sebastopol) for organic chicken and Liberty (Petaluma) for ducks. To delve deeper into what happens to meats between farm and restaurant, you can take a Saturday class at the Fatted Calf Charcuterie in the Oxbow Public Market. Classes that often sell out include Pig + Woman + Knife, a class in hog butchery "taught by women for women."

Seafood

Seafood from local waters abounds, from farm-raised scallops to line-caught California salmon. Around Thanksgiving, California's famous Dungeness crab begins appearing on menus, either steamed whole, in salads, or as a featured ingredient in cioppino, a tomato-based seafood stew that originated in San Francisco. Also look for Hog Island Oysters, whose namesake producer raises more than 3 million oysters a year just south of Sonoma County in Tomales Bay.

Cheese

Restaurant cheese plates, often served before—or in lieu of—dessert, are a great way to acquaint yourself with excellent local cheeses. In Sonoma, Vella Cheese, just north of Sonoma Plaza on 2nd Street East, has been producing Dry Monterey Jack and other cheeses since 1931, the same year that the nearby Sonoma Cheese Factory, on Sonoma Plaza, got its start.

KIDS AND FAMILIES

The Wine Country isn't a particularly child-oriented destination. Don't expect to find tons of activities organized with kids in mind. That said, you'll find plenty of playgrounds (there's one in Sonoma Plaza, for instance), as well as the occasional family-friendly attraction.

Choosing a Place to Stay

If you're traveling with kids, always mention it when making your reservations. Most of the smaller, more romantic inns and bed-and-breakfasts discourage or prohibit children, and those places that do allow them may prefer to put such families in a particular cottage or room so that any noise is less disruptive to other guests. Larger hotels are a mixed bag. Some actively discourage children, whereas others are more welcoming. Of the large, luxurious hotels, Meadowood tends to be the most child-friendly.

Eating Out

Unless your kid is a budding Thomas Keller, it's best to call ahead to see if a restaurant can accommodate those under 12 with a special menu. You will find inexpensive cafés in almost every town, and places like Gott's Roadside, a retro burger stand in St. Helena, are big hits with kids.

Family-Friendly Attractions

One especially family-friendly attraction is the Charles M. Schulz Museum in Santa Rosa. Its intelligent exhibits generally appeal to adults; younger kids may or may not enjoy the level of detail. The sure bets for kids are the play area outside and the education room, where they can color, draw, and create their own cartoons. Another place for a family outing, also in Santa Rosa, is Safari West, an African wildlife preserve on 400 acres. The highlight is the two-hour tour of the property in open-air vehicles that sometimes come within a few feet of giraffes, zebras, and other animals. You can spend the night in tent-cabins here. At Sonoma Canopy Tours, north of Occidental, families zip-line through the redwoods together.

At the Wineries

Children are few and far between at most wineries, but well-behaved children will generally be greeted with a smile. Some wineries offer a small treat—grape juice or another beverage, or sometimes coloring books or a similar distraction.

When booking a tour, ask if kids are allowed (for insurance reasons, wineries sometimes prohibit children under a certain age), how long it lasts, and whether there's another tour option that would be more suitable.

A few particularly kid-friendly wineries include Calistoga's Castello di Amorosa (what's not to like about a 107-room medieval castle, complete with a dungeon?) and Sterling Vineyards, where a short aerial tram ride whisks visitors from the parking lot to the tasting room. In Sonoma County, Benziger conducts vineyard tours in a tractor-pulled tram, and its picnic grounds are kid-friendly. You'll find plenty of kids poolside at the Francis Ford Coppola Winery in Geyserville, and Honig Vineyard & Winery in Rutherford prides itself on making sure kids enjoy a visit as much as their parents do.

GREAT ITINERARIES

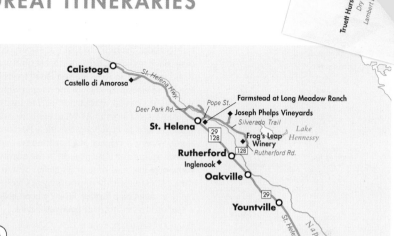

FIRST-TIMER'S NAPA TOUR

On this two-day Napa Valley survey you'll tour key wineries (some requiring an appointment), taste fine wine, learn some history, and shop and dine.

Day 1: History, Tasting, Shopping, Dining

Start your first morning at Napa's **Oxbow Public Market.** Down a brew at Ritual Coffee Roasters, then drive north on Highway 29. At Rutherford stop at film director Francis Ford Coppola's **Inglenook,** whose tour and exhibits provide a fascinating overview of Napa Valley wine making. Continue north on Highway 29 to St. Helena for lunch at **Farmstead at Long Meadow Ranch,** then visit Calistoga's over-the-top **Castello di Amorosa,** off Highway 29, or St. Helena's serene **Joseph Phelps Vineyards,** off the Silverado Trail.

Check into your St. Helena lodgings— luxurious **Meadowood Napa Valley** or pleasantly downscale **El Bonita Motel** are two good options. Poke around St. Helena's shops until dinner, perhaps at Meadowood, **Harvest Table,** or **Goose & Gander.**

Day 2: Winery and Art Tours, Lunch, and a Toast

Begin your day with coffee in St. Helena at **Model Bakery,** then drive south on Highway 29 and east on Rutherford Road to **Frog's Leap** (book the winery's entertaining tour in advance). Return to Highway 29 and drive south, then turn west on Highway 121. Stop for lunch at the **Boon Fly Café,** then continue west on Highway 121 to the **di Rosa** arts center and tour its gardens and galleries. Cross Highway 121 to **Domaine Carneros** and toast your trip with some sparkling wine.

SONOMA BACK ROADS TOUR

Stay strictly rural on this easygoing trek through forests, vineyards, and the occasional meadow.

Day 1: From Sebastopol to Forestville

Start day one at the **Barlow** artisan complex in Sebastopol. Have coffee and a pastry at **Taylor Maid Farms** and mosey around, then drive northwest on the Gravenstein Highway (Highway 116), stopping at **Dutton-Goldfield Winery**, at the intersection of the highway and Graton Road. From Dutton, take Graton Road west half a mile to Graton. Check out the shops and gallery on the hamlet's one-block main drag and have lunch at the **Willow Wood Market Cafe** or **Zosia Café and Kitchen**, which sit side-by-side.

After lunch, if the weather permits, walk a bit of the **West County Regional Trail** north from Graton Road a block west of the restaurants—the trailhead is just past Ross Road. Look for the plaques with historical tidbits about the railroad that once operated here. Back in the car, drive northeast on Ross Road and west on Ross Station Road to visit **Iron Horse Vineyards**, known for its sparkling wines. Afterward, backtrack to Highway 116 and turn north. At Martinelli Road, hang a right to reach Forestville's **Hartford Family Winery**, producer of Chardonnays and Pinots. Splurge on a night's rest at the nearby **Farmhouse Inn**, and dine at its stellar restaurant. (A less expensive option; stay in Guerneville at **AutoCamp Russian River** or **boon hotel + spa** and have dinner at **boon eat + drink**.)

Day 2: Healdsburg and Dry Creek

Start Day Two by taking Wohler Road and then Westside Road north to **Arista Winery**. After a tasting, continue on Westside to West Dry Creek Road, proceed north, and turn east at Lambert Bridge Road. Assemble a picnic at **Dry Creek General Store**, and continue north on Dry Creek Road to **Truett Hurst Winery**. Taste wines and choose one to have with your picnic here. Backtrack south on Dry Creek Road past the general store, turning east on Lytton Springs Road, which leads to **Ridge Vineyards**. End the day with a Cabernet.

THE ULTIMATE WINE TRIP, 4 DAYS

On this four-day extravaganza, you'll taste well-known and under-the-radar wines, bed down in plush hotels, and dine at restaurants operated by celebrity chefs. Appointments are required for some of the tastings.

Day 1: Sonoma County

Begin your tour in **Geyserville**, about 78 miles north of San Francisco on U.S. 101. Visit **Locals Tasting Room**, which pours the wines of special small wineries. Have lunch at nearby Diavolo or Catelli's, then head south on U.S. 101 and Old Redwood

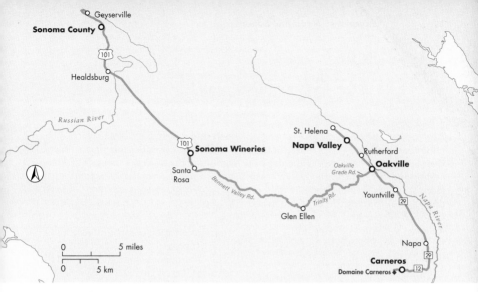

Highway to **Healdsburg**'s Jordan Vineyard & Winery for a 2 pm Library Tasting. From Jordan, head south to **Healdsburg Plaza** downtown. Explore the shops in the plaza area and have a "shrub" (vinegar-based soda) at **The Shed**; if you're up for more tasting, Banshee and Thumbprint Cellars are good options. **Hôtel Les Mars** and **h2hotel** are two well-located spots to spend the night. Have dinner at **Chalkboard**, **Bravas Bar de Tapas**, or **Campo Fina**, all close by.

Day 2: Sonoma Wineries
Interesting wineries dot the countryside surrounding Healdsburg, among them **Mauritson Wines** and **Trattore Farms** (the latter just barely in Geyserville). In the afternoon head south on U.S. 101 and east on scenic Highway 12 to Glen Ellen. Visit **Jack London State Historic Park**, the memorabilia-filled home of the famous writer. Dine at **Aventine Glen Ellen** or **Glen Ellen Star** and stay at the **Olea Hotel**.

Day 3: Napa Valley
Head east from Glen Ellen on Trinity Road, which twists and turns over the Mayacamas Mountains, eventually becoming the Oakville Grade. Unless you're the one driving, bask in the stupendous **Napa Valley** views. At Highway 29, drive north to **St. Helena**. Focus on history and architecture at **Charles Krug Winery** or let the art and wines at **Hall St. Helena** transport you. Take lunch downtown at **Cindy's Backstreet Kitchen** or **Cook St. Helena**. Check out St. Helena's shopping, then head south on Highway 29 to Yountville for more shopping. Start at **Hunter Gatherer**, at Madison and Washington Streets, and work your way south on Washington to **V Marketplace**.

Stay overnight at **Bardessono** or the **North Block Hotel**, both within walking distance of Yountville's famous restaurants. A meal at **The French Laundry** is many visitors' holy grail, but dining at **Bouchon**, **Bistro Jeanty**, or **Redd** will also leave you feeling well served.

Day 4: Oakville to Carneros
After breakfast, head north on Highway 29 to **Oakville**, where sipping wine at **Silver Oak**, **Nickel & Nickel**, or **B Cellars** will make clear why collectors covet Oakville Cabernet Sauvignons. Nickel & Nickel is on Highway 29; Silver Oak and B Cellars are east of it on Oakville Cross Road. Have a picnic at **Oakville Grocery**, in business on Highway 29 since 1881, or make reservations for lunch at **Mustards Grill**. After your meal, head south to Highway 121 and turn west to reach the Carneros District. Tour the **di Rosa** arts center (appointment required for the full tour), then repair across the street to **Domaine Carneros**, which makes French-style sparkling wines. There's hardly a more elegant way to bid a Wine Country adieu than from the château's vineyard-view terrace.

WHEN TO GO

Timing Your Trip

High season extends from April through October. In summer, expect the days to be hot and dry, and traffic heavy at the tasting rooms. Hotel rates are highest during peak harvest, in September and October. Then, and in summer, book lodgings well ahead. November, except for Thanksgiving week, and December before Christmas are less busy.

Climate

The weather in Napa and Sonoma is pleasant nearly year-round. Daytime temperatures average about 55°F in winter up into the 80s in summer, when readings in the 90s and higher are common. April, May, and October are milder but still warm. The rainiest months are usually from December through March.

Festivals and Seasonal Events

Auction Napa Valley. Dozens of events culminate in the Napa Valley's glitziest night—with an opulent dinner and an auction of rare wines and other coveted items to benefit nonprofit health and other programs. It's held on the first full weekend in June. ⊕ *auctionnapavalley.org*.

BottleRock Napa Valley. An end-of-May three-day food, wine, and music festival, BottleRock gets summer rolling (and rocking) with acts headlined by the likes of the Red Hot Chili Peppers and Maroon 5. Tickets sell out in early January when the lineup is announced. ⊕ *www.bottlerocknapavalley.com*.

Festival Napa Valley. This acclaimed mid-July event attracts international opera, theater, dance, and musical performers to Castello di Amorosa and other venues. ⊕ *www.festivalnapavalley.org*.

Flavor! Napa Valley Several days of dinners, cooking demonstrations, and wine-and-food tastings—many involving top chefs and winemakers—take place in late March. The event benefits the California campus of the Culinary Institute of America. ⊕ *www.flavornapavalley.com*.

Sonoma County Harvest Fair. This early fall festival at the county fairgrounds in Santa Rosa celebrates Sonoma agriculture with wine and olive-oil competitions, cooking demos, livestock shows, carnival rides, local entertainers, and the perennially popular Harvest Dog Dash. ⊠ *Santa Rosa* ⊕ *www.harvestfair.org*.

Sonoma Wine Country Weekend. Chefs, grape growers, and winemakers team up for this weekend of lunches, dinners, and wine tastings that culminates in a live auction of rare wines and other items. ⊕ *sonomawinecountryweekend.com*.

West of West Wine Festival. Wineries and grape growers along Sonoma County's coastline sponsor this early-August festival at The Barlow in Sebastopol. You can sample Chardonnays, Pinot Noirs, Syrahs, and other wines of small producers with no tasting rooms of their own. ⊕ *www.westsonomacoast.com*.

A Wine & Food Affair. For this November event, wineries prepare a favorite recipe and serve it with wine. Participants travel from winery to winery to sample the fare. This affair sells out every year. ⊕ *www.wineroad.com*.

Wine Road Barrel Tasting Weekends. In early March, more than 100 wineries open their cellars for tastings straight from barrel. ⊕ *www.wineroad.com*.

Winter Wineland. In mid-January, most northern Sonoma County wineries—including many not generally open to the public—offer tastings, seminars, and entertainment. ⊕ *www.wineroad.com*.

VISITING WINERIES AND TASTING ROOMS

Whether you're a serious wine collector making your annual pilgrimage to Northern California's Wine Country or a newbie who doesn't know the difference between Merlot and Mourvèdre but is eager to learn, you can have a great time touring Napa and Sonoma wineries. Your gateway to the wine world is the tasting room, where staff members—and occasionally even the winemaker—are almost always happy to chat with curious guests.

Tasting rooms range from the grand to the humble, offering everything from a few sips of wine to in-depth tours of the wine-making facilities and vineyards. First-time visitors frequently enjoy the history-oriented tours at Beaulieu, Beringer, Charles Krug, and Inglenook, or the ones at Mondavi and Korbel that highlight process as well. The environments at some wineries reflect their founders' other interests: horses at Nickel & Nickel and Tamber Bey, moviemaking at Francis Ford Coppola and Frank Family, art and architecture at Artesa and Hall St. Helena, and medieval history at the Castello di Amorosa.

To prepare yourself for your winery visits, we've covered the fundamentals: tasting rooms and what to expect, how to save money on tasting fees, and the types of tours typically offered by wineries. A list of common tasting terms will help you interpret what your mouth is experiencing as you sip. We've also provided a description of the major grape varietals, as well as the specific techniques employed to craft white, red, sparkling, and rosé wines. Because great wines begin in the vineyard, we've included a section on soils, climates, and organic and biodynamic farming methods. A handy Wine-Lover's Glossary of terms, from *acidity* to *zymology*, covers what you may come across in the tasting room or on a tour.

WINE TASTING 101

Don't be intimidated by sommeliers who toss aroun
tives as they swirl their glasses. At its core, wine
about determining which wines you like best. How
few basic tasting steps and a few key quality guid
your winery visit much more enjoyable and help you
wines you liked, and why, long after you return home. ■TIP→ **Above
all, follow your instincts at the tasting bar: there is no right or wrong
way to describe wine.**

If you watch the pros, you'll probably notice that they take time to
inspect, swirl, and sniff the wine before they get around to sipping it.
Follow their lead and take your time, going through each of the following steps for each wine. Starting with the pop of the cork and the splash-
ing of wine into a glass, all of your senses play a part in wine tasting.

USE YOUR EYES

Before you taste it, take a good look at the wine in your glass. Holding
the glass by the stem, raise it to the light. Whether it's white, rosé, or
red, your wine should be clear, without cloudiness or sediments, when
you drink it. Some unfiltered wines may seem cloudy at first, but they
will clear as the sediments settle.

In natural light, place the glass in front of a white background such as
a blank sheet of paper or a tablecloth. **Check the color.** Is it right for the
wine? A California white should be golden: straw, medium, or deep,
depending on the type. Rich, sweet, dessert wine will have more intense
color, but Chardonnay and Sauvignon Blanc will be paler. A rosé should
be a clear pink, from pale to deep, without too much red or any orange.
Reds may lean toward ruby or garnet coloring; some have a purple
tinge. They shouldn't be pale (the exception is Pinot Noir, which can
be quite pale yet still have character). In any color of wine, a brownish
tinge is a flaw that indicates the wine is too old, has been incorrectly
stored, or has gone bad. If you see brown, try another bottle.

BREATHE DEEP

After you have looked at the wine's color, **sniff the wine once or twice**
to see if you can identify any aromas. Then gently move your glass
in a circular motion to swirl the wine around. Aerating the wine this
way releases more of its aromas. (It's called "volatilizing the esters," if
you're trying to impress someone.) Stick your nose into the glass and
take another long sniff.

Wine should smell good to you. You might pick up the scent of apricots,
peaches, ripe melon, honey, and wildflowers in a white wine; black
pepper, cherry, violets, and cedar in a red. Rosés (which are made from
red wine grapes) smell something like red wine, but in a scaled-back
way, with hints of raspberry, strawberry, and sometimes a touch of rose
petal. You might encounter surprising smells, such as tar—which some
people actually appreciate in certain (generally expensive) red wines.

For the most part, a wine's aroma should be clean and pleasing to you, not "off." If you find a wine's odor odd or unpleasant, there's probably something wrong. A vinegar smell indicates that the wine has started to spoil. A rotten wood or soggy cardboard smell usually means that the cork has gone bad, ruining the wine. It's extremely rare to find these faults in wines poured in the tasting rooms, however, because staffers usually taste each bottle before pouring from it.

WINE CLUBS

If several of a winery's offerings appeal to you and you live in a state that allows you to order wines directly from wineries (most staffers have this information at the ready), consider joining its wine club. You'll receive offers for members-only releases, invitations to winery events, and a discount on all of your purchases.

JUST A SIP

Once you've checked its appearance and aroma, **take a sip**—not a swig or a gulp—of the wine. As you sip a wine, **gently swish it around in your mouth**—this releases more aromas for your nose to explore. Do the aroma and the flavor complement each other, improve each other? While moving the wine around in your mouth, also think about the way it feels: silky or crisp? Does it coat your tongue or is it thinner? Does it seem to fill your mouth with flavor or is it weak? This combination of weight and intensity is referred to as *body*: a good wine may be light-, medium-, or full-bodied.

The more complex a wine, the more flavors you will detect in the course of tasting. You might experience different things when you first take a sip (*up front*), when you swish (*in the middle* or *mid-palate*), and just before you swallow (*at the end* or *back-palate*).

SPIT OR SWALLOW?

You may choose to spit out the wine (into the dump bucket or a plastic cup) or swallow it. The pros typically spit, because they want to preserve their palates (and sobriety!) for the wines to come, but you'll find that swallowers far outnumber spitters in the winery tasting rooms. Either way, **pay attention to what happens after the wine leaves your mouth**—this is the finish, and it can be spectacular. What sensations stay behind or appear? Does the flavor fade away quickly or linger pleasantly? A long finish is a sign of quality; wine with no perceptible finish is inferior.

TASTING ROOMS AND WINERY TOURS

At most wineries, you'll have to pay for the privilege of tasting. Fees range from $15 to $25 for a standard tasting of some or all of a winery's current releases and from $20 to $50 (and up at high-end wineries) to taste reserve, estate, or library wines. To experience wine making at its highest level, consider splurging for a special tasting at one winery at least. In general, you'll find the fees higher in Napa than in Sonoma, though there are exceptions to this rule.

In tasting rooms, tipping is very much the exception rather than the rule. Most frequent visitors to the Wine Country never tip those pouring the wines in the tasting rooms, though if a server has gone out of his or her way to be helpful—by pouring special wines not on the list, for example—leaving $5 or so would be a nice gesture.

Many wineries are open to the public, usually daily from around 10 or 11 am to 5 pm. They may close as early as 4 or 4:30, especially in winter, so it's best to get a reasonably early start if you want to fit in more than a few spots. ■ TIP➜ **Most wineries stop serving new visitors from 15 to 30 minutes before the posted closing time, so don't expect to skate in at the last moment.**

IN THE TASTING ROOM

In most tasting rooms, a list of the wines available that day will be on the bar or offered by the server. The wines will be listed in a suggested tasting order, starting with the lightest-bodied whites and progressing to the most intense reds. Dessert wines will come at the end.

You'll usually find an assortment of the winery's current releases. There might also be a list of reserve (special in some way) or library (older) wines you can taste for a higher fee.

Don't feel the need to try all the wines you're offered. In fact, many wineries indicate at the bottom of the list that you're limited to four or five.

The server will pour you an ounce or so of each wine you select. There might be a plate of crackers on the bar; nibble them when you want to clear your palate before tasting the next selection. If you don't like a wine, or you've tasted enough, pour the rest into one of the dump buckets on the bar (if you don't see one, just ask).

TAKING A TOUR

Even if you're not a devoted wine drinker, seeing how grapes become wine can be fascinating. Tours tend to be most exciting (and most crowded) in September and October, when the harvest and crushing are under way. Depending on the size of the winery, tours range from a few people to large groups and typically last 30 minutes to an hour. ■ TIP➜ **Wear comfortable shoes, because you might be walking on wet floors or stepping over hoses or other equipment.**

Some winery tours are free, in which case you usually pay a separate fee to taste the wine. If you've paid for the tour—often from $10 to $30—your wine tasting is usually included in the price.

At large wineries, introductory tours are typically offered several times daily. Less frequent are specialized tours and seminars focusing on such subjects as growing techniques, sensory evaluation, wine blending, and food and wine pairing. These events typically cost from $30 to $75.

TOP CALIFORNIA GRAPE VARIETALS

Several dozen grape varietals are grown in the Wine Country, from favorites like Chardonnay and Cabernet Sauvignon to less familiar types like Albariño and Tempranillo. You'll likely come across many of the following varietals as you visit the wineries.

WHITE

Albariño. One of the most popular wine grapes in Spain (it's also a staple of Portuguese wine making), this cool-climate grape creates light, citrusy wines, often with overtones of mango or kiwi.

Chardonnay. California Chardonnays spent many years chasing big, buttery flavor, but the current trend is toward more restrained wines that let the grapes shine through. Because of Napa and Sonoma's warmer, longer growing seasons, Chardonnays from those regions will always be bolder than their counterparts in Burgundy.

Gewürztraminer. Cooler California climes such as the Russian River Valley are great for growing this German-Alsatian grape, which is turned into a boldly perfumed, fruity wine.

Marsanne. A white-wine grape of France's northern Rhône Valley, Marsanne can produce a dry or sweet wine depending on how it is handled.

Pinot Gris. Known in Italy as Pinot Grigio, this varietal yields a more deeply colored wine in California. It's not highly acidic and has a medium to full body.

Riesling. Also called White Riesling, this cool-climate German grape has a sweet reputation in America. When made in a dry style, though, it can be crisply refreshing, with lush aromas.

Roussanne. This grape from the Rhône Valley makes an especially fragrant wine that can achieve a balance of fruitiness and acidity.

Sauvignon Blanc. Hailing from Bordeaux and the Loire Valley, this white grape does very well almost anywhere in California. Wines made from this grape display a wide range of personalities, from herbaceous to tropical-fruity.

Viognier. Until the early 1990s, Viognier was rarely planted outside France's Rhône Valley, but today it's one of California's hottest white-wine varietals. Usually made in a dry style, the best Viogniers have an intense fruity or floral bouquet.

RED

Barbera. Prevalent in California thanks to 19th-century Italian immigrants, Barbera yields easy-drinking, low-tannin wines with big fruit and high acid.

Cabernet Franc. Most often used in blends, often to add complexity to Cabernet Sauvignon, this French grape can produce aromatic, soft, and subtle wines. An often earthy, or even stinky, aroma repels some drinkers and makes avid fans of others.

Cabernet Sauvignon. The king of California reds, this Bordeaux grape is at home in well-drained soils. At its best, the California version is dark, bold, and tannic, with black currant notes. On its own it can require a long aging period, so it's often softened with Cabernet Franc, Merlot, and other red varieties for earlier drinking.

Grenache. This Spanish grape, which makes some of the southern Rhône Valley's most distinguished wines, ripens best in hot, dry conditions. Done right, Grenache is dark and concentrated and improves with age.

Merlot. This blue-black Bordeaux varietal makes soft, full-bodied wine when grown in California. It's often fruity, and can be complex even when young.

Mourvèdre. A native of France's Rhône Valley, this grape makes wine that is deeply colored, very dense, and high in alcohol. When young it can seem harsh, but it mellows with aging.

Petite Sirah. Unrelated to the Rhône grape Syrah, Petite Sirah produces a hearty wine that is often used in blends.

Pinot Noir. The darling of grape growers in cooler parts of Napa and Sonoma, including the Carneros region and the Russian River Valley, Pinot Noir is also called the "heartbreak grape" because it's hard to cultivate. At its best it has a subtle but addictive earthy quality.

Sangiovese. Dominant in the Chianti region and much of central Italy, Sangiovese can, depending on how it's grown and vinified, be made into vibrant, light- to medium-bodied wines or complex reds.

Syrah. Another big California red, this grape originated in the Rhône Valley. With good tannins it can become a full-bodied, almost smoky beauty.

Tempranillo. The major varietal in Spain's Rioja region, sturdy Tempranillo makes inky purple wines with a beautifully rich texture. Wines made from this grape are great on their own but excel when paired with red-meat and game dishes.

Zinfandel. Celebrated as California's own (though it has distant old-world origins), Zinfandel is rich and spicy. Its tannins can make it complex and well suited for aging. When grown to extreme ripeness, the grape can produce wines with high alcohol levels.

HOW WINE IS MADE

THE CRUSH

The process of turning grapes into wine generally starts at the **crush pad,** where the grapes are brought in from the vineyards. Good winemakers carefully monitor their grapes throughout the year, but their presence is critical at harvest, when ripeness determines the proper day for picking. Once that day arrives, the crush begins.

Wineries pick their grapes by machine or by hand, depending on the terrain and on the type of grape. Some varietals are harvested at night with the help of powerful floodlights. Why at night? In addition to it being easier on the workers (daytime temperatures often reach 90°F

[32°C] or more in September), the fruit-acid content in the pulp and juice of the grapes peaks in the cool night air. The acids—an essential component during fermentation and aging, and an important part of wine's flavor—plummet in the heat of the day.

Grapes arrive at the crush pad in large containers called gondolas. Unless the winemaker intends to ferment the entire clusters, which is generally done only for red wines, they are dropped gently onto a conveyor belt that deposits them into a **stemmer-crusher,** which gently separates the grapes from their stems. Then the sorting process begins. At most wineries this is done by hand at sorting tables, where workers remove remaining stems and leaves and reject any obviously damaged berries. Because anything not sorted out will wind up in the fermenting tank, some wineries double or even triple sort to achieve higher quality. Stems, for instance, can add unwanted tannins to a finished wine. On the other hand, winemakers sometimes desire those tannins and allow some stems through. A few high-end wineries use electronic optical grape sorters that scan and assess the fruit. Berries deemed too small or otherwise defective are whisked away, along with any extraneous vegetal matter.

No matter the process used, the sorted grapes are then ready for transfer to a press or vat.

After this step, the production process goes one of four ways, depending on whether a white, red, rosé, or sparkling wine is being made.

WHITE WINES

The juice of white-wine grapes first goes to **settling tanks,** where the skins and solids sink to the bottom, separating from the free-run juice on top. The material in the settling tanks still contains a lot of juice, so after the free-run juice is pumped off, the rest goes into a **press.** A modern press consists of a perforated drum containing a Teflon-coated bag. As this bag is inflated like a balloon, it slowly pushes the grapes against the outside wall and the liquids are gently squeezed from the solids. Like the free-run juice, the press juice is pumped into a stainless-steel **fermenter.**

During fermentation, yeast feeds on the sugar in grape juice and converts it to alcohol and carbon dioxide. Wine yeast dies and fermentation naturally stops in two to four weeks, when the alcohol level reaches 15% (or sometimes more).

To prevent oxidation that damages wine's color and flavor and kills wild yeast and bacteria that produce off flavors, winemakers almost always add sulfur dioxide, in the form of sulfites, before fermenting. A winemaker may also encourage **malolactic fermentation** (or simply *malo*) to soften a wine's acidity or deepen its flavor and complexity. This is done either by inoculating the wine with lactic bacteria soon after fermentation begins or right after it ends, or by transferring the new wine to wooden vats that harbor the bacteria.

For richer results, free-run juice from Chardonnay grapes, as well as some from Sauvignon Blanc grapes, might be fermented in oak barrels.

In many cases the barrels used to make white wines, especially Sauvignon Blanc, are older, "neutral" barrels previously used to make other wines. These neutral barrels can add a fullness to a wine without adding any wood flavors. In recent years, wineries have begun using "concrete eggs" (egg-shape fermenting tanks made out of concrete), mostly to make white wines. Bigger than a barrel but smaller than most stainless tanks, the eggs, like barrels, are porous enough to "breathe," but unlike wood don't impart flavors or tannins to wines. The notion of fermenting wines in concrete receptacles may sound newfangled, but their use dates back to the 19th century (and some say even further).

When the wine has finished fermenting, whether in a tank or a barrel, it is generally **racked**—moved into a clean tank or barrel to separate it from any remaining grape solids. Sometimes Chardonnay and special batches of Sauvignon Blanc are left "on the lees"—atop the spent yeast, grape solids, and other matter that were in the fermenting tank—for extended periods of time before being racked to pick up extra complexity. Wine may be racked several times as the sediment continues to settle out.

After the first racking, the wine may be **filtered** to take out solid particles that can cloud the wine and any stray yeast or bacteria that can spoil it. This is especially common for whites, which may be filtered several times before bottling. Most commercial producers filter their wines, but many fine-wine makers don't, as they believe it leads to less complex wines that don't age as well.

White wine may also be **fined** by mixing in a fine clay called bentonite or albumen from egg whites. As they settle out, they absorb undesirable substances that can cloud the wine. As with filtering, the process is more common with ordinary table wines than with fine wines.

Winemakers typically blend several batches of wine together to balance flavor. Careful **blending** gives them an extra chance to create a perfect single-varietal wine or to combine several varietals that complement each other in a blend. Premium vintners also make unblended wines that highlight the attributes of grapes from a single vineyard.

New wine is stored in stainless-steel, oak, or concrete containers to rest and develop before bottling. This stage, called **maturation** or **aging,** may last anywhere from a few months to more than a year. Barrel rooms are kept dark to protect the wine from both light and heat, either of which can be damaging. Some wineries keep their wines in air-conditioned rooms or warehouses; others use long, tunnel-like caves bored into hillsides, where the wine remains at a constant temperature.

If wine is aged for any length of time before bottling, it will be racked and perhaps filtered several times. Once it is bottled, the wine is stored for **bottle aging.** This is done in a cool, dark space to prevent the corks from drying out; a shrunken cork allows oxygen to enter the bottle and spoil the wine. In a few months, most white wines will be ready for release.

RED WINES

Red-wine production differs slightly from that of white wine. Red-wine grapes are crushed in the same way, but the juice is not separated from the grape skins and pulp before fermentation. This is what gives red wine its color. After crushing, the red-wine **must**—the thick slurry of juice, pulp, and skins—is fermented in vats. The juice is "left on the skins" for varying amounts of time, from a few days to a few weeks, depending on the type of grape and on how much color and flavor the winemaker wants to extract.

Fermentation also extracts chemical compounds such as **tannins** from the skins and seeds, making red wines more robust than whites. In a red designed for drinking soon after bottling, tannin levels are kept down; they should have a greater presence in wine meant for aging. In a young red not ready for drinking, tannins feel dry or coarse in your mouth, but they soften over time. A wine with well-balanced tannin will maintain its fruitiness and backbone as its flavor develops. Without adequate tannins, a wine will not age well.

Creating the **oak barrels** that age the wine is a craft in its own right. At Demptos Napa Cooperage, a French-owned company that employs French barrel-making techniques, the process involves several elaborate production phases. The staves of oak are formed into the shape of a barrel using metal bands, and then the rough edges of the bound planks are smoothed. Finally, the barrels are literally toasted to give the oak its characteristic flavor, which will in turn be imparted to the wine.

At the end of fermentation, the free-run wine is drained off. The grape skins and pulp are sent to a press, where the remaining liquid is extracted. As with white wines, the winemaker may blend a little of the press wine into the free-run wine to add complexity. Otherwise, the press juice goes into bulk wine—the lower-quality, less expensive stuff.

Next up is **oak-barrel aging,** which takes from a half year to a year or longer. Oak, like grapes, contains natural tannins, and the wine extracts these tannins from the barrels. The wood also has countless tiny pores through which water slowly evaporates, making the wine more concentrated. To make sure the aging wine does not oxidize, the barrels have to be regularly **topped off** with wine from the same vintage.

New, or virgin, oak barrels impart the most tannins to a wine. With each successive use the tannins are diminished, until the barrel is said to be "neutral." Depending on the varietal, winemakers might blend juice aged in virgin oak barrels with juice aged in neutral barrels. In the tasting room you may hear, for instance, that a Pinot Noir was aged in 30% new oak and 70% two-year-old oak, meaning that the bulk of the wine was aged in oak used for two previous agings.

SPARKLING WINES

Despite the mystique surrounding them, sparkling wines are nothing more or less than wines in which carbon dioxide is suspended, making them bubbly. Good sparkling wine will always be fairly expensive because a great deal of work goes into making it.

White sparkling wines can be made from either white or black grapes. In France, Champagne is traditionally made from Pinot Noir or Chardonnay grapes, whereas in California sparkling wine might be made with Pinot Blanc, Riesling, or sometimes other white grapes.

The freshly pressed juice and pulp, or must, is **fermented with special yeasts** that preserve the characteristic fruit flavor of the grape variety used. Before bottling, this finished "still" wine (without bubbles) is mixed with a *liqueur de tirage,* a blend of wine, sugar, and yeast. This mixture causes the wine to ferment again—in the bottle, where it stays for up to 12 weeks. **Carbon dioxide,** a by-product of fermentation, is produced and trapped in the bottle, where it dissolves into the wine (instead of escaping into the air, as happens during fermentation in barrel, vat, or tank). This captive carbon dioxide transforms a still wine into a sparkler.

New bottles of sparkling wine are stored on their sides in deep cellars. The wine now ages *sur lie,* or "on the lees" (the dead yeast cells and other deposits trapped in the bottle). This aging process enriches the wine's texture and increases the complexity of its bouquet. The amount of time spent sur lie has a direct relation to its quality: the longer the aging, the more complex the wine.

The lees must be removed from the bottle before a sparkling wine can be enjoyed. This is achieved in a process whose first step is called **riddling.** In the past, each bottle, head tilted slightly downward, was placed in a riddling rack, an A-frame with many holes of bottleneck size. Riddlers gave each bottle a slight shake and a downward turn—every day, if possible. This continued for six weeks, until each bottle rested upside down in the hole and the sediment had collected in the neck, next to the cork. Today most sparkling wines are riddled in ingeniously designed machines called gyro palettes, which can handle 500 or more bottles at a time, though at a few wineries, such as Schramsberg, the work is still done by hand.

After riddling, the bottles are **disgorged.** The upside-down bottles are placed in a very cold solution, which freezes the sediments in a block that attaches itself to the crown cap that seals the bottle. The cap and frozen plug are removed, and the bottle is topped off with a wine-and-sugar mixture called **dosage** and recorked with the traditional Champagne cork. The dosage ultimately determines the sparkler's sweetness.

Most sparkling wines are not vintage dated but are *assembled* (the term sparkling-wine makers use instead of *blended*) to create a **cuvée,** a mix of different wines and sometimes different vintages consistent with the house style. However, sparkling wines may be vintage dated in particularly great years.

Sparkling wine may also be made by time- and cost-saving bulk methods. In the **Charmat process,** invented by Eugene Charmat early in the 20th century, the secondary fermentation takes place in large tanks

2

It's All on the Label

A wine's label will tell you a lot about what's inside. To decode the details, look for the following information:

■ **Alcohol content:** In most cases, U.S. law requires bottles to list the alcohol content, which typically hovers around 13% or 14%, but big red wines from California, especially Zinfandel, can soar to 16% or more.

■ **Appellation:** At least 85% of the grapes must have come from the AVA (American Viticultural Area) listed on the bottle. A bottle that says "Mt. Veeder," for example, contains mostly grapes that are grown in the compact Mt. Veeder appellation, but if the label says "California," the grapes could be from anywhere in the state.

■ **Estate or Estate Grown:** Wines with this label must be made entirely of grapes grown on land owned or farmed by the winery.

■ **Reserve:** An inexact term meaning "special" (and therefore usually costing more), *reserve* can refer to how or where the grapes were grown, how the wine was made, or even how long it was aged.

■ **Varietal:** If a type of grape is listed on the label, it means that at least 75% of the grapes in this wine are of that varietal. If there's none listed, it's almost certainly a blend of various types of grapes.

■ **Vineyard name:** If the label lists a vineyard, then at least 95% of the grapes used must have been harvested there. A vineyard name is more commonly, though not exclusively, found on higher-end bottles.

■ **Vintage:** If a year appears on the label, it means that at least 95% of the grapes were harvested in that year (85% if the wine is not designated with an AVA). If no vintage is listed, the grapes may come from more than one year's harvest.

rather than individual bottles. Basically, each tank is treated as one huge bottle. This comes at a price: although the sparkling wine may be ready in as little as a month, it has neither the complexity nor the bubble quality of traditional sparklers.

ROSÉ WINES

Rosé or blush wines are made from red-wine grapes, but the juicy pulp is left on the skins for a matter of hours—typically from 12 to 36—rather than days. When the winemaker decides that the juice has reached the desired color, it is drained off and filtered. Yeast is added, and the juice is left to ferment. Because the must stays on the skins for a shorter time, fewer tannins are leached from the skins, and the resulting wine is not as full flavored as a red. You might say that rosé is a lighter, fruitier version of red wine, not a pink version of white.

The range of tastes and textures is remarkable. Depending on how it's made, rosé of Cabernet Sauvignon, for instance, can have a velvety and almost savory taste, while rosé of Pinot Noir or Syrah might have a crisp and mineral taste.

Pinot Noir and Chardonnay are widely grown in the Russian River Valley.

GRAPE GROWING: THE BASICS

Most kinds of wine grapes are touchy. If the weather is too hot, they can produce too much sugar and not enough acid, resulting in overly alcoholic wines. Too cool and they won't ripen properly, and some will develop an unpleasant vegetal taste. And rain at the wrong time of year can wreak havoc on vineyards, causing grapes to rot on the vine. These and many other conditions must be just right to coax the best out of persnickety wine grapes, and Napa and Sonoma have that magical combination of sun, rain, fog, slope, and soil that allows many varieties of wine grape to thrive.

APPELLATIONS: LOCATION, LOCATION, LOCATION

California growers and winemakers generally agree that no matter what high-tech wine-making techniques might be used after the grapes are picked, in fact the wine is really made in the vineyard. This emphasis on *terroir* (a French term that encompasses a region's soil, microclimate, and overall growing conditions) reflects a belief that the quality of a wine is determined by what happens before the grapes are crushed.

In the United States, the Alcohol and Tobacco Tax and Trade Bureau (TTB) designates **appellations of origin** based on political boundaries or unique soil, climate, or other characteristics. California, for instance, is an appellation, as are Napa and Sonoma counties. More significantly to wine lovers, the TTB can designate a unique grape-growing region as an American Viticultural Area (AVA), more commonly called an appellation. Whether the appellation of origin is based on politics or terroir, it refers to the source of a wine's grapes, not to where it was made.

Different appellations—there are more than 100 AVAs in California, with 16 in the county of Napa alone—are renowned for different wines. The Napa Valley is known for Cabernet Sauvignon, for example, the Russian River Valley for Chardonnay and Pinot Noir, and the Dry Creek Valley for Zinfandel. Wineries can indicate the appellation on a bottle's label only if 85% of the grapes were grown in that appellation.

What makes things a little confusing is that appellations often overlap, allowing for increased levels of specificity. The Napa Valley AVA is, of course, part of the California appellation, but the Napa Valley AVA is itself divided into even smaller subappellations, the Oakville and Rutherford AVAs being among the most famous of these. There are even subappellations within subappellations. Over in Sonoma County, the Russian River Valley AVA contains the smaller Green Valley of the Russian River Valley AVA, which earned status as a separate viticultural area by virtue of its soils and a climate cooler and foggier than much of the rest of the Russian River Valley.

GEOLOGY 101

Wherever grapes are grown, geology matters. Grapevines are among the few plants that give their best fruit when grown in poor, rocky soil. On the other hand, grapes just don't like wet feet: the ideal vineyard soil is easily permeable by water for good drainage. Geologists do a brisk business advising growers.

Different grape varieties thrive in different types of soil. For instance, Cabernet Sauvignon does best in well-drained, gravelly soil. If it's too wet or contains too much heavy clay or organic matter, the soil will give the wine an obnoxious vegetative quality. Merlot, however, can grow in soil with more clay and still be made into a delicious, rich wine. Chardonnay likes well-drained vineyards but will also take heavy soil.

The soils below Napa Valley's crags and in the valleys of Sonoma County are dizzyingly diverse, which helps account for the unusually wide variety of grapes grown in such a small area. Some of the soils are composed of dense, heavy, sedimentary clays washed from the mountains; others are very rocky clays, loams, or silts of alluvial fans. These fertile, well-drained soils cover much of the valleys' floors. Other areas have soil based on serpentine, a rock that rarely appears aboveground. In all, there are about 60 soil types in the Napa and Sonoma valleys.

In Wine Country you'll hear a lot about limestone, a nutrient-rich rock in which grapevines thrive. Some California winemakers claim to be growing in limestone when they are not. In fact, only small patches of California's Wine Country have significant amounts of limestone. The term is often used to describe the streak of light-color, almost white soil that runs across the Napa Valley from the Palisades to St. Helena and through Sonoma County from the western flanks of the Mayacamas Mountains to Windsor. The band is actually made of volcanic material that has no limestone content.

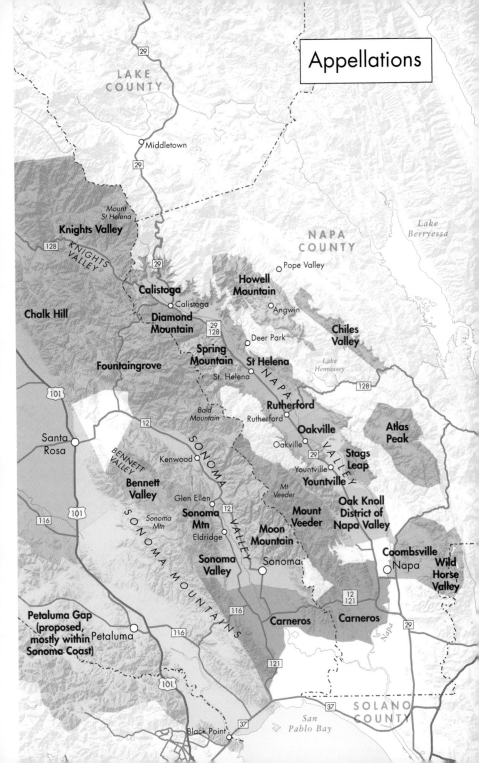

Appellations

LAKE COUNTY

[29] Middletown

[29]

Mount St Helena

NAPA COUNTY

Lake Berryessa

Knights Valley

[128] KNIGHTS VALLEY

Calistoga

Calistoga

Chalk Hill

Diamond Mountain

[29] [128]

Pope Valley

Howell Mountain

Angwin

Deer Park

Chiles Valley

Fountaingrove

Spring Mountain

St Helena

St. Helena

Lake Hennessey

[101]

[128]

[12]

Bald Mountain

Rutherford

Rutherford

Santa Rosa

BENNETT VALLEY

Kenwood

SONOMA

Oakville

Oakville

NAPA

Atlas Peak

[29]

Stags Leap

Yountville

Bennett Valley

Glen Ellen

Sonoma Mtn

[12]

Mt Veeder

Yountville

[116]

Sonoma Mtn

Eldridge

Moon Mountain

Mount Veeder

Oak Knoll District of Napa Valley

SONOMA MOUNTAINS

SONOMA VALLEY

Sonoma Valley

Sonoma

Coombsville

Napa

Wild Horse Valley

Petaluma Gap (proposed, mostly within Sonoma Coast)

[116] Petaluma

[116]

Carneros

Carneros

[12] [121]

[29]

[121]

[101]

[37]

Black Point [37]

Napa

San Pablo Bay

SOLANO COUNTY

DOWN ON THE FARM

Much like a fruit or nut orchard, a vineyard can produce excellent grapes for decades—even a century—if it's given the proper attention. The growing cycle starts in winter, when the vines are bare and dormant. While the plants rest, the grower works to enrich the soil and repair the trellising system (if there is one) that holds up the vines. This is when **pruning** takes place to regulate the vine's growth and the upcoming season's crop size.

In spring, the soil is aerated by plowing, and new vines go in. The grower trains established vines so they grow, with or without trellising, in the shape most beneficial for the grapes. **Bud break** occurs when the first bits of green emerge from the vines, and a pale green veil appears over the winter's gray-black vineyards. A late frost can be devastating at this time of year. Summer brings the flowering of the vines, when clusters of tiny green blossoms appear, and **fruit set,** when the grapes form from the blossoms. As the vineyards turn luxuriant and leafy, more pruning, along with leaf pulling, keeps foliage in check so the vine directs nutrients to the grapes, and so the sun can reach the fruit. As summer advances, the grower will **thin the fruit,** cutting off (or "dropping") some bunches so the remaining grapes intensify in flavor.

Fall is the busiest season in the vineyard. Growers and winemakers carefully monitor the ripeness of the grapes, sometimes with equipment that tests sugar and acid levels and sometimes simply by tasting them. As soon as the grapes are ripe, **harvest** begins amid the lush foliage. In California this generally happens in September and October, but sometimes a bit earlier or later, depending on the type of grape and the climatic conditions. Picking must be done as quickly as possible, within just a day or two, to keep the grapes from passing their peak. Most California grapes are harvested mechanically, but some are picked by hand. After harvest, the vines start to regenerate for the next year.

Many winemakers purchase at least some of their grapes. Some have negotiated long-term contracts with top growers, buying grapes from the same supplier year after year. This way, the winemaker can control the consistency and quality of the fruit, just as if it came from the winery's own vineyard. Other wineries buy from several growers, and many growers sell to more than one winery.

ORGANIC AND BIODYNAMIC

If, as many grape growers insist, a wine is only as good as the vineyard it comes from, those who have adopted organic and biodynamic agricultural methods may be on to something. But when using terms like *organic* and *biodynamic,* what do vintners mean? Although organic viticulture is governmentally recognized and regulated, it is vaguely defined and its value is hotly debated—just like the rest of organic farming. It boils down to a rejection of chemical fertilizers, pesticides, and fungicides. Biodynamic farmers also reject these artificial agents, and their vineyard maintenance involves metaphysical principles as well.

Even rarer than wines produced from organically grown grapes are completely organic wines. For a wine to be certified as organic, not only do the grapes have to come from organic vineyards, but the processing must use a minimum of chemical additives. Some winemakers argue that it is impossible to make truly fine wine without using additives like sulfur dioxide, an antioxidant that protects the wine's color, aroma, flavor, and longevity.

Very few producers make completely organic wine. To be called organic, a wine must contain certified organic grapes and have no added sulfites. (Remember that some wines made from certified organic grapes still contain naturally occurring sulfites.)

Biodynamic farmers view the land as a living, self-sustaining organism requiring a healthy, unified ecosystem to thrive. To nurture the soil, for instance, vineyard workers spray specially formulated herbal "teas" (the ingredients include yarrow, dandelion, valerian, and stinging nettle flowers) onto compost spread in the fields. Grazing animals such as sheep or goats maintain the ground cover between the vines (the animals' manure provides natural fertilizer), and natural predators, among them insect-eating bats, control pests that might damage the crop. Steiner and his successors believed that the movements of the sun and the moon influence plant development, so astronomical calendars play a role in the timing of many vineyard activities.

At its most elevated level, the biodynamic philosophy recognizes a farm as a metaphysical entity that requires its human inhabitants not merely to tend it but to form a spiritual bond with it, a notion that other organic farmers share in theory even if their methods sometimes diverge. Among wineries whose practices have been certified organic are Hall in the Napa Valley, and Preston of Dry Creek in Northern Sonoma County. The Napa Valley's Robert Sinskey Vineyards is certified both organic and biodynamic, as is the Sonoma Valley's Benziger Family Winery.

WINE-LOVER'S GLOSSARY

Wine making and tasting require specialized vocabularies. Some words are merely show-off jargon, but many are specific and helpful.

Acidity. The tartness of a wine, derived from the fruit acids of the grape. Acids stabilize a wine (i.e., preserve its character), balance its sweetness, and bring out its flavors. Tartaric acid is the major acid in wine, but malic, lactic, and citric acids also occur.

Aging. The process by which some wines improve over time, becoming smoother and more complex. Wine is often aged in oak vats or barrels, slowly interacting with the air through the pores in the wood. Sometimes wine is cellared for bottle aging. Age can diminish a wine's fruitiness and also dull its color: whites turn brownish, rosés orange, reds brown.

Alcohol. Ethyl alcohol is a colorless, volatile, pungent spirit that not only gives wine its stimulating effect and some of its flavor but also acts as a preservative, stabilizing the wine and allowing it to age. A wine's alcohol content must be stated on the label, expressed as a percentage of volume, except when a wine is designated table wine.

American Viticultural Area (AVA). More commonly termed an *appellation*. A region with unique soil, climate, and other conditions can be designated an AVA by the Alcohol and Tobacco Tax and Trade Bureau. When a label lists an AVA—Napa Valley or Mt. Veeder, for example—at least 85% of the grapes used to make the wine must come from that AVA.

Ampelography. The science of identifying varietals by their leaves, grapevines, and, more recently, DNA.

Appellation. *See American Viticultural Area.*

Aroma. The scent of young wine derived from the fresh fruit. It diminishes with fermentation and is replaced by a more complex bouquet as the wine ages. The term may also describe special fruity odors in a wine, such as black cherry, green olive, ripe raspberry, or apple.

Astringency. The puckery sensation produced in the mouth by the tannins in wine.

Balance. A quality of wine in which all desirable elements (fruit, acid, tannin) are present in the proper proportion. Well-balanced wine has a pleasing nose, flavor, and mouthfeel.

Barrel fermenting. The fermenting of wine in small oak barrels instead of large tanks or vats. This method keeps grape lots separate before blending the wine. The cost of oak barrels makes this method expensive.

Biodynamic. An approach to agriculture that focuses on regarding the land as a living thing; it generally incorporates organic farming techniques and the use of the astronomical calendar in hopes of cultivating a healthy balance in the vineyard ecosystem.

Blanc de blancs. Sparkling or still white wine made solely from white grapes.

Blanc de noirs. White wine made with red grapes by removing the skins during crush. Some sparkling whites, for example, are made with red Pinot Noir grapes.

Blending. The mixing of several wines to create one of greater complexity or appeal, as when a heavy wine is blended with a lighter one to make a more approachable medium-bodied wine.

Body. The wine's heft or density as experienced by the palate. *See also Mouthfeel.*

Bordeaux blend. A red wine blended from varietals native to France's Bordeaux region, the primary ones are Cabernet Sauvignon, Cabernet Franc, Malbec, Merlot, and Petit Verdot.

Bouquet. The odors a mature wine gives off when opened. They should be pleasantly complex and should give an indication of the wine's grape variety, origin, age, and quality.

Brix. A method of telling whether grapes are ready for picking by measuring their sugars. Multiplying a grape's Brix number by .55 approximates the potential alcohol content of the wine.

Brut. French term for the driest category of sparkling wine. *See also Demi-sec, Sec.*

Case. A carton of 12 bottles of wine (750 mL each). A magnum case contains six 1.5 L bottles. Most wineries will offer a discount if you purchase wine by the case (or sometimes a half case).

Cask. A synonym for *barrel*. More generally, any size or shape wine container made from wood staves.

Cellaring. Storage of wine in bottles for aging. The bottles are laid on their sides to keep the corks moist and prevent air leakage that would spoil the wine.

Champagne. The northernmost wine district of France, where the world's only genuine Champagne is made. The term is often used loosely in America to denote sparkling wines.

Cloudiness. The presence of particles that do not settle out of a wine, causing it to look and taste dusty or muddy. If settling and decanting do not correct cloudiness, the wine was badly made or is spoiled.

Complexity. The qualities of good wine that provide a multilayered sensory experience to the drinker. Balanced flavors, harmonious aromas or bouquet, and a long finish are components of complexity.

Corked. Describes wine that is flawed by the musty, wet-cardboard flavor imparted by cork mold, technically known as TCA, or 2,4,6-Trichloroanisole.

Crush. American term for the harvest season. Also refers to the year's crop of grapes crushed for wine.

Cuvée. Generally a sparkling wine, but sometimes a still wine, that is a blend of different wines and sometimes different vintages. Most sparkling wines are cuvées.

Decant. To pour a wine from its bottle into another container either to expose it to air or to eliminate sediment. Decanting for sediment pours out the clear wine and leaves the residue behind in the original bottle.

Demi-sec. French term that translates as "half-dry." It is applied to sweet wines that contain 3.5%–5% sugar.

Dessert wines. Sweet wines that are big in flavor and aroma. Some are quite low in alcohol; others, such as port-style wines, are fortified with brandy or another spirit and may be 17%–21% alcohol.

Dry. Having very little sweetness or residual sugar. Most wines are dry, although some whites, such as Rieslings, are made to be "off-dry," meaning "on the sweet side."

Estate bottled. A wine entirely made by one winery at a single facility. In general the grapes must come from the vineyards the winery owns or farms within the same appellation (which must be printed on the label).

Fermentation. The biochemical process by which grape juice becomes wine. Enzymes generated by yeast cells convert grape sugars into alcohol and carbon dioxide. Fermentation stops when either the sugar is depleted and the yeast starves or when high alcohol levels kill the yeast.

Fermenter. Any vessel (such as a barrel, tank, or vat) in which wine is fermented.

Filtering, Filtration. A purification process in which wine is pumped through filters to rid it of suspended particles.

Fining. A method of clarifying wine by adding egg whites, bentonite (a type of clay), or other natural substances to a barrel. As these solids settle to the bottom, they take various dissolved compounds with them. Most wine meant for everyday drinking is fined; however, better wines are fined less often.

Finish. Also known as *aftertaste*. The flavors that remain in the mouth after swallowing wine. A good wine has a long finish with complex flavor and aroma.

Flight. A few wines—usually from three to five—specially selected for tasting together.

Fortification. A process by which brandy or another spirit is added to a wine to stop fermentation and to increase its level of alcohol, as in the case of port-style dessert wines.

Fruity. Having aromatic nuances of fresh fruit, such as fig, raspberry, or apple. Fruitiness, a sign of quality in young wines, is replaced by bouquet in aged wines.

Fumé Blanc. A wine made with Sauvignon Blanc. Robert Mondavi coined the term to describe his oak-aged Sauvignon Blanc.

Green. Said of a wine made from unripe grapes, with a pronounced leafy flavor and a raw edge.

Horizontal tasting. A tasting of several different wines of the same vintage.

Late harvest. Wine made from grapes harvested later in the fall than the main lot, and thus higher in sugar levels. Many dessert wines are late harvest.

Lees. The spent yeast, grape solids, and tartrates that drop to the bottom of the barrel or tank as wine ages. Wine, particularly white wine, gains complexity when it is left on the lees for a time.

Library wine. An older vintage that the winery has put aside to sell at a later date.

Malolactic fermentation. A secondary fermentation that changes harsh malic acid into softer lactic acid and carbon dioxide. Wine is sometimes inoculated with lactic bacteria or placed in wooden containers that harbor the bacteria to enhance this process. Often referred to as *ML* or *malo*. Too much malo can make a wine heavy.

Meritage. A trademarked name for American (mostly California) Bordeaux blends that meet certain wine-making and marketing requirements and are made by member wineries of the Meritage Association.

Méthode champenoise. The traditional, time-consuming method of making sparkling wines by fermenting them in individual bottles. By agreement with the European Union, sparkling wines made in California this way are labeled *méthode traditionelle*.

Mouthfeel. Literally, the way wine feels in the mouth.

Must. The slushy mix of crushed grapes—juice, pulp, skin, seeds, and bits of stem—produced by the stemmer-crusher at the beginning of the wine-making process.

Neutral oak. The wood of older barrels or vats that no longer pass much flavor or tannin to the wine stored within.

New oak. The wood of a fresh barrel or vat that has not previously been used to ferment or age wine. It can impart desirable flavors and enhance a wine's complexity, but if used to excess it can overpower a wine's true character.

Nonvintage. A blend of wines from different years. Nonvintage wines have no date on their label.

Nose. The overall fragrance (aroma or bouquet) given off by a wine.

Oaky. A vanilla-woody flavor that develops when wine is aged in oak barrels. Leave a wine too long in a new oak barrel and that oaky taste overpowers the other flavors.

Organic viticulture. The technique of growing grapes without the use of chemical fertilizers, pesticides, or fungicides.

Oxidation. Undesirable flavor and color changes to juice or wine caused by too much contact with the air, either during processing or because of a leaky barrel or cork.

pH. Technical term for a measure of acidity. It is a reverse measure: the lower the pH level, the higher the acidity. Most wines range in pH from 2.9 to 4.2, with the most desirable level between 3.2 and 3.5.

Phylloxera. A disease caused by the root louse *Phylloxera vastatrix,* which attacks and ultimately destroys the roots. The pest is native to the United States; it traveled to France with American grapevines in the 19th century and devastated nonresistant vineyards.

Pomace. Spent grape skins and solids left over after the juice has been pressed, commonly returned to the fields as fertilizer.

Racking. Moving wine from one tank or barrel to another to leave unwanted deposits behind; the wine may or may not be fined or filtered in the process.

Residual sugar. The natural sugar left in a wine after fermentation, which converts sugar into alcohol. If the fermentation was interrupted or if the must has very high sugar levels, some residual sugar will remain, making a sweeter wine.

Rhône blend. A wine made from grapes hailing from France's Rhône Valley, such as Grenache, Syrah, Mourvèdre, or Viognier.

Rosé. Pink wine, usually made from red-wine grapes (of any variety). The juice is left on the skins only long enough to give it a tinge of color.

Rounded. Said of a well-balanced wine in which fruity flavor is nicely offset by acidity.

Sec. French for "dry." The term is generally applied within the sparkling or sweet categories, indicating the wine has 1.7%–3.5% residual sugar. Sec is drier than demi-sec but not as dry as brut.

Sediment. Dissolved or suspended solids that drop out of most red wines as they age in the bottle, thus clarifying their appearance, flavors, and aromas. Sediment is not a defect in an old wine or in a new wine that has been bottled unfiltered.

Sparkling wines. Wines in which carbon dioxide is dissolved, making them bubbly. Examples are French Champagne, Italian prosecco, and Spanish cava.

Sugar. Source of grapes' natural sweetness. When yeast feeds on sugar, it produces alcohol and carbon dioxide. The higher the sugar content of the grape, the higher the potential alcohol level or sweetness of the wine.

Sulfites. Compounds of sulfur dioxide almost always added before fermentation to prevent oxidation and to kill bacteria and wild yeasts that can cause off flavors.

Sustainable viticulture. A viticultural method that aims to bring the vineyard into harmony with the environment. Organic and other techniques are used to minimize agricultural impact and to promote biodiversity.

Table wine. Any wine that has at least 7% but not more than 14% alcohol by volume. The term doesn't necessarily imply anything about the wine's quality or price—both super-premium and jug wines can be labeled as table wine.

Tannins. You can tell when they're there, but their origins are still a mystery. These natural grape compounds produce a sensation of drying or astringency in the mouth and throat. Tannins settle out as wine ages; they're a big player in many red wines.

Tartaric acid, Tartrates. The principal acid of wine. Crystalline tartrates form on the insides of vats or barrels and sometimes in the bottle or on the cork. They look like tiny shards of glass but are not harmful.

Terroir. French for "soil." Typically used to describe the soil and climate conditions that influence the quality and characteristics of grapes and wine.

Varietal. A wine that takes its name from the grape variety from which it is predominantly made. According to U.S. law, at least 75% of a wine must come from a particular grape to be labeled with its variety name.

Veraison. The time during the ripening process when grapes change their color from green to red or yellow and sugar levels rise.

Vertical tasting. A tasting of several vintages of the same wine.

Vinification. The process by which grapes are made into wine.

Vintage. A given year's grape harvest. A vintage date on a label indicates the year the wine's grapes were harvested rather than the year the wine was bottled.

Viticulture. The cultivation of grapes.

Woody. A negative term describing excessively musty wood aromas and flavors picked up by wine stored in a wood barrel or cask for too long.

Yeast. A minute, single-celled fungus that germinates and multiplies rapidly as it feeds on sugar with the help of enzymes, creating alcohol and releasing carbon dioxide in the process of fermentation.

Zymology. The science of fermentation.

NAPA VALLEY

WELCOME TO NAPA VALLEY

TOP REASONS TO GO

★ **Wine tasting:** Whether you're on a pilgrimage to famous Cabernet houses or searching for hidden-gem wineries and obscure varietals, the valley supplies plenty of both.

★ **Fine dining:** It may sound like hype, but a meal at one of the valley's top-tier restaurants can be a revelation—about the level of artistry intuitive chefs can achieve and how well quality wines pair with food.

★ **Art and architecture:** Several wineries are owned by art collectors whose holdings grace indoor and outdoor spaces, and the valley contains remarkable specimens of winery architecture.

★ **Spa treatments:** Work-hard, play-hard types and inveterate sybarites flock to spas for pampering.

★ **Balloon rides:** By the dawn's early light, hot-air balloons soar over the vineyards, a magical sight from the ground and even more thrilling from above. Afterward, enjoy a champagne brunch.

Mount
St. Helena

Robert Louis
Stevenson
State Park

Aetna Springs

THE PALISADES

29

128

6 Calistoga

29
128

Bothe-Napa
State Park

Deer
Park

Bale Grist Mill
State Historic
Park

Charles Krug
Winery

Beringer Vineyards

5

St. Helena

Sugarloaf Ridge
State Park

Bald
Mountain

1 **Napa.** The valley's largest town has wineries and tasting rooms in both its urban and rural sectors, and downtown has evolved into a shopping and fine-dining haven.

2 **Yountville.** Several must-visit restaurants are located in this small town whose other delights include its well-groomed main street. Downtown has many tasting rooms; most of Yountville's wineries are to the east, with a few to the north and south.

3 **Oakville.** With a population of less than 100, this town is all about its vineyards, mostly of Cabernet. Fans of this noble grape could get lost for several days here sampling the terrific wines made from it.

4 **Rutherford.** "It takes Rutherford dust to grow great Cabernet," a legendary winemaker once said, and with several dozen wineries in this appellation, there are plenty of opportunities to ponder what this means.

5 **St. Helena.** Genteel St. Helena's Main Street evokes images of classic Americana; its wineries range from valley stalwarts Beringer and Charles Krug to boutique wineries tucked away in the hills.

6 **Calistoga.** Founded by Sam Brannan in the 19th century, this spa town still has its Old West–style false fronts, but it's now also home to luxurious lodgings and spas with 21st-century panache.

GETTING ORIENTED

From the air, the Napa Valley reveals itself as a tiny sliver, just 5 miles across at its widest, running 30 miles from southeast to northwest between the Vaca Range to the east and the Mayacamas Mountains to the west. The main towns—from south to north, Napa, Yountville, Oakville, Rutherford, St. Helena, and Calistoga—straddle Highway 29, known for most of this stretch as the St. Helena Highway.

With more than 500 wineries and many of the biggest brands in the business, the Napa Valley is the Wine Country's star. Napa, the largest town, lures visitors with cultural attractions and (relatively) reasonably priced accommodations. A few miles north, compact Yountville is packed with top-notch restaurants and hotels, and Oakville and Rutherford are extolled for their Cabernet Sauvignon–friendly soils. Beyond them, St. Helena teems with elegant boutiques and restaurants, and casual Calistoga, known for its spas and hot springs, has the feel of an Old West frontier town.

The Napa Valley contains only about an eighth of the acreage planted in Bordeaux, but past volcanic and other seismic activity have bequeathed the valley diverse soils and microclimates that provide winemakers with the raw materials to craft wines of consistently high quality. More land is devoted to Cabernet Sauvignon and Chardonnay than any other varietals, but Cabernet Franc, Merlot, Pinot Noir, Petite Sirah, Sauvignon Blanc, Syrah, Zinfandel, and other wines are also made here. In terms of output, though, the valley's reputation far exceeds the mere 4% of California's total wine-grape harvest it represents.

So what makes the Napa Valley one of the state's top tourist destinations and a playground for San Francisco Bay Area residents? For one thing, variety: for every blockbuster winery whose name you'll recognize from the shelves of wine stores and the pages of *Wine Spectator*—Robert Mondavi, Beringer, and Caymus, to name a very few—you'll also find low-frills operations that will warmly invite you into their modest tasting rooms. The local viticulture has in turn inspired a robust passion for food, and several marquee chefs have solidified the valley's position as one of the country's great restaurant destinations. You will also get a glimpse of California's history, from wine cellars dating back

to the late 1800s to the flurry of Steamboat Gothic
ing up Calistoga. Binding all these temptations tog
scenic beauty of the place. Much of Napa Valley's la
in orderly, densely planted rows of vines. Even the cli
as the warm summer days and refreshingly cool eveni
for grape growing also make perfect weather for trave

PLANNER

WHEN TO GO

The Napa Valley is a year-round destination whose charms vary depending on the season. Watching the misty winter fog rising on a rainy day off dark, gnarly grapevines, for example, can be just as captivating a moment as witnessing a summer sunset backlighting flourishing vineyard rows. Because the Napa Valley is the most-visited Wine Country locale, summers draw hordes of tourists, making late spring and early fall, when it's less crowded and temperatures are often cooler, among the best times to come. Harvesttime—from August into November, depending on the grape type and the year's weather—is the best time to visit to see wine making in action. Weekends can be busy year-round. To avoid heavy traffic on summer weekends, it almost always works best to arrive by midmorning, especially if you need to be back in San Francisco by early evening.

PLANNING YOUR TIME

First things first: even in a month it's impossible to "do" the Napa Valley—there are simply too many wineries here. Many visitors find that tasting at three or at most four a day and spending quality time at each of them, with a leisurely lunch to rest the palate, is preferable to cramming in as many visits as possible. You can, of course, add variety with a spa treatment (these can take up to a half day), a balloon ride (expect to rise early and finish in the late morning), shopping, or a bicycle ride.

You can maximize your time touring wineries with a few simple strategies. If you'll be visiting a big operation such as Mondavi, Beringer, or Castello di Amorosa, try to schedule that stop early in the day and then smaller wineries after lunch; you're less likely to be held up by the crowds that way. Even during the week in summertime, the afternoon traffic on Highway 29 can be heavy, so after 3 pm try to avoid wineries along this stretch. Plan your visits to wineries on or just off the Silverado Trail for later in the day, though even there you may find the going slow heading south from Rutherford.

The town of Napa is the valley's most affordable base, and it's especially convenient if most of your touring will be in the southern half. If you'll be dining a lot in Yountville, staying there is a good idea because you can walk or take the Yountville Trolley back to your lodging. Calistoga is the most affordable base in the northern Napa Valley, though it's not always convenient for touring southern Napa wineries.

GETTING HERE AND AROUND

BUS TRAVEL

VINE Bus 29 Express brings passengers from the BART (Bay Area Rapid Transit) El Cerrito Del Norte station and the Vallejo Ferry Terminal. VINE Bus 25 travels between the towns of Napa and Sonoma. VINE Bus 10 and (weekdays only) Bus 29 run between Napa and Calistoga, with one stop or more in Yountville, Oakville, Rutherford, St. Helena, and Calistoga. Bus 10 operates on Sunday, but other VINE buses do not. *For more information about arriving by bus, see Bus Travel in the Travel Smart chapter.*

Contacts VINE. ☎ *707/251-2800, 800/696-6443* ⊕ *www.ridethevine.com.*

CAR TRAVEL

Traveling by car is the most convenient way to tour the Napa Valley. Both of the main routes from San Francisco into the valley will get you here in about an hour in normal traffic. You can head north across the Golden Gate Bridge and U.S. 101, east on Highway 37 and then Highway 121, and north on Highway 29; or east across the San Francisco–Oakland Bay Bridge and north on Interstate 80, west on Highway 37, and north on Highway 29.

Highway 29 can become congested, especially on summer weekends. Traffic can be slow in St. Helena during morning and afternoon rush hours, though a recent street-widening project south of downtown has alleviated some of the backup. You may find slightly less traffic on the Silverado Trail, which roughly parallels Highway 29 between Napa and Calistoga. Cross streets connect the two highways like rungs on a ladder every few miles, making it easy to cross from one to the other.

■TIP→ Although the Silverado Trail can get busy in the late afternoon, it's often a better option than Highway 29 if you're traveling between, say, St. Helena or Calistoga and the city of Napa.

For information about car services and limos, see Getting Here and Around in the Travel Smart chapter.

RESTAURANTS

Dining out is one of the deep pleasures of a Napa Valley visit. Cuisine here tends to focus on seasonal produce, some of it from gardens the restaurants maintain themselves, and many chefs endeavor to source their proteins locally, too. The French Laundry, the Restaurant at Meadowood, La Toque, Bouchon, Bistro Jeanty, Redd, Solbar, Restaurant at Auberge du Soleil, Press, and Terra often appear at the top of visitors' agendas, and rightfully so: in addition to stellar cuisine they all have sommeliers or waiters capable of helping you select wines that will enhance your enjoyment of your meal immeasurably, and the level of service matches the food and surroundings. Another two dozen restaurants provide experiences nearly on a par with those at the above establishments, so if your favorite is booked when you visit you'll still have plenty of options. *Restaurant reviews have been shortened. For full information, visit Fodors.com.*

HOTELS

With the price of accommodations at high-end inns and hotels *starting* at more than $1,000 a night, when it comes to Napa Valley lodging the question at first glance seems to be how much are you willing to pay? If you have the means, you can ensconce yourself between plush linens at exclusive hillside retreats with fancy architecture and even fancier amenities, and you're more or less guaranteed to have a fine time. As with Napa Valley restaurants, though, the decor and amenities the most stylish hotels and inns provide have upped the ante for all hoteliers and innkeepers, so even if you're on a budget you can live swell. Many smaller inns and hotels and even the motels provide pleasant stays for a fairly reasonable price. The main problem with these establishments is that they often book up quickly, so if you're visiting between late May and October, it's wise to reserve your room as far ahead as possible. *Hotel reviews have been shortened. For full information, visit Fodors.com.*

WHAT IT COSTS				
	$	$$	$$$	$$$$
Restaurants	under $16	$16–$22	$23–$30	over $30
Hotels	under $201	$201–$300	$301–$400	over $400

Restaurant prices are the average cost of a main course at dinner, or if dinner isn't served, at lunch. Hotel prices are the lowest cost of a standard double room in high season.

APPELLATIONS

Nearly all of Napa County, which stretches from the Mayacamas Mountains in the west to Lake Berryessa in the east, makes up the Napa Valley American Viticultural Area (AVA). This large region is divided into many smaller AVAs, or subappellations, each with its own unique characteristics.

Los Carneros AVA stretches west from the Napa River across the southern Napa Valley into the southern Sonoma Valley. Pinot Noir and Chardonnay are the main grapes grown in this cool, windswept region just north of San Pablo Bay, but Merlot, Syrah, and, in the warmer portions, Cabernet Sauvignon, also do well here. Four of the subappellations north of the Carneros District—Oak Knoll, Oakville, Rutherford, and St. Helena—stretch clear across the valley floor. Chilled by coastal fog, the **Oak Knoll District of Napa Valley AVA** has some of the coolest temperatures. The **Oakville AVA,** just north of Yountville, is studded with both big-name wineries such as Robert Mondavi and Silver Oak and awe-inspiring boutique labels, among them the super-exclusive Screaming Eagle. Oakville's gravelly, well-drained soil is especially good for Cabernet Sauvignon.

A sunny climate and well-drained soil make **Rutherford AVA** one of the best locations for Cabernet Sauvignon in California, if not the world. North of Rutherford, the **St. Helena AVA** is one of Napa's toastiest, as the slopes surrounding the narrow valley reflect the sun's heat. Bordeaux

Napa Valley Wine Train passengers get up-close vineyard views from vintage Pullman cars.

varietals are the most popular grapes grown here—particularly Cabernet Sauvignon, but also Merlot. Just north, at the foot of Mt. St. Helena is the **Calistoga AVA**; Cabernet Sauvignon does well here, but also Zinfandel, Syrah, and Petite Sirah.

The **Stags Leap District AVA**, a small district on the eastern side of the valley, is marked by dramatic volcanic palisades. As with the neighboring **Yountville AVA**, Cabernet Sauvignon and Merlot are by far the favored grapes. In both subappellations, cool evening breezes encourage a long growing season and intense fruit flavors. Some describe the resulting wines as "rock soft" or an "iron fist in a velvet glove." Also on the valley's eastern edge is the **Coombsville AVA.** Cabernet Sauvignon grows on the western-facing slopes of the Vaca Mountains, with Merlot, Chardonnay, Syrah, and Pinot Noir more prevalent in the cooler lower elevations.

The **Mt. Veeder** and **Spring Mountain AVAs** each encompass parts of the mountains that give them their names. Both demonstrate how stressing out grapevines can yield outstanding results; the big winner is Cabernet Sauvignon. Growing grapes on these slopes takes a certain recklessness—or foolhardiness, depending on your point of view—since many of the vineyards are so steep that they have to be tilled and harvested by hand.

The great variety of the climates and soils of the remaining subappellations—the **Atlas Peak, Chiles Valley, Diamond Mountain District, Howell Mountain,** and **Wild Horse Valley AVAs**—explains why vintners here can make so many different wines, and make them so well, in what in the end is a relatively compact region.

NAPA

46 miles northeast of San Francisco.

After many years as a blue-collar burg detached from the Wine Country scene, the Napa Valley's largest town (population about 80,000) has evolved into one of its shining stars. Masaharu Morimoto and other chefs of note operate restaurants here, several swank hotels and inns can be found downtown and beyond, and nightlife options include the West Coast edition of the famed Blue Note jazz club. A walkway that follows the Napa River has made downtown more pedestrian-friendly, and the Oxbow Public Market, a complex of high-end food purveyors, is popular with locals and tourists.

The market is named for the nearby oxbow bend in the Napa River, a bit north of where Napa was founded in 1848. The first wood-frame building was a saloon, and the downtown area still projects an old-river-town vibe. Many Victorian houses have survived, some as bed-and-breakfast inns, and in the original business district a few older buildings have been preserved. Some of these structures, along with a few newer ones, were heavily damaged during a magnitude 6.0 earthquake in 2014.

Napans are rightly proud of how the city pulled together following the quake; visitors will find little lingering evidence of the temblor. Another cause for celebration is the return of Copia, the homage to food and wine spearheaded by the late vintner Robert Mondavi. Copia, now the Napa campus of the Culinary Institute of America, whose West Coast headquarters is in St. Helena, kick-started Napa's renaissance in the early 2000s but then closed for eight years. It hosts cooking demonstrations and other activities open to the public and has a shop and a restaurant.

■ TIP→ **If based in Napa, in addition to exploring the wineries amid the surrounding countryside, plan on spending at least a half a day strolling the downtown area.**

GETTING HERE AND AROUND

To get to downtown Napa from Highway 29, take the 1st Street exit and head east on 2nd Street, following the signs for Central Napa. Most of the town's sights and many of its restaurants are clustered in an easily walkable area around Main Street (you'll find street parking and garages nearby). Most wineries with Napa addresses are on or just off Highway 29 or the parallel Silverado Trail, the exception being the ones in the Carneros District or Mt. Veeder AVA. Most of these are on or just off Highway 121. VINE Bus 29 Express serves Napa from BART light-rail's El Cerrito Del Norte station and the San Francisco Ferry's Vallejo terminal. Bus 10 passes by some downtown sights.

ESSENTIALS

Contact Do Napa. ☎ *707/257–0322* ⊕ *www.donapa.com.*

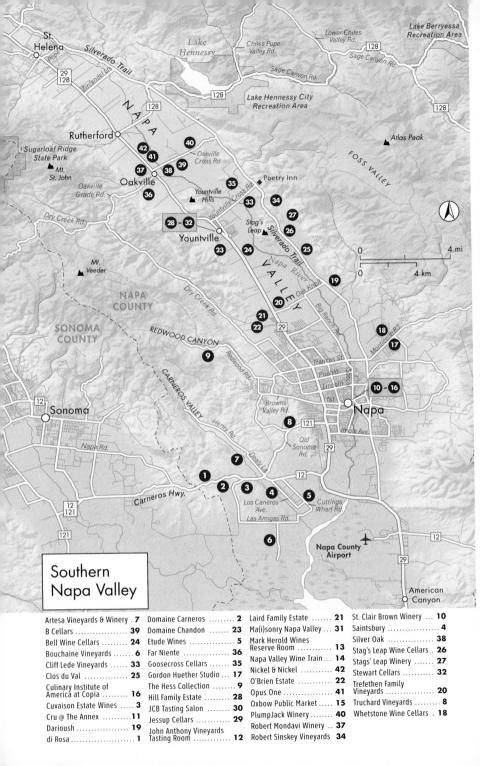

Southern Napa Valley

EXPLORING

TOP ATTRACTIONS

Artesa Vineyards & Winery. From a distance the modern, minimalist architecture of Artesa blends harmoniously with the surrounding Carneros landscape, but up close its pools, fountains, and the large outdoor sculptures by resident artist Gordon Huether of Napa make a vivid impression. So, too, do the wines: mostly Chardonnay and Pinot Noir but also Cabernet Sauvignon, Merlot, and other limited releases like Albariño and Tempranillo. You can sample wines by themselves without a reservation or, at tastings for which a reservation is required, paired with chocolate, cheese, or tapas. ■TIP→ The tour, conducted daily, explores wine making and the winery's history. ✉ *1345 Henry Rd., off Old Sonoma Rd. and Dealy La.* ☎ *707/224–1668* ⊕ *www.artesawinery.com* ✉ *Tastings $25–$60, tour $40 (includes tasting).*

Fodor's Choice ★ Bouchaine Vineyards. Tranquil Bouchaine lies just north of the tidal sloughs of San Pablo Bay—to appreciate the off-the-beaten-path setting, step out on the tasting-room deck and scan the skies for hawks and golden eagles soaring above the vineyards. The alternately breezy and foggy weather in this part of the Carneros works well for the Burgundian varietals Pinot Noir and Chardonnay. Since 2014, these account for most of Bouchaine's wines, but also look for Pinot Blanc, Pinot Gris, Pinot Meunier, Riesling, and Syrah. ■TIP→ Bay Areans come here to enjoy the easygoing pace and "Napa wines at Sonoma prices"—the excellent $50 Chardonnay from Hyde Vineyard, whose counterparts from other wineries go for double or more, is but one example. ✉ *1075 Buchli Station Rd., off Duhig Rd., south of Hwy. 121* ☎ *707/252–9065* ⊕ *www.bouchaine.com* ✉ *Tasting $25.*

Fodor's Choice ★ Cru @ The Annex. Prepare for a multisensory, multilabel experience at this tasting room adjacent to the main Oxbow market buildings. The snazzy space successfully integrates Mexican blankets, a backlit laser-etched Napa Valley wall map, outré lighting fixtures, and large monitors screening silent video art. Personable hosts stimulate your taste buds with wines from three labels produced by St. Helena's Vineyard 29 winery. Keith Emerson makes Sauvignon Blanc, Pinot Noir, Merlot, and Cabernet Sauvignon for Cru, whose flights are paired with lightly spiced popcorns, and Philippe Melka, a preeminent wine-making consultant, crafts collector-quality estate-grown Cabernets for Aida and Vineyard 29. Tastings are by the glass, flight, or bottle; one flight showcases the three labels' Cabernets. Walk-ins are welcome, but reservations are recommended, especially on weekends. ■TIP→ In good weather enjoy Napa River and Oxbow Commons views from the outdoor patio. ✉ *Oxbow Public Market, 1046 McKinstry St., at 1st St.* ☎ *707/927–2409* ⊕ *www.cruattheannex.com* ✉ *Tastings $29–$75.*

Culinary Institute of America at Copia. In fall 2016 the institute reopened the long-dormant Copia facility for wine and food education, whose founders included the late vintner Robert Mondavi. Honoring Copia's original mission and its own, the CIA offers public classes and demonstrations involving food and wine pairings, sparkling wines, ancient

CLOSE UP

Top Tastings and Tours

TASTINGS

Joseph Phelps Vineyards, St. Helena. Tastings at Phelps unfold like everything else here: with class, grace, and precision—an apt description of the wines themselves.

O'Brien Estate, Napa. The superb wines, self-contained location, and genial hosts make a stop at this Oak Knoll District winery the highlight of many a Wine Country vacation.

Silver Oak, Oakville. The sole wine produced here is a Cabernet Sauvignon blend available for tasting in a stone building constructed of materials from a 19th-century flour mill.

TOURS

Beringer Vineyards, St. Helena. Of several Napa wineries with tours focusing on the history of California wine making, Beringer has perhaps the prettiest site.

Schramsberg, Calistoga. Deep inside 19th-century caves created by Chinese laborers, you'll learn all about crafting *méthode traditionelle* sparkling wines. Back aboveground, you'll taste some.

SETTING

Barnett Vineyards, St. Helena. Arrive early at this producer atop Spring Mountain to bask in northern Napa Valley views rivaling those from a balloon.

Hall St. Helena. A glass-walled tasting area perched over the vineyards provides a dramatic setting for sampling award-winning Cabernets.

FOOD PAIRING

B Cellars, Oakville. An open kitchen dominates the B Cellars tasting space, a clear indication that this boutique winery takes the relationship between food and wine seriously.

VGS Chateau Potelle, St. Helena. Sophisticated whimsy is on full display at this tasting room where wines are paired exceedingly well with a top chef's small bites.

---

grains, cheeses, pasta, and sauces. One class explores the Napa Valley's history through eight glasses of wine, and children join their parents for Family Funday workshops about making mac and cheese and nutritious lunches. A store sells cookbooks, wines and sauces, and artisanal kitchenware, and there's a full-service restaurant. Plans are afoot to open a museum of culinary arts, to install tasting stands operated by area wineries, and to relocate the Wine Hall of Fame and a significant wine collection from the CIA's St. Helena campus. ⊠ *500 1st St., near McKinstry St.* ☎ *707/967–2500* ⊕ *www.ciaatcopia.com* ✒ *Facility free, demonstrations from $15.*

Darioush. Exceptional hospitality and well-balanced wines from southern Napa Valley grapes are the hallmarks of this winery whose dramatic architecture recalls the ancient Persian capital Persepolis. Several wines, including the signature Napa Valley Cabernet Sauvignon, combine grapes grown high on Mt. Veeder with valley-floor fruit, the former providing tannins and structure, the latter adding mellower, savory notes. Viognier, Chardonnay, Merlot, Pinot Noir, and a Cab-Shiraz blend are among the other wines made here. ■TIP→ On weekdays walk-in parties

The main château at Domaine Carneros sits high on a hill.

can taste at the bar, but an appointment is required on weekends and always for seated tastings that include cheese-wine pairings. ⊠ *4240 Silverado Trail, near Shady Oaks Dr.* ☎ *707/257–2345* ⊕ *www.darioush.com* 🎫 *Tasting $40–$300.*

Fodor'sChoice
★
di Rosa. A formidable array of artworks from the 1960s to the present by Northern California artists is displayed on this 217-acre property. The works can be found not only in galleries and in the former residence of its late founder, Rene di Rosa, but also throughout the surrounding landscape. Some works were commissioned especially for di Rosa, among them Paul Kos's meditative *Chartres Bleu,* a video installation in a chapel-like setting that replicates a stained-glass window from the cathedral in Chartres, France. ■TIP→ You can view the current temporary exhibition and a few permanent works at the Gatehouse Gallery, but to experience the breadth of the collection you'll need to book a tour. ⊠ *5200 Sonoma Hwy./Hwy. 121* ☎ *707/226–5991* ⊕ *www.dirosaart.org* 🎫 *Gatehouse Gallery $5, tours $12–$15* ⊗ *Closed Mon. and Tues.*

Domaine Carneros. A visit to this majestic château is an opulent way to enjoy the Carneros District—especially in fine weather, when the vineyard views are spectacular. The château was modeled after an 18th-century French mansion owned by the Taittinger family. Carved into the hillside beneath the winery, the cellars produce sparkling wines reminiscent of those made by Taittinger, using only Los Carneros AVA grapes. The winery sells flights and glasses of its sparklers, Chardonnay, Pinot Noir, and other wines. Enjoy them all with cheese and charcuterie plates, caviar, or smoked salmon. Seating is in the Louis XV–inspired salon or on the terrace overlooking the vines. The tour covers traditional methods of making sparkling wines. Both tours and tastings are by appointment only. ⊠ *1240 Duhig Rd., at Hwy. 121* ☎ *707/257–0101, 800/716–2788* ⊕ *www.domainecarneros.com* ⌣ *Tastings $10–$250, tour $50.*

Etude Wines. You're apt to see or hear hawks, egrets, Canada geese, and other wildlife on the grounds of Etude, known for its sophisticated Pinot Noirs. Although the winery and its light-filled tasting room are in Napa County, the grapes for its flagship Carneros Estate Pinot Noir come from the Sonoma portion of Los Carneros, as do those for the rarer Heirloom Carneros Pinot Noir. Chardonnay, Pinot Blanc, Pinot Noir, and other wines are poured daily at the tasting bar and in good weather on the patio. Pinot Noirs from Carneros, the Sonoma Coast, Oregon, and Santa Barbara County are compared at the Study of Pinot Noir sessions ($50), for which reservations are required. ■TIP→ Single-vineyard Napa Valley Cabernets are another Etude emphasis; those from Rutherford and Oakville are particularly good. ⊠ *1250 Cuttings Wharf Rd., 1 mile south of Hwy. 121* ☎ *707/257–5782* ⊕ *www.etudewines.com* ⌣ *Tastings $20–$50.*

The Hess Collection. About 9 miles northwest of Napa, up a winding road ascending Mt. Veeder, this winery is a delightful discovery. The limestone structure, rustic from the outside but modern and airy within, contains Swiss owner Donald Hess's world-class art collection, including large-scale works by contemporary artists such as Andy Goldsworthy, Anselm Kiefer, and Robert Rauschenberg. Cabernet Sauvignon is a major strength, and the 19 Block Cuvée, Mount Veeder, a Cabernet blend, shows off Malbec and other estate varietals. Tastings outdoors in the garden and the courtyard take place from spring to fall, with cheese or nuts and other nibbles accompanying the wines. ■TIP→ Among the wine and food pairings offered year-round, most of which involve a guided tour of the art collection, is a fun one showcasing locally made artisanal chocolates. ⊠ *4411 Redwood Rd., west off Hwy. 29 at Trancas St./Redwood Rd. exit* ☎ *707/255–1144* ⊕ *www.hesscollection.com* ⌣ *Tastings $25–$175, art gallery free.*

FodorśChoice
★

Mark Herold Wines Reserve Room. Mark Herold, whose debut Merus Cabernet vintage led to prestigious wine-making and consulting opportunities, sold that cult brand in 2008 and now makes Cabernets bearing his name. Seated tastings of his collector-quality wines unfold at a sliver of a space in downtown Napa. You can sip the flagship White Label Cabernet Sauvignon with ($75) or without ($50) small bites from chef Curtis Di Fede of Miminashi restaurant. The two other Cabs, Uproar and Brown Label, are served at these sessions and an introductory one ($30). All tastings include a Sauvignon Blanc or other white. Reservations are recommended for all tastings and required 72 hours ahead for chef's tasting. ■TIP→ While contractually prohibited from producing Cabernet, Herold developed wines from mostly Spanish and Rhône varietals. These zesty, agreeably priced wines can be sampled at his laid-back lair at 710 1st Street, near the Oxbow market. ⊠ *926 Franklin St., on pedestrian alley between 1st and 2nd Sts.* ☎ *707/227–1284* ⊕ *www.markheroldwines.com/visit-us/reserve-room* ⌣ *Tastings $30–$75.*

Both the art and the wine inspire at the Hess Collection.

Fodor'sChoice
★ **O'Brien Estate.** Barb and Bart O'Brien live on and operate this 40-acre Oak Knoll District estate, where in good weather guests sip wines at an outdoor tasting area adjoining the vineyard that produces the fruit for them. It's a singular setting in which to enjoy Merlot, Cabernet Sauvignon, Bordeaux-style red blends, Sauvignon Blanc, and Chardonnay wines that indeed merit the mid-90s scores they garner from critics. Club members snap up most of the bottlings, with the rest sold at intimate tastings held four times daily (reservations are required; book well ahead). All visits include vineyard and winery tours and an account of Barb and Bart's interesting path to winery ownership. ■TIP→ The superb wines and genial hosts make a stop here the highlight of many a Wine Country vacation. ✉ *1200 Orchard Ave., off Solano Ave.* ☎ *707/252–8463* ⊕ *www.obrienestate.com* ✉ *Tasting $55.*

Fodor'sChoice
★ **Oxbow Public Market.** The market's two dozen stands provide an introduction to northern California's diverse artisanal food products. Swoon over decadent charcuterie at the Fatted Calf (great sandwiches too), slurp oysters at Hog Island, or chow down on duck or salmon tacos at C Casa. You can sample wine (and cheese) at the Oxbow Cheese & Wine Merchant, ales at Fieldwork Brewery's taproom, and barrel-aged cocktails and handcrafted vodkas at the Napa Valley Distillery. Napa Bookmine is among the few nonfood vendors here. ■TIP→ If you don't mind eating at the counter, you can select a steak at the Five Dot Ranch meat stand and pay $8 above market price ($12 with two sides) to have it grilled on the spot, a real deal for a quality slab. ✉ *610 and 644 1st St., at McKinstry St.* ⊕ *www.oxbowpublicmarket.com.*

CLOSE UP

The Paris Wine Tasting of 1976

The event that changed the California wine industry forever took place half a world away, in Paris. To celebrate the American Bicentennial, Steven Spurrier, a British wine merchant, sponsored a comparative blind tasting of California Cabernet Sauvignon and Chardonnay wines against Bordeaux Cabernet blends and French Chardonnays. The tasters were French and included journalists and producers.

AND THE WINNERS WERE...
The 1973 Stag's Leap Wine Cellars Cabernet Sauvignon came in first among the reds, and the 1973 Chateau Montelena Chardonnay edged out the French and other California whites. The so-called Judgment of Paris stunned the wine establishment, as it was the first serious challenge to the supremacy of French wines. When the shouting died down, the rush was on. Tourists and winemakers streamed into the Napa Valley and interest grew so strong it helped revitalize Sonoma County's wine industry as well.

Saintsbury. Back in 1981, when Saintsbury released its first Pinot Noir, Los Carneros had yet to earn its current reputation as a setting in which the often finicky varietal could prosper. This pioneer helped disprove the conventional wisdom that only the French could produce great Pinot Noir, and with their subtlety and balance Saintsbury's wines continue to please. In recent years the winery has expanded its reach to the Green Valley of the Russian River Valley, the Sonoma Coast, and Mendocino County's Anderson Valley with equally impressive results. Named for the English author and critic George Saintsbury (he wrote *Notes on a Cellar-Book*), this unpretentious operation also makes Chardonnay and Pinot Gris. Tastings are by appointment only. ■ TIP→ **When the weather cooperates, tastings take place in a rose garden.** ⊠ *1500 Los Carneros Ave., south off Hwy. 121 and east (left) on Withers Rd. for entrance* ☎ *707/252-0592* ⊕ *www.saintsbury.com* ⊠ *Tastings $35–$100.*

Stag's Leap Wine Cellars. A 1973 Stag's Leap Wine Cellars S.L.V. Cabernet Sauvignon put this winery and the Napa Valley on the enological map by placing first in the famous Judgment of Paris tasting of 1976. The grapes for that wine came from a vineyard visible from the stone-and-glass Fay Outlook & Visitor Center, which has broad views of a second fabled Cabernet vineyard (Fay) and the promontory that gives both the winery and the Stags Leap District AVA their names. The top-of-the-line Cabernets from these vineyards are poured at the $45 Estate Collection Tasting. Among the other options are a cave tour and tasting and special wine and food pairings. ⊠ *5766 Silverado Trail, at Wappo Hill Rd.* ☎ *707/261-6410* ⊕ *www.cask23.com* ⊠ *Tasting $45, tours (with tastings by appointment only) $75 and up.*

Stags' Leap Winery. A must for history buffs, this winery was established in 1893 in a bowl-shape valley in the Vaca Mountains foothills. Three years earlier its original owners erected the Manor House, which reopened in 2016 after restoration of its castlelike stone facade and redwood-paneled interior. The home, whose open-air porch seems out of a flapper-era movie set, hosts elegant, appointment-only seated tastings of equally refined wines by the Bordeaux-born Christophe Paubert. Estate Cabernet Sauvignons, Merlot, and Petite Sirah, one of the latter from vines planted in 1929, are the calling cards. Paubert also makes a blend of these three grapes, along with Viognier, Chardonnay, and rosé. Some tastings take place on the porch, others inside; all include a tour of the property and tales of its storied past. ⊠ *6150 Silverado Trail, ¾ mile south of Yountville Cross Rd.* ☎ *800/395–2441* ⊕ *stagsleap.com* ✒ *Tastings $65–$150.*

Fodor's Choice **Trefethen Family Vineyards.** Superior estate Chardonnay, Cabernet Sau-
★ vignon, and Pinot Noir are Trefethen's trademark. To find out how well they age—and what Napa Valley Pinot Noir from grapes grown north of the Carneros district tastes like—pay for the reserve tasting, which includes pours of limited-release wines and one or two older vintages. The terra-cotta-color historic winery on-site, built in 1886, was designed with a gravity-flow system, with the third story for crushing, the second for fermenting the resulting juice, and the first for aging. The wooden building, whose ground floor served for years as the tasting room, suffered severe damage in the 2014 Napa earthquake. After major renovations, it reopened in 2017. The winery's appointment-only tastings also take place at the early-1900s Arts and Crafts–style Villa Trefethen. ⊠ *1160 Oak Knoll Ave., off Hwy. 29* ☎ *866/895–7696* ⊕ *www.trefethen.com* ✒ *Tastings $25–$40.*

Fodor's Choice **Whetstone Wine Cellars.** Pinot Noir, Syrah, Chardonnay, and Viognier are
★ the specialties of this boutique appointment-only winery with a tasting room inside a 19th-century French-style château. Hamden McIntyre, whose other Napa Valley wineries include the majestic Inglenook in Rutherford and Greystone (now the Culinary Institute of America) in St. Helena, designed this less showy yet still princely 1885 stone structure. The tree-shaded front lawn is a civilized spot in good weather to enjoy a full tasting or a glass of wine. The influence of winemaker Jamey Whetstone's mentor Larry Turley, known for velvety Zinfandels, is most evident in the Pinot and the Syrah, but their élan is Whetstone's alone. ⊠ *1075 Atlas Peak Rd., off Monticello Rd.* ☎ *707/254–0600* ⊕ *www.whetstonewinecellars.com* ✒ *Tastings $20–$75.*

WORTH NOTING

Clos du Val. A Napa Valley mainstay since the early 1970s, Clos du Val built its reputation on its intense reserve Cabernet Sauvignon, made with estate Stags Leap District fruit. Over the years the winery's owners "grew the brand" in ways many observers felt diluted the quality. Steve Tamburelli, formerly of the much-admired Chappellet winery and since 2014 the president here, has refocused on estate grown, small-lot wines. Although known for Cabernet, the winery also produces Merlot, Petit Verdot, and Pinot Noir reds, along with whites that include Chardonnay and a Gewürztraminer, Chardonnay, and Sauvignon Blanc blend. On a sunny day, this last wine is perfect for enjoying in the shady olive grove beside the tasting room. ⊠ *5330 Silverado Trail, just south of Capps Dr.* ☎ *707/261–5251, 800/993–9463* ⊕ *www.closduval.com* ✒ *Tastings from $35.*

Cuvaison Estate Wines. The flagship Carneros Chardonnay is the star at Cuvaison (pronounced "coo-vay-ZON"), whose tasting room was constructed from inventively recycled materials. The winery also makes Sauvignon Blanc, Pinot Noir, and Syrah under its own label, and Brandlin Cabernet Sauvignons and Zinfandels from a historic Mt. Veeder estate 1,200 feet above the Napa Valley floor. Some wines can be purchased only at the winery, or sometimes online. All tastings (by appointment only) are sit-down style, either indoors or, in good weather, on an outdoor patio whose lounge chairs and vineyard views encourage you to take the time to savor the wines. Tours, which take place on weekend mornings, are also by appointment. ■ TIP➔ The late Andy Warhol created silkscreen prints of grapes for Cuvaison labels that have only now been used for a commemorative Chardonnay-Cabernet boxed set. ✉ *1221 Duhig Rd., at Hwy. 121* ☎ *707/942–2455* ⊕ *www.cuvaison. com* 🍷 *Tasting $25, tour $30.*

Gordon Huether Studio. Local multimedia artist Gordon Huether has made a name for himself at home and internationally with his large-scale sculptures and installations. His Napa 9/11 Memorial anchors a section of Main Street downtown, across the street his music-inspired wall installations pep up the Blue Note Napa jazz club, and several outdoor sculptures grace Artesa Winery, where he's long been the artist in residence. On weekdays his studio 3 miles northeast of town is open for drop-in visits, where you can see scale models of his latest projects— among them a commission for the Salt Lake City airport—and glimpse his staff (and sometimes the artist himself) at work. ✉ *1821 Monticello Rd., near Atlas Peak Rd.* ☎ *707/255–5954* ⊕ *www.gordonhuether.com* 🌙 *Closed weekends.*

John Anthony Vineyards Tasting Room. Cabernet Sauvignon from Coombsville and Oak Knoll, two southern Napa Valley appellations, is the specialty of John Anthony Truchard, who presents his wines by the glass, flight, or bottle at a rustic-chic storefront tasting room in downtown Napa. As a farmer Truchard emphasizes matching the right varietal and clone, or variant of it, to the right vineyard. Having done so, he creates only 100% single-varietal wines—no blending of Cabernet with Merlot, for instance—meant to be "as beautiful as the vineyards they come from." The Syrah also stands out among the reds. La Dame Michele, a sparkling wine made from Pinot Noir grapes, and the Church Vineyard Sauvignon Blanc are the lighter wines to seek out. ✉ *1440 First St., at Franklin St.* ☎ *707/265–7711* ⊕ *www.johnanthonyvineyards.com* 🍷 *Tastings $10–$80.*

Laird Family Estate. By its account the Laird family has amassed the Napa Valley's largest vineyard holdings. Nearly all the grapes the Lairds farm are sold to other wineries—the family also makes the wines for many of them—but 2% are withheld for wines guests can sip at a vineyard-view indoor-outdoor tasting space off Highway 29. Wines of note include the Cold Creek Chardonnay from the Los Carneros AVA's Sonoma County side, the Phantom Ranch Pinot Noir from the appellation's Napa side, and the Mast Ranch Cabernet Sauvignon, from a hillside property far west in the Yountville AVA. ■ TIP➔ The outdoor west-facing patio here, pleasant at any hour, is best enjoyed in the late afternoon as the sun sets over the Mayacamas Mountains. ✉ *5055 Solano Ave., off Hwy. 29* ☎ *877/297–4902 Ext. 26* ⊕ *www. lairdfamilyestate.com* 🍷 *Tastings $20–$30.*

Napa Valley Wine Train. Several century-old restored Pullman railroad cars and a two-story 1952 Vista Dome car with a curved glass roof travel a leisurely, scenic route between Napa and St. Helena. All trips include a well-made lunch or dinner. Guests on the Quattro Vino tour enjoy a four-course lunch and tastings at four wineries, with stops at one or two wineries incorporated into other tours. Murder-mystery plays are among the regularly scheduled special events. ■ TIP➔ **It's best to make this trip during the day, when you can enjoy the vineyard views.** ✉ *1275 McKinstry St., off 1st St.* ☎ *707/253–2111, 800/427–4124* ⊕ *www.winetrain.com* 🍷 *From $146.*

St. Clair Brown Winery. Tastings at this women-run "urban winery" a few blocks north of downtown take place in an intimate, light-filled greenhouse or in the colorful culinary garden outside. Winemaker Elaine St. Clair, well regarded for her stints at Domaine Carneros and Black Stallion, produces elegant wines—crisp yet complex whites and smooth, French-style reds whose stars include a Cabernet Sauvignon and a Syrah from grapes grown in the Coombsville appellation. You can taste the wines solo or paired with appetizers that might include duck-confit bruschetta or the addictive almonds roasted with rosemary, lemon zest, and lemon olive oil. ■ TIP➔ **Wines are poured by the glass or half glass, or in four-wine flights.** ✉ *816 Vallejo St., off Soscol Ave.* ☎ *707/255–5591* ⊕ *www.stclairbrownwinery.com* 🍷 *Tastings $7–$25* ☉ *Closed Mon.–Wed.; spring–fall, call or check website for expanded hrs.*

Truchard Vineyards. Diversity is the name of the game at this family-owned winery on prime acreage amid the Carneros region's rolling hills. Major Napa Valley vintners purchase most of the grapes grown here, but some of the best are held back for estate-only wines—the Chardonnays and Pinot Noirs the region is known for, along with Roussannes, Zinfandels, Merlots, Syrahs, Cabernet Sauvignons, and a few others. You must call ahead to tour or taste, but if you do, you'll be rewarded with a casual but informative experience tailored to your interests. The tour takes in the vineyards and the wine cave. ■ TIP➔ **Climb the small hill near the winery for a photo-op view of the pond and the pen of Angora goats over the ridge.** ✉ *3234 Old Sonoma Rd., off Hwy. 121* ☎ *707/253–7153* ⊕ *www.truchardvineyards.com* 🍷 *Tasting $30.*

WHERE TO EAT

$

AMERICAN

Fodor's Choice

★

✗ **Alexis Baking Company and Café.** Visitors instantly take to this endearing spot for coffee and pastries, full breakfasts (served all day), and lunches with sandwiches served on homemade potato buns. The namesake owner, who opened her bakery in 1985, sets the tone—the scones, blueberry muffins, lemon-ricotta pancakes, egg sandwiches, and other menu items are prepared with care and offered in bonhomie. **Known for:** homemade soups; homespun vibe; breakfast until 3 daily except Sunday (until 2). Ⓢ *Average main: $10* ✉ *1517 3rd St.* ☎ *707/258–1827* ⊕ *www.abcnapa.com.*

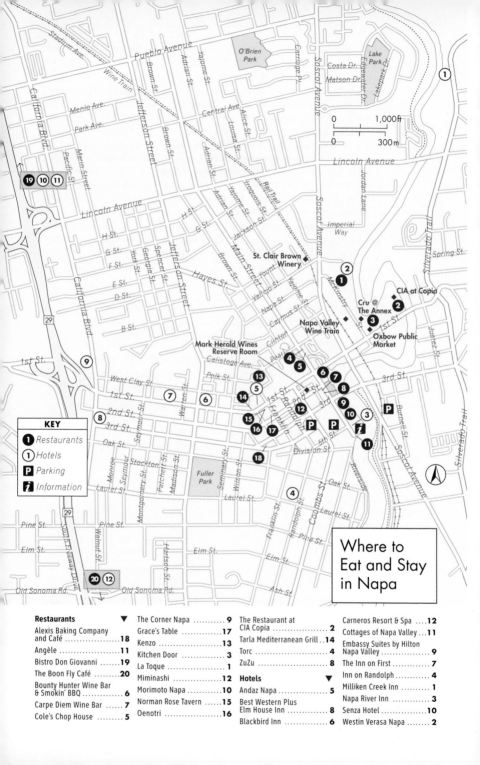

Where to Eat and Stay in Napa

KEY
- **1** Restaurants
- **1** Hotels
- **P** Parking
- **i** Information

Restaurants ▼		
Alexis Baking Company and Café 18	The Corner Napa 9	The Restaurant at CIA Copia 2
Angèle 11	Grace's Table 17	Tarla Mediterranean Grill ..14
Bistro Don Giovanni 19	Kenzo 13	Torc 4
The Boon Fly Café 20	Kitchen Door 3	ZuZu 8
Bounty Hunter Wine Bar & Smokin' BBQ 6	La Toque 1	
Carpe Diem Wine Bar 7	Miminashi 12	**Hotels ▼**
Cole's Chop House 5	Morimoto Napa 10	Andaz Napa 5
	Norman Rose Tavern 15	Best Western Plus Elm House Inn 8
	Oenotri 16	Blackbird Inn 6

Carneros Resort & Spa 12	
Cottages of Napa Valley ...11	
Embassy Suites by Hilton Napa Valley 9	
The Inn on First 7	
Inn on Randolph 4	
Milliken Creek Inn 1	
Napa River Inn 3	
Senza Hotel 10	
Westin Verasa Napa 2	

$$$
FRENCH

✕ **Angèle.** A vaulted wood-beam ceiling and paper-top tables spaced close together set the scene for romance at this softly lit French bistro inside an 1890s boathouse. Look for clever variations on classic dishes such as the croque monsieur (grilled Parisian ham and Gruyère) and wild-mushroom tartine for lunch, coq au vin for dinner, and French onion soup (*c'est magnifique!*) at both. **Known for:** classic bistro cuisine; romantic setting; outdoor seating in good weather under bright-yellow umbrellas. $ *Average main: $28* ✉ *540 Main St., at 5th St.* ☎ *707/252–8115* ⊕ *www.angelerestaurant.com.*

$$$
ITALIAN

✕ **Bistro Don Giovanni.** The chefs at this boisterous bistro with a roadhouse feel prepare inventive, comforting Cal-Italian food. Regulars, some since the restaurant's mid-1990s debut, favor the fritto misto (lightly battered deep-fried calamari, onions, fennel, and rock shrimp), spinach ravioli with lemon-cream or tomato sauce, slow-braised lamb shank with Tuscan-bean ragout, and wood-fired pizza with Italian ham, egg, wild mushrooms, artichokes, mozzarella, and truffle pecorino. **Known for:** robust cuisine; patio and lawn dining in good weather. $ *Average main: $25* ✉ *4110 Howard La., off Hwy. 29* ☎ *707/224–3300* ⊕ *www.bistrodongiovanni.com.*

$$
MODERN
AMERICAN

✕ **The Boon Fly Café.** This small spot that melds rural charm with industrial chic serves updated American classics such as fried chicken (free-range in this case), burgers (with Kobe beef), and pork chops (with lush tomato fondue). The flatbreads, including a smoked salmon one made with fromage blanc, Parmesan, lemon crème fraîche, and capers, are worth a try. **Known for:** open all day; signature doughnuts for breakfast; cocktail selection and wines by the glass. $ *Average main: $22* ✉ *Carneros Inn, 4048 Sonoma Hwy.* ☎ *707/299–4870* ⊕ *www. boonflycafe.com* ☞ *Reservations for dinner only.*

$$
AMERICAN

✕ **Bounty Hunter Wine Bar & Smokin' BBQ.** Every dish on the small menu at this triple-threat wine store, wine bar, and restaurant is a standout, including the pulled-pork and beef brisket sandwiches served with three types of barbecue sauce, the meltingly tender St. Louis–style ribs, and the signature beer-can chicken (only Tecate will do). The space is whimsically rustic, with stuffed game trophies mounted on the wall and leather saddles standing in for seats at a couple of tables. **Known for:** lively atmosphere; combo plates; good sides and sauces. $ *Average main: $18* ✉ *975 1st St., near Main St.* ☎ *707/226–3976* ⊕ *www.bountyhunterwinebar.com.*

$$
MODERN
AMERICAN
Fodor'sChoice
★

✕ **Carpe Diem Wine Bar.** Patrons at this restaurant's sociable happy hour wash down nibbles such as truffle popcorn, tacos, and harissa-spiced house fries with draft-beer and weekly wine specials. Those who remain for dinner graze on ahi tuna tartare, house-made burrata, brick-oven flatbreads topped with roasted wild mushrooms and other ingredients, and larger plates that include an ostrich burger smothered in triple-cream Brie. **Known for:** small plates; artisanal cheeses and charcuterie; wines and draft beers. $ *Average main: $19* ✉ *1001 2nd St., at Brown St.* ☎ *707/224–0800* ⊕ *www.carpediemwinebar.com* ☾ *Closed Sun. No lunch.*

$$$$
STEAKHOUSE
Fodor'sChoice
★

✕ **Cole's Chop House.** When only a thick, flawlessly cooked New York or porterhouse (dry-aged by the eminent Allen Brothers of Chicago) will do, this steak house inside an 1886 stone building is the best choice in town. New Zealand lamb chops are the non-beef favorite, with oysters Rockefeller, creamed spinach, grilled asparagus with hollandaise, all prepared with finesse, among the options for starters and sides. **Known for:** borderline-epic wine list. [$] *Average main: $38* ✉ *1122 Main St., at Pearl St.* ☎ *707/224–6328* 🌐 *www.coleschophouse.com* ⏲ *No lunch.*

$$$ MODERN AMERICAN Fodor's Choice ★ 🍴 **The Corner Napa.** Equal parts 21st-century gentleman's club and brooding urban loft, this downtown restaurant seduces with a suave palette of marble, leather, bronze, and polished walnut surfaces. Chef Dustin Falcon's cuisine similarly enchants, with pickled pearl onions, apple, sherry, and candied pecans elevating a garden beets salad, and Sicilian pistachio, Medjool dates, spiced yogurt, and fried naan balls playing well with each other and their dish's centerpiece, pan-seared Spanish octopus. **Known for:** contemporary decor; international wine list; specialty cocktails and rare spirits. [$] *Average main: $28* ✉ *660 Main St., near 5th St.* ☎ *707/927–5552* 🌐 *www.cornerbarnapa.com* ⏲ *Closed Mon. No lunch Tues.–Sat.*

$$$ ECLECTIC 🍴 **Grace's Table.** A dependable, varied, three-squares-a-day menu makes this modest corner restaurant occupying a brick-and-glass storefront many Napans go-to choice for a simple meal. Iron-skillet corn bread with lavender honey and butter shows up at all hours, with chilaquiles scrambled eggs a breakfast favorite, savory fish tacos a lunchtime staple, and cassoulet and pork osso buco risotto popular for dinner. **Known for:** congenial staffers; good beers on tap; eclectic menu focusing on France, Italy, and the Americas. [$] *Average main: $24* ✉ *1400 2nd St., at Franklin St.* ☎ *707/226–6200* 🌐 *www.gracestable.net.*

$$$$ JAPANESE 🍴 **Kenzo.** A rotating series of all-star Tokyo-based chefs supplies the seasonally changing multicourse *kaiseki* menus at the downtown Napa restaurant opened by the Japanese founder of Kenzo Estate Winery. Delicate preparations such as straw-smoked sashimi, eel and rice wrapped in bamboo leaf, and steamed turnip dumpling with Dungeness crab sauce were among the highlights of the three prix-fixe menus ($225–$270, service included) when the restaurant debuted in late 2016. **Known for:** beautiful, spare aesthetic; delicate preparations; three prix-fixe menus. [$] *Average main: $225* ✉ *1339 Pearl St., at Franklin St.* ☎ *707/294–2049* 🌐 *kenzonapa.com* ⏲ *Closed Mon. No lunch.*

$$ ECLECTIC 🍴 **Kitchen Door.** Todd Humphries has overseen swank Manhattan, San Francisco, and Napa Valley kitchens, but for his casual Oxbow-market restaurant he set more modest goals, focusing on multicultural comfort cuisine. The signature dishes include a silky cream of mushroom soup whose triumph lies in its magical stock and soupçon of marsala, with pizzas and flatbreads, chicken pho, rice bowls, Kobe-style burgers, and duck banh mi sandwiches (voluptuous duck jus) among the other customer favorites. **Known for:** communal atmosphere; river-view patio. [$] *Average main: $18* ✉ *Oxbow Public Market, 610 1st St., at McKinstry St.* ☎ *707/226–1560* 🌐 *www.kitchendoornapa.com.*

$$$$ MODERN AMERICAN Fodor's Choice ★ 🍴 **La Toque.** Chef Ken Frank's La Toque is the complete package: his imaginative modern American cuisine, served in a formal dining space, is complemented by a wine lineup that earned the restaurant a coveted *Wine Spectator* Grand Award. Built around seasonal local ingredients, the prix-fixe menu, which changes frequently, might include potato rösti with caviar, sole with eggplant and almond-hazelnut *picada* sauce, and five-spice Liberty Farm duck breast with black trumpet mushrooms.

Known for: elaborate preparations; astute wine pairings. $ *Average main: $80* ⊠ *Westin Verasa Napa, 1314 McKinstry St., off Soscol Ave.* ☎ *707/257–5157* ⊕ *www.latoque.com* ☾ *No lunch.*

$$$
JAPANESE
Fodor'sChoice
★

✕ **Miminashi.** Japanese *izakaya*—gastropubs that serve appetizers downed with sake or cocktails—provided the inspiration for chef Curtis Di Fede's buzz-worthy downtown Napa restaurant. Ramen, fried rice, and yakitori anchor the menu, whose highlights include smoked-trout potato croquettes, crispy skewered chicken skin, and the ooh-inspiring *okonomiyaki* pancake with bacon and cabbage, topped by dried fermented tuna flakes. **Known for:** soft-serve ice cream for dessert and from to-go window; wines and sakes that elevate the cuisine. $ *Average main: $28* ⊠ *821 Coombs St., near 3rd St.* ☎ *707/254–9464* ⊕ *miminashi.com* ☾ *No lunch weekends.*

$$$$
JAPANESE

✕ **Morimoto Napa.** *Iron Chef* star Masaharu Morimoto is the big name behind this downtown Napa hot spot where everything is delightfully overdone, right down to the desserts. Organic materials such as twisting grapevines above the bar and rough-hewn wooden tables seem simultaneously earthy and modern, creating a fitting setting for the gorgeously plated Japanese fare, from sashimi served with grated fresh wasabi to elaborate concoctions that include sea-urchin carbonara made with udon noodles. **Known for:** elaborate concoctions; gorgeous plating; omakase menu. $ *Average main: $36* ⊠ *610 Main St., at 5th St.* ☎ *707/252–1600* ⊕ *www.morimotonapa.com.*

$$
AMERICAN
FAMILY

✕ **Norman Rose Tavern.** If downtown Napa had its own version of the casual, something-for-everyone bar in *Cheers*, it would be "The Rose." Salads, burgers, chili, and sandwiches—all a cut above what you might expect from a tavern—are on the menu, with beer-batter fish-and-chips and meat loaf wrapped in pork belly among the larger plates. **Known for:** rollicking happy hour (weekdays 3–6 pm); truffle-and-Parmesan fries. $ *Average main: $17* ⊠ *1401 1st St., at Franklin St.* ☎ *707/258–1516* ⊕ *www.normanrosenapa.com.*

$$$
ITALIAN

✕ **Oenotri.** Often spotted at local farmers' markets and his restaurant's gardens, Oenotri's ebullient chef-owner and Napa native Tyler Rodde is ever on the lookout for fresh produce to incorporate into his rustic southern-Italian cuisine. His restaurant, a brick-walled contemporary space with tall windows and wooden tables, is a lively spot to sample house-made salumi and pastas, thin-crust pizzas, and entrées that might include roasted squab, Atlantic salmon, or pork sausage. **Known for:** fresh ingredients; Margherita pizza with San Marzano tomatoes. $ *Average main: $26* ⊠ *1425 1st St., at Franklin St.* ☎ *707/252–1022* ⊕ *www.oenotri.com.*

$$$
MODERN
AMERICAN

✕ **Restaurant at CIA Copia.** The chefs at CIA Copia toil in a gleaming open kitchen bordering a cheery dining room that neatly splits the difference between fancy restaurant and upscale cafeteria. The menu of mostly small, shareable plates changes based in part on what's in the culinary garden out front, but the early favorites included rainbow trout with pistachio, mussels in bourbon-laced bouillabaisse, and porcini-crusted hanger steak. **Known for:** wine, beer, craft cocktails; outdoor patio and olive grove seating; unusual shared-dining experience. $ *Average main: $23* ⊠ *Culinary Institute of America at Copia, 500 1st St., near McKinstry St.* ☎ *707/967–2555* ⊕ *www.ciarestaurantgroup.com/the-restaurant-at-cia-copia* ☾ *Closed Mon.*

$$$ MEDITERRANEAN 🍴 **Tarla Mediterranean Grill.** You can build a meal at Tarla by combining traditional Mediterranean mezes (small plates)—stuffed grape leaves with fresh tzatziki, perhaps, and spanakopita—with contemporary creations such as kale salad with Granny Smith apples. Entrées include updates of moussaka and other mainstays, along with fancifully modern items like beef short ribs braised with a pomegranate-wine sauce. **Known for:** sidewalk seating; no corkage on Tuesday. [$] *Average main: $23* ✉ *Andaz Napa, 1480 1st St., at School St.* ☎ *707/255–5599* 🌐 *www.tarlagrill.com.*

$$$$ MODERN AMERICAN Fodor's Choice ★ 🍴 **Torc.** *Torc* means "wild boar" in an early Celtic dialect, and owner-chef Sean O'Toole, who formerly helmed kitchens at top Manhattan, San Francisco, and Yountville establishments, occasionally incorporates the restaurant's namesake beast into his eclectic offerings. O'Toole and his team enhance dishes such as roast chicken—recently prepared with Florence fennel, hedgehog mushroom, pickle lily, and bergamot—with style and precision. **Known for:** gracious service; specialty cocktails; Bengali sweet-potato pakora and deviled-egg appetizers. [$] *Average main: $33* ✉ *1140 Main St., at Pearl St.* ☎ *707/252–3292* 🌐 *www.torcnapa.com* 🕒 *Closed Tues. No lunch weekdays.*

$$$ SPANISH Fodor's Choice ★ 🍴 **ZuZu.** At festive ZuZu the focus is on tapas, paella, the signature suckling pig, and other Spanish favorites often downed with cava or sangria. Regulars revere the paella, made with Spanish *bomba* rice, and small plates that might include white anchovies with sliced egg and rémoulade on grilled bread. **Known for:** singular flavors and spicing; Latin jazz on the stereo; sister restaurant La Taberna for bar bites three doors south. [$] *Average main: $29* ✉ *829 Main St., near 3rd St.* ☎ *707/224–8555* 🌐 *www.zuzunapa.com* 🕒 *No lunch weekends.*

WHERE TO STAY

$$$ HOTEL Fodor's Choice ★ 🏨 **Andaz Napa.** Part of the Hyatt family, this boutique hotel with an urban-hip vibe has luxurious rooms with flat-screen TVs, laptop-size safes, and white-marble bathrooms stocked with high-quality bath products. **Pros:** proximity to downtown restaurants, theaters, and tasting rooms; access to modern fitness center; complimentary beverage upon arrival; complimentary snacks and nonalcoholic beverages in rooms. **Cons:** parking can be a challenge on weekends; unremarkable views from some rooms. [$] *Rooms from: $359* ✉ *1450 1st St.* ☎ *707/687–1234* 🌐 *andaznapa.com* 🛏 *141 rooms* 🍽 *No meals.*

$$ HOTEL Fodor's Choice ★ 🏨 **Best Western Plus Elm House Inn.** In a region known for over-the-top architecture and amenities (and prices to match), this inn delivers style and even a touch of class at affordable rates. **Pros:** polite staff; generous continental breakfasts; complimentary freshly baked cookies in lobby. **Cons:** hot tub but no pool; about a mile from downtown; some road noise in street-side rooms. [$] *Rooms from: $259* ✉ *800 California Blvd.* ☎ *707/255–1831* 🌐 *bestwesternelmhouseinn.com* 🛏 *22 rooms* 🍽 *Breakfast.*

$$ B&B/INN 🏨 **Blackbird Inn.** Arts and Crafts style infuses this home from the turn of the last century, from the lobby's enormous fieldstone fireplace to the lamps that cast a warm glow over the impressive wooden staircase. **Pros:** gorgeous architecture and period furnishings; convenient to downtown Napa; free afternoon wine service. **Cons:** must be booked well in advance; some rooms are on the small side. [$] *Rooms from:*

At fascinating di Rosa the art treasures can be found indoors and out.

$229 ⊠ 1755 1st St. ☎ 707/226–2450, 888/567–9811 ⊕ *www.black-birdinnnapa.com* ☞ *8 rooms* ⦿| *Breakfast.*

$$$$
RESORT
Fodor's Choice
★

☖ **Carneros Resort & Spa.** Freestanding board-and-batten cottages with rocking chairs on each porch are simultaneously rustic and chic at this luxurious property made even more so by a $6.5 million makeover that should be complete by 2017's end. **Pros:** cottages have lots of privacy; beautiful views from hilltop pool and hot tub; heaters on private patios. **Cons:** a long drive to destinations up-valley. Ⓢ *Rooms from: $600* ⊠ *4048 Sonoma Hwy./Hwy. 121* ☎ 707/299–4900, 888/400–9000 ⊕ *www.thecarnerosinn.com* ☞ *86 rooms* ⦿| *No meals.*

$$$
B&B/INN

☖ **Cottages of Napa Valley.** Although contemporary design touches, plush new furnishings, and up-to-date bathrooms ensure a cozy, 21st-century experience, most of the accommodations here date back to the 1920s, and include the cottage in which Hollywood legends Clark Gable and Carole Lombard reportedly canoodled back in the day. **Pros:** private porches and patios; basket of Bouchon pastries each morning; kitchen with utensils in each cottage. **Cons:** hum of highway traffic. Ⓢ *Rooms from: $395* ⊠ *1012 Darms La.* ☎ 707/252–7810 ⊕ *www.napacottages.com* ☞ *9 rooms* ⦿| *Breakfast.*

$$
HOTEL

☖ **Embassy Suites by Hilton Napa Valley.** Set on 7 landscaped acres near Highway 29, the Mediterranean-style Embassy Suites represents a good value for the Napa Valley, all the more so if you are using or earning Hilton reward points. **Pros:** good value; resortlike ambience; rooms sensibly laid out. **Cons:** away from downtown; ongoing renovations well into 2018; unrenovated rooms are nondescript. Ⓢ *Rooms from: $279* ⊠ *1075 California Blvd.* ☎ 707/253–9540 ⊕ *www.embassysuitesnapa-hotel.com* ☞ *205 rooms* ⦿| *Breakfast.*

$$ B&B/INN Fodor's Choice ★ **The Inn on First.** Guests gush over this inn whose hosts-with-the-most owners make a stay here one to remember. **Pros:** full gourmet breakfast; varied room choices; away from downtown but not too far. **Cons:** no TVs; children under age 12 not permitted. [$] *Rooms from: $300* ✉ *1938 1st St.* ☎ *707/253–1331* 🌐 *www.theinnonfirst.com* 🛏 *10 rooms* 🍴 *Breakfast.*

$$ B&B/INN Fodor's Choice ★ **Inn on Randolph.** A few calm blocks from the downtown action, the restored Inn on Randolph is a sophisticated haven celebrated for its gourmet gluten-free breakfasts and snacks. **Pros:** quiet residential neighborhood; gourmet breakfasts; sophisticated decor; romantic setting. **Cons:** a bit of a walk from downtown. [$] *Rooms from: $299* ✉ *411 Randolph St.* ☎ *707/257–2886* 🌐 *www.innonrandolph.com* 🛏 *10 rooms* 🍴 *Breakfast.*

$$$ B&B/INN **Milliken Creek Inn.** Early-evening wine-and-cheese receptions set a romantic mood in this hotel's intimate lobby, whose terrace overlooks a lush lawn and the Napa River. **Pros:** soft-as-clouds beds; serene spa; breakfast delivered to your room or elsewhere on the beautiful grounds. **Cons:** expensive; road noise audible in outdoor areas. [$] *Rooms from: $379* ✉ *1815 Silverado Trail* ☎ *707/255–1197* 🌐 *www.millikencreekinn.com* 🛏 *12 rooms* 🍴 *Breakfast.*

$$ B&B/INN **Napa River Inn.** Part of a complex of restaurants, shops, a nightclub, and a spa, this waterfront inn is within easy walking distance of downtown hot spots. **Pros:** wide range of room sizes and prices; near downtown action; pet friendly. **Cons:** river views could be more scenic; some rooms get noise from nearby restaurants. [$] *Rooms from: $299* ✉ *500 Main St.* ☎ *707/251–8500, 877/251–8500* 🌐 *www.napariverinn.com* 🛏 *66 rooms* 🍴 *Breakfast.*

$$$ HOTEL Fodor's Choice ★ **Senza Hotel.** Exterior fountains, gallery-quality outdoor sculptures, and decorative rows of grapevines signal the Wine Country–chic aspirations of this boutique hotel operated by the owners of Hall Wines. **Pros:** high-style fixtures; fireplaces in all rooms; elegant atmosphere. **Cons:** just off highway; little of interest within walking distance; some bathrooms have no tub. [$] *Rooms from: $399* ✉ *4066 Howard La.* ☎ *707/253–0337* 🌐 *www.senzahotel.com* 🛏 *41 rooms* 🍴 *Breakfast.*

$$$ HOTEL **Westin Verasa Napa.** Near the Napa Valley Wine Train depot and the Oxbow market, this spacious mostly suites resort is sophisticated and relaxing. **Pros:** heated saline pool; most rooms have well-equipped kitchenettes (some have full kitchens); spacious double-headed showers. **Cons:** amenities fee added to room rate. [$] *Rooms from: $360* ✉ *1314 McKinstry St.* ☎ *707/257–1800, 888/627–7169* 🌐 *www.westinnapa.com* 🛏 *180 rooms* 🍴 *No meals.*

NIGHTLIFE AND PERFORMING ARTS

Because of Napa's size and proximity to San Francisco, a few downtown venues attract big-name performers. Wine bars here draw a younger and sportier crowd than elsewhere in the Napa Valley.

NIGHTLIFE

Fodor's Choice ★ **Blue Note Napa.** The famed New York jazz room's West Coast club hosts national headliners such as Chris Botti, Dee Dee Bridgewater, and Coco Montoya, along with local talents such as Lavay Smith &

Her Red Hot Skillet Lickers. Chef Jessica Sedlacek, formerly of The French Laundry and Bouchon in Yountville, supplies the culinary pizzazz—hearty entrées such as boneless crispy chicken and a massive pork chop, and lighter fare that includes raw oysters, chicken wings, and bacon-inflected potato fritters (an instant hit). ⊠ *Napa Valley Opera House, 1030 Main St., at 1st St.* ☎ *707/603–1258* ⊕ *www. bluenotenapa.com.*

Cadet Wine + Beer Bar. Cadet plays things urban-style cool with a long bar, high-top tables, an all-vinyl sound track, and a low-lit, generally loungelike feel. The two owners describe their outlook as "unabashedly pro-California," but their lineup of 150-plus wines and beers circles the globe. The crowd here is youngish, the vibe festive. ⊠ *930 Franklin St., at end of pedestrian alley between 1st and 2nd Sts.* ☎ *707/224–4400* ⊕ *www.cadetbeerandwinebar.com.*

JaM Cellars. Although it opens at 10 am daily for wine tasting, evening is the best time to visit this fun tasting room, especially during live-music events, mostly pop, rock, and soul. The California editions of JaM Butter Chardonnay and JaM Cabernet are sold nationally, but the subtler Napa Valley versions are only available here. ⊠ *1460 1st St., near School St.* ☎ *707/265–7577* ⊕ *www.jamcellars.com.*

Silo's. Dweezil Zappa and Tuck & Patti are among the recent headliners at this small club whose patrons sip wine and listen to accomplished musicians—mostly jazz, but also rock and blues—and sometimes spoken-word artists. ⊠ *Historic Napa Mill, 530 Main St., near 5th St.* ☎ *707/251–5833* ⊕ *www.silosnapa.com.*

PERFORMING ARTS

Uptown Theatre. At 860 seats, this art-deco former movie house attracts Ziggy Marley, Citizen Cope, Colbie Caillat, Napa Valley resident and winery owner Boz Scaggs, and other performers. ⊠ *1350 3rd St., at Franklin St.* ☎ *707/259–0123* ⊕ *www.uptowntheatrenapa.com.*

SPAS

The Spa at Napa River Inn. All stress will be under arrest after a massage, facial, or other treatment at this spa inside Napa's vaguely late-deco former police station. You can opt for therapeutic massages that might incorporate Swedish or other familiar techniques, or go more exotic with Adjust Your Ki, which involves Reiki, an ancient Japanese relaxation technique. The four-hour Royal Treatment pulls out all the stops with a full-body massage, foot rehab, exfoliation, a body wrap, and an antioxidant facial. ■ TIP➔ **If you're traveling with a dog in need of TLC, the spa will pamper your pet with a walk, a treat, and a mini massage while you're indulging yourself.** ⊠ *500 Main St., at 5th St.* ☎ *707/265–7537* ⊕ *www.napariverinn.com/the-spa* 🖫 *Treatments $25–$440.*

Few experiences are as exhilarating yet serene as an early-morning balloon ride above the vineyards.

SPORTS AND THE OUTDOORS

Balloons Above the Valley. This company's personable and professional pilots make outings a delight. Flights depart from the Napa Valley Marriott, in the city of Napa, and conclude with a champagne brunch there. You can extend the pleasure with packages that include a picnic lunch and winery tours. ✉ *Napa* ☎ *707/253–2222, 800/464–6824* ⊕ *www. balloonrides.com* ✈ *From $199.*

Fodor's Choice
★

Enjoy Napa Valley. Napa native Justin Perkins leads kayak and bicycle tours of downtown sights. On the easy history-oriented kayak tour Perkins points out the wildlife and regales paddlers with amusingly salacious tales of Napa's river-town past. The bicycle tour usually follows the Napa River Trail north from the Oxbow Public Market. ✉ *Tour meeting places vary* ☎ *707/227–7364* ⊕ *enjoy-napa-valley.com* ✈ *From $49.*

SHOPPING

Napa's most interesting shops and boutiques can be found downtown west of the Napa River, along Pearl and from 1st through 5th Streets between Main and about Franklin Streets.

Cake Plate. The charming Smith sisters keep their shop stocked with au courant women's and men's clothing and accessories, some by area designers. The goal is a look that's classic yet modern. ✉ *730 Main St., near 3rd St.* ☎ *707/226–2300.*

Copperfield's Books. Check the Napa page on this indie chain's website for readings or signings by local authors while you're in town. ✉ *Bel*

CLOSE UP

Wine Country Balloon Rides

Thought those vineyards looked beautiful from the highway? Try the view from a thousand feet up, serenely drifting along with the wind, the only sound the occasional roar of the burners overhead.

Many companies organize hot-air-ballooning trips over Napa and Sonoma, offering rides that usually cost between $200 and $250 per person for a one-hour flight, which typically includes brunch or lunch afterward. If you were hoping for the ultimate in romance—a flight with no one else but your sweetie (and an FAA-approved pilot) on board—be prepared to shell out two to four times as much.

Flights typically take off at the crack of dawn, when winds are the lightest, so be prepared to make an early start and dress in layers. Flights are dependent on weather, and if there's rain or too much fog, expect to be grounded. Hotels can hook you up with nearby companies, some of which will pick you up at your lodgings.

3

Aire Plaza, 3740 Bel Aire Plaza, off Trancas St., near Jefferson St. ☎ *707/252–8002* ⊕ *www.copperfieldsbooks.com/napa.*

Napa Bookmine. An indie shop with a second location in the Oxbow market, Napa Bookmine sells current magazines and new and used books and hosts author events. Specialties include children's and teen titles, travel books, and works by local writers. ⊠ *964 Pearl St., near Main St.* ☎ *707/265–8131* ⊕ *www.napabookmine.com.*

Shackford's Kitchen Store. This shop looks more like a hardware store than a low-key celebration of the art of cooking, but if you need kitchenware, accessories, or hard-to-find replacement items, you'll likely find what you're looking for. ⊠ *1350 Main St., at Caymus St.* ☎ *707/226–2132.*

Shop at CIA Copia. The shop at the Culinary Institute of America's Copia complex has the feel of a museum store—nearly every piece of kitchenware here is a work of art. Cookbooks, oils, and specialty food items are in the mix, too. ⊠ *500 1st St., near McKinstry St.* ☎ *707/967–2500* ⊕ *www.ciaatcopia.com.*

YOUNTVILLE

Fodor's Choice ★ *9 miles north of downtown Napa; 9 miles south of St. Helena.*

These days Yountville (population about 3,000) is something like Disneyland for food lovers. It all started with Thomas Keller's The French Laundry, one of the best restaurants in the United States. Keller is also behind two more casual restaurants a few blocks from his flagship, along with a very popular bakery. Perhaps by the time you read this, his proposed ice-cream shop will be open, too (permits can be hard to come by in this small town). And that's only the tip of the iceberg: you could stay here for a week and not exhaust all the options in this tiny town with a big culinary reputation.

Yountville is full of small inns and luxurious hotels catering to those who prefer to be able to walk rather than drive to their lodgings after dinner. Although visitors use Yountville as a home base, touring Napa Valley wineries by day and returning to town for dinner, you could easily while away a few hours in town, wandering through the many shops on or just off Washington Street, or visiting the many downtown tasting rooms.

Yountville is named for George C. Yount, who in 1836 received the first of several large Napa Valley land grants from the Mexican government. Yount is credited with planting the valley's first vinifera grapevines in 1838. The vines are long gone, but wisps of Yountville's 19th-century past bleed through, most notably along Washington Street, where a café at 6525 Washington occupies the former train depot, and shops and restaurants east of it inhabit the former Groezinger Winery. If you're up for a history walk, the visitor center of the Yountville Chamber of Commerce, a block to the south, has a good map.

GETTING HERE AND AROUND

If you're traveling north on Highway 29, take the Yountville exit, stay east of the highway, and take the first left onto Washington Street. Traveling south on Highway 29, turn left onto Madison Street and right onto Washington Street. Nearly all of Yountville's businesses and restaurants are clustered along a half-mile stretch of Washington Street. Yountville Cross Road connects downtown Yountville to the Silverado Trail, where you'll find many of the area's best wineries. VINE Bus 10 and Bus 29 stop in Yountville. The Yountville Trolley circles the downtown area and hits a few spots beyond.

Contact Yountville Trolley. ☎ *707/944–1234 (10 am–7 pm), 707/312–1509 (7 pm–11 pm)* ⊕ *www.ridethevine.com/yountville-trolley.*

ESSENTIALS

Contact Yountville Chamber Of Commerce. ✉ *6484 Washington St., at Oak Circle* ☎ *707/944–0904* ⊕ *yountville.com.*

EXPLORING

TOP ATTRACTIONS

Bell Wine Cellars. With vineyard and winery experience in South Africa, Europe, and California, a hand in the creation of the Carneros, Oakville, and Rutherford AVAs, and participation in research that led to the revival of Clone 6, a type of Cabernet Sauvignon, winemaker Anthony A. Bell had a varied career even before opening his namesake winery in 1991. Bell grows Chardonnay and Merlot on his Yountville property, but he's best known for Cabernet Sauvignons, particularly one from Clone 6 fruit grown in Rutherford. His winery, south of town down a long driveway off Washington Street, is a quiet, casual place to sip Old World–style wines made from carefully cultivated grapes. Tastings are by appointment only. ✉ *6200 Washington St., 1 mile south of town* ☎ *707/944–1673* ⊕ *www.bellwine.com* 🍷 *Tastings $20–$75, Grape to Glass tour and tasting $50.*

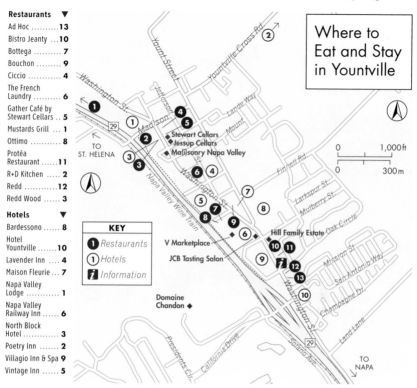

Where to Eat and Stay in Yountville

KEY

1 Restaurants
1 Hotels
i Information

V Marketplace
JCB Tasting Salon

Stewart Cellars
Jessup Cellars
Ma(i)sonry Napa Valley
Hill Family Estate
Domaine Chandon

0   1,000 ft
0   300 m

TO ST. HELENA

TO NAPA

Fodor's Choice
★ **Cliff Lede Vineyards.** Inspired by his passion for classic rock, owner and construction magnate Cliff Lede named the blocks in his Stags Leap District vineyard after hits by the Grateful Dead and other bands. The vibe at his efficient, high-tech winery is anything but laid-back, however. Cutting-edge agricultural and enological science informs the vineyard management and wine making here. Architect Howard Backen designed the winery and its tasting room, where Lede's Sauvignon Blanc, Cabernet Sauvignons, and other wines, along with some from sister winery FEL, which produces much-lauded Anderson Valley Pinot Noirs, are poured. ■**TIP➔ Walk-ins are welcome at the tasting bar, but appointments are required for the veranda outside and a nearby gallery that often displays rock-related art.** ⊠ *1473 Yountville Cross Rd., off Silverado Trail* ☎ *707/944–8642* ⊕ *cliffledevineyards. com* ⬚ *Tastings $30–$50.*

Goosecross Cellars. When Christi Coors Ficeli purchased this boutique winery in 2013 and commissioned a new barnlike tasting space, she and her architect had one major goal: bring the outside in. Large retractable west-facing windows open up behind the tasting bar to idyllic views of Cabernet vines—in fine weather, guests on the outdoor deck can practically touch them. Goosecross makes Chardonnay and Pinot Noir from Carneros grapes, but the soul of this cordial operation is

Domaine Chandon claims a prime piece of real estate.

its 9.2-acre estate vineyard, mostly Cabernet Sauvignon and Merlot with some Cabernet Franc and Petit Verdot. The Cab and Merlot are the stars, along with the Aeros Bordeaux-style blend of the best estate grapes. Aeros isn't usually poured, but a Howell Mountain Petite Sirah with expressive tannins (there's also a Howell Mountain Cabernet) often is. Visits to Goosecross are by appointment only. ✉ *1119 State La., off Yountville Cross Rd.* ☎ *707/944–1986, 800/276–9210* ⊕ *www. goosecross.com* ✉ *Tastings from $30.*

JCB Tasting Salon. Mirrors and gleaming surfaces abound in this eye-catching ode to indulgence named for its French owner, Jean-Charles Boisset (JCB). The JCB label first made its mark with sparkling wine, Chardonnay, and Pinot Noir, with Cabernet Sauvignon a more recent strong suit. In addition to providing a plush setting for sampling his wines, Boisset's downtown Yountville tasting space is also a showcase for home decor items from the likes of Lalique and Baccarat. The adjacent **Atelier by JCB** sells cheeses, charcuterie, and other gourmet foods, all quite good if in some cases *très cher* (very expensive). You can purchase them separately or assembled as a picnic. ✉ *6505 Washington St., at Mulberry St.* ☎ *707/934–8237* ⊕ *www.jcbcollection.com/location/ tasting-salon-yountville* ✉ *Tastings $30–$50.*

Fodor's Choice **Ma(i)sonry Napa Valley.** An art-and-design gallery that also pours the
★ wines of about two dozen limited-production wineries, Ma(i)sonry occupies a manor house constructed in 1904 from Napa River stone. Tasting flights of wines by distinguished winemakers such as Heidi Barrett, Philippe Melka, and Thomas Rivers Brown can be sampled in fair weather in the sculpture garden, in a private nook, or at the communal

CLOSE UP

A Scenic Southern Napa Drive

Wine, art, sweeping vistas, shopping, and more wine await on a scenic drive from the town of Napa up Mt. Veeder and down the Oakville Grade into Oakville, with a final stop in Yountville.

ART AND WINE IN NAPA

Head north from downtown Napa on Highway 29 to the Trancas Street/ Redwood Road exit and turn west (left) onto Trancas Street. After you cross over Highway 29, the road's name changes to Redwood. Continue west, bearing left at the fork when Redwood narrows from four lanes to two. From here, two signs point the way to the **Hess Collection.** Allow an hour or so to taste the wines and browse the modern art collection.

MAKING THE (OAKVILLE) GRADE

From Hess, backtrack on Redwood about 1¼ miles to Mt. Veeder Road and turn left. After a little more than 8 miles, turn right (east) onto Dry Creek Road. After ½ mile this road is signed as the Oakville Grade. The views east as you twist your way downhill to Highway 29 can be stunning, especially when a low-lying fog shrouds the valley floor. (If anyone in your party is prone to carsickness, take Redwood back to Highway 29 and turn north.) From the Oakville Grade, turn left (north) onto Highway 29 and right (east) in about ¼ mile onto Oakville Cross Road.

AMAZING CABERNETS

Head east on Oakville Cross, visiting either **Silver Oak** or, if you've reserved a tour and wine and food pairing ahead of time, **B Cellars.** Both wineries have enviable grape sources and highly skilled winemakers who blend amazing Cabernets.

YOUNTVILLE TEMPTATIONS

After your Oakville tasting, continue east on Oakville Cross, turning right (south) on the Silverado Trail and right again (west) onto Yountville Cross Road. Turn left at Yount Street, which leads into downtown **Yountville,** whose bakeries and boutiques tempt body and bank account. Washington Street, one block west of Yount, holds most of the action. To taste more wine, slip into the glam **JCB Tasting Salon** or Ma(i)sonry Napa Valley. Or drop by **Gather Café by Stewart Cellars,** where (until 3) you can have a light meal (and, if you'd like, a tasting). **Kollar Chocolates** in V Marketplace is another sweet option. Remain in Yountville for dinner, or return to Napa.

3

redwood table, and in any weather indoors among the contemporary artworks and well-chosen *objets*—which might include 17th-century furnishings, industrial lamps, or slabs of petrified wood. ■TIP→ Walk-ins are welcome, space permitting, but during summer, at harvest, and on weekends and holidays it's best to book in advance. ⊠ *6711 Washington St., at Pedroni St.* ☎ *707/944–0889* ⊕ *www.maisonry.com* 🍷 *Tasting $35–$55.*

Fodor's Choice ★ **Robert Sinskey Vineyards.** Although the winery produces a well-regarded Stags Leap Cabernet Sauvignon, two Bordeaux-style red blends (Marcien and POV), and white wines, Sinskey is best known for its intense, brambly Carneros District Pinot Noirs. All the grapes are grown in organic, certified biodynamic vineyards. The influence of

Robert's wife, Maria Helm Sinskey—a chef and cookbook author and the winery's culinary director—is evident during the tastings, which are accompanied by a few bites of food with each wine. ■TIP➜ **The Perfect Circle Tour ($95), offered daily, takes in the winery's gardens and ends with a seated pairing of food and wine. Even more elaborate, also by appointment, is the Chef's Table ($175), on Friday and weekends.** ✉ *6320 Silverado Trail, at Yountville Cross Rd., Napa* ☎ *707/944–9090* ⊕ *www.robertsinskey.com* ✉ *Tastings $40–$70, tour $95.*

Fodor'sChoice
★
Stewart Cellars. Three stone structures meant to mimic Scottish ruins coaxed into modernity form this complex that includes public and private tasting spaces, a bright outdoor patio, and a café with accessible vegan- and carnivore-friendly cuisine. The attention to detail in the ensemble's design mirrors that of the wines, whose grapes come from Stagecoach, Beckstoffer Las Piedras (for the intense Nomad Cabernet), and other coveted vineyards. Although Cabernet is the focus, winemaker Blair Guthrie, with input from consulting winemaker Paul Hobbs, also makes Chardonnay, Pinot Noir, and Merlot. ■TIP➜ **On sunny days this is a good stop around lunchtime, when you can order a meal from the café and a glass of wine from the tasting room—for permit reasons this must be done separately—and enjoy them on the patio.** ✉ *6752 Washington St., near Pedroni St.* ☎ *707/963–9160* ⊕ *www. stewartcellars.com* ✉ *Tastings $35–$85.*

■ QUICK
BITES
Bouchon Bakery. To satisfy that craving you didn't know you had—but soon will—for macarons, stock up on hazelnut, pistachio, chocolate-dipped raspberry, and several other flavors at this bakery associated with the Thomas Keller restaurant of the same name. The brownies, pastries, and other baked goods are equally alluring. **Known for: textbook golden-brown croissants; well-made espresso drinks; lemon and other tarts.** ✉ *6528 Washington St., at Yount St.* ☎ *707/944–2253* ⊕ *www.bouchonbakery.com.*

WORTH NOTING

Domaine Chandon. On a knoll shaded by ancient oak trees, this French-owned maker of sparkling wines claims one of Yountville's prime pieces of real estate. Chandon is best known for bubblies, but the still wines—Cabernet Sauvignon, Chardonnay, Pinot Meunier, and Pinot Noir—are also worth a try. You can sip by the flight or by the glass at the bar, or begin there and sit at tables in the lounge and return to the bar as needed; in good weather, tables are set up outside. For the complete experience, order a cheese board or other hors d'oeuvres on the lounge menu. ✉ *1 California Dr., off Hwy. 29* ☎ *707/204–7530, 888/242–6366* ⊕ *www.chandon.com* ✉ *Tastings $9–$40.*

Hill Family Estate. For years Doug Hill produced grapes for prominent Napa Valley wineries, but at the urging of his son, Ryan, the family established its own line of Merlot, Cabernet Sauvignon, and other wines. Crafted by Alison Doran, a protégé of the late Napa winemaker André Tchelistcheff, these are refined wines you can sample in the family's downtown tasting salon, a mélange of antiques alongside baseball, surfing, and other memorabilia—even a classic Fender guitar—ingeniously

HIT THE (VINE) TRAIL

The Napa Valley Vine Trail is a planned 47-mile scenic path that backers hope will eventually run the length of the valley. As 2017 dawned, about 13 miles had been completed, including a mostly flat 9-mile paved stretch between northern Yountville and Napa's Oxbow Commons.

FOLLOW THE TRACKS
For most of the way this section of the path follows the same route as the Napa Valley Wine Train. In Yountville, pick up the trail near the traffic light at Madison Street and Highway 29, just west of R+D Kitchen restaurant. This portion ends in Napa at Vallejo Street west of Soscol Avenue near St. Clair Brown Winery's greenhouse, though after a short break in the trail you can continue south 3 more miles. (Head east across Soscol and immediately south on McKinstry Street at the Westin hotel.)

MARKERS, STATIONS
Markers along the trail let riders, walkers, and joggers know where they are, and interpretive signs convey a bit of history. Bike stations—there's one at 1046 McKinstry Street outside the Oxbow Public Market's Cru @ The Annex tasting room—have bike racks, pumps, and tools for minor repairs. Get more information and rent bikes and helmets at Napa Valley Bike Tours, at 6500 Washington Street in Yountville. The Vine Trail's website (⊕ vinetrail.org) has a downloadable map.

3

stained in Hill red wine. In summer and early fall, entertaining "secret garden" tours (by appointment, weather permitting) are conducted of **Jacobsen Orchards,** a small nearby farm that grows produce for The French Laundry and other top restaurants. ✉ 6512 Washington St., at Mulberry St. ☎ 707/944–9580 ⊕ www.hillfamilyestate.com 🎟 Tastings $20, garden tour $65 (includes tasting).

Jessup Cellars. This winery's downtown Yountville tasting room attracts a loyal following for its upbeat vibe, smartly curated art gallery, and the lush red wines of its The Art of the Blend Series. Three of the series' wines—Table for Four, Juel, and Manny's Blend, with, respectively, Cabernet Sauvignon, Merlot, and Zinfandel as the lead grape—are among Jessup's most popular offerings. Their success spawned two additional blends, Graziella (Cabernet and Sangiovese) and Rougette (Grenache). Winemaker Rob Lloyd also crafts Chardonnay, Merlot, and Pinot Noir from southern Napa Valley vineyards with maritime climates, sourcing Zinfandel and Petite Sirah from hotter northern locales and Cabernet from both. ■TIP→ **Jessup's gallery often hosts evening events, including art openings, live music, and film screenings, many of which sell out well in advance.** ✉ 6740 Washington St., at Pedroni St. ☎ 707/944–8523, 888/537–7879 ⊕ jessupcellars.com 🎟 Tastings $10–$30.

WHERE TO EAT

$$$$
MODERN
AMERICAN
Fodor's Choice
★

✕ **Ad Hoc.** At this low-key dining room with zinc-top tables and wine served in tumblers, superstar chef Thomas Keller offers a single, fixed-price menu nightly, with a small but decadent Sunday brunch. The dinner selection might include smoked beef short ribs with creamy herb rice and charred broccolini, or sesame chicken with radish kimchi and fried rice. **Known for:** casual cuisine; great price for a Thomas Keller meal; don't-miss buttermilk-fried-chicken night. $ *Average main: $55* ✉ *6476 Washington St., at Oak Circle* ☎ *707/944–2487* ⊕ *www.adhocrestaurant.com* ☺ *No lunch Mon.–Sat.; no dinner Tues. and Wed.* ☞ *Call a day ahead to find out the next day's menu.*

$$$
FRENCH
Fodor's Choice
★

✕ **Bistro Jeanty.** Escargots, cassoulet, *daube de boeuf* (beef stewed in red wine), and other French classics are prepared with the utmost precision at this country bistro whose lamb tongue and other obscure delicacies delight daring diners. Regulars often start with the rich tomato soup in a flaky puff pastry before proceeding to sole meunière or coq au vin, completing the French sojourn with warm apple tarte tatin and other authentic desserts. **Known for:** traditional preparations; oh-so-French ambience. $ *Average main: $27* ✉ *6510 Washington St., at Mulberry St.* ☎ *707/944–0103* ⊕ *www.bistrojeanty.com.*

$$$
ITALIAN

✕ **Bottega.** At his downtown trattoria, chef Michael Chiarello transforms local ingredients into regional Italian dishes with a twist. A potato gnocchi first course might be served with pumpkin *fonduta* (Italian-style fondue) and roasted root vegetables, and main courses such as grilled acorn-fed pork shoulder with a honey-mustard glaze might be accompanied by stewed plums and crispy black kale. **Known for:** rustic yet sophisticated cuisine; open kitchen; Italian and California wines. $ *Average main: $26* ✉ *6525 Washington St., near Mulberry St.* ☎ *707/945–1050* ⊕ *www.botteganapavalley.com* ☺ *No lunch Mon.*

$$$
FRENCH
Fodor's Choice
★

✕ **Bouchon.** The team that created The French Laundry is also behind this place, where everything—the lively and crowded zinc-topped bar, the elbow-to-elbow seating, the traditional French onion soup—could have come straight from a Parisian bistro. Roasted chicken with leeks and oyster mushrooms and steamed mussels served with crispy, addictive *frites* (french fries) are among the perfectly executed entrées. **Known for:** bistro classics; rabbit and salmon rillettes. $ *Average main: $27* ✉ *6534 Washington St., near Humboldt St.* ☎ *707/944–8037* ⊕ *www. bouchonbistro.com.*

$$
MODERN ITALIAN

✕ **Ciccio.** The ranch of Ciccio's owners, Frank and Karen Altamura, supplies some of the vegetables and herbs for the modern Italian cuisine prepared in the open kitchen of this remodeled former grocery store. Seasonal growing cycles dictate executive chef Polly Lappetito's menu, with Tuscan kale and white-bean soup, wood-fired sardines with salsa verde, and a mushroom, Taleggio, and crispy-sage pizza among the frequent offerings. **Known for:** Negroni bar; prix-fixe chef's dinner; mostly Napa Valley wines, some from owners' winery. $ *Average main: $19* ✉ *6770 Washington St., at Madison St.* ☎ *707/945–1000* ⊕ *www. ciccionapavalley.com* ☺ *Closed Mon. and Tues. No lunch* ☞ *No reservations, except for prix-fixe chef's dinner (required; for 4–10 guests).*

$$$$ AMERICAN Fodor's Choice ★ 🍴 **The French Laundry.** An old stone building laced with ivy houses chef Thomas Keller's destination restaurant. Some courses on the two prix-fixe menus, one of which highlights vegetables, rely on luxe ingredients such as *calotte* (cap of the rib eye); other courses take humble elements like fava beans and elevate them to art. **Known for:** signature starter "oysters and pearls"; intricate flavors; superior wine list. [$] *Average main: $310* ✉ *6640 Washington St., at Creek St.* ☎ *707/944–2380* 🌐 *www.frenchlaundry.com* 🕒 *No lunch Mon.–Thurs.* 👔 *Jacket required* ☞ *Reservations essential weeks ahead (call or check website for precise instructions).*

$ MODERN AMERICAN 🍴 **Gather Café by Stewart Cellars.** Most dishes at chef Sarah Heller's street-side café at the Stewart Cellars tasting room are vegetarian-friendly, and carnivores can add proteins such as egg, chicken breast, or rock shrimp as desired. Sweet and savory Belgian waffles for breakfast or lunch are among the hits with local workers, along with Thai and spicy kale Caesar salads, brown-rice burrito bowls, and the soup du jour. **Known for:** healthful fast-food cuisine; wine available (separately) from tasting room; freshly pressed juice of the day. [$] *Average main: $9* ✉ *6752 Washington St., near Pedroni St.* ☎ *707/963–9160* 🌐 *www.stewartcellars.com* 🕒 *Closed Mon. and Tues. in winter. No dinner.*

$$$ AMERICAN 🍴 **Mustards Grill.** Cindy Pawlcyn's Mustards fills day and night with fans of her hearty cuisine, equal parts updated renditions of traditional American dishes—what Pawlcyn dubs "deluxe truck stop classics"—and fanciful contemporary fare. Barbecued baby back pork ribs and a lemon-lime tart piled high with brown-sugar meringue fall squarely in the first category, with sweet corn tamales with tomatillo-avocado salsa and wild mushrooms representing the latter. **Known for:** roadhouse setting; convivial mood; hoppin' bar. [$] *Average main: $27* ✉ *7399 St. Helena Hwy./Hwy. 29, 1 mile north of Yountville, Napa* ☎ *707/944–2424* 🌐 *www.mustardsgrill.com.*

$ ITALIAN 🍴 **Ottimo.** Chef Michael Chiarello opened this casual "multifaceted culinary experience" (*ottimo* is Italian for "optimal") across from his other restaurant, Bottega. The stations include a bakery, a *birreria* (craft brewery whose beers are made from grapes and rice), a *mozzeria* (fresh mozzarella stand) and pizzeria, a wine bar, and a tasting bar for preserves, pickled products, and oils and vinegars. **Known for:** pizzas and pastries; artisanal coffees and cold-pressed juices; gelati and desserts. [$] *Average main: $10* ✉ *V Marketplace, 6525 Washington St., across from Bottega entrance* ☎ *707/944–0102.*

$ LATIN AMERICAN Fodor's Choice ★ 🍴 **Protéa Restaurant.** A meal at Yountville's The French Laundry motivated Puerto Rico–born Anita Cartagena to pursue a career as a chef, which she did for several years at nearby Ciccio and elsewhere before opening this perky storefront serving Latin-inspired multi-culti fast-food cuisine. What's in season and the chef's whims determine the order-at-the-counter fare, but Puerto Rican rice bowls (often with pork), empanadas, and sweet-and-sour ramen stir-fries make regular appearances. **Known for:** patio and rooftop seating; beer and wine lineup; eager-to-please staff. [$] *Average main: $13* ✉ *6488 Washington St., at Oak Circle* ☎ *707/415–5035* 🌐 *www.proteayv.com.*

$$ ECLECTIC 🍴 **R+D Kitchen.** As the name suggests, the chefs here are willing to experiment, starting with sushi plates that include hiramasa rolls topped with rainbow-trout caviar. Among the items served at both lunch and dinner are the Greek-style rotisserie chicken in egg-lemon sauce, the buttermilk fried-chicken sandwich topped with Swiss, and a slow-roasted pork sandwich with avocado and slaw. **Known for:** good value; cheerful service; Dip Duo (guac and pimento cheese with chips) patio appetizer with wine or specialty cocktails. [$] *Average main: $19* ✉ *6795 Washington St., at Madison St.* ☎ *707/945–0920* 🌐 *rd-kitchen.com/locations/yountville.*

$$$ MODERN AMERICAN Fodor's Choice ★ 🍴 **Redd.** Chef Richard Reddington's culinary influences include California, Mexico, Europe, and Asia, but his dishes, like his minimalist dining room, feel modern and unfussy. The glazed pork belly with apple puree, set amid a pool of soy caramel, is an example of the East-meets-West style, and the seafood preparations—among them petrale sole, clams, and chorizo poached in a saffron-curry broth—exhibit a similar transcontinental dexterity. **Known for:** five-course tasting menu; street-side outdoor patio; cocktails and small plates at the bar. [$] *Average main: $30* ✉ *6480 Washington St., at Oak Circle* ☎ *707/944–2222* 🌐 *www.reddnapavalley.com.*

$$ ITALIAN 🍴 **Redd Wood.** Chef Richard Reddington's casual restaurant specializes in thin-crust wood-fired pizzas and contemporary variations on rustic Italian classics. With sausage soup laced with cabbage and turnip, pizzas such as the white anchovy with herb sauce and mozzarella, and the pork-chop entrée enlivened by persimmon, Redd Wood does for Italian comfort food what nearby Mustards Grill does for the American version: it spruces it up but retains its innate pleasures. **Known for:** industrial decor; easygoing service. [$] *Average main: $21* ✉ *North Block Hotel, 6755 Washington St., at Madison St.* ☎ *707/299–5030* 🌐 *www.redd-wood.com.*

WHERE TO STAY

$$$$ RESORT Fodor's Choice ★ 🏨 **Bardessono.** Although Bardessono bills itself as the "greenest luxury hotel in America," there's nothing spartan about its accommodations; arranged around four landscaped courtyards, the rooms have luxurious organic bedding, gas fireplaces, and huge bathrooms with walnut floors. **Pros:** large rooftop lap pool; excellent spa, with in-room treatments available. **Cons:** expensive; limited view from some rooms. [$] *Rooms from: $700* ✉ *6526 Yount St.* ☎ *707/204–6000* 🌐 *www.bardessono.com* 🛏 *62 rooms* 🍽 *No meals.*

$$$$ HOTEL 🏨 **Hotel Yountville.** The landscaped woodsy setting, resortlike pool area, glorious spa, and exclusive yet casual ambience of the Hotel Yountville attract travelers wanting to get away from it all yet still be close—but not too close—to fine dining and tasting rooms. **Pros:** chic rooms; close to Yountville fine dining; glorious spa. **Cons:** occasional service lapses unusual at this price point. [$] *Rooms from: $625* ✉ *6462 Washington St.* ☎ *707/967–7900, 888/944–2885 for reservations* 🌐 *www.hotelyountville.com* 🛏 *80 rooms* 🍽 *No meals.*

$$$ B&B/INN 🏨 **Lavender Inn.** On a quiet side street around the corner from The French Laundry, the Lavender Inn feels at once secluded and centrally located. **Pros:** reasonable rates for Yountville; in a residential area but close to restaurants and shops; friendly staff. **Cons:** hard to book in high season; lacks amenities of larger properties. [$] *Rooms from: $315*

✉ *2020 Webber St.* ☎ *707/944–1388, 800/533–4140* 🌐 *www.lavendernapa.com* 🛏 *9 rooms* 🍴 *Breakfast.*

$$ B&B/INN 🏨 **Maison Fleurie.** A stay at this comfortable inn places you within easy walking distance of Yountville's fine restaurants. **Pros:** smallest rooms a bargain; outdoor hot tub; pool (open in season); free bike rental. **Cons:** breakfast room can be crowded at peak times. [$] *Rooms from: $219* ✉ *6529 Yount St.* ☎ *707/944–2056, 800/788–0369* 🌐 *www.maisonfleurienapa.com* 🛏 *13 rooms* 🍴 *Breakfast.*

$$$ HOTEL 🏨 **Napa Valley Lodge.** Clean rooms in a convenient motel-style setting draw travelers willing to pay more than at comparable lodgings in the city of Napa to be within walking distance of Yountville's tasting rooms, restaurants, and shops. **Pros:** clean rooms; filling continental breakfast; large pool area. **Cons:** no elevator; lacks amenities of other Yountville properties. [$] *Rooms from: $350* ✉ *2230 Madison St.* ☎ *707/944–2468, 888/944–3545* 🌐 *www.napavalleylodge.com* 🛏 *55 rooms* 🍴 *Breakfast.*

$$ HOTEL 🏨 **Napa Valley Railway Inn.** Budget-minded travelers and those with kids appreciate these very basic accommodations—inside actual railcars—just steps away from most of Yountville's best restaurants. **Pros:** central location; quaint appeal. **Cons:** office is sometimes unstaffed; parking-lot side gets some noise. [$] *Rooms from: $210* ✉ *6523 Washington St.* ☎ *707/944–2000* 🌐 *www.napavalleyrailwayinn.com* 🛏 *9 rooms* 🍴 *No meals.*

$$$$ HOTEL 🏨 **North Block Hotel.** With chic Tuscan style, this 20-room hotel has dark-wood furniture and a brown and sage decor. **Pros:** extremely comfortable beds; attentive service; room service by Redd Wood restaurant. **Cons:** outdoor areas get some traffic noise. [$] *Rooms from: $420* ✉ *6757 Washington St.* ☎ *707/944–8080* 🌐 *northblockhotel.com* 🛏 *20 rooms* 🍴 *No meals.*

$$$$ B&B/INN Fodor's Choice ★ 🏨 **Poetry Inn.** All the rooms at this splurge-worthy hillside retreat have full vistas of the lower Napa Valley from their westward-facing balconies; indoors, the polished service, comfortably chic decor, and amenities that include a private spa and a fully stocked wine cellar only add to the exquisite pleasure of a stay here. **Pros:** perfect for special occasions; valley views; discreet, polished service; gourmet breakfasts. **Cons:** pricey; party types might find the atmosphere too low-key. [$] *Rooms from: $1,025* ✉ *6380 Silverado Trail* ☎ *707/944–0646* 🌐 *poetryinn.com* 🛏 *5 rooms* 🍴 *Breakfast.*

$$$$ RESORT 🏨 **Villagio Inn & Spa.** A multimillion-dollar renovation that kicked into high gear in 2017 will transform this downtown property into a slick yet inviting haven of tranquillity. **Pros:** central location; steps from restaurants and tasting rooms; 13,000-square-foot spa. **Cons:** sometimes bustling with large groups; highway noise audible from some balconies and patios. [$] *Rooms from: $575* ✉ *6481 Washington St.* ☎ *707/944–8877, 800/351–1133* 🌐 *www.villagio.com* 🛏 *112 rooms* 🍴 *Breakfast.*

$$$$ RESORT 🏨 **Vintage Inn.** Amid downtown Yountville's 22-acre Vintage Estate complex, this recently renovated property (sister to the Villagio Inn & Spa) consists of two-story villas whose top-floor guest rooms have vaulted beam ceilings. **Pros:** private patios and balconies; nostalgia-inducing contemporary design; secluded feeling yet near shops, tasting rooms, and restaurants. **Cons:** highway noise is audible in some exterior rooms. [$] *Rooms from: $595* ✉ *6541 Washington St.* ☎ *707/944–1112* 🌐 *www.vintageinn.com* 🛏 *80 rooms* 🍴 *Breakfast.*

3

SPAS

North Block Spa. "Relax. Just Do It," reads a sign along the staircase to the North Block Hotel's softly lit basement spa—and the well-trained massage and other therapists ensure you do. Signature treatments include a foot and back exfoliation followed by a massage; a full-body scrub with a blend of walnut-shell powder, sweet almond, and blood orange prior to a massage involving pink grapefruit; and a "Playful Passion" session (for hotel guests only) that includes couples exfoliating each other, receiving dual massages, and playing a sensual game after relaxation sets in. Facials, acupuncture, skin regimens, and "Stiletto Blues" therapy for ladies betrayed by tall, pointy heels are among the other treatments. ⊠ *North Block Hotel, 6757 Washington St., near Madison St.* ☎ *707/944–8080* ⊕ *northblockhotel.com/spa* ✉ *Treatments $140–$425.*

Fodor's Choice **The Spa at Bardessono.** Many of this spa's patrons are hotel guests who
★ take their treatments in their rooms' large, customized bathrooms—all of them equipped with concealed massage tables—but the main facility is open to guests and nonguests alike. An in-room treatment popular with couples starts with massages in front of the fireplace and ends with a whirlpool bath and a split of sparkling wine. For the two-hour Yountville Signature treatment, which can be enjoyed in-room or at the spa, a shea-butter-enriched sugar scrub is applied, followed by a massage with antioxidant Chardonnay grape-seed oil and a hydrating hair and scalp treatment. The spa engages massage therapists skilled in Swedish, Thai, and several other techniques. In addition to massages, the services include facials, waxing, and other skin-care treatments, as well as manicures and pedicures. ⊠ *Bardessono Hotel, 6526 Yount St., at Mulberry St.* ☎ *707/204–6050* ⊕ *www.bardessono.com/spa* ✉ *Treatments $60–$630.*

Spa Villagio. Five private spa suites complete with flat-screen TVs and wet bars are among the amenities that set the 13,000-square-foot spa at the Villagio Inn apart from its peers. Popular with couples, the suites also have separate relaxation lounges, indoor and outdoor fireplaces, steam showers, saunas, and couples' tubs. Retreats in the suites also include food and sparkling wine. The signature treatments involve the experiences and products of the internationally respected skin-care company ESPA. A salt-and-oil scrub and an aromatherapy massage are the centerpieces of the four-hour Detox Duo that leaves some patrons glowing for days. Body treatments, facials, and massages are among the à la carte services. ⊠ *6481 Washington St., at Oak Circle* ☎ *707/948–5050, 800/351–1133* ⊕ *www.villagio.com/spavillagio* ✉ *Treatments $85–$675.*

SPORTS AND THE OUTDOORS

BALLOONING

Napa Valley Aloft. Between 8 and 12 passengers soar over the Napa Valley in balloons that launch from downtown Yountville. Rates include preflight refreshments and a huge breakfast. ⊠ *V Marketplace, 6525 Washington St., near Mulberry St.* ☎ *707/944–4400, 855/944–4408* ⊕ *www.nvaloft.com* ✉ *From $220.*

Napa Valley Balloons. The valley's oldest balloon company offers trips that are elegant from start to finish. Satisfied customers include Chelsea Clinton and *Today* show host Matt Lauer. ✉ *Domaine Chandon, 1 California Dr., at Solano Ave., west of Hwy. 29* ☏ *707/944–0228, 800/253–2224* ⊕ *www.napavalleyballoons.com* ✉ *$215 per person.*

BICYCLING

Napa Valley Bike Tours. With dozens of wineries within 5 miles, this shop makes a fine starting point for guided and self-guided vineyard and wine-tasting excursions. The outfit also rents bikes. ✉ *6500 Washington St., at Mulberry St.* ☏ *707/944–2953* ⊕ *www.napavalleybiketours.com* ✉ *From $124 (½-day guided tour).*

SHOPPING

Finesse, the Store. This small store sells chef Thomas Keller logo items such as The French Laundry hats and aprons, Ad Hoc wine tumblers, and Bouchon Bakery milk bottles, all displayed with high style. You can also buy cookbooks, cookware sets, and mixes. ✉ *6540 Washington St., near Humboldt St.* ☏ *707/363–9552* ⊕ *store.tkrg.com* ⊙ *Closed Tues. and Wed.*

Hunter Gatherer. A Napa Valley play on the classic general store, Colby Hallen's high-end lifestyle shop sells women's clothing and accessories from designers such as Frēda Salvador and Emerson Fry. She carries some men's items, too, along with everything from ceramic flasks and small gifts and cards to artisanal honey and Vintner's Daughter Active Botanical Serum face oil. ✉ *6795 Washington St., Bldg. B, at Madison St.* ⊕ *www.huntergatherernapavalley.com.*

Kelly's Filling Station and Wine Shop. The fuel is more than petrol at this gas station–convenience store whose design recalls the heyday of Route 66 travel. The shop inside sells top-rated wines, hot dogs, fresh scones from nearby R+D Kitchen, gourmet chocolates, and ice cream. Gas up, grab some picnic items, order coffee, espresso, or a cool drink to go, and be ever-so-merrily on your way. ✉ *6795 Washington St., at Madison St.* ☏ *707/944–8165.*

Kollar Chocolates. The aromas alone will lure you into this shop whose not-too-sweet, European-style chocolates are made on-site with imaginative ingredients. The artisanal truffles, many incorporating local ingredients, include lavender milk chocolate, chai milk chocolate, and espelette chili dark chocolate. ✉ *V Marketplace, 6525 Washington St.* ☏ *707/738–6750* ⊕ *www.kollarchocolates.com.*

V Marketplace. This two-story redbrick market, which once housed a winery, a livery stable, and a brandy distillery, now contains clothing boutiques, art galleries, a chocolatier, and food, wine, and gift shops. Celebrity chef Michael Chiarello operates a restaurant (Bottega), a tasting room for his wines, and Ottimo, with pizza, fresh mozzarella, and other stands plus retail items. Show some love to the shops upstairs, especially Knickers and Pearls (lingerie and loungewear), Montecristi Panama Hats (Johnny Depp found one he liked), and Lemondrops (kids' clothing and toys). ✉ *6525 Washington St., near Mulberry St.* ☏ *707/944–2451* ⊕ *www.vmarketplace.com.*

OAKVILLE

2 miles northwest of Yountville.

Barely a blip on the landscape as you drive north on Highway 29, Oakville is marked only by its grocery store. The town's small size belies the big mark it makes in the wine-making world. Slightly warmer than Yountville and Carneros to the south, but a few degrees cooler than Rutherford and St. Helena to the north, the Oakville area benefits from gravelly, well-drained soil. This allows roots to go deep—sometimes more than 100 feet—so that the vines produce intensely flavored fruit. Cabernet Sauvignon from the most famous vineyard here, To Kalon, at the base of the Mayacamas range, goes into many top-rated wines from winemakers throughout the valley. Big-name wineries within this appellation include Silver Oak, Far Niente, and Robert Mondavi.

GETTING HERE AND AROUND

If you're driving along Highway 29, you'll know you've reached Oakville when you see the Oakville Grocery on the east side of the road. Here the Oakville Cross Road provides access to the Silverado Trail (head east). Oakville wineries are scattered along Highway 29, Oakville Cross Road, and the Silverado Trail in roughly equal measure.

You can reach Oakville from the town of Glen Ellen in Sonoma County by heading east on Trinity Road from Highway 12. The twisting route, along the mountain range that divides Napa and Sonoma counties, eventually becomes the Oakville Grade. The views of both valleys on this drive are breathtaking, though the continual curves make it unsuitable for those who suffer from motion sickness. VINE Bus 10 serves Oakville.

EXPLORING

TOP ATTRACTIONS

B Cellars. The chefs take center stage in the open-hearth kitchen of this boutique winery's hospitality house, and with good reason: creating food-friendly wines is B Cellars's raison d'être. Visits to the Oakville facility—all steel beams, corrugated metal, and plate glass yet remarkably cozy—begin with a tour of the winery's culinary garden and caves. Most guests return to the house to sample wines paired with small bites, with some visitors remaining in the caves for exclusive tastings of Cabernet Sauvignons from several historic vineyards of Andy Beckstoffer, a prominent grower. Kirk Venge, whose fruit-forward style well suits the winery's food-oriented approach, crafts these and other wines, among them red and white blends and single-vineyard Cabernets from other noteworthy vineyards. ■ TIP➔ **The B Cellars wine and food pairings, all strictly by appointment, are outstanding.** ✉ *703 Oakville Cross Rd., west of Silverado Trail* ☎ *707/709–8787* ⊕ *www.bcellars.com* ✉ *Tastings $37–$135.*

Fodor'sChoice **Far Niente.** Guests arriving at Far Niente are welcomed by name and
★ treated to a glimpse of one of the Napa Valley's most beautiful properties. By appointment only, small groups are escorted through the historic 1885 stone winery, including some of the 40,000 square feet of aging caves, for a lesson on the labor-intensive method of making

Far Niente ages its Cabernets and Chardonnays in 40,000 square feet of caves.

Far Niente's flagship wines: a Cabernet Sauvignon blend and a Chardonnay. Next on the agenda is a peek at the Carriage House, which holds a gleaming collection of classic cars. The seated tasting of wines and cheeses that follows concludes on a sweet note with Dolce, a late-harvest wine made from Semillon and Sauvignon Blanc grapes. ⊠ *1350 Acacia Dr., off Oakville Grade Rd.* ☎ *707/944–2861* ⊕ *www.farniente. com* ✉ *Tasting and tour $75.*

Fodor's Choice
★
Nickel & Nickel. A corral out front and a farm-style windmill add horse-country flair to this winery, which makes smooth, almost sensual, single-vineyard Cabernet Sauvignons. Some of Nickel & Nickel's best derive from the home-base Oakville AVA—in particular the John C. Sullenger Vineyard, which surrounds the property—with impressive Cabernets from other Napa Valley appellations supplying the contrast. Tastings, all by appointment, begin with Chardonnay in the immaculate 1884 Sullenger House, followed by a tour of a rebuilt 18th-century barn and underground aging caves. Tasting of more wines resumes back at the house. ■TIP→ **Cabernet lovers won't want to miss this sister winery to elegant Far Niente.** ⊠ *8164 St. Helena Hwy./Hwy. 129, north of Oakville Cross Rd.* ☎ *707/967–9600* ⊕ *www.nickelandnickel.com* ✉ *Tasting and tour $75.*

Fodor's Choice
★
Silver Oak. The first review of this winery's Napa Valley Cabernet Sauvignon declared the debut 1972 vintage not all that good and, at $6 a bottle, overpriced. Oops. The celebrated Bordeaux-style Cabernet blend, still the only Napa Valley wine bearing its winery's label each year, evolved into a cult favorite, and Silver Oak founders Ray Duncan and Justin Meyer received worldwide recognition for their signature use

The design of the Opus One winery combines space-age and Mayan elements.

of exclusively American oak to age the wines. At the Oakville tasting room, constructed out of reclaimed stone and other materials from a 19th-century Kansas flour mill, you can sip the current Napa Valley vintage, its counterpart from Silver Oak's Alexander Valley operation, and a library wine without an appointment. One is required for tours, private tastings, and food-wine pairings. ⊠ *915 Oakville Cross Rd., off Hwy. 29* ☎ *707/942–7022* ⊕ *www.silveroak.com* ⊒ *Tastings $30–$75, tour $50 (includes tasting).*

WORTH NOTING

QUICK BITES

Oakville Grocery. Built in 1881 as a general store, Oakville Grocery carries high-end groceries and prepared foods. On summer weekends the place is often packed with customers stocking up on picnic provisions—meats, cheeses, breads, and gourmet sandwiches—but during the week it serves as a mellow pit stop to sip an espresso out front, have a picnic out back, or taste wines next door. ⊠ *7856 St. Helena Hwy./Hwy. 29, at Oakville Cross Rd.* ☎ *707/944–8802* ⊕ *www.oakvillegrocery.com.*

Opus One. In 1979 the Napa Valley's Robert Mondavi and France's Baron Philippe de Rothschild joined forces to produce a single wine: Opus One, a Bordeaux blend that was the first of Napa's ultrapremium wines. Tours here focus on the combination of agriculture, science, and technology required to create Opus One and conclude with a tasting of the current vintage. ■TIP→ You can taste the wine without touring, but as with the tour you'll need a reservation. ⊠ *7900 St. Helena*

Hwy./Hwy. 29, at Oakville Cross. Rd. ☎ *707/944–9442, 800/292–6787* ⊕ *www.opusonewinery.com* ✉ *Tasting $50, tours $85–$140.*

PlumpJack Winery. With its metal chandelier and wall hangings, the tasting room at this casual winery looks like a stage set for a modern Shakespearean production. (The name "PlumpJack" is a nod to Shakespeare's Falstaff.) A youngish crowd assembles here to sample vintages that include the citrusy reserve Chardonnay and a Merlot that's blended like a Cab, providing sufficient tannins to ensure ageability. The Syrah, from Atlas Peak and Carneros grapes, is available only through the winery. ■TIP→ **The Hilltop Tasting (reservations required) takes in the cellar and grounds and ends with a seated tasting overlooking the vineyards. Limited to six guests, it books up quickly in summer.** ✉ *620 Oakville Cross Rd., off Silverado Trail* ☎ *707/945–1220* ⊕ *www.plumpjackwinery.com* ✉ *Tastings $50–$65.*

Robert Mondavi Winery. The arch at the center of the sprawling Mission-style building frames the lawn and the vineyard behind, inviting a stroll under the arcades. You can head for one of the walk-in tasting rooms, but if you've not toured a winery before, the 90-minute Signature Tour and Tasting ($40, reservation recommended) is a good way to learn about enology, as well as the late Robert Mondavi's role in California wine making. Those new to tasting should consider the 45-minute Wine Tasting Basics experience ($25, by appointment). Serious wine lovers can opt for the appointment-only $55 Exclusive Cellar tasting, during which a server pours and explains limited-production, reserve, and older-vintage wines. ■TIP→ **Concerts take place in summer on the lawn; call ahead for tickets.** ✉ *7801 St. Helena Hwy./Hwy. 29* ☎ *888/766–6328* ⊕ *www.robertmondaviwinery.com* ✉ *Tastings and tours $20–$55.*

RUTHERFORD

2 miles northwest of Oakville.

The spot where Highway 29 meets Rutherford Road in the tiny community of Rutherford may well be the most significant wine-related intersection in the United States. With its singular microclimate and soil, Rutherford is an important viticultural center, with more big-name wineries than you can shake a corkscrew at, including Beaulieu, Inglenook, Mumm Napa, and St. Supéry.

Cabernet Sauvignon is king here. The soil is ideal for those vines, and since this part of the valley gets plenty of sun, the grapes develop intense flavors. Legendary winemaker André Tchelistcheff's famous claim that "it takes Rutherford dust to grow great Cabernet" is quoted by just about every winery in the area that produces the stuff. That "Rutherford dust" varies from one part of the region to another, but the soils here are primarily gravel, sand, and loam, a well-drained home for Cabernet Sauvignon grapes, which don't like to get their feet wet.

GETTING HERE AND AROUND

Wineries around Rutherford are dotted along Highway 29 and the parallel Silverado Trail just north and south of Rutherford Road/Conn Creek Road, which connect these two major thoroughfares. VINE Bus 10 serves Rutherford.

ESSENTIALS

Contact **Rutherford Dust Society.** ☎ *707/987–9821* ⊕ *www.rutherforddust.org.*

EXPLORING

TOP ATTRACTIONS

Caymus Vineyards. This winery's Special Selection Cabernet Sauvignon remains the only two-time *Wine Spectator* Wine of the Year honoree. In good weather you can sample the latest vintage and a few other wines outdoors in a landscaped area in front of the tasting room. Chuck Wagner started making wine on this property in 1972 and still oversees Caymus production, which includes a Napa Valley Zinfandel available for tasting only at the winery. His children craft most of the other wines in the Wagner Family of Wines portfolio, among them the oaked and unoaked Mer Soleil Chardonnays and the Emmolo Sauvignon Blanc and Merlot. Especially on weekends, it's wise to make an appointment to taste here. ✉ *8700 Conn Creek Rd., off Rutherford Rd.* ☎ *707/967–3010* ⊕ *www.caymus.com* ☜ *Tasting $50.*

FAMILY
Fodor'sChoice
★
Frog's Leap. John Williams, owner of Frog's Leap, maintains a sense of humor about wine that translates into an entertaining yet informative experience—if you're a novice, the tour here is a fun way to begin your education. You'll taste wines that might include Zinfandel, Merlot, Chardonnay, Sauvignon Blanc, and an estate-grown Cabernet Sauvignon. The winery includes a barn built in 1884, 5 acres of organic gardens, an eco-friendly visitor center, and a frog pond topped with lily pads. Reservations are required for all visits here. ■TIP→ The tour is recommended, but you can also just sample wines either inside or on a porch overlooking the garden. ✉ *8815 Conn Creek Rd.* ☎ *707/963–4704, 800/959–4704* ⊕ *www.frogsleap.com* ☜ *Tastings $20–$25; tour $25.*

FAMILY
Honig Vineyard & Winery. Sustainable farming is the big story at this family-run winery. The Eco Tour, offered seasonally, focuses on the Honig family's environmentally friendly farming and production methods, which include using biodiesel to fuel the tractors, monitoring water use in the vineyard and winery, and generating power for the winery with solar panels. The family produces only Sauvignon Blanc and Cabernet Sauvignon. By appointment, you can taste whites and reds at a standard tasting for $30; the reserve tasting ($60) pairs single-vineyard Cabernets with small bites. ✉ *850 Rutherford Rd., near Conn Creek Rd.* ☎ *800/929–2217* ⊕ *www.honigwine.com* ☜ *Tastings $30–$60, tour $45.*

Inglenook. Filmmaker Francis Ford Coppola began his wine-making career in 1975, when he bought part of the historic Inglenook estate. Over the decades he reunited the original property acquired

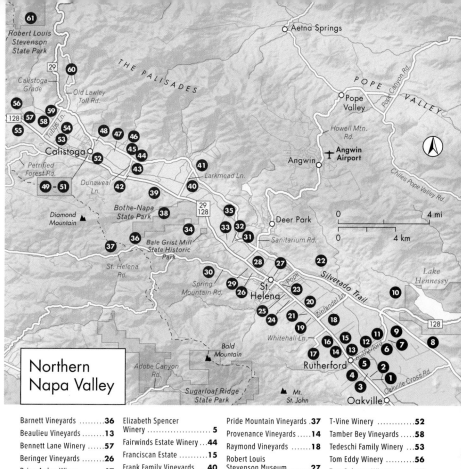

Northern Napa Valley

Round Pond Estate makes sophisticated wines and extra-virgin olive oils.

by Inglenook founder Gustave Niebaum, remodeled Niebaum's ivy-covered 1880s château, and purchased the rights to the Inglenook name. The Inglenook Experience ($50), an escorted tour of the château, vineyards, and caves, ends with a seated tasting of wines paired with artisanal cheeses. Among the topics discussed are the winery's history and the evolution of Coppola's signature wine, Rubicon, a Cabernet Sauvignon–based blend. The Heritage Tasting ($45), which also includes a Rubicon pour, is held in the opulent Pennino Salon. Reservations are required for some tastings and tours, and are recommended for all. ■TIP→ **Walk-ins can sip wines by the glass or bottle at The Bistro, a wine bar with a picturesque courtyard.** ⊠ *1991 St. Helena Hwy./Hwy. 29, at Hwy.128* ☎ *707/968–1100, 800/782–4266* ⊕ *www.inglenook. com* ▧ *Tastings $45–$50, private experiences from $75.*

Mumm Napa. In Mumm's light-filled tasting room or adjacent outdoor patio you can enjoy bubbly by the flight, but the sophisticated sparkling wines, elegant setting, and vineyard views aren't the only reasons to visit. An excellent gallery displays original Ansel Adams prints and presents temporary exhibitions by premier photographers. Winery tours cover the major steps in making sparklers. For a leisurely tasting of several vintages of the top-of-the-line DVX wines, book an Oak Terrace tasting ($50; reservations recommended Friday through Sunday). ■TIP→ **Carlos Santana fans may want to taste the sparklers the musician makes in collaboration with Mumm's winemaker, Ludovic Dervin.** ⊠ *8445 Silverado Trail, 1 mile south of Rutherford Cross Rd.* ☎ *707/967–7700, 800/686–6272* ⊕ *www.mummnapa.com* ▧ *Tastings $20–$50, tour $40 (includes tasting).*

Piña Napa Valley. The Piña family, whose Napa Valley heritage dates to the 1850s, is known locally as much for its first-rate vineyard-management company as its modest winery that specializes in single-vineyard, 100% Cabernet Sauvignon wines. Winemaker Anna Monticelli crafts robust Cabs from mostly hillside fruit, all estate grown. Though she doesn't blend in other varietals, commonly done to soften Cabernet, Piña doesn't release its wines until age has mellowed them. If he's not busy elsewhere, Larry Piña, the winery's genial managing partner and among his family's seventh generation involved in the wine business, often drops by the no-frills barrel-room tasting area. Appointments aren't not necessary, but it's good to call 30 minutes ahead to make sure there's space. ■TIP→ A short hillside path behind the barrel room leads to a picnic platform with views west to Rutherford. ⊠ *8060 Silverado Trail, 0.2 miles north of Skellenger La.* ☎ *707/738–9328* ⊕ *pinanapavalley.com* ✉ *Tasting $20.*

Provenance Vineyards. Far northwest in the Rutherford appellation, Provenance makes first-rate Bordeaux-style wines from estate grapes and others sourced from top valley vineyards. Because the Cabernet Sauvignons poured in the Reserve Tasting ($30) hail from different subappellations, sampling them provides the opportunity to learn what makes a Yountville or Oakville Cab different from a Howell or Diamond Mountain one. Provenance also produces the single annual bottling of the separately labeled Hewitt Cabernet Sauvignon from a nearby estate vineyard. A recent Hewitt vintage was designated the top Cabernet in the world by *Wine Spectator* magazine. Oak-barrel staves from Provenance's first vintage (1999) were shaved, sanded, and polished to create the tasting room floor; in good weather many patrons never see it, opting instead to sip on the merry patio out front. The seated indoor tastings of several Hewitt vintages require a reservation. Hewitt tastings are by appointment only. ⊠ *1695 St. Helena Hwy./Hwy. 29, near Mee La.* ☎ *707/968–3633* ⊕ *provenancevineyards.com* ✉ *Provenance tastings $25–$30, Hewitt tasting $75.*

Round Pond Estate. Sophisticated wines come from Round Pond, but the estate also produces premium olive oils, most from olives grown and crushed on the property. Informative olive-related seminars pass through the high-tech mill, followed by tastings of the aromatic oils, both alone and with house-made red-wine vinegars. To sample the wines, head across the street to the winery; the basic tasting includes a Sauvignon Blanc and Round Pond's well-rounded reds. The flagship Estate Cabernet Sauvignon has the structure and heft of the classic 1970s Rutherford Cabs but acknowledges 21st-century palates with smoother, if still sturdy, tannins. The estate tasting pairs small morsels with the wines. Tastings and tours are by appointment only (24–48 hours in advance). ■TIP→ The full Il Pranzo lunch incorporates products made and produce grown on-site, as does the well-attended Sunday brunch. ⊠ *875 Rutherford Rd., near Conn Creek Rd.* ☎ *707/302–2575, 888/302–2575* ⊕ *www.roundpond.com* ✉ *Wine tastings $40–$65, barrel tour and tasting $85; olive mill tour and tasting $70.*

St. Supéry Estate Vineyards & Winery. The French fashion company Chanel purchased St. Supéry in late 2015, adding further glamour to this appointment-only winery whose Rutherford vineyards surround its immaculate hospitality center and production facility. St. Supéry makes two widely distributed wines, a Sauvignon Blanc and a Cabernet Sauvignon, but tastings here focus on limited-production efforts from the Rutherford property and the 1,500-acre Dollarhide Ranch on Howell Mountain. The Divine Estate Tasting ($45) includes whites and reds; you can also opt for an all-Cabernet tasting ($50). Among the specialized experiences, the popular Aromatherapy with a Corkscrew involves blind sniffing and tasting to learn how to identify citrus, tropical, and other aromas in wines. ■TIP➜ **In fine weather, sipping Sauvignon Blanc outside and playing pétanque (like boccie), feels like a mini-excursion to the old country.** ⊠ *8440 St. Helena Hwy./ Hwy. 29, near Manley La.* ☎ *707/963—4507* ⊕ *www.stsupery.com* ⌘ *Tastings $45–$125.*

WORTH NOTING

Beaulieu Vineyard. The influential André Tchelistcheff (1901–1994), who helped define the California style of wine making, worked his magic here for many years. BV, founded in 1900 by Georges de Latour and his wife, Fernande, is known for its widely distributed Chardonnay, Pinot Noir, and Cabernet Sauvignon wines, but many others are produced in small lots and are available only at the winery. The most famous of the small-lot wines is the flagship Georges de Latour Private Reserve Cabernet Sauvignon, first crafted by Tchelistcheff himself in the late 1930s. Reservations are required for some tastings here. ■TIP➜ **Book a Retrospective Reserve Tasting ($75) to taste the current Georges de Latour and older vintages of it and other limited-production wines.** ⊠ *1960 St. Helena Hwy./Hwy. 29, at Hwy. 128* ☎ *707/967–5233, 800/264–6918 ext. 5233* ⊕ *www.bvwines.com* ⌘ *Tastings $25–$125.*

Cakebread Cellars. Jack and Dolores Cakebread were among the wave of early-1970s vintners whose efforts not only raised the Napa Valley's wine-making profile but also initiated what became known as the Wine Country lifestyle. Guests at standard tastings sample Chardonnay and Cabernet Sauvignon, which helped establish the company, along with Merlot, Pinot Noir, Syrah, and other current releases made in smaller lots. At any tasting you'll learn about the winery's interesting history—Jack was a photographer whose mentors included Ansel Adams—but book a tour for deeper insight. Cakebread makes so many different wines, some available only here or online, that you can opt for all-red or all-white tastings, or one focusing on single-vineyard, library, and limited-production wines. All tours and tastings are by appointment. ⊠ *8300 St. Helena Hwy./Hwy. 29, near Glos La.* ☎ *707/963–5222 for info, 800/588–0298 for reservations* ⊕ *www. cakebread.com* ⌘ *Tastings $15–$45, tour $25.*

Elizabeth Spencer Winery. Although its first vintage (1998) debuted long after those of neighbors Inglenook and Beaulieu, this winery owned by wife and husband Elizabeth Pressler and Spencer Graham lays claim to a slice of Rutherford history: for most of the year, guests

CLOSE UP

Prohibition and Depression

The National Prohibition Act, which passed in 1919 under the popular name of the Volstead Act, had far-reaching effects on California wineries. Prohibition forced many to shut down altogether, but some, particularly Napa operations such as Beaulieu Vineyards, Beringer, and (on the St. Helena site now occupied by the Culinary Institute of America) the Christian Brothers, stayed in business by making sacramental wines. Others took advantage of the exception permitting home wine making and sold grapes and in some cases do-it-yourself kits with "warnings" about the steps that would result in grape juice turning into wine. A few wineries kept their inventories in bond, storing their wine in warehouses certified by the Department of Internal Revenue and guaranteed secure by bonding agencies. Magically, wine flowed out the back doors of the bonded warehouses into barrels and jugs brought by customers, and just as magically it seemed to replenish itself. Now and then a revenuer would crack down, but enforcement seems to have been lax at best.

STRUGGLE AND SURVIVAL

Prohibition, which ended in 1933, did less damage in the Napa Valley, where grapes thrive but fruit trees grow poorly on the rocky and gravelly slopes, benchlands, and alluvial fans, than it did in Sonoma County, where plum, walnut, and other orchards had replaced many vineyards. Fewer Napa growers had been able to convert to other crops, and more had been able to survive with sacramental wine, so more vineyards could be brought back to fine-wine production after repeal. Several major wineries survived Prohibition, including Inglenook and Charles Krug (acquired in the 1940s by the Cesare Mondavi family), which made some amazingly good wines during this period. Nevertheless, the wine industry struggled well into the 1960s to regain its customer base.

3

gain entry to the courtyard tasting area via the town's 1872 redbrick former post office. Varietal and geographical variety is a major goal, with Cabernet Sauvignon, Grenache, Merlot, Pinot Noir, and Syrah among the reds winemaker Sarah Vandenriessche crafts from Napa, Sonoma, and Mendocino county grapes. Whites include Chardonnay, Marsanne, Riesling, and Sauvignon Blanc. All tastings, one of current releases, the other focusing on earlier ones, are seated. In winter, staffers move the courtyard's black-metal chairs and tables into a nearby warehouse space made slightly snug by its fireplace. Appointments, though not required, are recommended. ⊠ *1165 Rutherford Rd., at Hwy. 29* 🖷 *707/963–6067* ⊕ *www.elizabethspencerwines.com* 🖾 *Tastings $25–$40.*

Hall Rutherford. The appointment-only sister winery to Hall St. Helena provides an exclusive, elegant wine and food pairing atop a Rutherford hillside. The visit includes a peek at the production facility's ornate stainless-steel aging tanks and the 14,000 square feet of caves under the Sacrashe vineyard, from whose steep slopes and rocky soils come grapes for some of Hall's best Cabernet Sauvignons. A tunnel lined with hand-stamped bricks salvaged from Habsburg-era Austrian buildings leads to a regal tasting room lit by a chandelier by artist Donald Lipski. Designed to mimic the roots of the grapevines above, it's adorned with nearly 2,000 Swarovski crystals. Tastings are by appointment only and focus on single-appellation wines. ✉ *56 Auberge Rd., off Silverado Trail* ☎ *707/967–2626* ⊕ *www.hallwines. com/hall-rutherford* ✉ *Tasting, tour, and wine-food pairing $125.*

Sequoia Grove. A stand of sequoias shades the outdoor areas and woodsy tasting room of this Cabernet Sauvignon producer. A standard tasting ($25) includes the Napa Valley Cabernet—a blend with grapes from several vineyards—along with wines that might include Sauvignon Blanc, Chardonnay, Merlot, or Syrah. You can also request a tasting of single-vineyard Cabernets (price varies depending on what's being poured). A Taste for Cabernet ($50), a thoughtful seminar focused on the output of five vineyards, provides surprising insights into which tastes—sweet, sour, bitter, salty, and umami—best complement Cabernet Sauvignon. ✉ *8338 St. Helena Hwy./Hwy. 29, near Bella Oaks La.* ☎ *707/944–2945, 800/851–7841* ⊕ *www.sequoia-grove.com* ✉ *Tastings $25–$50.*

WHERE TO EAT AND STAY

$$$$
MODERN
AMERICAN
Fodor'sChoice
★

✕ **Restaurant at Auberge du Soleil.** Possibly the most romantic roost for a dinner in all the Wine Country is a terrace seat at the Auberge du Soleil resort's illustrious restaurant, and the Mediterranean-inflected cuisine more than matches the dramatic vineyard views. The prix-fixe dinner menu, which relies largely on local produce, might include veal sweetbreads and chanterelles in a caramelized shallot sauce or prime beef pavé with hearts of palm, lobster mushrooms, and bok choy. **Known for:** polished service; comprehensive wine list; over-the-top weekend brunch. 🅢 *Average main: $115* ✉ *Auberge du Soleil, 180 Rutherford Hill Rd., off Silverado Trail* ☎ *707/963–1211, 800/348–5406* ⊕ *www. aubergedusoleil.com.*

$$$
AMERICAN
Fodor'sChoice
★

✕ **Rutherford Grill.** Dark-wood walls, subdued lighting, and red leather banquettes make for a perpetually clubby mood at this trusty Rutherford hangout. Many entrées—steaks, burgers, fish, succulent rotisserie chicken, and barbecued pork ribs—emerge from an oak-fired grill operated by master technicians. **Known for:** French dip sandwich; reasonably priced wine list. 🅢 *Average main: $29* ✉ *1180 Rutherford Rd., at Hwy. 29* ☎ *707/963–1792* ⊕ *www.rutherfordgrill.com.*

$$$$
RESORT
Fodor'sChoice
★

🛏 **Auberge du Soleil.** Taking a cue from the olive-tree-studded landscape, this hotel with a renowned restaurant and spa cultivates a luxurious look that blends French and California style. **Pros:** stunning views over the valley; spectacular pool and spa areas; the most expensive suites are fit for a superstar. **Cons:** stratospheric prices; least expensive rooms get some noise from the bar and restaurant. 🅢 *Rooms from: $875* ✉ *180 Rutherford Hill Rd.* ☎ *707/963–1211, 800/348–5406* ⊕ *www.aubergedusoleil.com* ⤴ *50 rooms* ⫿⊙⫿ *Breakfast.*

ST. HELENA

Fodor's Choice *2 miles northwest of Rutherford.*

★ Downtown St. Helena is the very picture of good living in the Wine Country: sycamore trees arch over Main Street (Highway 29), where visitors flit between boutiques, cafés, and storefront tasting rooms housed in sun-faded redbrick buildings. The genteel district pulls in rafts of tourists during the day, though like most Wine Country towns St. Helena more or less rolls up the sidewalks after dark.

The Napa Valley floor narrows between the Mayacamas and Vaca mountains around St. Helena. The slopes reflect heat onto the vineyards below, and since there's less fog and wind, things get pretty toasty. This is one of the valley's hottest AVAs, with midsummer temperatures often reaching the mid-90s. Bordeaux varietals are the most popular grapes grown here—especially Cabernet Sauvignon but also Merlot, Cabernet Franc, and Sauvignon Blanc. High-profile wineries bearing a St. Helena address abound, with Beringer, Charles Krug, and Ehlers Estate among the ones whose stories begin in the 19th century. The successes of relatively more recent arrivals such as Stony Hill, Rombauer, Duckhorn, Hall, Phelps, and a few dozen others have only added to the town's enological cachet.

GETTING HERE AND AROUND
The stretch of Highway 29 that passes through St. Helena is called Main Street, and many of the town's shops and restaurants are clustered on two pedestrian-friendly blocks between Pope and Adams Streets. Wineries are found both north and south of downtown along Highway 29 and the Silverado Trail, but some of the less touristy and more scenic spots are on the eastern and western slopes of Spring Mountain. VINE Bus 10 and Bus 29 stop along Main Street.

ESSENTIALS
Contact **St. Helena Chamber of Commerce.** ⊠ *657 Main St., at Vidovich La.* ☎ *707/963–4456* ⊕ *www.sthelena.com.*

EXPLORING

TOP ATTRACTIONS
Barnett Vineyards. Scenic Spring Mountain Road winds past oaks and madrones and, in the springtime, sprays of wildflowers to this winery's lofty east-facing hillside setting. Arrive a little early to give yourself more time to bask in perspectives on the northern Napa Valley rivaling those from a balloon. When the weather's fine, tastings are held outside to take advantage of the views across the valley to Howell Mountain and beyond; if not, they're held in the atmospheric wine-aging cave. Barnett's winemaker, David Tate, makes restrained, beautifully balanced wines: Chardonnay and Pinot Noir with fruit sourced from prestigious vineyards, and Cabernet Franc, Cabernet Sauvignon, and Merlot from the steeply terraced mountain estate. Quietly dazzling, they'll draw your attention from those vistas. Tastings are by appointment. ⊠ *4070 Spring Mountain Rd., at Napa–Sonoma county line* ☎ *707/963–7075* ⊕ *www.barnettvineyards.com* 🍷 *Tasting $50.*

inger Vineyards. Brothers Frederick and Jacob Beringer opened the ~~~nery~~~ that still bears their name in 1876. One of California's earliest ~~~nded~~~ wineries, it is the oldest one in the Napa Valley never to have ~~~issed~~~ a vintage—no mean feat, given Prohibition. Frederick's grand ~~~hine~~~ House Mansion, built in 1884, serves as the reserve tasting room. ~~~Here~~~, surrounded by Belgian art-nouveau hand-carved oak and walnut furniture and stained-glass windows, you can sample wines that include a limited-release Chardonnay, a few big Cabernets, and a Sauterne-style dessert wine. A less expensive tasting takes place in the original stone winery. Reservations are required for some tastings and recommended for tours. ■ TIP→ **The one-hour Taste of Beringer ($50) tour of the property and sensory gardens surveys the winery's history and wine making and concludes with a seated wine and food pairing.** ✉ *2000 Main St./ Hwy. 29, near Pratt Ave.* ☎ *707/963–8989, 866/708–9463* ⊕ *www. beringer.com* ✍ *Tastings $25–$125, tours $30–$50.*

Charles Krug Winery. A historically sensitive renovation of its 1874 Redwood Cellar Building transformed the former production facility of the Napa Valley's oldest winery into an epic hospitality center. Charles Krug, a Prussian immigrant, established the winery in 1861 and ran it until his death in 1892. Italian immigrants Cesare Mondavi and his wife, Rosa, purchased Krug in 1943, and operated it with their sons Peter and Robert (who later opened his own winery). Krug, still run by Peter's family, specializes in small-lot Yountville and Howell Mountain Cabernet Sauvignons and makes Chardonnay, Merlot, Pinot Noir, Sauvignon Blanc, Zinfandel, and a Zinfandel port. The tour is by appointment only. ■ TIP→ **To sample the small-lot Cabernets, book a Family Reserve & Limited Release Tasting ($40).** ✉ *2800 Main St./Hwy. 29, across from the Culinary Institute of America* ☎ *707/967–2229* ⊕ *www.charleskrug.com* ✍ *Tastings $20–$40, tour $60 (includes tasting).*

Fodor'sChoice ★ **Corison Winery.** Respected for two 100% Cabernet Sauvignons, Corison Winery harks back to simpler days, with tastings amid oak barrels inside an unadorned, barnlike facility. The straightforward approach suits the style of Cathy Corison, one of the Napa Valley's first women owner-winemakers, who eschews blending because she believes her sunny St. Helena AVA vineyards (and other selected sites) can ripen Cabernet better than anywhere else in the world. Critics tend to agree, often waxing ecstatic about these classic wines. Library tastings start with a tour of the winery and the estate's Kronos Vineyard. They include both recent releases and older vintages, which together illustrate her consistency as a winemaker and how gracefully her wines mature. Tastings are by appointment. ✉ *987 St. Helena Hwy., at Stice La.* ☎ *707/963–0826* ⊕ *www.corison.com* ✍ *Tasting $55.*

Culinary Institute of America at Greystone. The West Coast headquarters of the country's leading school for chefs is in the 1889 Greystone Cellars, an imposing building once the world's largest stone winery. On the ground floor you can check out the quirky Corkscrew Museum and browse the Spice Islands Marketplace shop, stocked with gleaming gadgets and many cookbooks. The Bakery Café by illy serves soups, salads, sandwiches, and baked goods. One-day and multiday cooking and

The Culinary Institute's well-stocked Spice Islands store tempts aspiring chefs.

beverage classes take place weekly, public cooking demonstrations on weekends. Students run the Gatehouse Restaurant, which serves lunch and dinner except during semester breaks. ⊠ *2555 Main St./Hwy. 29* ☎ *707/967–1100* ⊕ *www.ciachef.edu/california* ✉ *Museum free, cooking demonstrations $25, class prices vary.*

Duckhorn Vineyards. Merlot's moment in the spotlight may have passed, but you wouldn't know it at Duckhorn, whose fans gladly pay top dollar for some of the world's finest wines from this varietal. You can taste Merlot, Sauvignon Blanc, Cabernet Sauvignon, and other wines in the airy, high-ceilinged tasting room, which looks like a fine-dining restaurant; you'll be seated at a table and served by staffers who make the rounds to pour. In good weather, you may do your sipping on a fetching wraparound porch overlooking a vineyard. "Elevated" experiences include a tasting of estate and single-vineyard wines offered twice daily, as well as a once-a-day (except Saturday) private hosted tasting. All tastings are by appointment. ⊠ *1000 Lodi La., at Silverado Trail N* ☎ *707/963–7108* ⊕ *www.duckhorn.com* ✉ *Tastings $35–$85.*

Ehlers Estate. New and old blend seamlessly at this winery whose 1886 tasting room's contemporary furnishings and changing artworks benefit from the gravitas and sense of history the original stone walls and exposed redwood beams impart. Winemaker Kevin Morrisey crafts complex Cabernet Sauvignon and other Bordeaux-style wines made from 100% organically and biodynamically farmed estate grapes. Seated, appointment-only tastings focus on the growing practices and the winery's fascinating history, including Prohibition hijinks and

ST. HELENA HISTORY

Unlike many other parts of the Napa Valley, where milling grain was the primary industry until the late 1800s, St. Helena took to vines almost instantly. The town got its start in 1854, when Henry Still built a store. Still wanted company, so he donated land lots on his town site to anyone who wanted to erect a business. Soon he was joined by a wagon shop, a shoe shop, hotels, and churches. Dr. George Crane planted a vineyard in 1858, and was the first to produce wine in commercially viable quantities. Charles Krug followed suit a couple of years later, and other wineries soon followed.

In the late 1800s, phylloxera began to destroy France's vineyards, and Napa Valley wines caught the

world's attention. The increased demand for Napa wines spawned a building frenzy in St. Helena. Many of the mansions still gracing the town's residential neighborhoods were built around this time. During the same period, some entrepreneurs attempted to turn St. Helena into an industrial center to supply specialized machinery to local viticulturists. Several stone warehouses were built near the railroad tracks downtown. Other weathered stone buildings on Main Street, mostly between Adams and Spring Streets and along Railroad Avenue, date to the same era. Modern facades sometimes camouflage these old-timers, but you can study the old structures by strolling the back alleys.

the property's late-20th-century revival by a dynamic French couple. ■TIP➜ Croissants are served at the Start Your Day tasting, which commences at 9:30 am. ✉ *3222 Ehlers La., at Hwy. 29* ☎ *707/963–5972* ⊕ *www.ehlersestate.com* ✉ *Tasting $35.*

Fodor's Choice **Hall St. Helena.** The Cabernet Sauvignons produced here are works of art
★ and the latest in organic-farming science and wine-making technology. A glass-walled tasting room allows guests to see in action some of the high-tech equipment winemaker Steve Leveque employs to craft wines that also include Merlot, Cabernet Franc, and Sauvignon Blanc. Westward from the second-floor tasting area, rows of neatly spaced Cabernet vines capture the eye, and beyond them the tree-studded Mayacamas Mountains. The main guided tour takes in the facility, the grounds, and a restored 19th-century winery, passing by artworks—inside and out—by John Baldessari, Jaume Plensa, Jesús Moroles, and other contemporary talents. ■TIP➜ Among the engaging seminars here is the Ultimate Cabernet Experience ($125), the winery's flagship tasting of current and library releases, as well as wines still aging in barrel. ✉ *401 St. Helena Hwy./Hwy. 29, near White La.* ☎ *707/967–2626* ⊕ *www.hallwines.com* ✉ *Tastings $40–$250, tours $40–$50.*

Fodor's Choice **Joseph Phelps Vineyards.** An appointment is required for tastings at the
★ winery started by the late Joseph Phelps, but it's well worth the effort—and all the more so since an inspired renovation of the main redwood structure, a classic of 1970s Northern California architecture. Known for wines crafted with grace and precision, Phelps does produce fine whites, but the blockbusters are red, particularly the Cabernet Sauvignon and the luscious-yet-subtle Bordeaux-style blend called Insignia.

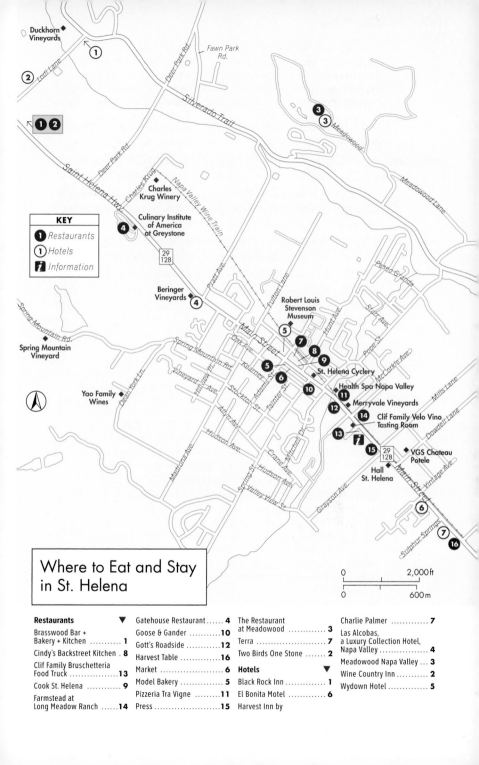

KEY

- **1** *Restaurants*
- **1** *Hotels*
- **i** *Information*

Where to Eat and Stay in St. Helena

In good weather, one-hour seated tastings take place on a terrace overlooking vineyards and oaks. At 90-minute tastings as thoughtfully conceived as the wines, guests explore such topics as wine and cheese pairing, wine blending, and the role oak barrels play in wine making. Participants in the blending seminar mix the various varietals that go into the Insignia blend. ⊠ *200 Taplin Rd., off Silverado Trail* ☎ *707/963–2745, 800/707–5789* ⊕ *www.josephphelps.com* ✍ *Tastings and seminars $75–$200.*

QUICK BITES

Napa Valley Olive Oil Manufacturing Company. "There's a crazy little shack beyond the tracks," the song goes, but in this case the barnlike building east of the railroad tracks sells tickle-your-taste-buds olive oils and vinegars, along with cheeses, meats, breads, and other delectables to take on the road or enjoy at picnic tables right outside. This is old Napa—no frills, cash only—with a shout-out to old Italy. **Known for:** a fun stop even if you're not buying, though something will likely tempt you. ⊠ *835 Charter Oak Ave., off Main St.* ☎ *707/963–4173* ⊕ *oliveoilsainthelena.com.*

Pride Mountain Vineyards. This winery 2,200 feet up Spring Mountain straddles Napa and Sonoma counties, confusing enough for visitors but even more complicated for the wine-making staff: government regulations require separate wineries and paperwork for each side of the property. It's one of several amusing Pride Mountain quirks, but winemaker Sally Johnson's "big red wines," including a Cabernet Sauvignon that earned 100-point scores from a major wine critic two years in a row, are serious business. At tastings and on tours you can learn about the farming and cellar strategies behind Pride's acclaimed Cabs (the winery also produces Syrah, a Cab-like Merlot, Viognier, and Chardonnay among others). The tour, which takes in vineyards and caves, also includes tastings of wine still in barrel. ■ TIP➔ **The views here are knock-your-socks-off gorgeous.** ⊠ *4026 Spring Mountain Rd., off St. Helena Rd. (extension of Spring Mountain Rd. in Sonoma County)* ☎ *707/963–4949* ⊕ *www.pridewines.com* ✍ *Tastings $20–$75.*

Rombauer Vineyards. The great-aunt of winery founder Korner Rombauer defined generations of American home cuisine with her best-selling book *The Joy of Cooking,* but he can lay claim to a similar triumph. "Iconic" is an adjective often associated with Rombauer Chardonnays, particularly the flagship Carneros bottling. Although often described simply as "buttery," at their best the wines express equal parts ripeness, acidity, and creaminess, with vanilla accents courtesy of skillful oak aging. You can learn about these famous Chards at the tasting bar, on tours of caves that extend more than a mile, or over a glass sipped on the vineyard-view porch or while strolling the landscaped grounds. Rombauer, which requires reservations for all visits, also makes Sauvignon Blanc, Zinfandel, Cabernet Sauvignon, Merlot, and dessert wines. ■ TIP➔ **Picnicking is permitted on a first-come, first-served basis.** ⊠ *3522 Silverado Trail N, ¾ mile north of Glass Mountain Rd.* ☎ *800/622–2206* ⊕ *rombauer.com* ✍ *Tastings $9–$30, cave tour $60 (includes tasting).*

Spring Mountain Vineyard. Hidden off a winding road behind a security gate, the family-owned Spring Mountain Vineyard has the feeling of a private country estate, even though it's only a few miles from downtown St. Helena. Chardonnay, Sauvignon Blanc, Pinot Noir, and Syrah wines are produced in limited quantities, but the calling card here is Cabernet Sauvignon—big and chewy, reflecting its mountain origin. A tasting of current releases ($40) gives you a good sense of these wines' charms. The estate tasting ($75) includes a meander through the elegant property, from the 19th-century caves to the beautifully preserved 1885 mansion. Other tastings explore library vintages of Cabernet Sauvignon ($100) and a vertical selection of the signature Bordeaux blend, Elivette ($200). All visits require an appointment. ⊠ *2805 Spring Mountain Rd., off Madrona Ave.* ☎ *707/967–4188, 877/769–4637* ⊕ *www. springmountainvineyard.com* ✎ *Tastings $40–$200.*

Stony Hill Vineyard. Few wineries embrace low-tech more than Stony Hill, an ageless wonder whose longtime winemaker crafts Old World–style Chardonnays and other whites sommeliers love. The magic takes place in a *Hobbit*-like cellar, itself worth the steep drive up Spring Mountain's eastern slope. Crammed with barrels—many a half-century old—it's a reminder that savvy and restraint are as crucial to wine making as fancy gadgets. Private tours (reservations required) begin at the home of founders Fred and Eleanor McCrea, whose first Chardonnay debuted in 1952. (Gewürztraminer, White Riesling, and a lean Cabernet are among the other wines made.) After walking the grounds and touring the winery, guests taste a few wines, often ending with Semillon du Soleil, a dessert one made from grapes dried in the sun after harvesting. ⊠ *3331 St. Helena Hwy. N , near Bale Grist Mill* ☎ *707/963–2636* ⊕ *stonyhillvineyard.com* ✎ *Tour $45 (includes tasting).*

Fodor'sChoice
★
Tres Sabores Winery. A long, narrow lane with two sharp bends leads to splendidly workaday Tres Sabores, where the sight of sheep, guinea hens, pomegranate and other trees and plants, a slew of birds and bees, and a heaping compost pile help reinforce a simple point: despite the Napa Valley's penchant for glamour this is, first and foremost, farm country. Owner-winemaker Julie Johnson specializes in single-vineyard wines that include Cabernet Sauvignon, Sauvignon Blanc, and a quietly stunning Zinfandel made from Rutherford bench grapes. She also excels with Petite Sirah from dry-farmed Calistoga fruit and makes a zippy red blend called Por Qué No? (Why not?). *Tres sabores* is Spanish for "three flavors," which to Johnson represents the land, her vines, and her input as winemaker. Tastings here, all by appointment, are informal and often held outside. ⊠ *1620 S. Whitehall La., off Hwy. 29* ☎ *707/967–8027* ⊕ *www.tressabores.com* ✎ *Tasting $40.*

Trinchero Napa Valley. Sipping this winery's Malbec or Forté blend (Malbec, Petit Verdot, and Cabernet Franc), it seems inconceivable that the Sutter Home White Zinfandel craze a quarter century ago made possible these willfully tannic wines. Over the years, the Trinchero family, owners of Sutter Home and nearly four dozen other brands, assembled a quality portfolio of estate vineyards, from which winemaker Mario Monticelli crafts wines that truly live up to the term "terroir-driven." The wowsers include the Single Vineyard Collection reds—four Cabs, a Petit Verdot, two Merlots, and the Malbec—all but one Merlot from the Napa Valley's Atlas Peak, Mt. Veeder, Rutherford, and St. Helena subappellations. All are served in local designer Erin Martin's exuberant tasting room, which began hosting guests in 2016. ⊠ *3070 St. Helena Hwy. N, near Ehlers La.* ☎ *707/963–1160* ⊕ *www.trincheronapavalley.com* ✉ *Tastings $30–$40.*

Fodor'sChoice
★
VGS Chateau Potelle. Sophisticated whimsy is on full display at the Chateau Potelle tasting room. Jean-Noel Fourmeaux, its bon vivant owner, fashioned this jewel of a space out of a nondescript 1950s bungalow south of downtown St. Helena. Decorated with contemporary art, some of it wine-themed, the residence is now the scene of leisurely paced sit-down tastings accompanied by gourmet bites from Napa's La Toque restaurant. Fourmeaux prefers fruit grown at higher elevations, because he believes the relatively lengthy time grapes take to ripen in a cooler environment produces more complex and flavorful wines. And his Cabernet Sauvignon, Zinfandel, Merlot, Petite Sirah, and other reds support this thesis. The Inevitable blend of Chardonnay, Gewürztraminer, and Viognier stars among the whites. Tastings are by appointment only. ■ TIP➔ Be sure to ask what "VGS" stands for. ⊠ *1200 Dowdell La., at Hwy. 29* ☎ *707/255–9440* ⊕ *www.vgschateaupotelle. com* ✉ *Tasting $60.*

WORTH NOTING

Clif Family Velo Vino Tasting Room. Cyclists swarm to the tasting room of Gary Erickson and Kit Crawford, best known for the Clif energy bar, a staple of many a pedaling adventure. Cycling trips through Italian wine country inspired the couple to establish a Howell Mountain winery and organic farm whose bounty they share at this merry hangout. The King of the Mtn. Tasting ($40) of estate Cabernets shows winemaker Laura Barrett at her most nuanced, but she crafts whites and reds for all palates. Some wines are offered as flights, others as 2- or 4-ounce pours. If hungry, you can pair the wines with soups, salads, and *bruschette* (open-face grilled-bread sandwiches) from the Bruschetteria food truck parked outside. ■ TIP➔ Tasting-room staffers arrange Wine Country bike rides: one easy, one challenging, and both memorable. ⊠ *709 Main St./Hwy. 29, at Vidovich La.* ☎ *707/968–0625* ⊕ *www. cliffamily.com* ✉ *Tastings $25–$60.*

Franciscan Estate. Light streams through the full-length clerestory window of this bustling winery's main tasting space. You can also sip wines in small, private rooms and, on weekends in summer and fall, on an outdoor patio. Winemaker Janet Myers's best reds—among them the Oakville Cabernet Sauvignon and the Cabernet-heavy Magnificat blend—are bold yet smooth, with just enough tannins to build character but not overwhelm. The Cuvée Sauvage Chardonnay, fermented using only natural yeasts, is another standout, with two Sauvignon Blanc–based blends among the other crowd-pleasing whites. Franciscan also pours the complex red wines—including the truly lofty Cabernet Sauvignon Elevation 1550—of its separate Mount Veeder Winery. ■ TIP➔ On Friday, Franciscan offers a three-course lunch paired with top Franciscan vintages ($135). ⊠ *1178 Galleron Rd., at Hwy. 29* ☎ *707/967–3830* ⊕ *www.franciscan.com* ✉ *Tastings $20–$40, blending and sensory seminars $50.*

Franciscan Estate's Cuvée Sauvage Chardonnay contributed to a revival in California of fermenting wines with natural instead of commercial yeasts.

Merryvale Vineyards. Chardonnay and Cabernet Sauvignon are this winery's claims to fame, with Merlot and small-lot Cabernet Franc and Malbec among the other wines made. The winery has been in existence as Merryvale since 1991, but the building it occupies, the former Sunny St. Helena Winery, dates to just after Prohibition. No reservations are needed for the Signature Flight ($30) of current releases or the Reserve Tasting ($50) of winery and wine-club exclusive bottlings. They are required a day ahead, though, for the wine and artisanal cheese pairing and for private tastings of Profile, a Cabernet Sauvignon–heavy Bordeaux-style blend of each vintage's best grapes. ⊠ *1000 Main St., at Charter Oak Ave.* ☎ *707/963–7777* ⊕ *www.merryvale.com* ✉ *Tastings $30–$125.*

Pestoni Family Estate Winery. A 19th-century wine-bottling contraption, a Prohibition-era safe with tales to tell, and photos and documents spanning five generations enhance a visit to this winery, formerly known as Rutherford Grove, run by the descendants of Albino Pestoni, their Swiss-Italian forebear. Pourers share the Pestoni story while dispensing wines made from grapes grown in choice vineyards the family has acquired over the decades. The Howell Mountain Merlots and Cabernet Sauvignons at reserve tastings ($40) always stand out. Estate tastings ($20) often include Sauvignon Blanc, Sangiovese, and Cabernet grown on the Pestonis' Rutherford Bench property. The 1892 field blend from Lake County heirloom grapes—Zinfandel, Cabernet, and Petite Sirah—commemorates the year Albino entered the wine business. ■TIP➜ **After a tasting flight, guests are welcome to picnic in the winery's tree-shaded area.** ⊠ *1673 St. Helena Hwy. S/Hwy. 29, near Galleron Rd.* ☎ *707/963–0544* ⊕ *www.pestonifamily.com* ✉ *Tastings $20–$40.*

Tastings in Raymond's atmospheric Barrel Cellar include wines that are still aging.

Raymond Vineyards. All the world's a stage to Jean-Charles Boisset, Raymond's charismatic owner—even his vineyards, where his five-act Theater of Nature includes a series of gardens and displays that explain biodynamic agriculture. The theatrics continue indoors in the disco-dazzling Crystal Cellar tasting room (chandelier and other accoutrements by Baccarat), along with several other spaces, some sedate and others equally expressive. Despite goosing up the glamour—gal pals out for a fun afternoon love this place—Boisset and winemaker Stephanie Putnam, formerly of Hess and Far Niente, have continued the winery's tradition of producing reasonably priced premium wines. The Cabernet Sauvignons and Merlots often surprise. ■**TIP→ Concerned about dogs being left in hot cars during tastings, Boisset established the on-site Frenchie Winery, where canines lounge in comfort while their guardians sip wine.** ⊠ *849 Zinfandel La., off Hwy. 29* ☎ *707/963–3141* ⊕ *www.raymondvineyards.com* ⊠ *Tastings $25–$85, tour and tasting $50.*

Robert Louis Stevenson Museum. The rare manuscripts, first editions, photographs, childhood toys, and other artifacts at this small museum document the life and literary career of Robert Louis Stevenson (*Treasure Island, Kidnapped*). One exhibit examines the months Stevenson, at the time impoverished, spent in an abandoned miners' bunkhouse north of Calistoga. The interlude later became the inspiration for the author's book *The Silverado Squatters.* ⊠ *1490 Library La., at Adams St.* ☎ *707/963–3757* ⊕ *www.stevensonmuseum.org* ⊠ *Free.*

Yao Family Wines. While playing for the NBA's Houston Rockets, the team's superstar center and future Hall of Famer Yao Ming became captivated by high-end Cabernets sipped at fine-dining spots after games. Before retiring from basketball, the Shanghai-born player was introduced to Thomas Hinde, a notable Napa Valley winemaker who helped him develop two upscale Cabernets, Yao Ming Napa Valley and Yao Ming Family Reserve. The Cabs, aged in 100% new oak for 18–24 months, are exquisite. These wines and the Sauvignon Blanc and Bordeaux-style red blend of the more moderately priced Napa Crest line can be tasted at Yao's contempo-chic storefront space near Gott's Restaurant. Memorabilia on display sheds light on Yao's sports career and his philanthropic work in support of endangered species, clean drinking water, and other causes. ✉ *929 Main St., at Charter Oak Ave.* ☎ *707/968–5874* 🌐 *www.yaofamilywines.com* 🎟 *Tastings $35–$80.*

WHERE TO EAT

$$$ ITALIAN 🍴 **Brasswood Bar + Bakery + Kitchen.** After Napa Valley fixture Tra Vigne lost its lease, many staffers regrouped a few miles north at the restaurant (the titular Kitchen) of the Brasswood complex, which also includes a bakery, shops, a gallery, and a wine-tasting room. Along with dishes developed for the new location, chef David Nuno incorporates Tra Vigne favorites such as *arancini* (mozzarella-stuffed risotto balls) into his Mediterranean-leaning menu. **Known for:** top-tier mostly Napa-Sonoma wine list; no corkage on first bottle. [$] *Average main: $28* ✉ *3111 St. Helena Hwy. N, near Ehlers La.* ☎ *707/968–5434* 🌐 *www.brasswood.com.*

$$ MODERN AMERICAN Fodor's Choice ★ 🍴 **Cindy's Backstreet Kitchen.** At her up-valley outpost, Cindy Pawlcyn serves variations on the comfort food she made popular at Mustards Grill, but spices things up with dishes influenced by Mexican, Central American, and occasionally Asian cuisines. Along with staples such as meat loaf with garlic mashed potatoes and beef and duck burgers served with impeccable fries, the menu might include a rabbit tostada or curried chicken salad. **Known for:** warm pineapple upside-down cake; ethereal parfait. [$] *Average main: $22* ✉ *1327 Railroad Ave., at Hunt St., 1 block east of Main St.* ☎ *707/963–1200* 🌐 *www.cindysbackstreetkitchen.com.*

$ ITALIAN 🍴 **Clif Family Bruschetteria Food Truck.** Although it does venture out for special events, this walk-up spot for Italian-inflected fast food has a steady gig outside the Clif Family tasting room. Order a tomato, mushroom, pork, or other bruschetta, then enjoy it on the back patio or indoors, purchasing a glass or flight of wine, an espresso, or other beverage separately. **Known for:** canny flavor combos; soups and salads; hot link in a pretzel bun. [$] *Average main: $11* ✉ *Clif Family Velo Vino Tasting Room, 709 Main St./Hwy. 29, at Vidovich La.* ☎ *707/968–0625 for tasting room* ⏲ *Closed Mon. No dinner Thurs.–Tues.* ☞ *Truck hours Thurs.–Tues. 11–4:30, Wed. 11–7.*

$$ ITALIAN Fodor's Choice ★ 🍴 **Cook St. Helena.** A curved marble bar spotlit by contemporary art-glass pendants adds a touch of style to this downtown restaurant whose northern Italian cuisine pleases with similarly understated sophistication. Mussels with house-made sausage in a spicy tomato broth, chopped salad with pancetta and pecorino, and the daily changing risotto are among the dishes regulars revere. **Known for:** top-quality ingredients; reasonably priced local and international wines; Cook Tavern two doors down for beer, wine, and cocktail-friendly small plates. [$] *Average main: $22* ✉ *1310 Main St., near Hunt Ave.* ☎ *707/963–7088* 🌐 *www.cooksthelena.com.*

\$\$\$
MODERN
AMERICAN
✕ **Farmstead at Long Meadow Ranch.** Housed in a high-ceilinged former barn, Farmstead revolves around an open kitchen where executive chef Stephen Barber's team prepares meals with grass-fed beef and lamb, fruits and vegetables, eggs, olive oil, wine, honey, and other ingredients from parent company Long Meadow Ranch. Entrées might include wood-grilled trout with fennel, brussels sprouts, pears, and hazelnuts, or a pork chop with broccolini, jalapeño grits, and apple chutney. **Known for:** Tuesday fried-chicken night; house-made charcuterie; seasonal cocktails. $ *Average main: $24* ✉ *738 Main St., at Charter Oak Ave.* ☎ *707/963–4555* ⊕ *www.longmeadowranch.com/ farmstead-restaurant.*

\$\$\$\$
MODERN
AMERICAN
✕ **Gatehouse Restaurant.** Gung-ho Culinary Institute of America students in their final semester run this restaurant in a historic stone structure. A great Wine Country value, the three- or four-course prix-fixe meals—oft-changing, nicely plated dishes such as crab risotto, pancetta-wrapped quail, and crispy-skin California trout—emphasize local ingredients, some so much so they're grown on-site or across the street at the CIA's student-tended garden at Charles Krug Winery. **Known for:** passionate service; many repeat customers; patio seating in good weather. $ *Average main: $42* ✉ *2555 Main St., near Deer Park Rd.* ☎ *707/967–2300* ⊕ *www.ciagatehouserestaurant.com* ⊘ *Closed Sun. and Mon. and during semester breaks (check website or call for updates).*

\$\$\$
MODERN
AMERICAN
Fodor'sChoice
★
✕ **Goose & Gander.** The pairing of food and drink at G&G is as likely to involve cool cocktails as wine. Main courses such as grilled sturgeon, pork loin with sweet-potato hash, and Wagyu beef with Bordelaise sauce work well with starters that might include lamb merguez toast and mushroom soup from wild and cultivated fungi. **Known for:** intimate main dining room with fireplace; alfresco dining on patio in good weather; basement bar among Napa's best drinking spots. $ *Average main: $29* ✉ *1245 Spring St., at Oak St.* ☎ *707/967–8779* ⊕ *www. goosegander.com.*

\$
AMERICAN
✕ **Gott's Roadside.** A 1950s-style outdoor hamburger stand goes upscale at this spot whose customers brave long lines to order breakfast sandwiches, juicy burgers, root-beer floats, and garlic fries. Choices not available a half century ago include the ahi tuna burger and the chili-spice-marinated chicken breast served with Mexican slaw. **Known for:** tasty (if pricey) 21st-century diner cuisine; shaded picnic tables (arrive early or late for lunch to get one); second branch at Napa's Oxbow Public Market. $ *Average main: $13* ✉ *933 Main St./Hwy. 29* ☎ *707/963–3486* ⊕ *www.gotts.com* ↝ *Reservations not accepted.*

\$\$\$
MODERN
AMERICAN
✕ **Harvest Table.** Five culinary gardens at the Harvest Inn by Charlie Palmer supply produce and herbs for the seasonal, haute-rustic cuisine executive chef Levi Mezick prepares at its restaurant. Truffle chicken for two quickly became the signature entrée, with pan-roasted shrimp and grits, juicily crunchy pig's-ear salad, and roasted carrots served with buttermilk, vadouvan, and granola favorites among the smaller plates. **Known for:** local wines and spirits; outdoor dining in summer; chocolate peanut bar and pot de crème. $ *Average main: $29* ✉ *1 Main St., near Sulphur Springs Ave.* ☎ *707/967–4695* ⊕ *www.harvesttablenapa. com* ⊘ *No lunch Thurs.; no dinner Mon.*

$$$ AMERICAN 🍴 **Market.** Ernesto Martinez, this understated eatery's Mexico City–born chef-owner, often puts a clever Latin spin on American classics. Although he plays things straight with the Caesar salad, fish-and-chips, and braised short ribs, the fried chicken comes with cheddar-jalapeño corn bread, and the fried calamari owes its piquancy to the accompanying peppers, nopales cactus, chipotle aioli, and avocado tomatillo sauce. **Known for:** dependable cuisine; Sunday brunch. [$] *Average main: $25* ✉ *1347 Main St., near Hunt Ave.* ☎ *707/963–3799* 🌐 *marketsthelena.com.*

$ BAKERY 🍴 **Model Bakery.** Thanks to plugs by Oprah and celeb chef Michael Chiarello, each day's batch of doughnutlike English muffins here sells out quickly, but the scones, croissants, breads, and other baked goods also inspire. Breakfast brings pastries and sandwiches with scrambled eggs, bacon, and Canadian ham, with the lunch menu expanding to include soups, salads, pizzas, and more sandwiches, turkey panini, Italian hoagies, muffalettas, and Cubanos among them. **Known for:** signature English muffins; people-watching at outdoor tables; second Oxbow market location. [$] *Average main: $10* ✉ *1357 Main St., near Adams Ave.* ☎ *707/963–8192* 🌐 *www.themodelbakery.com* 🕓 *No dinner.*

$ PIZZA 🍴 **Pizzeria Tra Vigne.** Crisp, thin-crust Neapolitan-style pizzas, among them the unusual Positano, with sautéed shrimp, crescenza cheese, and fried lemons, are the specialties of this spiffed-up, family-friendly offshoot of the famous, now departed, Tra Vigne restaurant. Hand-pulled mozzarella, braised rabbit pappardelle, and a few other beloved Tra Vigne dishes are on the menu, along with salads, pizzas, and pastas. **Known for:** amiable service; no corkage fee for first bottle. [$] *Average main: $14* ✉ *1016 Main St., at Charter Oak Ave.* ☎ *707/967–9999* 🌐 *www.travignerestaurant.com.*

$$$$ MODERN AMERICAN 🍴 **Press.** Few taste sensations surpass the combination of a sizzling steak and a Napa Valley red, a union the chef and sommeliers at Press celebrate with a reverence bordering on obsession. Grass-fed beef cooked on the cherry-and-almond-wood-fired grill and rotisserie is the star—especially the rib eye for two—but the cooks also prepare pork chops, free-range chicken, fish, and even vegetarian dishes such as carrot and yellow-eye bean cassoulet. **Known for:** extensive wine cellar; impressive cocktails; casual-chic ambience. [$] *Average main: $48* ✉ *587 St. Helena Hwy./Hwy. 29, at White La.* ☎ *707/967–0550* 🌐 *www.pressstheleena.com* 🕓 *Closed Tues. No lunch.*

$$$$ MODERN AMERICAN Fodor's Choice ★ 🍴 **The Restaurant at Meadowood.** Chef Christopher Kostow has garnered rave reviews—and three Michelin stars for several years running—for creating a unique dining experience. Patrons choosing the Tasting Menu option ($275 per person) enjoy their meals in the dining room, its beautiful finishes aglow with warm lighting, but up to four guests can select the Counter Menu ($500 per person) for the chance to sit in the kitchen and watch Kostow's team prepare the food. **Known for:** complex cuisine; first-class service; romantic setting. [$] *Average main: $275* ✉ *900 Meadowood La., off Silverado Trail N* ☎ *707/967–1205, 800/458–8080* 🌐 *www.therestaurantatmeadowood.com* 🕓 *Closed Sun. No lunch* ☞ *Jacket suggested but not required.*

$$$$ MEDITERRANEAN Fodor's Choice ★

🍴 **Terra.** In an 1884 fieldstone building, chef Hiro Sone gives an unexpected twist to Italian and southern French cuisine, though for a few dishes, among them the signature sake-marinated black cod in a shiso broth, he draws on his Japanese background. Homey yet elegant desserts, courtesy of Sone's wife, Lissa Doumani, might include a chocolate mousseline with chocolate–peanut butter crunch and toasted marshmallow. **Known for:** prix-fixe menu; old-school romance and service; Bar Terra for cocktails, lighter fare à la carte. [$] *Average main: $85* ✉ *1345 Railroad Ave., off Hunt Ave.* ☎ *707/963–8931* 🌐 *www.terrarestaurant.com* 🕒 *Closed Tues. No lunch.*

$$$ JAPANESE Fodor's Choice ★

🍴 **Two Birds One Stone.** Sang Yoon and Douglas Keane, who became friends while on TV's *Top Chef Masters,* teamed up on this restaurant, loosely inspired by Japanese yakitori establishments, in a contemporary space within a historic winery. Small plates such as green-onion-and-ginger meatballs, "ham and eggs" (custardlike smoked duck ham and jidori-chicken eggs), and silken tofu (amid chilled shiitake broth, sea grapes, and salmon roe) add up to entrée equivalents. **Known for:** complex, unusual flavors; Japanese, American whiskeys; exclusive local wines on tap. [$] *Average main: $28* ✉ *Freemark Abbey Winery, 3020 St. Helena Hwy., near Lodi La.* ☎ *707/302–3777* 🌐 *www.twobirdsonestonenapa.com* 🕒 *Closed Tues. and Wed. No lunch Mon. and Thurs.*

WHERE TO STAY

$$$ B&B/INN

🏨 **Black Rock Inn.** Owner Jeff Orlik provides his guests such a gracious, thoughtful experience that they gush poetic about his suites, his gourmet breakfasts, but most of all his passion for ensuring a memorable time for everyone. **Pros:** winning host; gorgeous retreat; a gourmet breakfast to remember. **Cons:** rooms fill up quickly in season; somewhat pricey. [$] *Rooms from: $350* ✉ *3100 N. Silverado Trail* ☎ *707/968–7893* 🌐 *www.blackrockinn.net* 🛏 *5 rooms* 🍽 *Breakfast.*

$ HOTEL

🏨 **El Bonita Motel.** The tidy rooms at this roadside motel are nice enough for budget-minded travelers, and the landscaped grounds and picnic tables put this property a cut above similar accommodations. **Pros:** cheerful rooms; hot tub; microwaves and mini-refrigerators. **Cons:** road noise is a problem in some rooms. [$] *Rooms from: $196* ✉ *195 Main St./Hwy. 29* ☎ *707/963–3216, 800/541–3284* 🌐 *www.elbonita.com* 🛏 *52 rooms* 🍽 *Breakfast.*

$$$ HOTEL

🏨 **Harvest Inn by Charlie Palmer.** Although this inn sits just off Highway 29, its patrons remain mostly above the fray, strolling 8 acres of landscaped gardens, enjoying views of the vineyards adjoining the property, partaking in spa services, and drifting to sleep in beds adorned with fancy linens and down pillows. **Pros:** garden setting; spacious rooms; well-trained staff. **Cons:** some lower-price rooms lack elegance; high weekend rates. [$] *Rooms from: $354* ✉ *1 Main St.* ☎ *707/963–9463, 800/950–8466* 🌐 *www.harvestinn.com* 🛏 *78 rooms* 🍽 *Breakfast.*

$$$$ HOTEL

🏨 **Las Alcobas, a Luxury Collection Hotel, Napa Valley.** Upscale-casual luxury is the goal of this hillside beauty next door to Beringer Vineyards and six blocks north of Main Street shopping and dining. **Pros:** pool,

CLOSE UP

A Great Northern Napa Drive

Dean & DeLuca in St. Helena opens early, making it a fine starting point for a day of exploring the northern Napa Valley. Purchase some food and drink, then drive north on Highway 29 and then Highway 128 to Tubbs Lane and turn east (right).

A TASTE AND A HIKE
A mile east of Highway 128 on the left side of Tubbs you'll see the entrance to **Chateau Montelena,** which opens at 9:30. Enjoy a wine tasting, then continue east on Tubbs to Highway 29, also signed as Lake County Highway, and turn left. The route winds steeply up the slopes of Mt. St. Helena until you reach the crest, where parking lots on either side of the road invite you to hike a bit in **Robert Louis Stevenson State Park,** named for the author who squatted here during a period of impoverishment.

LUNCH AND A SPARKLER
Backtrack to **Calistoga** on Highway 29 and enjoy lunch at **Solbar.** If you've made a reservation for a tour at **Schramsberg** (the last one's at 2:30), head south on Highway 29 to Peterson Road, where you'll turn right and then quickly right again onto narrow Schramsberg Road. If sparkling wines aren't your thing, opt for **Castello di Amorosa,** off Highway 29 half a mile north of Schramsberg. Either experience should leave you in a bubbly mood.

SHOP MAIN, DRINK AT GOOSE
Return to Highway 29 and turn right to reach **St. Helena.** You'll have an hour or two to browse the shops and galleries along Main Street before they close for the evening. Numerous dining options await in St. Helena, but wherever you're going, stop beforehand at the handsome basement bar at **Goose & Gander** for a well-crafted cocktail.

3

spa, and fitness center; vineyard views from most rooms; chef Chris Cosentino's Acacia House restaurant. **Cons:** pricey. $ *Rooms from: $575* ⌨ *1915 Main St.* ☏ *707/963–7000* ⊕ *www.lasalcobasnapavalley.com* ⟿ *68 rooms* |○| *Breakfast.*

$$$$
RESORT
Fodor'sChoice
★

✴ **Meadowood Napa Valley.** Founded in 1964 as a country club, Meadowood has evolved into a five-star resort, a gathering place for Napa's wine-making community, and a celebrated dining destination. **Pros:** superb restaurant; hiking trails; gracious service; all-organic spa. **Cons:** very expensive; far from downtown St. Helena. $ *Rooms from: $650* ⌨ *900 Meadowood La.* ☏ *707/963–3646, 800/458–8080* ⊕ *www.meadowood.com* ⟿ *85 rooms* |○| *No meals.*

$$$
B&B/INN

✴ **Wine Country Inn.** Vine-covered hills surround the rooms and cottages of this retreat that, since its founding in 1975, has built up a loyal following due to its thoughtful staff and pastoral setting. **Pros:** upgrades under new ownership; good-size swimming pool; vineyard views from most rooms. **Cons:** some rooms let in noise from neighbors. $ *Rooms from: $329* ⌨ *1152 Lodi La., east of Hwy. 29* ☏ *707/963–7077, 888/465–4608* ⊕ *www.winecountryinn.com* ⟿ *29 rooms* |○| *Breakfast.*

$$$ HOTEL Fodor's Choice ★ 🏨 **Wydown Hotel.** A smart boutique-hotel option near downtown shopping and dining, the Wydown delivers comfort with a heavy dose of style. **Pros:** well run; eclectic decor; downtown location; quiet atrium rooms. **Cons:** lacks the amenities of larger properties. [$] *Rooms from: $329* ✉ *1424 Main St.* ☎ *707/963–5100* 🌐 *www.wydownhotel.com* 🛏 *12 rooms* 🍴 *No meals.*

NIGHTLIFE AND PERFORMING ARTS

Cameo Cinema. The art-nouveau Cameo Cinema, built in 1913 and now beautifully restored, screens first-run and art-house movies, and occasionally hosts live performances. ✉ *1340 Main St., near Hunt Ave.* ☎ *707/963–9779* 🌐 *www.cameocinema.com.*

SPAS

Health Spa Napa Valley. The focus at this local favorite is on health, wellness, and fitness, so there are personal trainers offering advice and an outdoor pool where you can swim laps in addition to the extensive regimen of massages and body treatments. The Harvest Mud Wrap, for which clients are slathered with grape-seed mud and French clay, is a more indulgent, less messy alternative to a traditional mud bath. Afterward, you can take advantage of the sauna, hot tub, and eucalyptus steam rooms. ■ **TIP→ Longtime patrons book treatments before noon to take advantage of the all-day access.** ✉ *1030 Main St., at Pope St.* ☎ *707/967–8800* 🌐 *www.napavalleyspa.com* 🎟 *Treatments $20–$525.*

SPORTS AND THE OUTDOORS

BICYCLING

St. Helena Cyclery. Rent hybrid and road bikes by the hour or day at this shop that has a useful "Where to Ride" page on its website (see the About tab). ✉ *1156 Main St., at Spring St.* ☎ *707/963–7736* 🌐 *www.sthelenacyclery.com* 🎟 *From $15 per hr, $45 per day.*

SHOPPING

St. Helena's coolest stores are clustered around the 1200 and 1300 blocks of Main Street, where 19th-century redbrick buildings recall the town's past and make it an agreeable place to while away an afternoon.

ART GALLERIES

Ærena Galleries & Gardens. This airy gallery exhibits abstract and contemporary realist paintings, works on paper, and sculpture. ✉ *1354 Main St., near Adams St.* ☎ *707/603–8787* 🌐 *www.aerenagalleries.com.*

CLOTHING AND ACCESSORIES

Footcandy. Precariously steep stilettos and high-heeled boots are elevated to an art form here. You'll also find swingin' handbags and other accessories. ✉ *1239 Main St., at Hunt Ave.* ☎ *707/963–2040* 🌐 *www.footcandyshoes.com.*

Pearl Wonderful Clothing. Sweet Pearl carries the latest in women's fashions in a space that makes dramatic use of the section of the historic stone building the shop occupies. Celebs find bags, shoes, jewelry, and outfits here—and you might, too. ⊠ *1219C Main St.* ☎ *707/963–3236* ⊕ *pearlwonderfulclothing.com.*

FOOD AND WINE

Dean & Deluca. The specialty grocery chain's Napa Valley branch sells kitchenware and has a large wine selection, but most visitors come for the produce, prepared foods, and deli items to picnic in style. ⊠ *607 St. Helena Hwy./Hwy. 29, at White La.* ☎ *707/967–9980* ⊕ *www.deandeluca.com.*

3

Woodhouse Chocolate. Elaborate confections made on the premises are displayed like miniature works of art at this shop that resembles an 18th-century Parisian salon. ⊠ *1367 Main St., at Adams St.* ☎ *707/963–8413, 800/966–3468* ⊕ *www.woodhousechocolate.com.*

HOUSEHOLD ITEMS

Acres Home and Garden. Part general store, part gift shop, Acres sells bulbs, gardening implements, and home decor items "for the well-tended life." ⊠ *1219 Main St., near Spring St.* ☎ *707/967–1142* ⊕ *www.acreshomeandgarden.com.*

Jan de Luz. Fine French table linens and high-quality items for home and garden fill this shop where you can also pick up dish towels too pretty to actually use and monogrammed seersucker pajamas and other items indispensable to a life properly lived. ⊠ *1219 Main St., at Spring St.* ☎ *707/963–1550* ⊕ *www.jandeluz.com.*

Spice Islands Marketplace. This fun store sells cookbooks, kitchenware, and many other things related to cooking. ⊠ *Culinary Institute of America, 2555 Main St./Hwy. 29* ☎ *888/424–2433, 707/967–2309* ⊕ *www.ciachef.edu/california.*

CALISTOGA

3 miles northwest of St. Helena.

The false-fronted shops, 19th-century buildings, and unpretentious cafés lining the main drag of Lincoln Avenue give Calistoga a slightly rough-and-tumble feel that's unique in the Napa Valley. With Mt. St. Helena rising to the north and visible from downtown, Calistoga looks a bit like a cattle town tucked into a remote mountain valley.

In 1859 Sam Brannan—Mormon missionary, entrepreneur, and vineyard developer—learned about a place in the upper Napa Valley, called Agua Caliente by settlers, that was peppered with hot springs and even had its own "old faithful" geyser. He snapped up 2,000 acres of prime property and laid out a resort. Planning a place that would rival New York's famous Saratoga Hot Springs, he built an elegant hotel, bathhouses, cottages, stables, an observatory, and a distillery (the last a questionable choice for a Mormon missionary). Brannan's gamble didn't pay off as he'd hoped, but Californians kept coming to "take the waters," supporting small hotels and bathhouses built wherever a hot spring bubbled to the surface. In the 21st century, Calistoga began to get back to its roots, with new luxury properties springing up and old standbys getting a sprucing up. At the Brannan Cottage Inn *(see Where to Stay, below)*, you can spend a night in part of the only Sam Brannan cottage still on its original site.

GETTING HERE AND AROUND

To get here from St. Helena or anywhere else farther south, take Highway 29 north and then turn right on Lincoln Avenue. Alternately, you can head north on Silverado Trail and turn left on Lincoln. VINE Bus 10 and Bus 29 serve Calistoga.

ESSENTIALS

Contact **Calistoga Chamber of Commerce.** ⌧ *1133 Washington St., near Lincoln Ave.* ☎ *707/942–6333* ⊕ *www.visitcalistoga.com.*

EXPLORING

TOP ATTRACTIONS

Fodor's Choice
★

Bennett Lane Winery. The stated goal of Rob Hunter, Bennett Lane's winemaker, is "to create the greatest Cabernet Sauvignon in the world." At this winery's tastefully casual salon in the far northern Napa Valley you can find out how close he and associate winemaker Rachel Gondouin have come. Although it's known for Cabernet, Bennett Lane also makes other reds, a sparkling wine, Chardonnay, and the Maximus White Feasting Wine, a blend of Sauvignon Blanc, Chardonnay, and Muscat. Signature flight tastings, indoors at the bar and, in pleasant weather, outdoors at tables with Calistoga Palisades views, survey the winery's white and red wines. There's also a Cab-focused reserve tasting. Tastings are by appointment only. ■ TIP→ **Given the quality of their grapes, the Napa Valley Cabernet and Cab-heavy Maximus Red Feasting Wine are relative bargains.** ⌧ *3340 Hwy. 128, 3 miles north of downtown* ☎ *877/629–6272* ⊕ *www.bennettlane.com* 🍷 *Tastings $20–$45.*

Ca' Toga Galleria d'Arte. The boundless wit, whimsy, and creativity of the Venetian-born Carlo Marchiori, this gallery's owner-artist, finds expression in paintings, watercolors, ceramics, sculptures, and other artworks. Marchiori often draws on mythology and folktales for his inspiration. A stop at this magical gallery may inspire you to tour **Villa Ca' Toga,** the artist's fanciful Palladian home, a tromp-l'oeil tour de force open for tours from May through October on Saturday mornings only, by appointment. ⌧ *1206 Cedar St., near Lincoln Ave.* ☎ *707/942–3900* ⊕ *www.catoga.com* ☉ *Closed Tues. and Wed.*

Fodor's Choice
★

Davis Estates. Owners Mike and Sandy Davis transformed a ramshackle property into a plush winery whose predominantly Bordeaux-style wines live up to the magnificent setting. In fashioning the couple's haute-rustic appointment-only hospitality center, the celebrated Wine Country architect Howard Backen incorporated cedar, walnut, and other woods. In fine weather, many guests sit on the open-air terrace's huge swinging sofas, enjoying broad valley views while tasting wines by Cary Gott. The winemaker, who counts Ram's Gate and Round Pond among previous clients, makes Sauvignon Blanc, Viognier, and Chardonnay

The astounding Castello di Amorosa has 107 rooms.

whites, with Pinot Noir, Merlot, and Cabernet-heavy blends among the reds. The wines can be paired with small bites by Michael Caldwell, the executive chef. Tastings are by appointment only. ■TIP→ **Philippe Melka, an elite consultant, crafts two collector-quality wines labeled Phase V, a Cabernet and a Petite Sirah.** ⊠ *4060 Silverado Trail N, near Larkmead La.* ☎ *707/942–0700* ⊕ *www.davisestates.com* 🖂 *Tastings $60–$225* ⊘ *Closed Mon.*

Jericho Canyon Vineyard. It takes a Polaris all-terrain vehicle to tour the vineyards at this family-owned winery whose grapes grow on hillsides that slope as much as 55 degrees. The rocky, volcanic soils of this former cattle ranch yield intensely flavored berries that winemaker Nicholas Bleecher, the son of the founders, transforms in consultation with blending specialist Michel Rolland into the flagship Jericho Canyon Cabernet Sauvignon and other wines. The nuances of sustainable farming in this challenging environment are among the topics covered on the Polaris tour, which also takes in the caves. All tours (there's one on foot as well), by appointment only, conclude with a tasting that begins with Sauvignon Blanc or rosé and includes the current flagship Cabernet and an older vintage. ⊠ *3322 Old Lawley Toll Rd., off Hwy. 29* ☎ *707/331– 9076* ⊕ *jerichocanyonvineyard.com* 🖂 *Tastings and tours from $50.*

Fodor's Choice ★ Schramsberg. On a Diamond Mountain site first planted to grapes in the early 1860s, Schramsberg produces sparkling wines using the *méthode traditionnelle* (aka *méthode champenoise*). A fascinating tour covering Schramberg's history and wine-making techniques precedes the tasting. In addition to glimpsing the winery's historic architecture you'll visit caves, some dug in the 1870s by Chinese laborers, where

2 million–plus bottles are stacked in gravity-defying configurations. Tastings include generous pours of very different bubblies. To learn more about them, consider attending the session at which the wines are paired with cheeses; not held every day, this tasting focuses on the ways wine influences our experience of food and vice versa. All visits here are by appointment. ✉ *1400 Schramsberg Rd., off Hwy. 29* ☎ *707/942–4558, 800/877–3623* ⊕ *www.schramsberg.com* 🔖 *Tastings and tours $65–$120.*

Storybook Mountain Vineyards. Tucked into a rock face in the Mayacamas range, this winery established in 1976 occupies a picture-perfect site with rows of vines rising steeply in dramatic tiers. Zinfandel is king—there's even a Zin Gris, a dry rosé of Zinfandel grapes. Tastings, all by appointment, are preceded by a low-key tour that includes a short walk up the hillside and a visit to the atmospheric tunnels, parts of which have the same rough-hewn look as they did when Chinese laborers dug them by hand around 1888. Jerry Seps, who started Storybook with his wife, Sigrid, continues to make the wines, these days with their daughter, Colleen. ✉ *3835 Hwy. 128, 4 miles northwest of town* ☎ *707/942–5310* ⊕ *www.storybookwines.com* 🔖 *Tasting and tour $25* ☉ *Closed Sun.*

Tom Eddy Winery. If you miss the driveway to Tom and Kerry Eddy's hillside slice of paradise, you'll soon find yourself in Sonoma County—their tree-studded 22-acre property, home to deer, wild turkeys, and a red-shouldered hawk, is that far north. Tom, the winemaker, and Kerry, a sommelier and talented sculptor (look for her works in the wine-aging cave), pour their wines by appointment only. Except for the estate Kerry's Vineyard Cabernet Sauvignon, they're made from grapes sourced from as near as Calistoga and, in the case of the Sauvignon Blanc, as far away as New Zealand. The current president of the Calistoga Winegrowers Association and a winery and wine-making consultant, Tom also makes other Cabernets, Chardonnay, Petit Verdot, Petite Sirah, Pinot Noir, and Syrah. A visit here is enchanting. ✉ *3870 Hwy. 128, 4¼ miles north of downtown* ☎ *707/942–4267* ⊕ *tomeddywinery.com* 🔖 *Tastings $50–$75.*

Venge Vineyards. As the son of Nils Venge, the first winemaker to earn a 100-point score from the wine critic Robert Parker, Kirk Venge had a hard act to follow. Now a consultant to exclusive wineries himself, Kirk is an acknowledged master of balanced, fruit-forward Bordeaux-style blends. At his casual ranch-house tasting room you can sip wines that might include the estate Bone Ash Cabernet Sauvignon, an Oakville Merlot, a Syrah from the Stagecoach Vineyard in the Vaca hills, and the Silencieux Cabernet, a blend of grapes from several appellations. Tastings are by appointment only. ■TIP→ **With its views of the well-manicured Bone Ash Vineyard and, west across the valley, Diamond Mountain, the ranch house's porch would make for a magical perch even if Venge's wines weren't works of art in themselves.** ✉ *4708 Silverado Trail, 1½ miles south of downtown, near Dunaweal La.* ☎ *707/942–9100* ⊕ *www.vengevineyards.com* 🔖 *Tasting $25* ☉ *Reservations recommended 3–4 wks in advance for weekend visits.*

Vincent Arroyo Winery. Fans of this down-home winery's fl. Sirah snap it up so quickly that visitors to the plywood-ing room have to buy "futures" of wines still aging in same holds true of the other small-lot wines. The namesal original winemaker quit his mechanical engineering caree to become a farmer, replacing a prune orchard with plantings of Petite Sirah and Cabernet Sauvignon, these days with Zinfandel the winery's top sellers. Later came more acreage and other varietals, including Merlot, Tempranillo, Sangiovese, and Chardonnay—all dry-farmed. Current winemaker Matthew Moye also crafts several of the red blends that Arroyo originated, along with Petite Sirah and sometimes Chardonnay ports. The presentation here, experienced by appointment only, is charmingly old-school, with Arroyo, his daughter, Adrian, and Moye (her husband) often on hand. ⊠ *2361 Greenwood Ave., off Hwy. 29* ☎ *707/942–6995* ⊕ *www.vincentarroyo.com* 🍷 *Tasting $10.*

WORTH NOTING

Brian Arden Wines. This winery—a contemporary stone, glass, and metal facility a quarter mile south of the Solage resort—takes its name from its son (Brian Harlan) and father (Arden Harlan) vintners. Brian, who makes the wines, has early memories of a 19th-century Lake County Zinfandel vineyard his family still farms, but his passion for the grape grew out of wine-related work in the restaurant industry. In addition to the expected Cabernet Sauvignon, in this case an exemplary one from a labor-intensive vineyard up Howell Mountain, Brian also makes Cabernet Franc, Sangiovese, Zinfandel from the family ranch, Sauvignon Blanc, and a blend called B.A. Red that changes each vintage. These wines and a few others are poured in the tasting room or on an outdoor patio with Calistoga Palisades views. ⊠ *331 Silverado Trail, near Rosedale Rd.* ☎ *707/942–4767* ⊕ *www.brianardenwines.com* 🍷 *Tastings $20–$50* ☺ *Closed Wed.*

Castello di Amorosa. An astounding medieval structure complete with drawbridge and moat, chapel, stables, and secret passageways, the Castello commands Diamond Mountain's lower eastern slope. Some of the 107 rooms contain replicas of 13th-century frescoes (cheekily signed, "[the-artist's-name].com"), and the dungeon has an iron maiden from Nuremberg, Germany. You must pay for a tour to see most of Dario Sattui's extensive eight-level property, though with a basic tasting you'll have access to part of the complex. Bottlings of note include several Italian-style wines, including La Castellana, a robust "super Tuscan" blend of Cabernet Sauvignon, Sangiovese, and Merlot; and Il Barone, a deliberately big Cab made largely from Rutherford grapes. ■TIP→ **The two-hour Royal Food & Wine Pairing Tour by sommelier Mary Davidek ($85, by appointment only) is among the Wine Country's best.** ⊠ *4045 N. St. Helena Hwy./Hwy. 29, near Maple La.* ☎ *707/967–6272* ⊕ *www.castellodiamorosa.com* 🍷 *Tastings $25–$35, tours $40–$85 (include tastings).*

Chateau Montelena. Set amid a bucolic northern Calistoga landscape, this winery helped establish the Napa Valley's reputation for high-quality wine making. At the pivotal Paris tasting of 1976, the Chateau Montelena 1973 Chardonnay took first place, beating out four white

Burgundies from France and five other California Chardonnays, an event immortalized in the 2008 movie *Bottle Shock*. A 21st-century Napa Valley Chardonnay is always part of a Current Release Tasting ($25)—the winery also makes Sauvignon Blanc, Riesling, a fine estate Zinfandel, and Cabernet Sauvignon—or you can opt for a Limited Release Tasting ($50) focusing more on Cabernets. The walking Estate Tour takes in the grounds and covers the history of this stately property whose stone winery building was erected in 1888. Guests board a vehicle for the seasonal Vineyard Tour. Tours and some tastings require a reservation. ⊠ *1429 Tubbs La., off Hwy. 29* ☎ *707/942–5105* ⊕ *www. montelena.com* 🍷 *Tastings $25–$75, tours $40–$78.*

Fairwinds Estate Winery. A sleeper pick with a tasting bar made of concrete and repurposed glass, Fairwinds Estate pours its wines and those of other boutique producers. Tastings also take place in labyrinthine caves nearby. Todd Heth makes the wines for Fairwinds (Cabernet, Petit Verdot, Carmenere, and others) and sister operation Valley Floor Vineyard (Cabernet). Nearby Kenefick Ranch, which sells grapes to Caymus, Phelps, and other brands of renown, reserves some fruit for its estate portfolio (Cabernet Franc, Cabernet Sauvignon, Merlot, and a blend of these and Petit Verdot). Canard specializes in Cabernet Sauvignon and makes great old-vine Zinfandel. White blends, Chardonnay, and rosés are among the lighter wines poured here. Because the wineries make small quantities, the tasting lineup changes frequently. ■TIP→ **The shady picnic area makes this a good midday stop.** ⊠ *4550 Silverado Trail N, near Dunaweal La.* ☎ *707/341–5300* ⊕ *www.fairwindsestatewinery.com* 🍷 *Tastings $20–$50.*

Frank Family Vineyards. As a former Disney film and television executive, Rich Frank knows a thing or two about entertainment, and it shows in the chipper atmosphere that prevails in the winery's bright-yellow Craftsman-style tasting room. The site's wine-making history dates back to the 19th century, and portions of an original 1884 structure, reclad in stone in 1906, remain standing today. From 1952 until 1990, Hanns Kornell made sparkling wines on this site. Frank Family makes sparklers itself, but the high-profile wines are the Cabernet Sauvignons, particularly the Rutherford Reserve and the Winston Hill red blend, which appear on many Napa Valley restaurants' wine lists. Tastings are mostly sit-down affairs. Reservations are required from Friday through Sunday; in summer they're wise on other days, too. ⊠ *1091 Larkmead La., off Hwy. 29* ☎ *707/942–0859* ⊕ *www.frankfamilyvineyards.com* 🍷 *Tastings $40–$70.*

Kelly Fleming Wines. Given her previous career designing concept restaurants, it's fitting that upon opening her own winery Kelly Fleming gravitated toward food-friendly Cabernet Sauvignon and that her facility's stone design, by Taylor Lombardo Architects of San Francisco and Napa, was implemented with the utmost precision. A similar attention to detail is in evidence in the vineyards, green and well pruned even during the dog days of summer, and in the wine made from those grapes, the elegant, aromatic estate Cabernet. Appointment-only visits to the Tuscan-inspired winery, which sits amid 300 acres in Calistoga's eastern foothills, less than 12 of them planted to grapes, begin with Sauvignon Blanc and a tour of the production facility and caves, followed by Big Pour Napa Red, a Bordeaux-style blend, and the Cabernet. Small bites accompany the wines. ✉ *2339 Pickett Rd., off Silverado Trail* ☎ *707/942–6849* ⊕ *www.kellyflemingwines. com* ☕ *Tasting and tour $75.*

Robert Louis Stevenson State Park. Encompassing the summit of Mt. St. Helena, this mostly undeveloped park is where Stevenson and his bride, Fanny Osbourne, spent their honeymoon in an abandoned bunkhouse of the Silverado Mine. This stay in 1880 inspired the writer's travel memoir *The Silverado Squatters*, and Spyglass Hill in *Treasure Island* is thought to be a portrait of Mt. St. Helena. A marble memorial marks the site of the bunkhouse. The 10-mile trail is steep and lacks shade in spots, but the summit is often cool and breezy. ■TIP→ **Bring plenty of water, and dress in layers.** ✉ *Hwy. 29, 7 miles north of town* ☎ *707/942–4575* ⊕ *www.parks.ca.gov/?page_id=472* ☕ *Free.*

Sharpsteen Museum of Calistoga History. Walt Disney animator Ben Sharpsteen, who retired to Calistoga, founded this museum whose centerpiece is an intricate diorama depicting the Calistoga Hot Springs Resort during its 19th-century heyday. One exhibit examines the indigenous Wappo people who once lived here, and another focuses on Sharpsteen's career as an animator. ✉ *1311 Washington St., at 1st St.* ☎ *707/942– 5911* ⊕ *www.sharpsteenmuseum.org* ☕ *$3.*

FAMILY **Sterling Vineyards.** Instead of driving to the tasting room here, you board an aerial tram to reach pristine white buildings, which recall those of Greek islands. (The founder often vacationed on Mykonos.) The ride is spectacular, the wines less so. ✉ *1111 Dunaweal La., off Hwy. 29* ☎ *707/942–3300, 800/726–6136* ⊕ *www.sterlingvineyards.com* ☕ *Tastings $29–$49 (includes tram ride, self-guided tour).*

T-Vine Winery. Robust reds reflecting "a sense of place" are the calling cards of this winery that provides a break from Cabernet, with Zinfandels, a Grenache, and wines from less common varietals. The latter include a Carignane from a 140-year-old vineyard east of San Francisco and a Charbono from Calistoga's Frediani Vineyard, itself more than a century old. Winemaker Bertus van Zyl gooses up the Grenache, also from Frediani vines, with a year in 50% new French oak, producing a more tannic wine than one usually expects of this grape. Although the wines derive from Northern California legacy vineyards, they're poured in a barn-moderne tasting room whose tall plate-glass windows and outdoor patio have views east to the Calistoga Palisades. ✉ *810 Foothill Blvd./Hwy. 29, near Lincoln Ave.* ☎ *707/942–1543* ⊕ *www. tvinewinery.com* ☕ *Tastings $30–$45.*

Tamber Bey Vineyards. Endurance riders Barry and Jennifer Waitte share their passion for horses and wine at their glam-rustic winery north of Calistoga. Their 22-acre Sundance Ranch remains a working equestrian facility, but the site has been revamped to include a state-of-the-art winery with separate fermenting tanks for grapes from Tamber Bey's vineyards in Yountville, Oakville, and elsewhere. The winemakers produce three Chardonnays and a Sauvignon Blanc, but the stars are several subtly powerful reds, including the flagship Oakville Cabernet

Sauvignon and a Yountville Merlot. A recent vintage of the top-selling wine, the Rabicano blend, contained Cabernet Sauvignon, Merlot, Petit Verdot, and Cabernet Franc. Visits to taste or tour require an appointment. ⊠ *1251 Tubbs La., at Myrtledale Rd.* ☎ *707/942-2100* ⊕ *www. tamberbey.com* ✉ *Tastings $35-$65, tour $10 extra.*

Tedeschi Family Winery. Time-travel back to the days when the Napa Valley "lifestyle" revolved around a family rolling up its collective sleeves to grow grapes, make wines, and pour them at a slab of wood held up by used oak barrels. The first Tedeschi arrived in the valley in 1919 from Pisa, Italy, and the grandparents of the current winemaker, Mario, and general manager, his amiable brother Emilio, purchased the Calistoga property, then an orchard, in the 1950s. The Estate Cabernet, among Mario's best, is made from an acre of grapes grown on-site, with fruit for Sauvignon Blanc, Merlot, Petite Sirah, and other wines coming from Napa Valley and Sonoma County sources. ■TIP→ **An appointment to taste is required, but it's possible to make one same-day (just call ahead).** ⊠ *2779 Grant St., at Greenwood Ave., Napa* ☎ *707/337-6835* ⊕ *www.tedeschifamilywinery.com* ✉ *Tastings $20-$30.*

Twomey Cellars. A fortuitous acquisition led to the creation of this winery and its flagship Merlot. Parent company Silver Oak purchased Soda Canyon Ranch Vineyard as a primary fruit source for its flagship Napa Valley Cabernet. Then-winemaker Daniel Baron soon realized that a few blocks of Merlot clones were among the world's finest and proposed a stand-alone wine. Silver Oak only makes Cabernet, so the Twomey label was launched to explore new varietals and vineyards. Since 2012, Jean Claude Berrouet, responsible for decades of vintages at France's Château Petrus, has consulted on the Merlot, which is made at Twomey's Calistoga location. Tastings of Sauvignon Blanc and Pinot Noirs made by Erin Miller at the company's Healdsburg winery precede the Merlot. ⊠ *1183 Dunaweal La., off Hwy. 29* ☎ *707/942-7026* ⊕ *www. twomey.com* ✉ *Tasting $15.*

Vermeil Wines. Sports memorabilia fills the tasting room of Dick Vermeil, the former football broadcaster and Super Bowl–winning NFL coach. Unlike many sports figures who jump into the wine business with no previous connection, Vermeil, a Calistoga native, has roots going back four generations, when his ancestors owned part of what's now the Frediani Vineyard northeast of downtown. Thomas Rivers Brown, a major talent, oversees the wine making for a lineup that focuses on Cabernet Sauvignon and other Bordeaux varietals. The Jean Louis Vermeil Cabernet Sauvignon and the Frediani Vineyard Cabernet Franc are two to watch out for, along with the Charbono, a red varietal rarely planted in California. ⊠ *1255 Lincoln Ave., at Cedar St.* ☎ *707/341-3054* ⊕ *www. vermeilwines.com* ✉ *Tastings $20-$45.*

Von Strasser Winery & Lava Vine Winery. In 2016 Rudy von Strasser, a winemaker whose single-vineyard Diamond Mountain Cabernet Sauvignons have earned decades of acclaim and high-90s wine scores, acquired Lava Vine Winery, a valley-floor establishment known for its partylike atmosphere and eclectic wine roster. To some insiders the coupling seemed an odd match, but von Strasser, who now makes the wines for both labels, welcomed the opportunity to extend his range. For Lava Vine he'll be making Sauvignon Blanc, Viognier, Grenache, Petite Sirah, and anything else that captures his fancy. ⊠ *965 Silverado Trail N, near Brannan St.* ☎ *707/942–9500* ⊕ *vonstrasser.com* ▧ *Tastings $20–$50.*

WHERE TO EAT

$$
ITALIAN

✕ **Bosko's Trattoria.** Affable Bosko's provides tasty Italian cuisine at a fair price. Specialties include house-made pastas and thin-crust pizzas cooked in a wood-fired oven. **Known for:** good value. $ *Average main: $17* ⊠ *1364 Lincoln Ave., at Washington St.* ☎ *707/942–9088* ⊕ *www.boskos.com.*

$
BARBECUE

✕ **Buster's Southern BarBeQue & Bakery.** A roadside stand at the west end of Calistoga's downtown, Buster's lives up to its name with barbecue basics, sweet-potato pies, and corn bread muffins. Local-fave sandwiches at lunch include the tri-tip, spicy hot links, and pulled pork, with tri-tip and pork or beef ribs the hits at dinner. **Known for:** mild and searing-hot sauces; slaw, baked beans, and other sides. $ *Average main: $12* ⊠ *1207 Foothill Blvd./Hwy. 29, at Lincoln Ave.* ☎ *707/942–5605* ⊕ *www.busterssouthernbbq.com* ☞ *Closes in early evening (7 in winter, 8 in summer).*

$$$
AMERICAN

✕ **Calistoga Inn Restaurant & Brewery.** When the weather's nice, the inn's outdoor patio and beer garden are a swell place to hang out and sip some microbrews. Among the beer-friendly dishes, the garlic-crusted calamari appetizer and the country paella entrée stand out, along with the Reuben and chicken club sandwiches, the pizzas, and the burger topped with Tillamook cheddar and applewood-smoked bacon. **Known for:** pleasing decor; kid-friendly patio; wine and beer flights. $ *Average main: $24* ⊠ *1250 Lincoln Ave., at Cedar St.* ☎ *707/942–4101* ⊕ *www. calistogainn.com.*

$$$
MODERN
AMERICAN
Fodor's Choice
★

✕ **Calistoga Kitchen.** Rick Warkel, a chef and caterer with a fine local pedigree, delivers farm-to-table perfection—but only 3½ days a week—on the ground floor of a two-story bungalow. His small menu changes seasonally but items often seen include roast-duck soup, whose aromatics, powered by star anise, evoke a Chinese restaurant, and two farm-raised rabbit dishes: gumbo with okra and andouille sausage, and cacciatore with creamy polenta. **Known for:** imaginative, well-plated cuisine; intimate indoor dining; lively outdoor spaces. $ *Average main: $27* ⊠ *1107 Cedar St., at Lincoln Ave.* ☎ *707/942–6500* ⊕ *www.calistogakitchen.com* ☾ *Closed Mon.–Wed. No lunch Thurs.; no dinner Sun.*

$$$
MODERN
AMERICAN
Fodor's Choice
★

✕ **Evangeline.** Brandon Sharp, formerly of nearby Solbar, opened this restaurant whose gas-lamp-style lighting fixtures, charcoal-black hues, and bistro cuisine evoke old New Orleans with a California twist. Executive chef Gustavo Rios puts a jaunty spin on dishes that might include shrimp étouffée or grilled salmon with a chicory salad; the elaborate weekend brunch, with everything from buttermilk waffles to shrimp po'boys, is an up-valley favorite. **Known for:** outdoor courtyard; palate-cleansing Sazeracs and signature old-fashioneds; gumbo ya-ya and addictive fried pickles. $ *Average main: $24* ⊠ *1226 Washington St., near Lincoln Ave.* ☎ *707/341–3131* ⊕ *www.evangelinenapa.com* ☾ *No lunch weekdays.*

$$ MODERN AMERICAN 🍴 **Johnny's Restaurant & Bar.** Across the lobby from the Mount View Hotel's fine-dining restaurant, whose executive chef also developed the menu here, casual Johnny's serves comfort cuisine a cut well above typical tavern fare. Fried-chicken sliders with buttermilk slaw, brioche croque madame, pan-roasted chicken, and shaved-apple salad with chèvre make this a good stop for lunch, a low-key dinner, or to catch sports events on any of several large TVs. **Known for:** raw bar; weekday happy hour (3–6 pm); brunch daily (until 4 on weekends). [$] *Average main: $21* ✉ *Mount View Hotel & Spa, 1457 Lincoln Ave., near Fair Way* ☎ *707/942–5938* 🌐 *www.johnnyscalistoga.com.*

$$ MODERN AMERICAN 🍴 **Sam's Social Club.** Tourists, locals, and spa guests—some of the latter in bathrobes after treatments—assemble at this resort restaurant for breakfast, lunch, bar snacks, or dinner. Lunch options include pizzas, sandwiches, an aged-cheddar burger, and entrées such as chicken paillard, with the burger reappearing for dinner along with grilled salmon, rib-eye steak frites, and similar fare, perhaps preceded by oysters and other cocktail-friendly starters. **Known for:** casual atmosphere; active patio scene; thin-crust lunch pizzas. [$] *Average main: $22* ✉ *Indian Springs Resort and Spa, 1712 Lincoln Ave., at Wappo Ave.* ☎ *707/942–4969* 🌐 *www.samssocialclub.com.*

$$$$ MODERN AMERICAN Fodor's Choice ★ 🍴 **Solbar.** As befits a restaurant at a spa resort, the sophisticated menu at Solbar is divided into "healthy, lighter dishes" and "hearty cuisine," with the stellar wine list's many half-bottle selections encouraging moderation, too. On the lighter side, grilled yellowfin tuna might come with charred carrots, mole amarillo, and toasted pumpkin seeds, with heartier options recently including a wood-grilled pork tenderloin with jasmine rice, chili-laced cashews, and mustard greens. **Known for:** stylish dining room; festive outdoor patio; Sunday brunch. [$] *Average main: $33* ✉ *Solage Calistoga, 755 Silverado Trail, at Rosedale Rd.* ☎ *877/684–9146* 🌐 *www.solagecalistoga.com/solbar.*

$$ JAPANESE 🍴 **Sushi Mambo.** Preparations are traditional and unconventional at this sushi and country-Japanese restaurant whose owner vows diners will not leave hungry. They don't lack for choice either, and though the menu's diversity may daunt you into sticking to the familiar, consider ordering offbeat items like the Fungus Among Us (tempura mushrooms stuffed with spicy tuna), Batman Roll (eel and cream cheese), and Hottie (panko deep-fried shrimp with spicy crabmeat). **Known for:** upbeat vibe and offbeat items; vegetarian options; dessert mochi. [$] *Average main: $19* ✉ *1631 Lincoln Ave., at Wappo Ave.* ☎ *707/942–4699* 🌐 *www.napasushi.com.*

$$$ FRENCH 🍴 **Veraison.** Chef James Richmond aims to prepare "good, tasty, contemporary but not too complicated French food," which he serves in a softly lit space off the Mount View Hotel's lobby. Steak tartare, veal sweetbreads with a wild-mushroom glaze, slow-braised short rib with horseradish crème, and seared sea scallop with blood sausage are among the dishes frequently on the menu. **Known for:** oysters on the half shell and house-made charcuterie to start; wine pairings; cassoulet, duck confit, and other daily specials. [$] *Average main: $28* ✉ *Mount View Hotel & Spa, 1457 Lincoln Ave., near Fair Way* ☎ *707/942–5938* 🌐 *www.veraisoncalistoga.com* 🕒 *No lunch.*

Almost half the lodgings at the posh Calistoga Ranch have private hot tubs.

WHERE TO STAY

$ Best Western Plus Stevenson Manor. Budget travelers get what they pay
HOTEL   for—and a little bit more—at this motel a few blocks from Calistoga's
downtown. **Pros:** great price for region, especially midweek and off-
season; nice pool area; complimentary full breakfast. **Cons:** weekends
pricey in high season. $ *Rooms from: $175* ✉ *1830 Lincoln Ave.*
☎ *707/942–1112, 800/780–7234* ⊕ *www.stevensonmanor.com* ↩ *34
rooms* ❄ *Breakfast.*

$$ Brannan Cottage Inn. A 2014 renovation injected glamour and vin-
B&B/INN   tage-yet-modern style into this small inn whose centerpiece is an
1860s cottage from Calistoga's original spa era. **Pros:** short walk
from downtown; plush mattresses; helpful staff. **Cons:** noise from
neighbors can be heard in some rooms; showers but no bathtubs in
some rooms. $ *Rooms from: $299* ✉ *109 Wappo Ave., at Lincoln
Ave.* ☎ *707/942–4200* ⊕ *www.brannancottageinn.com* ↩ *6 rooms*
❄ *Breakfast.*

$$$$ Calistoga Ranch. Spacious cedar-shingle lodges throughout this posh
RESORT   wooded property have outdoor living areas, and even the restaurant,
Fodor's Choice   spa, and reception space have outdoor seating and fireplaces. **Pros:**
★   many lodges have private hot tubs on the deck; lovely hiking trails on
the property; guests have reciprocal privileges at Auberge du Soleil and
Solage Calistoga. **Cons:** innovative indoor-outdoor organization works
better in fine weather than in rain or cold. $ *Rooms from: $895* ✉ *580
Lommel Rd.* ☎ *707/254–2800, 855/942–4220* ⊕ *www.calistogaranch.
com* ↩ *50 guest lodges* ❄ *No meals.*

$$$ B&B/INN 🏨 **Cottage Grove Inn.** A long driveway lined with freestanding, elm-shaded cottages with rocking chairs on their porches looks a bit like Main Street USA, but inside each skylighted building you'll find all the perks necessary for a romantic weekend getaway. **Pros:** bicycles available for rent; plenty of privacy; huge bathtubs. **Cons:** no pool. [$] *Rooms from: $350* ✉ *1711 Lincoln Ave.* ☎ *707/942–8400, 800/799–2284* 🌐 *www.cottagegrove.com* 🛏 *16 rooms* 🍴 *Breakfast.*

$$ B&B/INN Fodor's Choice ★ 🏨 **Embrace Calistoga.** Extravagant hospitality defines the Napa Valley's luxury properties, but Embrace Calistoga—the renamed Luxe Calistoga still run by the same attentive owners—takes the prize in the "small lodging" category. **Pros:** attentive owners; marvelous breakfasts; restaurants, tasting rooms, and shopping within walking distance. **Cons:** the hum of street traffic. [$] *Rooms from: $269* ✉ *1139 Lincoln Ave.* ☎ *707/942–9797* 🛏 *5 rooms* 🍴 *Breakfast.*

$$ RESORT 🏨 **Indian Springs Resort and Spa.** Stylish Indian Springs—operating as a spa since 1862—ably splits the difference between laid-back and chic in accommodations that include lodge rooms, dozens of suites, 14 duplex cottages, three stand-alone bungalows, and two houses. **Pros:** palm-studded grounds with outdoor seating areas; on-site Sam's Social Club restaurant; enormous mineral pool. **Cons:** lodge rooms are small. [$] *Rooms from: $239* ✉ *1712 Lincoln Ave.* ☎ *707/942–4913* 🌐 *www.indianspringscalistoga.com* 🛏 *113 rooms* 🍴 *No meals.*

$$ B&B/INN Fodor's Choice ★ 🏨 **Meadowlark Country House.** Two charming European gents run this laid-back but sophisticated inn on 20 wooded acres just north of downtown. **Pros:** charming innkeepers; tasty sit-down breakfasts; welcoming vibe that attracts diverse guests. **Cons:** clothing-optional pool policy isn't for everyone. [$] *Rooms from: $270* ✉ *601 Petrified Forest Rd.* ☎ *707/942–5651, 800/942–5651* 🌐 *www.meadowlarkinn.com* 🛏 *10 rooms* 🍴 *Breakfast.*

$$ B&B/INN 🏨 **Mount View Hotel & Spa.** Although it's in a 1912 building that's been designated a National Historic Landmark, the Mount View skews modern, with a cheery lobby and a boutique, slightly Euro feel. **Pros:** full-service spa; spacious suites and cottages; off-season and Internet specials. **Cons:** outside noise can be heard in some rooms; ground-floor rooms are dark; some rooms feel cramped. [$] *Rooms from: $209* ✉ *1457 Lincoln Ave.* ☎ *707/942–6877, 800/816–6877* 🌐 *www.mountviewhotel.com* 🛏 *33 rooms* 🍴 *Breakfast.*

$$$$ RESORT Fodor's Choice ★ 🏨 **Solage Calistoga.** The aesthetic at this 22-acre property is Napa Valley barn meets San Francisco loft: guest rooms have high ceilings, polished concrete floors, recycled walnut furniture, and all-natural fabrics in soothingly muted colors. **Pros:** great service; complimentary bikes; separate pools for kids and adults. **Cons:** vibe may not suit everyone. [$] *Rooms from: $530* ✉ *755 Silverado Trail* ☎ *855/942–7442, 707/226–0800* 🌐 *www.solagecalistoga.com* 🛏 *89 rooms* 🍴 *No meals.*

NIGHTLIFE

The restaurant bars at Solbar, the Calistoga Inn, and Sam's Social Club are good stops for a nightcap. Susie's has a more traditional barlike feel.

Hydro Bar & Grill. Open until midnight on Friday and Saturday with live music, this may well be Calistoga's premier all-purpose nightspot. That's not saying much, but the vibe is festive. Except for the burger, a local fave, it's best to dine elsewhere. ⊠ *1403 Lincoln Ave., at Washington St.* ☎ *707/942–9777.*

Susie's Bar. Calistoga's entrant in the dive-bar sweepstakes is on the demure side, but it's a good place to toss back a top-shelf cocktail or a local brew at well below resort prices after other nightspots have thrown in the bar towel. ⊠ *1365 Lincoln Ave., at Washington St.* ☎ *707/942–6710* ⊕ *susiescalistoga.com.*

SPAS

Dr. Wilkinson's Hot Springs Resort. Newer, fancier establishments may have eclipsed Dr. Wilkinson's, but loyal fans appreciate its reasonable prices and unpretentious vibe. The mud baths here are a mix of volcanic ash and Canadian peat, warmed by the spa's own hot springs. Fun fact: back in 1952, "The Works"—a mud bath, steam room, blanket wrap, and a massage—cost $3.50; the charge now is $144. ⊠ *1507 Lincoln Ave., at Fair Way* ☎ *707/942–4102* ⊕ *www.drwilkinson.com* ✎ *Treatments $69–$179.*

Indian Springs Spa. Even before Sam Brannan constructed a spa on this site in the 1860s, the Wappo Indians were building sweat lodges over its thermal geysers. Treatments include a Calistoga-classic, pure volcanic-ash mud bath followed by a mineral bath, after which clients are wrapped in a flannel blanket for a 15-minute cool-down session or until called for a massage if they've booked one. Facials using Osmosis, Intraceuticals, and Organic Male products are another specialty. Spa clients have access to the Olympic-size mineral-water pool, kept at 92°F in summer and a toasty 102°F in winter. ⊠ *1712 Lincoln Ave., at Wappo Ave.* ☎ *707/942–4913* ⊕ *www.indianspringscalistoga.com* ✎ *Treatments $95–$275.*

Fodor'sChoice ★ **Spa Solage.** This eco-conscious spa has reinvented the traditional Calistoga mud and mineral-water therapies. Case in point: the hour-long "Mudslide," a three-part treatment that includes a mud body mask (in a heated lounge), a soak in a thermal bath, and a power nap in a sound-vibration chair. The mud here is a mix of clay, volcanic ash, and essential oils. Traditional spa services—combination Shiatsu-Swedish and other massages, full-body exfoliations, facials, and waxes—are available, as are fitness and yoga classes. ⊠ *755 Silverado Trail, at Rosedale Rd.* ☎ *707/226–0825, 855/790–6023* ⊕ *www.solagecalistoga.com/spa* ✎ *Treatments $110–$510.*

SPORTS AND THE OUTDOORS

BICYCLING

Calistoga Bikeshop. Options here include regular and fancy bikes that rent for $28 and up for two hours, and there's a self-guided Cool Wine Tour ($110) that includes tastings at three or four small wineries. ✉ *1318 Lincoln Ave., near Washington St.* ☎ *707/942–9687* ⊕ *www.calisto-gabikeshop.net.*

SHOPPING

A stroll of the 1300 and 1400 blocks of Lincoln Avenue downtown will take you past most of Calistoga's best shops, with the remaining ones nearby. One outlier, Calistoga Pottery, can be found off Highway 29 just south of Lincoln.

A Man's Supply. Devoted to "class act" guys, this fun space stocks masculine outdoor clothing and gear and casual everyday wear. In addition to wallets and hats, accessories include cigars, knives, and manly-man gadgets. ✉ *1343 Lincoln Ave., near Washington St.* ☎ *707/942–2280* ⊕ *amanssupply.com.*

Calistoga Pottery. You may recognize the dinnerware and other pottery sold by owners Jeff and Sally Manfredi—their biggest customers are the area's inns, restaurants, and wineries. Works by a few other potters are also sold here. ✉ *1001 Foothill Blvd./Hwy. 29, 500 ft south of Lincoln Ave.* ☎ *707/942–0216* ⊕ *www.calistogapottery.com* ☉ *Closed Sun.*

Enoteca Wine Shop. The extensive tasting notes posted alongside nearly all of the wines sold here—among them some hard-to-find bottles from Napa, Sonoma, and around the world—help you make a wise choice. ✉ *1348-B Lincoln Ave.* ☎ *707/942–1117* ⊕ *www.enotecawine-shop.com.*

SONOMA VALLEY

WELCOME TO SONOMA VALLEY

TOP REASONS TO GO

★ **California and wine history:** Sonoma's mission and nearby sites shine a light into California's history; at Buena Vista you can explore the wine industry's roots.

★ **Literary and other trails:** Work off the wine and fine cuisine—and just enjoy the scenery—while hiking the trails of Jack London and Sugar Loaf Ridge state parks; the former contains the ruins of London's Wolf House.

★ **Peaceful Glen Ellen:** As writers from Jack London to M.F.K. Fisher discovered, peaceful Glen Ellen is a good place to decompress and tap into one's creativity. (Hunter S. Thompson found it too sedate.)

★ **Seated Pinot Noir tastings:** Patz & Hall, Sojourn, the Donum Estate, and other wineries host seated tastings focusing on high-quality Pinots from Los Carneros and beyond.

★ **Wineries with a view:** The views from the outdoor tasting spaces at Gundlach Bundschu, Ram's Gate, and Kunde encourage lingering over a glass of your favorite varietal.

1 Sonoma. The Wine Country's oldest town has it all: fine dining, historical sites, and wineries from down-home to high style. Much of the activity takes place around Sonoma Plaza, where in 1846 some American settlers declared independence from Mexico and established the California Republic. The republic only lasted a month, but during the next decade, Count Agoston Haraszthy laid the foundation for modern California wine making. Much of the southern Sonoma Valley, including the western section of Los Carneros AVA, has a Sonoma address.

2 Glen Ellen. Sonoma Creek snakes through Glen Ellen's tiny "downtown," 8 miles northwest of Sonoma Plaza off Highway 12. The lodgings here are small, and the town, home to Jack London State Park, has retained its rural character.

3 **Kenwood.** St. Francis and a few other name wineries straddle Highway 12 in Kenwood, whose vague center lies about 5 miles north of Glen Ellen. At Kunde Family Estate you can survey the whole Kenwood scene during a Mountain Top Tasting; back down on the ground, most of the action takes place on or just off Highway 12.

GETTING ORIENTED

The Sonoma Valley lies just north of San Pablo Bay, itself an extension of the larger San Francisco Bay. The largest town, Sonoma, about 41 miles north of San Francisco's Golden Gate Bridge, is bisected by Highway 12, which continues north to Glen Ellen and Kenwood. About 11,000 people live in Sonoma proper, with another 22,000 within its orbit; Glen Ellen has about 800 residents; and Kenwood a little more than 1,000.

Trinity Rd.

Mt. Veeder

NAPA COUNTY

Sonoma Highway

SONOMA COUNTY

12

VALLEY OF THE MOON

Agua Caliente

Gehricke Rd.

Boyes Hot Springs

Arnold Dr.

El O Verano

Castle Rd.

Sonoma

Napa St.

1

MacArthur

Old Winery Rd.

Denmark St.

Napa Rd.

Broadway

5th St. W.

5th St. E.

8th St. E.

Temelec

Watmaugh

Napa Rd.

Stage Gulch

116

12 121

Bonness Rd.

Carneros Highway

VALLEY

Arnold Dr.

121

0   2 mi

0   2 km

Sears Point Rd.   37

37

The birthplace of modern California wine making, the Sonoma Valley seduces with its unpretentious attitude and pastoral landscape. Tasting rooms, restaurants, and historical sites abound near Sonoma Plaza, but beyond downtown Sonoma the wineries and attractions are spread out along gently winding roads. Sonoma County's half of the Carneros District lies within Sonoma Valley, whose other towns of note include Glen Ellen and Kenwood.

Sonoma Valley tasting rooms are often less crowded than those in Napa or northern Sonoma County, especially midweek, and the vibe here, though sophisticated, is definitely less sceney. That's not to suggest that the Sonoma Valley is undiscovered territory. On the contrary, along Highway 12, the main corridor through the Sonoma Valley, you'll spot classy inns, restaurants, and spas in addition to wineries. In high season Glen Ellen and Kenwood are filled with well-heeled wine buffs, and the best restaurants can be crowded.

The historic Sonoma Valley towns offer glimpses of the past. Sonoma, with its tree-filled central plaza, is rich with 19th-century buildings. Two names pop up on many plaques affixed to them: General Mariano Guadalupe Vallejo, who in the 1830s and 1840s was Mexico's highest-ranking military officer in these parts, and Count Agoston Haraszthy, who opened Buena Vista Winery in 1857. Glen Ellen, meanwhile, has a special connection with the author Jack London. Kenwood claims a more recent distinction: in 1999 its Chateau St. Jean winery was the first one in Sonoma County to earn a "Wine of the Year" award from *Wine Spectator* magazine, one of several signs that Sonoma Valley wine making had come of age.

Bounded by the Mayacamas Mountains on the east and Sonoma Mountain on the west, this scenic valley extends north from San Pablo Bay nearly 20 miles to the eastern outskirts of Santa Rosa. The varied terrain, soils, and climate—cooler in the south because of the bay influence and hotter toward the north—allow grape growers to raise cool-weather varietals such as Chardonnay and Pinot Noir as well as Cabernet Sauvignon and other heat-seeking grapes.

PLANNER

WHEN TO GO
The best time to visit the Sonoma Valley is between late spring and early fall, when the weather is warm and wineries bustle with activity. September and October, when grape harvesting and crushing are in full swing, are the busiest months. Especially at this time—and on all summer weekends—lodging prices tend to be at their highest. Tasting rooms throughout the Sonoma Valley are generally not too crowded during the week, even in high season, except perhaps on holiday Mondays.

PLANNING YOUR TIME
You can hit the Sonoma Valley's highlights in a day or two—a half or a full day exploring western Carneros District wineries and some in Sonoma proper, and the same amount of time to check out Glen Ellen and Kenwood. Most visitors stay in Sonoma. Traffic usually isn't an issue, except on Highway 12 north of Sonoma Plaza (though a recent road-widening has mitigated congestion during most of the day) and the intersection of Highways 116 and 121 during the morning and afternoon commutes.

Several star wineries—Patz & Hall, Scribe, and Sojourn among them—accept visitors by appointment only. On weekdays you may be able to reserve a space on short notice, but for weekend visits, especially during the summer and early fall, booking ahead is essential even when food pairings (which wineries need time to plan for) are not involved. A good strategy year-round is to book appointment-only wineries in the morning; this gives you more flexibility in the afternoon should lunch or other stops take longer than expected.

GETTING HERE AND AROUND
BUS TRAVEL
VINE Bus 25 travels between downtown Napa and Sonoma, where Sonoma Transit buses provide service within Sonoma and to Glen Ellen and Kenwood. *For more information about arriving by bus, see Bus Travel in the Travel Smart chapter. For more information about local bus service, see the Bus Travel sections for the individual towns in this chapter.*

CAR TRAVEL
Traveling by car is the easiest way to tour the Sonoma Valley. Highway 12, also called the Sonoma Highway, is the main thoroughfare through the valley, running north–south through Sonoma, Glen Ellen, and Kenwood into Santa Rosa. Arnold Drive heads north from Highway 121 in southern Sonoma to Glen Ellen. On the north side of town it reconnects with (and dead-ends at) Highway 12. A turn left (north) leads to Kenwood.

From San Francisco: To get to the Sonoma Valley from San Francisco, travel north on U.S. 101 to the Highway 37 turnoff (Exit 460A), driving east for about 7 miles to Highway 121, the main route through the Carneros District. Highway 12 leads north from Highway 121 into the town of Sonoma.

From the Napa Valley: Highway 29 heads south from the town of Napa. Turn west onto Highway 121/12 and drive north on Highway 12 when it splits off from Highway 121. A more adventurous route (not for the carsick) leads west over the Mayacamas range on highly scenic—but slow and winding—Oakville Grade Road, which turns into Trinity Road before it reaches Highway 12 in Glen Ellen. If coming to the Sonoma Valley from Calistoga, travel north a few miles on Highway 128 and then west on Petrified Forest Road and later Calistoga Road to reach Highway 12 in Santa Rosa. From there, head south into the valley.

Avoiding confusion: In the Carneros District, Highway 121 is often signposted as the Carneros Highway, the Sonoma Highway, or Arnold Drive. The multiple names can lead to confusion. The Gloria Ferrer winery gives its address as 23555 Carneros Highway, for instance; the listed address of Cornerstone, across the road, is 23570 Arnold Drive.

RESTAURANTS

With Sonoma's Friday farmers' market arguably the Wine Country's best, it's not surprising that farm-to-table influences can be felt not only at fancy establishments but also ethnic and comfort-food venues. Fine dining in the Sonoma Valley is generally low-key, with the major exception being Santé, the tony restaurant inside the Fairmont Sonoma Mission Inn & Spa. Santé and Cafe La Haye, El Dorado Kitchen, Harvest Moon Cafe, and Oso Sonoma, all in Sonoma, turn out thoughtful, complex cuisine that emphasizes locally produced meat, fish, cheese, vegetables, and fruit. Manuel Azevedo serves winning Portuguese-influenced dishes at LaSalette and the less formal Tasca Tasca, separate spots near Sonoma Plaza. Aventine Glen Ellen, inside a former sawmill and gristmill, is the best place for Italian. Glen Ellen Star is its town's other must-do, but you can't go wrong at any of the fine-dining restaurants here, among them Yeti for Indian and Himalayan cuisine. El Molino Central—as with Yeti, modern in its use of organic ingredients but traditional in its preparations—is the top stop in Sonoma for Mexican, and the Fremont Diner south of town takes comfort food to interesting places. *Restaurant reviews have been shortened. For full information, visit Fodors.com.*

HOTELS

Sonoma has the valley's most varied accommodations, with motels and small inns, vacation condos, and boutique hotels all in the mix. Small inns are the norm in Glen Ellen and Kenwood. Spa lovers have two high-end choices at either end of the valley: the large and splashy Fairmont Sonoma Mission Inn & Spa in Sonoma and the Mediterranean-style Kenwood Inn and Spa, in Kenwood.

For weekend stays in all towns it's wise to book a month or more ahead from late May through October. Most small lodgings require a two-night minimum stay on weekends at this time, three if Monday is a holiday. *Hotel reviews have been shortened. For full information, visit Fodors.com.*

WHAT IT COSTS			
	$	**$$**	**$$$**	**$$$$**
Restaurants	under $16	$16–$22	$23–$30	over $30
Hotels	under $201	$201–$300	$301–$400	over $400

Restaurant prices are the average cost of a main course at dinner, or if dinner isn't served, at lunch. Hotel prices are the lowest cost of a standard double room in high season.

VISITOR INFORMATION

Contacts Sonoma Valley Visitors Bureau. ⊠ *Sonoma Plaza, 453 1st St. E, Sonoma* ☎ *707/996–1090* ⊕ *www.sonomavalley.com.*

APPELLATIONS

Although Sonoma *County* is a large, diverse growing region that encompasses several different appellations, the much smaller Sonoma *Valley,* at the southern end of Sonoma County, is comparatively compact and consists mostly of the **Sonoma Valley AVA,** which stretches northwest from San Pablo Bay toward Santa Rosa. The weather and soils here are unusually diverse. Pinot Noir and Chardonnay vineyards are most likely to be found in the AVA's southernmost parts, the sections cooled by fog from San Pablo Bay. (This part of the Sonoma Valley AVA overlaps with the Sonoma County portions of **Los Carneros AVA.**) Zinfandel, Cabernet Sauvignon, and Sauvignon Blanc grapes are more plentiful farther north, near Glen Ellen and Kenwood, both of which tend to be a few degrees warmer.

The **Sonoma Mountain AVA** rises to the west of Glen Ellen on the western border of the Sonoma Valley AVA. Benefiting from a sunny location and rocky soil, the vineyards here produce deep-rooted vines and intensely flavored grapes that are made into complex red wines, especially Cabernet Sauvignon. Opposite Sonoma Mountain southeast across the Sonoma Valley lies the **Moon Mountain District Sonoma County AVA.** This mountainside sliver, on the western slopes of the Mayacamas Mountains (just west of the Napa Valley's Mt. Veeder subappellation), contains some of California's oldest Zinfandel and Cabernet Sauvignon vines. The heavily sloped, rocky soils here produce smaller berries than vines on the valley floor, and the higher skin-to-juice ratio yields intense flavor.

Portions of the **Sonoma Coast AVA** overlap Los Carneros and the Sonoma Valley. The tiny **Bennett Valley AVA,** also part of the Sonoma Valley AVA, falls within the city of Santa Rosa *(see Chapter 5).*

SONOMA

Fodor's Choice *14 miles west of Napa; 45 miles northeast of San Francisco.*

★ One of the few towns in the valley with multiple attractions not related to food and wine, Sonoma has plenty to keep you busy for a couple of hours before you head out to the wineries. And you needn't leave town to taste wine: about three dozen tasting rooms do business on or near Sonoma Plaza, a few of them pouring wines from more than one winery.

The valley's cultural center, Sonoma, founded in 1835 when California was still part of Mexico, is built around tree-filled Sonoma Plaza. If you arrive from the south, on wide Broadway (Highway 12), you'll be retracing the last stretch of what long ago was California's most important road—El Camino Real, or "the royal road," the only overland route through the state. During California's Spanish and Mexican periods, it ran past all of the state's 21 missions: beginning at San Diego de Alcalá (1769) and ending at Mission San Francisco Solano (1823). This last mission still sits in the center of Sonoma.

GETTING HERE AND AROUND
Highway 12 from the south (San Francisco) or north (Santa Rosa) is the main route into the town of Sonoma. For several blocks south of Sonoma Plaza, the street's name changes to Broadway. There are two- and three-hour unmetered parking spaces around the plaza, and free all-day parking can be found off 1st Street East a third of a block north of the plaza. Once you've parked, a pleasant stroll takes you past many of the town's restaurants, shops, and tasting rooms. High-profile and boutique wineries can be found a mile or so east; arrow-shape signs on East Spain Street and East Napa Street will direct you.

Napa County VINE buses travel between Napa and Sonoma. Sonoma Transit buses connect Sonoma with other Sonoma County towns.

EXPLORING

TOP ATTRACTIONS
CocoaPlanet Chocolate Factory & Tasting Room. Anne McKibben believes that chocolate should have more taste and less sugar. With that objective in mind, the chocolatier and her husband, Jeffrey, patented a technology that enables her to strategically deposit drops of salted caramel, Mandarin orange, vanilla espresso, and other fillings into her chocolates in smaller amounts than traditional candies. As a result, CocoaPlanet chocolates are low in calories yet bursting with flavor. To learn more about these treats, visit the combination factory, tasting room, and mini French café the couple opened several blocks south of Sonoma Plaza. You can have a few nibbles for free or order "flights" of chocolates. Tours are by appointment only. ⊠ *921 Broadway, at W. MacArthur St.* ☎ *707/343–7453* ⊕ *www.cocoaplanet.com* 🍽 *Tastings free–$11, tour free.*

CLOSE UP

Top Tastings and Tours

TASTINGS

Lasseter Family Winery, Glen Ellen. A visit to the immaculately groomed vineyard paradise of Pixar producer John Lasseter and his wife feels like a special occasion.

Scribe, Sonoma. The 1915 Mission Revival–style hacienda here overlooks vineyards with Riesling, Sylvaner, and other grapes German immigrants planted in Sonoma a century and a half ago.

TOURS

Benziger Family Winery, Glen Ellen. On this winery's tram tour, you'll learn about Benziger's unique microclimates and deep commitment to biodynamic farming principles.

Buena Vista Winery, Sonoma. Tours of this winery founded in 1857 pass through caves dug by Chinese laborers, and there's a high-tech museum of wine-making tools.

SETTING

Kunde Estate Winery & Vineyards, Kenwood. The Mountain Top Tastings passenger-van tour here winds 1,400 feet above the valley floor. On a shaded deck you'll enjoy memorable vistas while sipping reserve wines.

FOOD PAIRING

Patz & Hall, Sonoma. The gourmet small bites at a Salon Tasting at this respected winery show just how food-friendly its Chardonnays and Pinot Noirs are.

St. Francis Winery, Kenwood. The five petite plates of this famous winery's executive chef pair well with its Zins, Cabs, and other wines.

Walt Wines, Sonoma. Small bites from The Girl & the Fig help illustrate the range of flavors of Walt Pinot Noirs, whose grape sources range from Oregon to California's Central Coast.

4

Cornerstone Sonoma. Huge Adirondack chairs bookend this collection of tasting rooms and design, housewares, and gift shops. The main draws, though, are the ¼-acre Sunset Test Gardens, which debuted in 2016, and nine unrelated landscape installations. Sunset divides its section into five "rooms"—Farm Garden, Gathering Space, Backyard Orchard, Flower Room, and Cocktail Garden—intended to expand visitors' agri-lifestyle horizons. The installations make artistic and political statements that inspire on levels beyond the agrarian. Chateau Sonoma, Artefact Design & Salvage, and Nomad Chic are three shops worth checking out. ■TIP➜ The Poseidon Vineyard & Obsidian Ridge tasting room is the best of the wine stops here. ✉ *23570 Arnold Dr./Hwy. 121, across from the Gloria Ferrer winery* ☎ *707/933–3010* ⊕ *www. cornerstonesonoma.com* ✉ *Free.*

Fodor'sChoice ★ **The Donum Estate.** Anne Moller-Racke, the founder of this prominent Chardonnay and Pinot Noir producer, calls herself a winegrower in the French *vigneron* tradition that emphasizes agriculture—selecting vineyards with the right soils, microclimates, and varietals, then farming with precision—over wine-making wizardry. The Donum Estate, which by mid-2017 should be occupying a new hilltop tasting room with views of Los Carneros, San Pablo Bay, and beyond, farms two vineyards surrounding the structure, along with one in the Russian River Valley and another in Mendocino County's Anderson Valley. All the wines exhibit the "power yet elegance" that sealed the winery's fame in the 2000s. Tastings are by appointment only. ■ TIP➡ **Large museum-quality contemporary outdoor sculptures, the showstopper being the Beijing-born artist Ai Weiwei's 12 cast metal heads of the Chinese zodiac, add a touch of high culture to a visit here.** ✉ *24520 Ramal Rd., off Hwy. 121/12* ☎ *707/939–2290* ⊕ *www.thedonumestate.com* ☜ *Tasting $50.*

Gundlach Bundschu. "Gun lock bun shoe" gets you close to pronouncing this winery's name correctly, though everyone here shortens it to Gun Bun. The Bundschu family, which has owned most of this property since 1858, makes reds that include Cabernet Franc, Cabernet Sauvignon, Merlot, and a Bordeaux-style blend of each vintage's best grapes. Gewürztraminer, Chardonnay, and two rosés are also in the mix. Parts of the 1870 stone winery where standard tastings ($20) unfold are still used for wine making. For a more comprehensive experience, book a cave tour ($40), a Pinzgauer vehicle vineyard tour ($60), or a Heritage Reserve ($85) pairing of limited-release wines with small gourmet bites. Some tastings and all tours are by appointment only. ■ TIP➡ **On some summer days you can enjoy the outdoor Vista Courtyard's broad vineyard views while tasting wines paired with cheese and charcuterie ($30).** ✉ *2000 Denmark St., at Bundschu Rd., off 8th St. E, 3 miles southeast of Sonoma Plaza* ☎ *707/938–5277* ⊕ *www.gunbun.com* ☜ *Tastings $20–$30, tours $40–$85 (include tastings).*

Pangloss Cellars Tasting Lounge. The high-ceilinged tasting room of this winery named for the optimistic doctor from Voltaire's satire *Candide* occupies a restored circa-1900 stone building across from Sonoma Plaza. Originally a general store, it's a striking setting to enjoy wines by Erich Bradley, also the winemaker at nearby Sojourn Cellars. The Pangloss roster—white and red blends plus Sauvignon Blanc, Chardonnay, Pinot Noir, Zinfandel, and Cabernet Sauvignon—aims to represent the range of Sonoma County's viticultural portfolio. (A recent red-blend vintage containing Cab, Pinot, Zin, Merlot, and Mourvèdre did this all in one bottle.) Without a reservation you can sip wines by the flight or glass in the lounge area, or taste at the bar, but you'll need one for a private Cellar tasting of wines and local cheeses and charcuterie. ✉ *35 E. Napa St., at 1st St. E* ☎ *707/933–8565* ⊕ *www.panglosscellars.com* ☜ *Tastings $25–$50.*

Fodor'sChoice
★

Patz & Hall. Sophisticated single-vineyard Chardonnays and Pinot Noirs are the trademark of this respected winery whose tastings take place in a fashionable single-story residence 3 miles southeast of Sonoma Plaza. It's a Wine Country adage that great wines are made in the vineyard—the all-star fields represented here include Hyde, Durell, and Gap's Crown—but winemaker James Hall routinely surpasses peers with access to the same fruit, proof that discernment and expertise (Hall is a master at oak aging) play a role, too. You can sample wines at the bar and on some days on the vineyard-view terrace beyond it, but to learn how food friendly these wines are, consider the Salon Tasting, at which they're paired with gourmet bites crafted with equal finesse. Tastings are by appointment only. ✉ *21200 8th St. E, near Peru Rd.* ☎ *707/265–7700* ⊕ *www.patzhall.com* ☜ *Tastings $30–$60.*

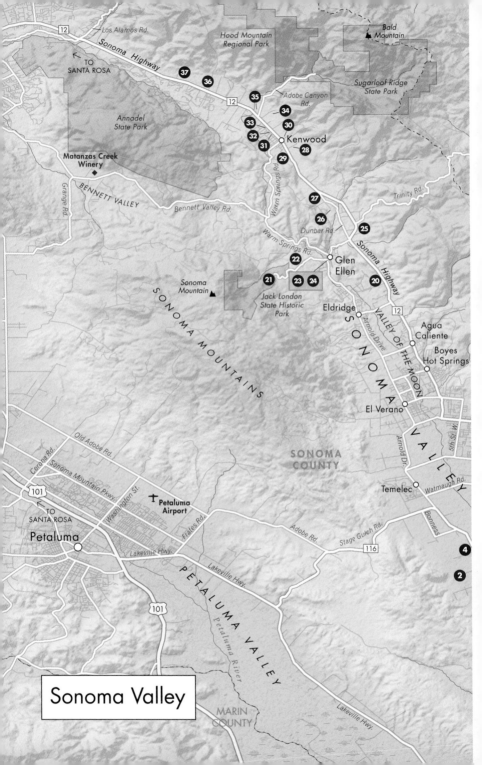

Sonoma Valley

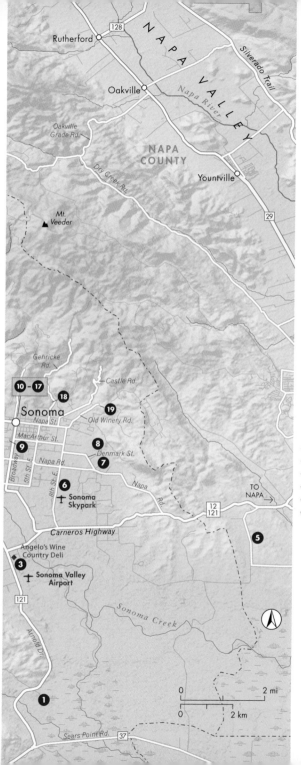

Ram's Gate Winery. Stunning views, ultrachic architecture, and wines made from grapes grown by acclaimed producers make a visit to Ram's Gate an event. The welcoming interior spaces—think Restoration Hardware with a dash of high-style whimsy—open up to the entire western Carneros. In fine weather you'll experience the cooling breezes that sweep through the area while sipping sophisticated wines, mostly Pinot Noirs and Chardonnays, but also Pinot Blanc, Sauvignon Blanc, Cabernet Sauvignon, and Syrah. With grapes sourced from the Sangiacomo, Hudson, and other illustrious vineyards, winemaker Jeff Gaffner focuses on creating balanced wines that express what occurred in nature that year. All visits are by appointment only. ■TIP→ You can sip current releases at the tasting bar ($40), take a tour and taste ($65), or tour and enjoy wines paired with food ($90). ✉ *28700 Arnold Dr./ Hwy. 121* ☎ *707/721–8700* ⊕ *www.ramsgatewinery.com* ✉ *Tastings $40–$90; tour $65 (includes tasting)* ☉ *Closed Tues. and Wed.*

Fodor'sChoice **Scribe.** Andrew and Adam Mariani, sons of California walnut grow-
★ ers, established Scribe in 2007 on land first planted to grapes in 1858 by Emil Dresel, a German immigrant. Dresel's claims to fame include cultivating Sonoma's first Riesling and Sylvaner, an achievement the brothers honor by growing both varietals on land he once farmed. Using natural wine-making techniques they craft bright, terroir-driven wines from those grapes, along with Chardonnay, Pinot Noir, Syrah, and Cabernet Sauvignon. In restoring their property's 1915 Mission Revival–style hacienda the brothers preserved various layers of history—original molding and light fixtures, for instance, but also fragments of floral-print wallpaper and 1950s newspapers. Now a tasting space, the hacienda served during Prohibition as a bootleggers' hideout, and its basement harbored a speakeasy: two intriguing tales among many associated with this historic site. Tastings are by appointment only. ✉ *2100 Denmark St., off Napa Rd.* ☎ *707/939–1858* ⊕ *scribewinery.com* ✉ *Tasting price varies; contact winery.*

Fodor'sChoice **Sojourn Cellars.** Superior fruit sources and a winemaker with a wisely
★ light touch have earned Sojourn Cellars high ratings from major wine critics for its Chardonnay, Pinot Noir, and Cabernet Sauvignon wines. The initial releases of this winery founded in 2001 were Cabernets, but it's best known these days for nine well-balanced Pinot Noirs from the Sonoma Coast and Russian River Valley appellations. The four Chardonnays all hail from the Sonoma Coast, with the grapes for the four Cabernets from the Napa and Sonoma valleys. In part because winemaker Erich Bradley uses oak in such a consistent way, the informative tastings (by appointment only) at Sojourn's homey bungalow just east of Sonoma Plaza focus on the subtle variations caused by climate, terrain, and clone type depending on the grape sources. ✉ *141 E. Napa St., ½ block east of Sonoma Plaza* ☎ *707/938–7212* ⊕ *www.sojourncellars. com* ✉ *Tasting $35.*

Sonoma Plaza. Dating to the Mission era, Sonoma Plaza is surrounded by 19th-century adobes, atmospheric hotels, and the swooping marquee of the Depression-era Sebastiani Theatre. A statue on the plaza's northeastern side marks the spot where California proclaimed its independence from Mexico on June 14, 1846. Despite its historical roots,

Sonoma Mission was the last of California's 21 missions.

the plaza is not a museum piece. On summer days it's a hive of activity, with children blowing off steam in the playground, couples enjoying picnics from gourmet shops, and groups listening to live music at the small amphitheater. The stone **City Hall** is also here. If you're wondering why the 1906 structure looks the same from all angles, here's why: its four sides were purposely made identical so that none of the plaza's merchants would feel that City Hall had turned its back to them. ⊠ *North end of Broadway/Hwy. 12, bordered by E. Napa St., 1st St. E, E. Spain St., and 1st St. W.*

NEED A BREAK

Sweet Scoops. The scent of waffle cones baking in back draws patrons into this family-run parlor serving artisanal ice cream made fresh daily. Butter brickle, Mexican chocolate, and salted caramel ice cream are among the 180 alternating flavors that include sorbets, sometimes sherbets, and always a vegan option. **Known for:** shakes, floats, and sundaes; local ingredients, from CocoaPlanet chocolates to Gloria Ferrer sparkling wines; peppy decor and staffers; husband and wife owners (he makes the ice cream, and she runs the business). ⊠ *408 1st St E, near E. Spain St.* ☎ *707/721–1187* ⊕ *www.sweetscoopsicecream.com.*

Fodor'sChoice ★

Texture Wines. Collectors of artisanal Chardonnay and Pinot Noir ring the bell at an old stone building's speakeasylike side door to gain entrée to exclusive seated tastings of refined small-lot wines by Erich Bradley, one of Sonoma County's most accomplished winemakers. "At their finest," says Bradley, Chardonnay and Pinot Noir "provide important, seminal moments for devout wine lovers." The winemaker "aspires to reach those heights"—and does—with three handcrafted Sonoma Coast Chardonnays and two Anderson Valley (Mendocino County) Pinot Noirs served with small bites. Tastings take place in an elegant room lit softly by a beaded chandelier. With a slight minerality, the wines exhibit Bradley's Burgundian influences while still expressing the brightness and fullness of their California origins. Tastings are by appointment only. ✉ *35 E. Napa St., at 1st St. E* ☎ *707/939–7406* ⊕ *www.texturewines.com* 🍷 *Tasting $45.*

Fodor'sChoice **Three Sticks Wines.** Pinot Noir artiste Bob Cabral, formerly of the exclu-
★ sive Williams Selyem Winery, makes Pinots and Chardonnays from the prized Durell and Gap's Crown vineyards of Bill Price, the owner of Three Sticks Winery. Cabral also makes other Pinots and Chardonnays, along with Rhône-style wines that bear the Castañeda label in honor of the restored 1842 Vallejo-Castañeda Adobe, where the winery pours its wines. San Francisco–based designer Ken Fulk transformed the structure, Sonoma's longest occupied residence, into a showcase both lavish and refined. Seated private tastings unfold at a long elm table inside the adobe or, weather permitting, at a cast stone table under a willow-covered arbor. In either setting a tasting here (by appointment only) feels like a special occasion. ✉ *143 W. Spain St., at 1st St. W* ☎ *707/996–3328* ⊕ *www.threestickswines.com* 🍷 *Tastings $40–$200.*

Fodor'sChoice **Walt Wines.** You could spend a full day sampling wines in the tast-
★ ing rooms bordering or near Sonoma Plaza, but be sure not to miss Walt, which specializes in Pinot Noir from Sonoma County, Mendocino County (just to the north), California's Central Coast, and Oregon's Willamette Valley. Walk-ins are welcome to taste several wines inside a mid-1930s Tudor-inspired home or, weather permitting, at backyard tables beneath a tall, double-trunk redwood tree. To see how winemaker Megan Gunderson Paredes's wines pair with food—in this case small bites from The Girl & the Fig across the street—make a reservation for the Root 101: A Single Vineyard Exploration. At both tastings you'll learn about the origins of this sister winery to Hall St. Helena. ✉ *380 1st St. W, at W. Spain St.* ☎ *707/933–4440* ⊕ *www.waltwines. com* 🍷 *Tastings $30–$60.*

Fodor'sChoice **Westwood Estate.** This winery's 23 acres of vineyards in the Annadel
★ Gap of the northern Sonoma Valley occupy a zone hospitable to cool-climate grapes such as Pinot Noir, along with Syrah and other Rhône varietals. Ben Cane, Westwood's winemaker, fashions the remarkable fruit grown here into exciting, thought-provoking wines. Because the estate ones all come from the same vineyard, the focus is on which Pinot Noir or Rhône clones (variants of each varietal) they derive from and how Cane applies oak aging to bring out bring out the best in each. Westwood's small tasting room, just south of Sonoma Plaza, is staffed from Thursday through Sunday. Appointments aren't necessary, but it's a good idea to call ahead, especially on weekends. ■TIP➔ **Westwood is down a narrow alley east of the restaurant at 9 East Napa Street.** ✉ *Vine Alley Complex, 11 E. Napa St., No. 3, at Broadway* ☎ *707/933–7837* ⊕ *www.westwoodwine.com* 🍷 *Tastings $15–$50, depending on wines available* ⊙ *Closed Mon.–Wed. (appointments sometimes possible with notice).*

WORTH NOTING

Anaba Wines. Reprising the greatest hits of Burgundy (Chardonnay, Pinot Noir) and the Rhône (Grenache, Mourvèdre, Syrah, Viognier), Anaba tries to be all things to most wine drinkers and succeeds. Pinot Noirs from Dutton Ranch and Soberanes Vineyard, the latter in Monterey County's Santa Lucia Highlands AVA, are among the standouts, but all the wines, since 2014 made by Ross Cobb and Katy Wilson, both Pinot Noir pros, are thoughtfully crafted. The winery's bungalowlike tasting room sits at the northwest corner of the intersection of Highways 121 and 116. ■ TIP→ A side patio faces the vineyards; if you don't mind a little highway noise, on a sunny day it's not a bad spot for a picnic put together at the deli across the street or nearby Angelo's. ⊠ *60 Bonneau Rd., off Hwy. 116* ⊕ *707/996–4188 Ext. 106 for tours, 877/990–4188* ⊕ *www.anabawines.com* ⊠ *Tastings $15–$35, tour free* ⊙ *No tour Tues.–Thurs.*

QUICK BITES

Angelo's Wine Country Deli. Many Bay Area locals stop at this roadside shop to get their jerky fix or to pick up cheese, charcuterie, and huge sandwiches. **Known for:** beef jerky including Cajun, barbecue, and peppered; generous free samples. ⊠ **23400 Arnold Dr./Hwy. 121, near Wagner Rd.** ☎ **707/938–3688** ⊕ **angelossmokehouse.com/deli.htm.**

Buena Vista Winery. The birthplace of modern California wine making has been transformed into an entertaining homage to the accomplishments of the 19th-century wine pioneer Count Agoston Haraszthy. Tours pass through the original aging caves dug deep into the hillside by Chinese laborers, and banners, photos, and artifacts inside and out convey the history made on this site. Reserve tastings ($40) include library and current releases, plus barrel samples. The rehabilitated former press house (used for pressing grapes into wine), which dates to 1862, hosts the standard tastings. Chardonnay, Pinot Noir, several red blends, and a vibrant Petit Verdot are the strong suits here. Tours are by appointment only. ■ TIP→ The high-tech Historic Wine Tool Museum displays implements, some decidedly low-tech, used to make wine over the years. ⊠ *18000 Old Winery Rd., off E. Napa St.* ☎ *800/926–1266* ⊕ *www.buenavistawinery.com* ⊠ *Tastings $20–$50, tours $25–$40.*

Gloria Ferrer Caves and Vineyards. A tasting at Gloria Ferrer is an exercise in elegance: at tables inside the Spanish hacienda–style winery or outside on the terrace (no standing at the bar at Gloria Ferrer), you can take in vistas of gently rolling Carneros hills while sipping sparkling and still wines. The Chardonnay and Pinot Noir grapes from the surrounding vineyards are the product of old-world winemaking knowledge—the same family started the sparkling-wine maker Freixenet in 16th-century Spain—and contemporary soil management techniques and clonal research. The Daily Sparkling Tour covers *méthode champenoise* wine making, the Ferrer family's history, and the winery's vineyard sustainability practices. Other tours, one of which includes small bites, touch on these and other topics. ⊠ *23555 Carneros Hwy./Hwy. 121* ☎ *707/933–1917* ⊕ *www.gloriaferrer.com* ⊠ *Tastings $7–$75, tours $25–$60.*

CLOSE UP

Wine-Making Pioneer

Count Agoston Haraszthy arrived in Sonoma in 1857 and set out to make fine wine commercially. He planted European vinifera varietals rather than mission grapes (varietals brought to the Americas by Spanish missionaries) and founded Buena Vista Winery the year he arrived.

TWO BREAKTHROUGHS

Haraszthy deserves credit for two breakthroughs. At Buena Vista, he grew grapes on dry hillsides, instead of in the wetter lowlands, as had been customary in the Mission and Rancho periods. His success demonstrated that Sonoma's climate was moist enough to sustain grapes without irrigation. The innovative count was also the first to try aging his wine in redwood barrels, which were much less expensive than oak ones. More affordable barrels made it feasible to ratchet up wine production. For almost 100 years, redwood barrels would be the California wine industry's most popular storage method, even though redwood can impart an odd flavor.

ADAPTABLE ZINFANDEL

Despite producing inferior wines, the prolific mission grapes were preferred by California growers over better varieties of French, German, and Italian vinifera grapes through the 1860s and into the 1870s. But Haraszthy's success had begun to make an impression. A new red-wine grape, Zinfandel, was becoming popular, both because it made excellent Claret (as good red wine was then called) and because it had adapted to the area's climate.

BALANCE LOST

By this time, however, Haraszthy had disappeared, literally, from the scene. After a business setback during the 1860s, the count lost control of Buena Vista and ventured to Nicaragua to restore his fortune in the sugar and rum industries. While crossing a stream infested with alligators, the count lost his balance and plunged into water below. The body of modern California wine making's first promoter and pioneer was never recovered.

Ravenswood Winery. "No wimpy wines" is the punchy motto of this producer, famous for big, bold Zinfandels. Ravenswood also makes Petite Sirah and Bordeaux-style red blends; the whites include Chardonnay, Gewürztraminer, and lightly sparkling Moscato. You can taste flights of small-lot Zinfandels and Cabernets, some available only at the winery, without an appointment at the bar ($18) or, when the weather permits, outdoors on the terrace ($25). Reservations are required for the daily tour. Focusing on viticultural practices, it includes a barrel tasting of wines in the cellar. To learn even more about the wine-making process, make an appointment for one of the wine-blending sessions. ✉ *18701 Gehricke Rd., off E. Spain St.* ☎ *707/933–2332* ⊕ *www.ravenswood-winery.com* 🖰 *Tastings $18–$60, tour $25, blending session $75.*

Sonoma Mission. The northernmost of the 21 missions established by Franciscan friars in California, Sonoma Mission was founded in 1823 as Mission San Francisco Solano. It serves as the centerpiece of **Sonoma State Historic Park,** which includes several other sites in Sonoma and nearby Petaluma. Some early mission structures were destroyed, but all or part of several remaining buildings date to the days of Mexican rule

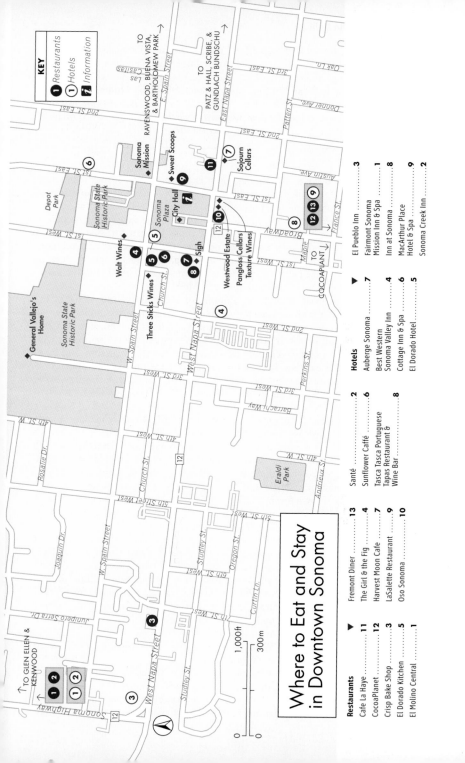

Where to Eat and Stay in Downtown Sonoma

KEY
- **1** Restaurants
- **①** Hotels
- **🛈** Information

Restaurants ▼
Cafe La Haye	11
CocoaPlanet	12
Crisp Bake Shop	3
El Dorado Kitchen	5
El Molino Central	1
Fremont Diner	13
The Girl & the Fig	4
Harvest Moon Cafe	7
LaSalette Restaurant	9
Oso Sonoma	10
Santé	2
Sunflower Caffé	6
Tasca Tasca Portuguese Tapas Restaurant & Wine Bar	8

Hotels ▼
Auberge Sonoma	7
Best Western Sonoma Valley Inn	4
Cottage Inn & Spa	6
El Dorado Hotel	5
El Pueblo Inn	3
Fairmont Sonoma Mission Inn & Spa	1
Inn at Sonoma	8
MacArthur Place Hotel & Spa	9
Sonoma Creek Inn	2

General Vallejo's Home

Sonoma State Historic Park

Depot Park

Sonoma State Historic Park

Walt Wines

Three Sticks Wines

Sonoma Plaza

City Hall

Sigh

Westwood Estate Pangloss Cellars Texture Wines

Sonoma Mission

Sweet Scoops

Sojourn Cellars

TO RAVENSWOOD, BUENA VISTA, & BARTHOLOMEW PARK →

TO PATZ & HALL, SCRIBE, & GUNDLACH BUNDSCHU →

TO COCOAPLANT ↓

TO GLEN ELLEN & KENWOOD

Eraldi Park

1,000ft
300m

over California. Worth a look are the **Sonoma Barracks,** a half block west of the mission at 20 East Spain Street, which housed troops under the command of General Mariano Guadalupe Vallejo, who controlled vast tracts of land in the region. **General Vallejo's Home,** a Victorian-era structure, is a few blocks west. ✉ *114 E. Spain St., at 1st St. E* ☎ *707/938–9560* 🌐 *www.parks.ca.gov/?page_id=479* 🎟 *$3, includes same-day admission to other historic sites.*

WHERE TO EAT

$$$ AMERICAN Fodor's Choice ★ 🍴 **Cafe La Haye.** The dining room is compact, the open kitchen even more so, but chef Jeffrey Lloyd turns out understated, sophisticated fare emphasizing local ingredients. Chicken, beef, pasta, and fish get deluxe treatment without fuss or fanfare—the daily roasted chicken and the risotto specials are always good. **Known for:** Napa-Sonoma wine list with clever French complements; signature butterscotch pudding dessert; owner Saul Gropman on hand to greet diners. [$] *Average main: $24* ✉ *140 E. Napa St., at 1st St. E* ☎ *707/935–5994* 🌐 *www.cafelahaye.com* 🕓 *Closed Sun. and Mon. No lunch.*

$ CAFÉ 🍴 **CocoaPlanet.** The stone, aluminum, and glass tasting space of the CocoaPlanet chocolate factory doubles as a gluten-free modern French café. Soups, salads, quiche, and pizza are on the menu, but the items locals return for are the *fromage grillé* (grilled cheese sandwich with Gruyère or sharp cheddar), croques monsieur or madame, and ham-and-cheese crepes. **Known for:** plates to share; mandarin orange–chocolate-almond cake; CocoaMint chocolate brownie. [$] *Average main: $14* ✉ *921 Broadway, at MacArthur St.* ☎ *707/343–7453* 🌐 *www.cocoaplanet.com* 🕓 *Closed Tues. and Wed.*

$ BAKERY 🍴 **Crisp Bake Shop.** Only in the Wine Country would your local pastry chef, in this case Andrea Koweek, have honed her skills at The French Laundry. Her croissants, cupcakes, mini-Bundt cakes, chocolate sea-salt cookies, and brioche sweet buns are so cute you'll struggle between taking a picture and taking that first bite, and her husband-chef, Moaya Scheiman, crafts their shop's savory breakfast and lunch fare with equal finesse. **Known for:** bacon, egg, and cheese breakfast pies; unusual sandwiches. [$] *Average main: $8* ✉ *720 W. Napa St./Hwy. 12, at 7th St. W* ☎ *707/933–9999* 🌐 *www.crispbakeshop.com.*

$$$ MODERN AMERICAN 🍴 **El Dorado Kitchen.** This restaurant owes its visual appeal to its clean lines and handsome decor, but the eye inevitably drifts westward to the open kitchen, where executive chef Armando Navarro's crew crafts dishes full of subtle surprises. The menu might include ahi tuna tartare with wasabi tobiko caviar as a starter, with paella awash with seafood and dry-cured Spanish chorizo sausage among the entrées. **Known for:** subtle tastes and textures; truffle-oil fries with Parmesan; spiced crepes and other desserts. [$] *Average main: $26* ✉ *El Dorado Hotel, 405 1st St. W, at W. Spain St.* ☎ *707/996–3030* 🌐 *www.eldoradosonoma.com/restaurant.*

$ MEXICAN 🍴 **El Molino Central.** Fans purchase Karen Waikiki's tortillas and tamales—handmade from stone-ground heritage corn and other organic ingredients—at Bay Area stores and farmers' markets. At her roadside restaurant, which has more tables outside than in, you can pick from the

El Dorado Kitchen's chef Armando Navarro crafts flavorful dishes full of subtle surprises.

full lineup, which includes the star tamales (chicken mole and Niman Ranch pork), tacos filled with beer-battered fish or crispy beef, and enchiladas and burritos. **Known for:** high-quality ingredients; authentic techniques; breakfast chilaquiles Merida, with soft-scrambled eggs and spicy roasted tomato. $ *Average main: $13* ⊠ *11 Central Ave., at Hwy. 12, Boyes Hot Springs* ☎ *707/939–1010* ⊕ *www.elmolinocentral.com.*

$$
SOUTHERN
✕ **Fremont Diner.** Locals mix with tourists at this retro-yet-au-courant roadhouse restaurant whose menu favors rock-around-the-clock Southern favorites. Hefty breakfasts of buttermilk pancakes and stone-ground grits with shrimp-sausage gravy and bacon ensure that no one goes hungry; ditto for the lunch and dinner lineup that includes oyster po'boys, chili cheese dogs, handmade hamburgers (no prefab patties here), and spicy fried Nashville chicken. **Known for:** down-home Southern cuisine with modern twists; small-batch brews; pecan pie; skillet-baked buttermilk cake with caramel. $ *Average main: $18* ⊠ *2698 Fremont Dr., at Hwy. 121* ☎ *707/938–7370* ⊕ *www.thefremontdiner.com* ☉ *No dinner Mon.–Wed.*

$$$
FRENCH
Fodor'sChoice
★
✕ **The Girl & the Fig.** At this hot spot for inventive French cooking inside the historic Sonoma Hotel bar you can always find a dish with owner Sondra Bernstein's signature figs on the menu, whether it's a fig-and-arugula salad or an aperitif blending sparkling wine with fig liqueur. Also look for duck confit, a burger with matchstick fries, and wild flounder meunière. **Known for:** wine list emphasis on Rhône varietals; artisanal cheese platters; croques monsieurs and eggs Benedict at Sunday brunch. $ *Average main: $24* ⊠ *Sonoma Hotel, 110 W. Spain St., at 1st St.* W ☎ *707/938–3634* ⊕ *www.thegirlandthefig.com.*

$$$
AMERICAN
Fodor's Choice
★

✕ **Harvest Moon Cafe.** Everything at this little restaurant with an odd, zigzag layout is so perfectly executed and the vibe is so genuinely warm that a visit here is deeply satisfying. The ever-changing menu might include homey dishes such as grilled half chicken with baked polenta or pan-seared Hawaiian ono with jasmine rice and eggplant. **Known for:** friendly service; back patio with central fountain. $ *Average main:* $25 ⊠ *487 1st St. W, at W. Napa St.* ☎ *707/933–8160* ⊕ *www.harvestmooncafesonoma.com* ☾ *Closed Tues. No lunch.*

$$$$
PORTUGUESE
Fodor's Choice
★

✕ **LaSalette Restaurant.** Born in the Azores and raised in Sonoma, chef-owner Manuel Azevedo serves three- and five-course prix-fixe meals inspired by his native Portugal. The wood-oven-roasted fish is always worth trying, and there are usually boldly flavored lamb and pork dishes, along with soups, stews, salted cod, and other hearty fare. **Known for:** authentic Portuguese cuisine; sophisticated spicing; olive-oil cake with queijo fresco (fresh cheese) ice cream. $ *Average main:* $55 ⊠ *452 1st St. E, near E. Spain St.* ☎ *707/938–1927* ⊕ *www. lasalette-restaurant.com.*

$$$$
MODERN
AMERICAN

✕ **Oso Sonoma.** Chef David Bush, who achieved national recognition for his food pairings at St. Francis Winery, owns this barlike small-plates restaurant whose menu evolves throughout the day. Lunch might see mole braised pork-shoulder tacos or an achiote chicken sandwich, with dinner fare perhaps of steamed mussels, harissa roasted salmon, or roasted forest mushrooms with baby spinach and polenta. **Known for:** bar menu between lunch and dinner; Korean soju cocktails; decor of reclaimed materials. $ *Average main:* $32 ⊠ *9 E. Napa St., at Broadway* ☎ *707/931–6926* ⊕ *www.ososonoma. com* ☾ *No lunch Mon.–Wed.*

$$$$
AMERICAN

✕ **Santé.** This elegant dining room developed into a destination restaurant by focusing on seasonal local ingredients. Dishes like the risotto appetizer with black truffles, Parmigiano-Reggiano cheese, and white-truffle foam recently spotted on the à la carte menu are sophisticated without being fussy, but the tasting menu's Wagyu beef sampler and other plates represent pure decadence. **Known for:** chef's tasting menu; excellent wines. $ *Average main:* $43 ⊠ *Fairmont Sonoma Mission Inn & Spa, 100 Boyes Blvd./Hwy. 12, 2½ miles north of Sonoma Plaza* ☎ *707/938–9000* ⊕ *www.santediningroom.com* ☾ *No lunch.*

$
AMERICAN

✕ **Sunflower Caffé.** Cheerful art and brightly painted walls set a jolly tone at this casual eatery whose assets include sidewalk seating with Sonoma Plaza views and the verdant patio out back. Omelets and waffles are the hits at breakfast, with the smoked duck breast sandwich, served on a baguette and slathered with caramelized onions, a favorite for lunch. **Known for:** combination café, gallery, and wine bar; local cheeses and hearty soups; free Wi-Fi. $ *Average main:* $13 ⊠ *421 1st St. W, at W. Spain St.* ☎ *707/996–6645* ⊕ *www.sonomasunflower.com* ☾ *No dinner.*

$
PORTUGUESE

✕ **Tasca Tasca Portuguese Tapas Restaurant & Wine Bar.** Late-night Sonoma dining—or nibbling, given the portion sizes—received a boost when Azores-born chef Manuel Azevedo opened this retro-contempo tavern dedicated to Portuguese small bites. Dividing his menu into five parts—Cheese, Garden, Sea, Land, Sweet—Azevedo, who also owns the nearby restaurant LaSalette, serves everything from hearty *caldo verde* stew, foie gras, and salted codfish cakes to São Jorge cheese topped with marmalade. **Known for:** Portuguese wines; dessert mousses and sorbets; good for lunch, open late. [$] *Average main: $15* ✉ *122 W. Napa St., near 1st St. W* ☎ *707/996–8272* 🌐 *www.tascatasca.com.*

WHERE TO STAY

$$$ RENTAL **Auberge Sonoma.** If you are traveling in a group of three or four, or just prefer lodgings that feel more like home, consider the two-bedroom suites at this charmer just off Sonoma Plaza. **Pros:** good value for couples traveling together; beautifully appointed; close to Sonoma Plaza shops, restaurants, and tasting rooms. **Cons:** two-night minimum (three on summer weekends). [$] *Rooms from: $360* ✉ *151 E. Napa St.* ☎ *707/939–5670 voice mail* 🌐 *www.aubergesonoma.com* 🛏 *3 rooms* 🍴 *No meals.*

$$ HOTEL **Best Western Sonoma Valley Inn.** A low(er)-budget option just off Sonoma Plaza, this motel has inviting, if not elegant, public areas, and the staff aim to please. **Pros:** good value; complimentary continental breakfast; within walking distance of Sonoma Plaza shops and restaurants; wine-tasting coupons; pool. **Cons:** small fitness center; public areas nicer than the rooms; convention facilities and rooms in front can be noisy; could use a remodel. [$] *Rooms from: $269* ✉ *550 2nd St. W* ☎ *800/334–5784, 707/938–9200* 🌐 *www.sonomavalleyinn.com* 🛏 *80 rooms* 🍴 *Breakfast.*

$$ B&B/INN Fodor's Choice ★ **Cottage Inn & Spa.** Delivering romance, relaxation, and Zen-like tranquillity is the innkeepers' goal at this courtyard complex 1½ blocks north of Sonoma Plaza. **Pros:** convenient yet quiet location; serene style; morning pastries and fresh-cut flowers; four suites with double Jacuzzi tubs. **Cons:** books up far ahead from late spring to early fall. [$] *Rooms from: $275* ✉ *310 1st St. E* ☎ *707/996–0719* 🌐 *www.cottageinnandspa.com* 🛏 *9 rooms* 🍴 *Breakfast.*

$$ HOTEL **El Dorado Hotel.** Guest rooms in this remodeled 1843 building strike a rustic-contemporary pose with their Restoration Hardware furnishings and new beds, but the Mexican-tile floors hint at Sonoma's Mission-era past. **Pros:** stylish for the price; on-site El Dorado Kitchen restaurant; handsome breakfast space; central location. **Cons:** rooms are small; street noise audible in some rooms. [$] *Rooms from: $250* ✉ *405 1st St. W* ☎ *707/996–3030* 🌐 *www.eldoradosonoma.com* 🛏 *27 rooms* 🍴 *No meals.*

$$ HOTEL **El Pueblo Inn.** A giant pepper tree and a few palms tower over the garden courtyard of this motel run by the third generation of the family that opened it in 1959. **Pros:** tree-shaded courtyard; festive pool area; thoughtful service; winery passes. **Cons:** basic decor; street noise an issue in some rooms; several blocks west of Sonoma Plaza. [$] *Rooms from: $204* ✉ *896 W. Napa St., off Hwy. 12 near Riverside Dr.* ☎ *707/996–3651* 🌐 *www.elpuebloinn.com* 🛏 *54 rooms* 🍴 *Breakfast.*

$$$ RESORT **Fairmont Sonoma Mission Inn & Spa.** The real draw at this Mission-style resort is the extensive spa with its array of massages and treatments, some designed for couples. **Pros:** enormous spa; destination restaurant; free shuttle to downtown. **Cons:** standard rooms on the smaller side; lacks intimacy of other similarly priced options. [$] *Rooms from: $399* ✉ *100*

Boyes Blvd./Hwy. 12, 2½ miles north of Sonoma Plaza ☏ *707/938–9000* ⊕ *www.fairmont.com/sonoma* ⟿ *226 rooms* ⭘ *No meals.*

$$
B&B/INN

☷ **Inn at Sonoma.** They don't skimp on the little luxuries here: wine and hors d'oeuvres are served every evening in the lobby, and the cheerfully painted rooms are warmed by gas fireplaces. **Pros:** last-minute specials are a great deal; free soda available in the lobby. **Cons:** on a busy street rather than right on the plaza. $ *Rooms from: $220* ⊠ *630 Broadway* ☏ *707/939–1340, 888/568–9818* ⊕ *www.innatsonoma.com* ⟿ *27 rooms* ⭘ *Breakfast.*

$$$
HOTEL
Fodor's Choice
★

☷ **MacArthur Place Hotel & Spa.** Guests at this 7-acre boutique property five blocks south of Sonoma Plaza bask in ritzy seclusion in plush accommodations set amid landscaped gardens. **Pros:** secluded garden setting; high-style furnishings; on-site steak house. **Cons:** a bit of a walk from the plaza; some traffic noise audible in street-side rooms. $ *Rooms from: $399* ⊠ *29 E. MacArthur St.* ☏ *707/938–2929, 800/722–1866* ⊕ *www.macarthurplace.com* ⟿ *64 rooms* ⭘ *Breakfast.*

$
B&B/INN
FAMILY

☷ **Sonoma Creek Inn.** The small but cheerful rooms at this motel-style inn are individually decorated with painted wooden armoires, cozy quilts, and brightly colored contemporary artwork. **Pros:** clean, well-lighted bathrooms; lots of charm for the price; popular with bicyclists. **Cons:** office not staffed 24 hours a day; a 10-minute drive from Sonoma Plaza. $ *Rooms from: $145* ⊠ *239 Boyes Blvd., off Hwy. 12* ☏ *707/939–9463, 888/712–1289* ⊕ *www.sonomacreekinn.com* ⟿ *16 rooms* ⭘ *No meals.*

NIGHTLIFE AND PERFORMING ARTS

On or near Sonoma Plaza, the full bars at El Dorado Kitchen and the Swiss Hotel are good bets, as are Tasca Tasca (for wine and beer) and Sigh (for sparkling wines). On Tuesday nights in summer, check out the evening farmers' market in the plaza.

Sigh. From the oval bar and walls the color of a fine Blanc de Blancs to retro chandeliers that mimic Champagne bubbles, everything about this sparkling-wine bar's frothy new space—it originally opened nearby in 2012—screams "have a good time." That owner Jayme Powers and her posse are trained in the fine art of *sabrage* (opening a sparkler with a saber) only adds to the festivity. ■ **TIP**➜ **Sigh opens at 11 am, so it's a good daytime stop, too.** ⊠ *120 W. Napa St., at 1st St. W* ☏ *707/996–2444* ⊕ *www.sighsonoma.com.*

Swiss Hotel. Old-timers head to the hotel's old-timey bar for a blast of Glariffee, a cold and potent cousin to Irish coffee that loosens the tongue. ⊠ *18 W. Spain St., at 1st St. W* ☏ *707/938–2884* ⊕ *www.swisshotelsonoma.com.*

Valley of the Moon Certified Farmers' Market. With live music, food vendors, and wine and beers poured, Tuesday Night on Sonoma Plaza (from 5:30 to sunset, May to October) is as much a block party as a chance to buy produce. It's a good place to chat up the locals. ⊠ *Sonoma Plaza, 453 1st St. E, at E. Napa St.* ☏ *707/694–3611* ⊕ *www.sonomaplazamarket.org* ⬗ *Free.*

SHOPPING

G's General Store. The inventory of this "modern general store" runs the gamut from cute bunny LED nightlights and Euro-suave kitchen utensils to bright-print shirts and a log-and-leather sofa fit for a ski chalet. The owner used to buy for Smith & Hawken and Williams-Sonoma, so expect upscale merch presented with style. ✉ *19 W. Napa St., near Broadway* ☎ *707/933–8082* ⊕ *www.ggeneralstore.com.*

Fodor'sChoice ★ **Sonoma Valley Certified Farmers Market.** To discover just how bountiful the Sonoma landscape is—and how talented its farmers and food artisans are—head to Depot Park, just north of the Sonoma Plaza, on Friday morning. This market is considered Sonoma County's best. ✉ *Depot Park, 1st St. W, at the Sonoma Bike Path* ☎ *707/538–7023* ⊕ *www.svcfm.org.*

Vella Cheese Company. North and east of Sonoma Plaza, this Italian cheese shop has been making superb cheeses, including raw-milk cheddars and several varieties of jack, since 1931. A bonus: plenty of free samples. ✉ *315 2nd St. E, ½ block north of E. Spain St.* ☎ *707/938–3232, 800/848–0505* ⊕ *vellacheese.com* ☾ *Closed Sun.*

SPAS

Willow Stream Spa at Fairmont Sonoma Mission Inn & Spa. With 40,000 square feet and 30 treatment rooms, the Wine Country's largest spa provides every amenity you could possibly want, including pools and hot tubs fed by local thermal springs. Although the place fills with patrons in summer and on some weekends, the vibe is always soothing. The signature bathing ritual includes an exfoliating shower, dips in two mineral-water soaking pools, an herbal steam, and a dry-salt sauna and rain tunnel. The regime draws to a close with cool-down showers. Other popular treatments involve alkaline baths, aloe-gel wraps, and massages in styles from Swedish to Thai. For a touch of the exotic designed to leave your skin luminous, try a caviar facial. The most requested room among couples is outfitted with a two-person copper bathtub. ✉ *100 Boyes Blvd./Hwy. 12, 2½ miles north of Sonoma Plaza* ☎ *707/938–9000* ⊕ *www.fairmont.com/sonoma/willow-stream* ⬚ *Treatments $65–$528.*

SPORTS AND THE OUTDOORS

Sonoma Valley Bike Tours. Just a mile south of Sonoma Plaza, this Napa Valley Bike Tours offshoot rents bikes, conducts guided bicycle tours of wineries, and has a self-guided-tour option. ✉ *1245 Broadway, at Woodworth La.* ☎ *707/996–2453* ⊕ *sonomavalleybiketours.com* ⬚ *Bike rentals from $30 for 2 hrs, guided tours from $144, self-guided tour $108.*

Wine Country Cyclery. You can rent comfort/hybrid, tandem, and road bikes by the hour or the day at this mellow shop west of the plaza. ✉ *262 W. Napa St., at 3rd St. W* ☎ *707/996–6800* ⊕ *winecountrycyclery.com* ⬚ *From $10 per hr, $30 per day.*

GLEN ELLEN

7 miles north of Sonoma.

Craggy Glen Ellen epitomizes the difference between the Napa and Sonoma valleys. Whereas small Napa towns like St. Helena get their charm from upscale boutiques and restaurants lined up along well-groomed sidewalks, Glen Ellen's crooked streets are shaded with stands of old oak trees and occasionally bisected by the Sonoma and Calabasas creeks. Tucked among the trees of a narrow canyon, where Sonoma Mountain and the Mayacamas pinch in the valley floor, Glen Ellen looks more like a town of the Sierra foothills gold country than a Wine Country village.

Wine has been part of Glen Ellen since the 1840s, when a French immigrant, Joshua Chauvet, planted grapes and later built a winery and the valley's first distillery. Machinery at the winery was powered by steam, and boilers were fueled with wood from local oaks. Other valley farmers followed Chauvet's example, and grape growing took off, although Prohibition took its toll on most of these operations. Today dozens of wineries in the area beg to be visited, but sometimes it's hard not to succumb to Glen Ellen's slow pace and simply lounge poolside at your lodging or linger over a leisurely picnic. The renowned cook and food writer M.F.K. Fisher, who lived and worked in Glen Ellen for 22 years until her death in 1992, would surely have approved. Hunter S. Thompson, who lived here for a spell before he became famous might not: he found the place too sedate. Glen Ellen's most famous resident, however, was Jack London, who epitomized the town's rugged spirit.

GETTING HERE AND AROUND

To get to Glen Ellen from Sonoma, drive west on Spain Street. After about a mile, take Highway 12 for 7 miles to Arnold Drive, which deposits you in the middle of town. Many of Glen Ellen's restaurants and inns are along a half-mile stretch of Arnold Drive. Sonoma Transit Bus 30 and Bus 38 serve Glen Ellen from Sonoma and Kenwood.

EXPLORING

TOP ATTRACTIONS

Fodor's Choice ★ **Benziger Family Winery.** One of the best-known Sonoma County wineries sits on a sprawling estate in a bowl with 360-degree sun exposure, the benefits of which are explored on tram tours that depart several times daily. Guides explain Benziger's biodynamic farming practices and provide a glimpse of the extensive cave system. The regular tram tour costs $25; another tour costing $50 concludes with a seated tasting. Known for Chardonnay, Cabernet Sauvignon, Merlot, Pinot Noir, and Sauvignon Blanc, the winery is a beautiful spot for a picnic. ■ TIP→ Reserve a seat on the tram tour through the winery's website or arrive early in the day on summer weekends and during harvest season. ⊠ *1883 London Ranch Rd., off Arnold Dr.* ☎ *707/935–3000, 888/490–2739* ⊕ *www. benziger.com* ✍ *Tastings $20–$40, tours $25–$50.*

Fodor's Choice ★ **Jack London State Historic Park.** The pleasures are pastoral and intellectual at author Jack London's beloved Beauty Ranch. You could easily spend the afternoon hiking some of the 30-plus miles of trails that loop through meadows and stands of oaks, redwoods, and other trees. Manuscripts and personal artifacts depicting London's travels are on view at the House of Happy Walls Museum, which provides an overview of the writer's life and literary passions. A short hike away lie the ruins of Wolf House, which burned down just before London was to move in. Also open to visitors are a few outbuildings and the restored Cottage, a wood-framed building where he penned many of his later works. He's buried on the property. ■ TIP→ Well-known performers headline the park's Broadway Under the Stars series, a hot ticket in summer. ⊠ *2400 London Ranch Rd., off Arnold Dr.* ☎ *707/938–5216* ⊕ *www.jacklondonpark.com* ☜ *Parking $10 ($5 walk-in or bike), includes admission to museum; cottage $4.*

Korbin Kameron Tasting Room. This winery with vineyards up 2,200 feet in the Mayacamas Mountains has a Glen Ellen address and a downtown tasting room, but the 186-acre property (10% planted to grapes) straddles the Sonoma and Napa valleys. At that elevation, well above the fog line, Bordeaux varietals like Cabernet Sauvignon, Merlot, and Cabernet Franc thrive in the rocky, volcanic soils, producing fruit with intense flavors and rockin' tannins. (If the word "brambly" in tasting notes perplexes you, the wines here are textbook examples.) You can sample current releases for $20, but for an inkling of how well these wines age, opt for the $35 tasting of several Cabernet vintages. ■ TIP→ Grapevines can't tell the difference between Napa and Sonoma. These are classic Mt. Veeder wines at Sonoma prices. ⊠ *13647 Arnold Dr., at Carquinez Ave.* ☎ *707/935–3888* ⊕ *www.korbinkameron.com* ☜ *Tastings $20–$35* ☉ *Closed Tues. and Wed.*

Lasseter Family Winery. Immaculately groomed grapevines dazzle the eye at John and Nancy Lasseter's secluded winery, and it's no accident: Phil Coturri, Sonoma Valley's premier organic and biodynamic vineyard manager, tends them. Even the landscaping, which includes an insectary to attract beneficial bugs, is meticulously maintained. Come harvesttime, winemaker Julia Lantosca oversees gentle processes that transform the fruit into wines of purity and grace: a Semillon–Sauvignon Blanc blend, two rosés, and Bordeaux and Rhône reds. As might be expected of a storyteller as accomplished as John, whose screenwriting credits include *Toy Story*, *Cars*, and other Pixar features, evocative labels illustrate the tale behind each wine. These stories are well told on tours that precede tastings of wines, paired with local artisanal cheeses, in an elegant room whose east-facing window frames vineyard and Mayacamas Mountains views. All visits are by appointment only. ⊠ *1 Vintage La., off Dunbar Rd.* ☎ *707/933–2814* ⊕ *www.lasseterfamilywinery.com* ☜ *Tastings (some with tours) $25–$45.*

Laurel Glen Vineyard. As a longtime wine-industry marketing director, Bettina Sichel knew the potential pitfalls of winery ownership, but when she discovered a uniquely situated volcanic-soiled Sonoma Mountain vineyard for sale, she plunged in enthusiastically. Because her 14 acres of Cabernet Sauvignon vines face east, the mountain shelters the grapes from hot late-afternoon sun and excessively cool Pacific influences. Sichel's impressive wine-making team includes Phil Coturri, an organic farming expert *Wine Spectator* magazine calls the "Wizard of Green," and winemaker Randall Watkins. Their efforts yield a complex estate

Benziger tram tours take to the fields to show biodynamic farming techniques in action.

Cabernet commanding nearly $40 a glass at posh big-city restaurants because it's *that* good. You can taste it, along with Counterpoint Cabernet and other small-lot wines from the same vineyard, with an appointment at Sichel's industrial-chic tasting room in downtown Glen Ellen. ✉ *969 Carquinez Ave., east of Arnold Dr.* ☎ *707/933–9877* ⊕ *www. laurelglen.com* 🍷 *Tastings $20–$50.*

NEED A BREAK

Horatius. The affable Horatio Gomes opened this natty, light-filled pit stop for pastries, soups, salads, sandwiches, desserts, beer, wine, and nitrogen-laced coffee. An offshoot of sorts of a successful event space he operated in San Francisco, it has the potential to evolve into a magnet for low-key performing arts activities. **Known for:** outdoor patio; great use of historic winery space; free Wi-Fi. ✉ *Jack London Village, 14301 Arnold Dr., ¾ mile south of downtown* ☎ *707/934–8496* ⊕ *www.horatius.com.*

Loxton Cellars. Back in the day when tasting rooms were low-tech and the winemaker often poured the wines, the winery experience unfolded pretty much the way it does at Loxton Cellars today. The personable Australia-born owner, Chris Loxton, who's on hand many days, crafts Zinfandels, Syrahs, and a Cabernet Sauvignon, all quite good, and some regulars swear by the delicate Pinot Noir from Russian River Valley grapes and the seductively smooth Syrah Port. You can sample a few current releases without an appointment, but one is needed to taste library- and limited-release wines. ■ TIP→ To learn more about Loxton's wine-making philosophy and practices, book a tour ($25), which is followed by a seated tasting. ✉ *11466 Dunbar Rd., at Hwy. 12* ☎ *707/935–7221* ⊕ *www.loxtonwines. com* 🍷 *Tastings $10–$20, tour $25.*

WORTH NOTING

B.R. Cohn. Classic-rock fans acknowledge this Glen Ellen winery's musical chops—Bruce Cohn, the longtime manager of the Doobie Brothers, founded it in 1984—but the enological pedigree is equally noteworthy: the first winemaker was the now-famous consultant Helen Turley, and Pinot Noir specialist Merry Edwards followed her. The wines, still crafted in Turley's fruit-forward style (by Marco DiGiulio since 2015) include Sauvignon Blanc, Chardonnay, and Riesling whites, and Cabernet Sauvignon, Malbec, and Zinfandel reds. A 1920s residence was expanded to create the tasting room, which bustles on most weekend afternoons. ■TIP➜ A gourmet shop near the patio outside the tasting room sells olive oil from the property's 19th-century olive trees, along with vinegars and other food items. ⊠ *15000 Sonoma Hwy./Hwy. 12, ½ mile north of Madrone Rd.* ☎ *707/938-4064* ⊕ *brcohn.com* ✉ *Tastings $20–$40.*

Quarryhill Botanical Garden. For three decades the late founder of this research botanical garden and her successors have journeyed to East Asia to collect the seeds of rare trees and plants with the goal of preserving them before they become extinct. The low-key facility, which takes its name from the quarry that once operated here, exhibits these plants on 25 acres little over a mile north of downtown Glen Ellen. There's also a heritage rose garden near the entrance. The colors at Quarryhill are the most vibrant in spring, but year-round a visit here makes for a pleasant break from wine touring. ⊠ *12841 Hwy. 12, ¼ mile north of Arnold Dr.* ☎ *707/996-3166* ⊕ *www.quarryhillbg.org* ✉ *$12.*

WHERE TO EAT

$$
ITALIAN
Fodor's Choice
★

✕ **Aventine Glen Ellen.** A Wine Country cousin to chef Adolfo Veronese's same-named San Francisco and Hollywood establishments, this Italian restaurant occupies an 1839 sawmill from California's Mexican period. Veronese's varied menu includes several pizzas (the seasonal one with black truffle honey, béchamel, and wild arugula is a savory masterpiece), an equal number of pasta dishes, a daily risotto, and several meat and fish entrées. **Known for:** chicken parmigiana the envy of local Sicilian grandmothers; outdoor patio overlooking Sonoma Creek. $ *Average main: $20* ⊠ *Jack London Village, 14301 Arnold Dr., ¾ mile south of downtown* ☎ *707/934-8911* ⊕ *www.aventinehospitality.com/ glen-ellen* ⊗ *Closed Mon. and Tues.*

$$
FRENCH

✕ **The Fig Cafe.** The compact menu at this cheerful bistro, a Glen Ellen fixture, focuses on California and French comfort food—pot roast and duck confit, for instance, as well as thin-crust pizza. Steamed mussels are served with crispy fries, which also accompany the sirloin burger, and weekend brunch brings out locals and tourists for French toast, corned-beef hash, and pizza with applewood-smoked bacon and poached eggs. **Known for:** casual ambience; no corkage fee, so good for enjoying your winery discoveries. $ *Average main: $18* ⊠ *13690 Arnold Dr., at O'Donnell La.* ☎ *707/938-2130* ⊕ *www.thefigcafe.com* ⊗ *No lunch weekdays.*

4

Jack London Country

The rugged, rakish author and adventurer Jack London is perhaps best known for his travels to Alaska and his exploits in the Pacific, which he immortalized in tales such as *The Call of the Wild, White Fang,* and *South Sea Tales.* But he loved no place so well as the hills of eastern Sonoma County, where he spent most of his thirties and where he died in 1916 at the age of 40.

Between 1905 and 1916 London bought seven parcels of land totaling 1,400 acres, which he dubbed Beauty Ranch. When he wasn't off traveling, he dedicated most of his time to cultivating the land and raising livestock. He also maintained a few acres of wine grapes for his personal use.

DREAMS AND MYSTERIES
In 1913, London rhapsodized about his beloved ranch near Glen Ellen, writing, "The grapes on a score of rolling hills are red with autumn flame. Across Sonoma Mountain wisps of sea fog are stealing. The afternoon sun smolders in the drowsy sky. I have everything to make me glad I am alive. I am filled with dreams and mysteries."

Much of Beauty Ranch is now preserved as Jack London State Historic Park, worth visiting not only for its museum and other glimpses into London's life but also for the trails that skirt vineyards and meander through a forest of Douglas fir, coastal redwoods, oak, and madrones. London and his wife spent two years here constructing their dream home, Wolf House, before it burned down one hot August night in 1913, just days before they were scheduled to move in. A look at the remaining stone walls and fireplaces gives you a sense of the building's grand scale. Within, a fireproof basement vault was to hold London's manuscripts. Elsewhere in the park stands the unusually posh pigsty that London's neighbors called the Pig Palace.

LEGACY VINEYARDS
Parts of Beauty Ranch are still owned by London's descendants, from whom Kenwood Vineyards leases and farms legacy vineyards producing Cabernet Sauvignon, Merlot, Syrah, and Zinfandel. The wines from Beauty Ranch are among the winery's best.

$$$
ECLECTIC
Fodor'sChoice
★

✕**Glen Ellen Star.** Chef Ari Weiswasser honed his craft at The French Laundry, Daniel, and other bastions of culinary finesse, but at his Wine Country boîte he prepares haute-rustic cuisine, much of it emerging from a wood-fired oven that burns a steady 600°F. Crisp-crusted, richly sauced Margherita and other pizzas thrive in the torrid heat, as do tender whole fish entrées and vegetables roasted in small iron skillets. **Known for:** kitchen-view counter for watching chefs cook; enclosed patio; Weiswasser's sauces, emulsions, and spices. $ *Average main: $28* ✉ *13648 Arnold Dr., at Warm Springs Rd.* ☎ *707/343–1384* ⊕ *glenellenstar.com* ⊗ *No lunch.*

$$$
INDIAN

✕**Yeti Restaurant.** Glen Ellen's finer restaurants all emphasize seasonal local produce, but instead of riffs on French, Italian, or California styles, the farm-to-table creations at Yeti fuse Indian and Himalayan cuisine. Start with samosas or tomato-based Himalayan pepper pot soup from Nepal—so warming on a chilly day—then proceed to curries, sizzling tandooris, or chicken, prawn, or vegetable biryanis upon ethereally aromatic saffron basmati rice. **Known for:** deck overlooking Sonoma Creek; international beer selection; smart wine choices at all price points. $ *Average main: $26* ✉ *Jack London Village, 14301 Arnold Dr., ¾ mile south of downtown* ☎ *707/996–9930* ⊕ *www.yetirestaurant.com.*

WHERE TO STAY

$$
B&B/INN

Beltane Ranch. On a slope of the Mayacamas range with gorgeous Sonoma Valley views, this 1892 ranch house shaded by ancient oak trees contains charmingly old-fashioned rooms, each individually decorated with antiques and original artworks. **Pros:** casual, friendly atmosphere; reasonable prices; beautiful grounds with ancient oak trees; working ranch, vineyard, and winery; owned by the same family for six generations. **Cons:** downstairs rooms get some noise from upstairs rooms; ceiling fans instead of air-conditioning. $ *Rooms from: $215* ✉ *11775 Sonoma Hwy./Hwy. 12* ☎ *707/833–4233* ⊕ *www.beltaneranch.com* ⤳ *6 rooms* ⦿| *Breakfast.*

$$
B&B/INN
Fodor'sChoice
★

Gaige House. Asian objets d'art and leather club chairs cozied up to the lobby fireplace are just a few of the graceful touches in this luxurious but understated bed-and-breakfast. **Pros:** beautiful lounge areas; lots of privacy; excellent service; full breakfasts, afternoon wine and appetizers. **Cons:** sound carries in the main house; the least expensive rooms are on the small side. $ *Rooms from: $275* ✉ *13540 Arnold Dr.* ☎ *707/935–0237, 800/935–0237* ⊕ *www.gaige.com* ⤳ *23 rooms* ⦿| *Breakfast.*

$$
B&B/INN
Fodor'sChoice
★

Olea Hotel. The husband-and-wife team of Ashish and Sia Patel operate this boutique lodging that's at once sophisticated and down-home country casual. **Pros:** beautiful style; welcoming staff; chef-prepared breakfasts; complimentary wine throughout stay. **Cons:** fills up quickly on weekends; minor road noise in some rooms. $ *Rooms from: $288* ✉ *5131 Warm Springs Rd., west off Arnold Dr.* ☎ *707/996–5131* ⊕ *www.oleahotel.com* ⤳ *15 rooms* ⦿| *Breakfast.*

KENWOOD

4 miles north of Glen Ellen.

Tiny Kenwood consists of little more than a few restaurants, shops, tasting rooms, and a historic train depot, now used for private events. But hidden in this pretty landscape of meadows and woods at the north end of Sonoma Valley are several good wineries, most just off the Sonoma Highway. Varietals grown here at the foot of the Sugarloaf Mountains include Sauvignon Blanc, Chardonnay, Zinfandel, and Cabernet Sauvignon.

GETTING HERE AND AROUND

To get to Kenwood from Glen Ellen, head northeast on Arnold Drive and north on Highway 12. Sonoma Transit Bus 30 and Bus 38 serve Kenwood from Glen Ellen and Sonoma.

EXPLORING

TOP ATTRACTIONS

B Wise Vineyards Cellar. The stylish roadside tasting room of this producer of small-lot reds sits on the valley floor, but B Wise's winery and vineyards occupy a prime spot high in the Moon Mountain District AVA. B Wise made its name crafting big, bold Cabernets. One comes from owner Brion Wise's mountain estate and another from the nearby Monte Rosso Vineyard, some of whose Cabernet vines are among California's oldest. These hearty mountain-fruit Cabs contrast with a suppler one from the Napa Valley's Coombsville AVA. Mark Herold, known for several cult wines, makes the Cabernets with Massimo Monticelli, who's responsible for the rest of the uniformly excellent lineup: Sonoma Coast Chardonnay; Russian River Valley, Sonoma Coast, and Willamette Valley (Oregon) Pinot Noir; and estate Syrah, Petite Sirah, Petit Verdot, and Zinfandel. ⊠ *9077 Sonoma Hwy., at Shaw Ave.* ☎ *707/282–9169* ⊕ *www.bwisevineyards.com* ☕ *Tasting $20.*

Chateau St. Jean. At the foot of the Mayacamas Mountains stretch the impeccably groomed grounds of Chateau St. Jean, an old-country estate. After a spin around the gardens, whose style harmonizes with the sprawling Mediterranean-style villa, step inside for a tasting of Chardonnay, Fumé Blanc, Pinot Gris, and other fine whites, along with reds that include Pinot Noir, Cabernet Sauvignon, Merlot, and Syrah. Picnicking is allowed in several areas; you can bring your own food or purchase cheese and charcuterie on-site. Some tastings are by appointment. ⊠ *8555 Sonoma Hwy./Hwy. 12* ☎ *707/257–5784* ⊕ *www.chateaustjean.com* ☕ *Tastings $15–$75.*

Kunde Estate Winery & Vineyards. On your way into Kunde you pass a terrace flanked by fountains, virtually coaxing you to stay for a picnic with views over the vineyard. Family owned for more than a century, Kunde prides itself on producing 100% estate wines from its 1,850-acre property, which rises 1,400 feet from the valley floor. Kunde's whites include several Chardonnays and a Sauvignon Blanc, with Cabernet Sauvignon, Merlot, and a Zinfandel from 1880s vines among the reds. Two wines of note available only through the winery, both in the Destination Series, are the Red Dirt Red blend of seven varietals and the Dunfillan Cuvée, made from Cabernet and Syrah grapes. ■ TIP→ Make a reservation for the Mountain Top Tasting, a tour by luxury van that ends with a sampling of reserve wines. ⊠ *9825 Sonoma Hwy./Hwy. 12* ☎ *707/833–5501* ⊕ *www.kunde.com* ☕ *Tastings $15–$50, Mountain Top Tasting $50, grounds and cave tour free.*

Landmark Vineyards. High-quality Chardonnays have always been Landmark's claim to fame, led by the flagship Overlook wine, with grapes from multiple vineyards going into each vintage. The winery also makes several single-vineyard Chardonnays, including ones from Rodgers Creek (Sonoma Coast) and Lorenzo Vineyard (Russian River Valley). Landmark's other specialty is Pinot Noir. As with the Chardonnays, there's an Overlook Pinot Noir using grapes from multiple sources, and winemaker Greg Stach crafts several single-vineyard wines, among them the highly praised Sonoma Coast Grand

Detour Pinot Noir. Stop here to sample wines, relax in the landscaped picnic area, and play a game of boccie ball with the craggy Mayacamas Mountains and Sugarloaf Ridge forming the backdrop. The estate tour and tasting is by appointment only. ■TIP➔ **On Saturday afternoon from mid-spring to early fall, you can tour the vineyards in a horse-drawn carriage.** ✉ *101 Adobe Canyon Rd., at Hwy. 12* ☎ *707/833–0053* ⊕ *www.landmarkwine.com* 🖫 *Tastings $15–$40, estate tour and tasting $35, carriage tour free.*

St. Francis Winery. Nestled at the foot of Mt. Hood, St. Francis has earned national acclaim for its wine and food pairings. With its red-tile roof and bell tower and views of the Mayacamas Mountains just to the east, the winery's California Mission–style visitor center occupies one of Sonoma County's most scenic locations. The charm of the surroundings is matched by the mostly red wines, including rich, earthy Zinfandels from the Dry Creek, Russian River, and Sonoma valleys. Chef Bryan Jones's five-course small bites and wine pairings ($68)—Liberty duck breast cassoulet with one of the Zins, for example—are offered from Thursday through Monday; pairings with cheeses and charcuterie ($35) are available daily. ✉ *100 Pythian Rd., off Hwy. 12* ☎ *888/675–9463, 707/833–0242* ⊕ *www.stfranciswinery.com* 🖫 *Tastings $15–$68.*

WORTH NOTING

Deerfield Ranch Winery. The focus at Deerfield is on producing "clean wines"—low in histamines and sulfites—the better to eliminate the headaches and allergic reactions some red-wine drinkers experience. Winemaker Robert Rex accomplishes this goal with no loss of flavor or complexity. Deerfield wines are bold and fruit-forward, with a long finish. The lush DRX and Meritage Bordeaux-style red blends invite contemplation about the vineyards, weather, and wine-making skills involved in their creation. To sip these and other wines, including a finely tuned blend of four white grapes, you walk deep into a 23,000-square-foot cave for a seated tasting in a relaxed, loungelike space. ■TIP➔ **Standard tastings ($15) include five wines; for an additional $5, you can sample more, including at least one older, library wine.** ✉ *10200 Sonoma Hwy./Hwy. 12* ☎ *707/833–5215* ⊕ *www.deerfieldranch.com* 🖫 *Tastings $15–$25.*

Kenwood Vineyards. The best of the Kenwood wines—Cabernet Sauvignons, Zinfandels, Syrahs, and Merlots—are made from Sonoma Mountain AVA grapes the winery farms on the author Jack London's old vineyard. Kenwood, established in 1970, is best known for these wines, its widely distributed Sauvignon Blanc, and the Artist Series Cabernet Sauvignon, named for the artworks commissioned for the labels. Collectively the Kenwood wines, made since 2003 by Pat Henderson, a protégé of the winery's locally beloved founder, the late Mike Lee, represent a survey of notable Sonoma County appellations and vineyards. A new tasting room is planned for a knoll with views across the estate; until its completion, tastings will take place in a redwood barn in which the property's original vintners began making wine in 1906. ✉ *9592 Sonoma Hwy./Hwy. 12* ☎ *707/282–4228* ⊕ *www.kenwoodvineyards. com* 🖫 *Tastings $15–$25.*

Ledson Winery & Vineyards. The outrageously ornate Normandy-style castle visible from the highway was intended as winery owner Steve Ledson's family home when construction began in 1989, but this 16,000-square-foot space has always been a hospitality center. Pourers stationed amid a warren of tasting spaces introduce guests to the several dozen largely single-varietal wines Ledson makes, everything from Zinfandel and Cabernet Sauvignon to Rhône varietals such as Syrah and Mourvèdre. **TIP→ The on-site market sells salads, sandwiches, artisanal cheeses, and other edibles you can enjoy on the picnic grounds here (no outside food, though).** ✉ *7335 Sonoma Hwy./Hwy. 12* ☎ *707/537–3810* 🌐 *www.ledson.com* 🎟 *Tastings $20–$50.*

Ty Caton Vineyards. In the late 1990s, when Ty Caton began planting Cabernet Sauvignon and other vines on his parents' 108-acre Moon Mountain property, the area hadn't yet received AVA designation, but he sensed that wines with flavors achievable nowhere else could be coaxed from this land. Time has proven him right. Caton makes 11 Cabernets from specific sections of the estate, along with small lots of Malbec, Merlot, Petite Sirah, and Syrah. These four grapes plus Cabernet and Petit Verdot go into his flagship Tytanium, a wine he feels best expresses what's special about his family's vineyard. You can sample Caton's wines—he also makes a Russian River Chardonnay and rosé of Syrah—at a valley-floor tasting room in Kenwood known for its convivial vibe. ✉ *8910 Sonoma Hwy./Hwy. 12, at Greene St.* ☎ *707/938–3224* 🌐 *www.tycaton.com* 🎟 *Tastings $15–$25.*

VJB Cellars. This Tuscan-inspired courtyard marketplace with tasting spaces and food shops is a fine spot to sip wines, enjoy a pizza or a deli sandwich, and just relax. Mostly from Italian varietals, some rare in these parts, the wines are, like the complex, less rustic than in the old country and clearly adapted for contemporary American tastes. This isn't always a bad thing, and the best vintages—the Barbera, the Sangiovese, and the especially the Montepulciano—are lively and clean on the palate. Reservations are required for seated tastings. **TIP→ For gourmet dolci, check out Wine Truffle Boutique, which sells chocolates, Italian gelato, and wine-infused sorbets.** ✉ *60 Shaw Ave., off Hwy. 12* ☎ *707/833–2300* 🌐 *www.vjbcellars.com* 🎟 *Tastings $15–$45.*

WHERE TO EAT AND STAY

$ ITALIAN 🍴 **Café Citti.** Classical music in the background, a friendly staff, and a roaring fire when it's cold outside keep this roadside café from feeling too spartan. Stand in line to order dishes such as roast chicken, pasta prepared with the sauce of your choice, and slabs of tiramisu for dessert, and someone will deliver your meal to a table indoors or on an outdoor patio. **Known for:** welcoming atmosphere; prepared salads and sandwiches; to-go winery picnics. [$] *Average main: $14* ✉ *9049 Sonoma Hwy./Hwy. 12* ☎ *707/833–2690* 🌐 *www.cafecitti.com.*

$ AMERICAN 🍴 **Palooza Gastropub & Wine Bar.** Palooza pleases with 16 beers on tap, jazzed-up pub grub, casual decor, and an often-packed covered outdoor patio. Pulled-pork sandwiches, falafel wraps, pan-seared salmon,

CLOSE UP

A Great Drive in Sonoma Valley

It's easy to zip through the Sonoma Valley in a day—the drive from Sonoma in the south to Kenwood in the north can be done in half an hour—but once you begin stopping at historic sites and wineries, your visit could easily be spread over two days.

BREAKFAST AND BUENA VISTA

To hit the highlights, start in the town of Sonoma. Have breakfast at Sunflower Caffé, on the western edge of Sonoma Plaza, or a few blocks west of the square at Crisp Bake Shop, on West Napa Street. From your breakfast spot, head east on East Napa Street and north on Old Winery Road to reach **Buena Vista Winery,** the birthplace of modern California wine making. (Alternatively, for sophisticated Chardonnays and Pinot Noirs, book a tasting at **Patz & Hall**; to reach its hospitality center, turn south from East Napa Street onto 8th Street East.)

WINE, FOOD, AND WINE

Enjoy your tasting, then backtrack to East Napa Street and head west. The road eventually becomes Highway 12, which you'll take west and north to photogenic **St. Francis Winery** for the 1 pm wine and food pairing (reserve a few days ahead). If you arrive early, ask about the self-guided vineyard tour, which ends at the culinary garden that supplies ingredients for the pairing. From St. Francis, head back south 2 miles on Highway 12 to **B Wise** (look for it on the right). Stop at this rustic-chic roadside tasting room for Moon Mountain District Cabernets and other wines.

LITERARY STROLL

From B Wise, continue south on Highway 12 and take Arnold Drive into the picturesque town of Glen Ellen. Turn right on London Ranch Road and wind your way uphill for a few minutes to reach **Jack London State Historic Park.** Take a short stroll through the grounds and observe the historic buildings near the parking area before the park closes at 5 pm.

KNOW MORE THAN JACK

Afterward, or as an alternative if the weather isn't cooperating, drop by **Jack London Village** on the southern edge of downtown Glen Ellen and check out the historical displays in the main building near the Sculpturesite Gallery. Some detail the lives of other famous Glen Ellen residents as diverse as "Hap" Arnold—Arnold Drive, on which the complex is located, is named for this aviation pioneer and World War II air force commander—and the author M.F.K Fisher. If you need a pick-me-up, have a nitrogen-infused iced coffee (or a regular cuppa) at **Horatius** here. Dine in town at **Aventine Glen Ellen** or **Glen Ellen Star**, or return to Sonoma on Highway 12.

4

fish and fries, blue-cheese-and-bacon burgers, and Chicago-style hot dogs are among the popular items, with fish tacos and shredded-kale and apple-spinach salads for those seeking lighter fare. **Known for:** many local brews; Sonoma Valley wines only; beer-battered fried pickles, mozzarella-ball appetizers. [$] *Average main: $14* ✉ *8910 Sonoma Hwy./Hwy. 12* ☎ *707/833–4000* 🌐 *www.paloozafresh.com.*

$$$$ B&B/INN **Kenwood Inn and Spa.** Fluffy feather beds, custom Italian furnishings, and French doors opening onto terraces or balconies lend this inn's uncommonly spacious guest rooms a particularly romantic air. **Pros:** large rooms; lavish furnishings; romantic. **Cons:** road or lobby noise in some rooms; expensive. [$] *Rooms from: $475* ✉ *10400 Sonoma Hwy./Hwy. 12* ☎ *800/353–6966* 🌐 *www.kenwoodinn.com* 🛏 *29 rooms* 🍴 *Breakfast.*

SPAS

Fodor's Choice ★ **Spa at Kenwood Inn.** A pretty setting, expert practitioners, and rejuvenating therapies using products from iS Clinical, Intraceuticals, and the French line Caudalíe make a visit to this spa an ethereal experience. Caudalíe's wine-based Vinothérapie treatments and its beauty products come together admirably in the delicious-sounding Honey Wine Wrap, which involves a warming, full-body slathering of wine yeast and honey, the better to rehydrate your parched and neglected skin. The Crushed Cabernet Scrub, designed to stimulate and soften your skin, raises the sweetness ante by adding brown sugar to the honey, along with crushed grape seeds and grape-seed oil. The spa's other services include massages and facials. ✉ *10400 Sonoma Hwy./Hwy. 12* ☎ *800/353–6966* 🌐 *www.kenwoodinn.com/spa.php* 🎫 *Treatments $149–$610.*

SPORTS AND THE OUTDOORS

Sugarloaf Ridge State Park. On a clear day you can see all the way to San Francisco and sometimes east to the Sierra mountains at this hilltop park on the Napa–Sonoma border. The easiest hiking trail follows Sonoma Creek for a mile from the visitor center; the hardest (8.2 miles) heads over Bald Mountain for those superlative views. Wildflower viewing is a major pastime from spring to early summer. You can mountain bike year-round. ✉ *2605 Adobe Canyon Rd., off Hwy. 12* ☎ *707/833–5712* 🌐 *www.sugarloafpark.org* 🎫 *$8.*

NORTHERN SONOMA, RUSSIAN RIVER, AND WEST COUNTY

WELCOME TO NORTHERN SONOMA, RUSSIAN RIVER, AND WEST COUNTY

TOP REASONS TO GO

★ **Back-roads biking:** The region's ultrascenic back roads include gentle hills and challenging terrain you can traverse with a guide or on your own.

★ **Diverse dining:** Area chefs tickle diners' palates with diverse offerings—everything from haute-French and Peruvian cuisine to playful variations on American standards.

★ **Hillside Cabs and old-vine Zins:** Alexander Valley hillside Cabernet Sauvignon and Dry Creek Valley old-vine Zinfandel grapes—as far as the eye can see in spots—thrive in the high heat here.

★ **Hip Healdsburg shopping:** Healdsburg wins the shopping wars fair and square, with more captivating galleries, design-oriented shops, and clothing stores than anywhere in the Wine Country.

★ **Pinot aplenty and Chardonnay, too:** Russian River Valley and Sonoma Coast wineries large and small produce some of California's most celebrated Pinot Noirs and Chardonnays.

1 **Healdsburg and Northern Sonoma.** An hour's drive north of the Golden Gate Bridge on U.S. 101 (when there's no traffic), Healdsburg has a compact downtown surrounding a tree-filled central plaza. Although its population is small, Healdsburg sprawls in all directions from the plaza, lending its address to many acclaimed wineries. North of the plaza 8 miles, more sedate Geyserville straddles U.S. 101.

2 **West County.** The Russian River Valley's hotter eastern portions lie within Healdsburg proper, but the bulk of the AVA stretches southwest into Forestville, Guerneville, Occidental, Sebastopol, Graton, and other small towns collectively known as West County. Its main roads include River Road, Highway 12, and Highway 116.

3 **Santa Rosa.** Sonoma County's largest city lies south of Healdsburg on U.S. 101 and north of the Sonoma Valley on Highway 12, which winds west from Santa Rosa into West County.

GETTING ORIENTED

Northern Sonoma County and Santa Rosa lie due north of San Francisco on U.S. 101. Highway 116 and Highway 12 lead west from U.S. 101 into Sebastopol, where 116 continues to north Forestville. River Road, often parallel to the Russian River, snakes west from U.S. 101 through Forestville and on to Guerneville, eventually dead-ending at the Pacific Ocean. From Guerneville the Bohemian Highway leads south into Occidental, then farther south to Freestone, where it joins Highway 12.

5

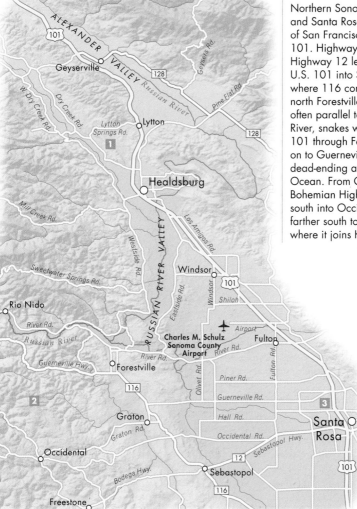

101

ALEXANDER VALLEY

Geyserville

128

Geysers Rd.

Russian River

Pine Flat Rd.

W. Dry Creek Rd.

Dry Creek Rd.

Lytton Springs Rd.

Lytton

1

128

Mill Creek Rd.

Healdsburg

Westside Rd.

Los Amigos Rd.

RUSSIAN RIVER VALLEY

Sweetwater Springs Rd.

Windsor

Eastside Rd.

Windsor

101

Shiloh

Rio Nido

River Rd.

Russian River

Charles M. Schulz Sonoma County Airport

Airport

River Rd.

Fulton

Guerneville Hwy.

Forestville

River Rd.

Olivet Rd.

Piner Rd.

Fulton Rd.

116

Graton

Graton Rd.

Guerneville Rd.

Hall Rd.

3

Santa Rosa

2

Occidental

Occidental Rd.

Sebastopol Hwy.

12

101

Bodega Hwy.

Sebastopol

Freestone

116

Sonoma County's northern and western reaches are a study in contrasts. Trendy hotels, restaurants, shops, and tasting rooms have transformed Healdsburg into a hot spot. Within a few miles, though, the chic yields to the bucolic, with only an occasional horse ranch, apple or peach orchard, or stand of oaks to interrupt the rolling vineyard hills. The Russian River, Dry Creek, and Alexander valleys are the grape-growing stars, but the Sonoma Coast and smaller appellations also merit investigation. Office parks and strip malls diminish Santa Rosa's appeal, but wineries, cultural attractions, and budget lodgings can be found within its borders.

Healdsburg is the most convenient base for exploring northern Sonoma County. Not only does it have an easily walkable town center, swanky hotels, and a remarkable restaurant scene, but it's also at the confluence of the Russian River, Dry Creek, and Alexander valleys. The wineries here produce some of the country's best Pinot Noirs, Cabernet Sauvignons, Zinfandels, and Chardonnays.

In the smaller West County towns of Forestville, Guerneville, and Sebastopol, high-style lodgings and fine dining are in shorter supply. Each town has a few charmers, however, along with wineries worth seeking out. The western reaches of Sonoma County, extending all the way to the Pacific Ocean, are more sparsely populated, although more and more vineyards are popping up where once stood orchards or ranches.

As the county's—and Wine Country's—largest city, workaday Santa Rosa may lack sex appeal, but it does contain the Charles M. Schulz Museum, Safari West, and other nonwine attractions, and dining and lodging options here tend to be more affordably priced than in the smaller towns.

Each of northern and western Sonoma County's regions claims its own microclimates, soil types, and most-favored varietals, but—except for urban Santa Rosa—all have something in common: peace and quiet. This area is less crowded than the Napa Valley and southern Sonoma. Healdsburg, in particular, is hardly a stranger to overnight visitors, but you'll find less company in many of the region's tasting rooms.

PLANNER

WHEN TO GO

High season runs from early June through October, but even then weekday mornings find many wineries blissfully uncrowded. Summers are warm and nearly always pleasant on the coast, and though inland the temperatures often reach 90°F, this is nothing a rosé of Pinot Noir can't cure. Fall brings harvest fairs and other celebrations. Things slow down during winter, but with smaller crowds come more intimate winery visits. Two big events that break up the winter are Winter Wineland, in January, and Barrel Tasting, on two weekends in early March *(see Festivals and Seasonal Events in the Experience Napa and Sonoma chapter for more information)*. Roads along the Russian River are prone to flooding during heavy rains, as are a few in the Alexander Valley. Spring, when the grapevines are budding but the crowds are still thin, is a good time to visit.

PLANNING YOUR TIME

With hundreds of wineries separated by miles of highway—Sonoma County is as big as Rhode Island—you could spend weeks here and not cover everything. To get a taste for what makes this region special, plan on a minimum of two or three days to hit the highlights. Healdsburg and the Russian River Valley are the must-sees, but it's worth venturing beyond them to the Alexander and Dry Creek valleys. If you still have time, head west toward the coast. Healdsburg makes a good base for Northern Sonoma and Russian River Valley touring, and Sebastopol, Forestville, and Guerneville are prime West County perches. Santa Rosa is convenient to both Northern Sonoma and the Russian River Valley, and it often has the best lodging rates.

GETTING HERE AND AROUND

SMART (Sonoma-Marin Area Rail Transit) commuter service is set to debut in 2017—of little use to wine tourists, however, until the tracks are extended to Healdsburg (a few years off)—but travel by car and to a lesser extent bus remains the best option for visitors. One alternative is to book a group or private tour *(see Winery Tours in the Travel Smart chapter for more tour information)*.

BUS TRAVEL

Sonoma County Transit provides transportation to all the main towns in this region, though except for the routes from Santa Rosa (which also operates its own bus line within city limits) to Healdsburg and to Sebastopol service isn't always frequent. Bus 60 travels from Santa Rosa to Healdsburg, where Bus 67, aka the Healdsburg Shuttle, loops through downtown. Buses 20, 22, 24, 26, and 28 serve Sebastopol and

5

other West County towns. *For more information about arriving by bus, see Bus Travel in the Travel Smart chapter. For more information about local bus service, see the Bus Travel sections for the individual towns in this chapter.*

CAR TRAVEL

Driving a car is by far the easiest way to get to and experience this region. From San Francisco, the quickest route to Northern Sonoma is north on U.S. 101 to Santa Rosa and Healdsburg. Highway 116 (aka Gravenstein Highway), heads west from U.S. 101, taking you through Sebastopol and the hamlets of Graton and Forestville before depositing you along the Russian River near Guerneville. Traffic can be slow on U.S. 101, especially around Petaluma and Santa Rosa during rush hour and on summer weekends. Parking can be difficult in downtown Healdsburg on busy summer and early fall weekends, when you may have to park in a lot or feed a meter.

RESTAURANTS

Each year at the Sonoma County Harvest Festival and seasonally at local farmers' markets, the remarkable output of Northern Sonoma's farms and ranches is on display. Local chefs often scour the markets for seafood, meats, cheeses, and produce, and many restaurants have their own gardens. With all these fresh ingredients at hand, it should come as no surprise that farm-to-table cuisine predominates here, especially among the high-profile restaurants. Wood-fired pizzas are another local passion, as is modern Italian. Good delis and groceries abound, several of them located conveniently near wineries that allow picnics. Except in the region's most expensive restaurants, it's fine to dress casually.

HOTELS

Healdsburg's hotels and inns set this region's standard for bedding down in style, with plush rooms that top $1,000 a night in a few cases. In the more affordable category are traditional bed-and-breakfast inns and small hotels, and there are even some inns and motels with down-to-earth prices. These last lodgings book up well in advance for high season, which is why Santa Rosa—just 15 miles away and home to decent chain and independent inns and hotels—is worth checking out year-round. Several secluded West County inns provide an elegant escape. Smaller properties throughout the region have two-night minimums on weekends (three nights on holiday weekends), though in winter this is negotiable. *Hotel reviews have been shortened. For full information, visit Fodors.com.*

WHAT IT COSTS				
	$	$$	$$$	$$$$
Restaurants	under $16	$16–$22	$23–$30	over $30
Hotels	under $201	$201–$300	$301–$400	over $400

Restaurant prices are the average cost of a main course at dinner, or if dinner isn't served, at lunch. Hotel prices are the lowest cost of a standard double room in high season.

APPELLATIONS

Covering about 329,000 acres, the **Northern Sonoma AVA,** itself within the larger Sonoma County "appellation of origin," a geopolitical designation, and the even larger multicounty **North Coast AVA,** is divided into subappellations. Three of the most important meet at Healdsburg: the Russian River Valley AVA, which runs southwest along the river; the Dry Creek Valley AVA, which runs northwest of town; and the Alexander Valley AVA, which extends to the east and north. Also in this far northern area are smaller AVAs whose names you're more likely to see on wine labels throughout the county than at the few visitable wineries within the appellations themselves: Knights Valley, Chalk Hill, and Fountaingrove, east and south of Alexander Valley; Rockpile, which slices northwest from the Dry Creek AVA to the Mendocino County line; and Pine Mountain–Cloverdale Peak, which extends from the Alexander Valley's northeastern tip into Mendocino County.

The cool climate of the low-lying **Russian River Valley AVA** is perfect for fog-loving Pinot Noir grapes as well as Chardonnay. Although three decades ago this area had as many farms, orchards, and redwood stands as vineyards, this is now one of Sonoma's most-recognized growing regions—with a significant subappellation of its own, the **Green Valley of the Russian River Valley AVA,** in the Forestville-Sebastopol area.

The **Dry Creek Valley AVA** is a small region—only about 16 miles long and 2 miles wide—but Zinfandel lovers know it well. The coastal hills temper the cooling influence of the Pacific Ocean, making it ideal for this varietal. Even more acres are planted to Cabernet Sauvignon, and you'll find Merlot, Chardonnay, Sauvignon Blanc, Syrah, and several other grape types growing in the diverse soils and climates (it's warmer in the north and cooler in the south).

Cabernet Sauvignon thrives in the warm **Alexander Valley AVA.** Sauvignon Blanc, Zinfandel, Petite Sirah, and Italian varietals such as Sangiovese do well, and certain cooler spots have proven hospitable to Chardonnay and Merlot.

Much of the **Sonoma Coast AVA,** which stretches the length of Sonoma County's coastline, lies within the Northern Sonoma AVA. The classic combination of hot summer days and cooling evening fog and breezes (in some spots even cooler than the Russian River Valley) inspired major wine-making operations, including the Napa Valley's Joseph Phelps Vineyards, to invest in acreage here. The hunch paid off for Phelps and other area winemakers, whose Pinots and Chardonnays have been the darlings of national wine critics for a decade. Because the Sonoma Coast AVA encompasses such varied terrain—its southeastern portion edges into the comparatively warmer Sonoma Valley, for instance— some West County growers and vintners have proposed subappellations that express what they promote as the "true" Sonoma Coast geology and microclimates. One subappellation granted approval was **Fort Ross– Seaview AVA,** whose hillside vineyards, mostly of Chardonnay and Pinot Noir, occupy hilly patches once thought too close to the Pacific Ocean to support grape growing. Fairly far along in the approval process—and perhaps official by the time you read this—is the **Petaluma Gap AVA,**

5

whose name references a gap in the Coast Range that permits cooling Pacific Ocean fog and wind to flow through. Except for a wee bit that edges into Marin County, as proposed the rest of this subappellation will lie within the Sonoma Coast AVA.

Mountains surround the idyllic **Bennett Valley AVA** on three sides. Part of the Sonoma Valley AVA *(see Chapter 4)*, it lies within the city of Santa Rosa. Coastal breezes sneak through the wind gap at Crane Canyon, making this area ideal for such cooler-weather grapes as Pinot Noir and Chardonnay, though Syrah, Cabernet Sauvignon, and Sauvignon Blanc also do well here.

HEALDSBURG AND NORTHERN SONOMA

Most of California's major grape varietals thrive in the disparate terrains and microclimates of Sonoma County's northern section, among them Zinfandel, which Italian immigrants such as Edoardo Seghesio planted in the Alexander Valley in the 1890s. Some of these vines survive to this day, but they were not the first grapes planted up this way. Five decades earlier, Cyrus Alexander, from whom the valley takes its name, planted grapevines on land now part of Alexander Valley Vineyards.

For years, most Alexander Valley grapes and those grown in the neighboring Dry Creek Valley found their way into bulk wines, and prune and other stone-fruit trees were far more common than grapevines. By the 1950s and '60s, though, pioneers such as Evelyn and Leo Trentadue had begun planting the first vines in the Geyserville area since the Prohibition era, and in 1972 David Stare opened Dry Creek Vineyard, the Dry Creek Valley's first new winery since Prohibition. A few years later in the Alexander Valley, Tom and Sally Jordan upped the ante when they set about producing French-style Chardonnays and Cabernet Sauvignons to rival those in the Napa Valley and France itself. More wineries followed, and by the early 2000s it was clear that Healdsburg, the area's winery hub, at the eastern edge of the Russian River Valley, was destined for stardom.

HEALDSBURG

17 miles north of Santa Rosa.

Fodor'sChoice Easily Sonoma County's ritziest town and the star of many a magazine
★ spread or online feature, Healdsburg is located at the intersection of the Dry Creek Valley, Russian River Valley, and Alexander Valley AVAs. Several dozen wineries bear a Healdsburg address, and around downtown's plaza you'll find fashionable boutiques, spas, hip tasting rooms, and art galleries, and some of the Wine Country's best restaurants. Star chef Kyle Connaughton, who opened SingleThread Farms Restaurant in late 2016 to much fanfare, has motivated his counterparts all over town to up their game. The celebrity buzz could shift to the art scene if new owners, among them Annie Leibovitz, are able to rehabilitate a former machine shop at 444 Healdsburg Avenue and convert it into a gallery.

CLOSE UP

Top Tastings and Tours

TASTINGS

Arista Winery, Healdsburg. Balanced, richly textured small-lot Pinot Noirs are the specialty of this winery with a picnic area and a Japanese garden.

Trattore Farms, Geyserville. Views of the northern Dry Creek Valley unfold at this hilltop winery specializing in Rhône-style whites and a mix of reds.

TOURS

Jordan Vineyard and Winery, Healdsburg. The pièce de résistance of the estate tour here is a Cabernet tasting at a 360-degree vista point overlooking acres of countryside.

SETTING

Iron Horse Vineyards, Sebastopol. The vine-covered hills and valleys surrounding this sparkling wine producer provide such compelling views that the winery hosts all its tastings outside.

Ridge Vineyards, Healdsburg. Outdoors in good weather and indoors year-round you can enjoy views of rolling vineyards while tasting intense Zinfandels and other well-rounded wines.

FOOD PAIRING

J Vineyards & Winery, Healdsburg. Marvelous morsels by executive chef Carl Shelton are paired with J's best sparkling and still wines in the plush Bubble Room.

JUST PLAIN FUN

Davis Family Vineyards, Healdsburg. On weekends from late spring to early fall, you can "get your BLT on" with sandwiches paired with superlative Pinot Noir, Syrah, and other wines.

Truett Hurst Winery, Healdsburg. A cool place to kick back—especially on weekends, when bands play—T-H has a creek-side tasting area that's a treat all its own.

5

Especially on weekends, you'll have plenty of company as you tour the downtown area. You could spend a day just exploring the tasting rooms and shops surrounding Healdsburg Plaza, but be sure to allow time to venture into the surrounding countryside. With orderly rows of vines alternating with beautifully overgrown hills, this is the setting you dream about when planning a Wine Country vacation. Many wineries here are barely visible, often tucked behind groves of eucalyptus or hidden high on fog-shrouded hills. Country stores and roadside farm stands alongside relatively untrafficked roads sell just-plucked fruits and vine-ripened tomatoes.

GETTING HERE AND AROUND

To get to Healdsburg from San Francisco, cross the Golden Gate Bridge and continue north on U.S. 101. About 65 miles from San Francisco, take the Central Healdsburg exit and follow Healdsburg Avenue a few blocks north to Healdsburg Plaza. Many hotels and restaurants are within a few blocks of the scenic town square. From Santa Rosa, the drive along U.S. 101 takes about 15 minutes in light traffic. Wineries bearing Healdsburg addresses can be as far apart as 20 miles, so you'll find a car handy. The Dry Creek Valley AVA and most of the Russian River Valley AVA are west of U.S. 101; most of the Alexander Valley AVA is east of the freeway. Sonoma County Transit Bus 60 serves Healdsburg from Santa Rosa; Bus 67, a shuttle, serves portions of downtown and vicinity but isn't convenient for winery touring.

Westside wineries: To get to wineries along Westside Road, head south on Center Street, then turn right at Mill Street. After Mill Street crosses under U.S. 101, its name changes to Westside Road. After about ½ mile, veer south to continue on Westside Road to reach the Russian River Valley wineries. Roughly following the curves of the Russian River, Westside Road passes vineyards, woods, and meadows along the way.

Eastside wineries: The route to wineries on Old Redwood Highway and Eastside Road is less scenic. Follow Healdsburg Avenue south to U.S. 101. Hop on the freeway, exiting after a mile at Old Redwood Highway. Bear right as you exit, and continue south. Just past the driveway that serves both Rodney Strong and J Vineyards, turn southwest to merge onto Eastside Road.

Dry Creek Valley and Alexander Valley wineries: To reach the wineries along Dry Creek Road and West Dry Creek Road, head north from the plaza on Healdsburg Avenue. After about a mile, turn west on Dry Creek Road. Roughly parallel to Dry Creek Road is West Dry Creek Road, accessible by the cross streets Lambert Bridge Road and Yoakim Bridge Road. For Alexander Valley wineries, continue north on Healdsburg Avenue past Dry Creek Road.

VISITOR INFORMATION
Healdsburg Chamber of Commerce & Visitors Bureau. ⊠ *217 Healdsburg Ave., at Matheson St.* ☎ *707/433–6935* ⊕ *www.healdsburg.com.*

EXPLORING
TOP ATTRACTIONS

Fodor's Choice
★

Acorn Winery. A throwback to the era when a hardworking couple forsook sensible careers and went all-in to become grape growers and vintners, this low-tech yet classy operation has earned high praise for wines that include Cabernet Franc, Sangiovese, Zinfandel, and the rare-in-America Italian varietal Dolcetto. The gracious Betsy and Bill Nachbaur share their output in a garage-style, appointment-only tasting room amid their Alegría Vineyard. Each Acorn wine is a field blend of multiple grape varietals grown side by side and then crushed and fermented together. In the wrong hands, this old-world approach produces muddled, negligible wines, but these, made by Bill in consultation with local winemaker Clay Mauritson, soar. ⊠ *12040 Old Redwood Hwy., south of Limerick La.* ☎ *707/433–6440* ⊕ *acornwinery.com* ☞ *Tasting $15.*

Fodor's Choice
★

Arista Winery. Brothers Mark and Ben McWilliams own this winery specializing in small-lot Pinot Noirs that was founded in 2002 by their parents. The sons have raised the winery's profile in several ways, most notably by hiring winemaker Matt Courtney, who has earned high praise from the *Wine Spectator* and other publications for his balanced, richly textured Pinot Noirs. Courtney shows the same

Healdsburg and
Northern Sonoma

deft touch with Arista's Zinfandels, Chardonnays, and a Riesling. One tasting focuses the regions from which the Arista sources its grapes, another on small-lot single-vineyard wines. Tastings are by appointment only. ■TIP➔ Guests who purchase a bottle are welcome to enjoy it in the picnic area, near a Japanese garden that predates the winery. ✉ 7015 *Westside Rd.* ☎ 707/473–0606 ⊕ *www.aristawinery. com* ✉ *Tastings $35–$65.*

Banshee Wines. Cool-climate Sonoma Coast wines are the focus of this winery whose downtown Healdsburg storefront—reclaimed wood floors, brass pendant chandeliers, plush leather seating, window banquettes, vinyl on the turntable—feels more fancy pad than tasting room. The House Flight includes the flagship Sonoma County Pinot Noir, a Sonoma Coast Chardonnay, and Mordecai, a multivarietal blend that's always heavy on the Cabernet Sauvignon and Syrah. Given their quality, these wines represent a bargain at under $30 apiece, but to sample Banshee at its best, opt for a Reserve Flight of single-vineyard Chardonnays and Pinot Noirs. Lead winemaker and co-owner Noah Dorrance displays a light touch with well-sourced grapes picked early to preserve acidity. The staffers know their wines and their winery and are happy to suggest your next tasting stops. ✉ *325 Center St., at North St.* ☎ 707/395–0915 ⊕ *www.bansheewines.com* ✉ *Tastings $15–$30.*

Fodor's Choice ★ **Comstock Wines.** Winemaker Chris Russi gained fans—collectors and wine critics alike—during previous stops at the Christopher Creek and Thomas George wineries, and with the high-quality purchased and estate-grown fruit at his disposal here, his posse will only expand. Refined Zinfandel is the specialty, some of it from the characterful old vines in front of the tasting room. The stunner is the Rockpile Zin, which Russi crafts in a softer, more elegant style than some of his peers. Russi also does well with purchased Pinot Noir and estate Sauvignon Blanc. Opened in 2015 in a contemporary barnlike structure, Comstock is the kind of place that encourages lingering, best done in fine weather at a Terrace Tasting, with vineyard and hillside views enhancing the pleasure of these remarkable wines. The tour and some tastings are by appointment only. ✉ *1290 Dry Creek Rd., 1 mile west of U.S. 101 (Dry Creek Rd. exit)* ☎ 707/723–3011 ⊕ *www.comstockwines.com* ✉ *Tastings $15–$50, tour $45 (includes tasting).*

Copain Wines. This winery whose name means "buddies" in French makes Chardonnays, Pinot Noirs, and Syrahs. Although Copain occupies an enviable slope in northern Sonoma County—one that begs guests to sit, sip, and take in the Russian River Valley view—for years most of its wines derived from grapes grown in hillside vineyards near the coast in Monterey and Mendocino counties. Wells Guthrie, the winemaker and cofounder, prefers those locations for their marine climates and rocky soils; following the winery's 2016 purchase by Jackson Family Wines (Guthrie remaining as winemaker), some Russian River Valley and Sonoma Coast wines are being introduced to the lineup. Tastings focus on the regions from which the winery sources its grapes, the individual vineyards, or multiple vintages of Guthrie's intuitive wines; all are by appointment only. ✉ *7800 Eastside Rd., near Ballard Rd.* ☎ 707/836–8822 ⊕ *www.copainwines.com* ✉ *Tastings $30–$60.*

Where to Eat and Stay in Downtown Healdsburg

KEY

- ● Restaurants
- ① Hotels
- 🅿 Parking
- 🛈 Information

Restaurants ▼

Baci Café & Wine Bar **4**

Barndiva **16**

Bravas Bar de Tapas **7**

Café Lucia **14**

Campo Fina **10**

Chalkboard **3**

Costeaux **1**

Downtown Bakery & Creamery **11**

Dry Creek Kitchen **13**

Guiso Latin Fusion **6**

KINSmoke **12**

Noble Folk Ice Cream and Pie Bar **15**

Shed Café **2**

SingleThread Farms Restaurant **8**

Sonoma Cider Taproom and Restaurant **18**

Spoonbar **17**

Valette **9**

Willi's Seafood & Raw Bar **5**

Hotels ▼

Best Western Dry Creek Inn **1**

Camellia Inn **5**

Healdsburg Inn on the Plaza **7**

h2hotel **8**

The Honor Mansion **2**

Hotel Healdsburg **6**

Hôtel Les Mars **3**

Madrona Manor **9**

SingleThread Farms Inn **4**

Fodor's Choice **Davis Family Vineyards.** On weekends from late spring to early fall,
★ this winery's large outdoor tasting space becomes party central as
guests heeding the invitation to "get your BLT on" enjoy sandwiches
prepared in a food truck operated by Zazu restaurant of Sebastopol.
Pinot Noir and Rhône-style wines are the specialty here. Owner-
winemaker Guy Davis crafts all the Pinots the same way—aiming
to let vineyard conditions and the specific clones, or variants, of
Pinot Noir find expression in bottle—and wine critics routinely
praise the results of this humble approach. Other reds include two
beautifully rendered Syrahs (great with the BLTs), a Zinfandel, and
the sultry Rockpile Ridge Cabernet Sauvignon. On the lighter side,
Davis makes Chardonnay, a sparkling wine, sometimes rosé, and the
flagship Cuvée Luke blend of Roussanne, Marsanne, and Viognier.
The wine and cheese pairing is by appointment only. ⊠ *52 Front St.,
at Hudson St.* ☏ *707/433–3858* ⊕ *www.davisfamilyvineyards.com*
🍷 *Tastings $10–$35.*

Fodor's Choice **Dry Creek Peach & Produce.** If you happen by this farm stand in the
★ summer, don't pass up the chance to sample the tree-ripened white
and yellow peaches, some of which may have been harvested moments
before you arrived. You can buy peaches in small quantities, as well as
organic peach jam. How good are these peaches? Customers include the
famed Chez Panisse Restaurant in Berkeley. ■TIP→ The stand is only
open from July to mid-September between noon and 5 on Wednesday,
Friday, and the weekend. ⊠ *2179 Yoakim Bridge Rd., near Dry Creek
Rd.* ☏ *707/433–8121* ⊕ *www.drycreekpeach.com* ☾ *Closed mid-Sept.–
June and Mon., Tues., and Thurs. July–mid-Sept.*

Dry Creek Vineyard. Sauvignon Blanc marketed as Fumé Blanc put Dry
Creek Vineyard on the enological map in the 1970s, but the winery
receives high marks as well for its Zinfandels, Bordeaux-style red
blends, and Cabernet Sauvignons. In the nautical-theme tasting room—
Dry Creek has featured sailing vessels on its labels since the 1980s—you
can choose an all–Sauvignon Blanc flight, an all-Zinfandel one, or a
mix of these and other wines. A vineyard walk and an insectary garden enhance a visit to this historic producer, a fine place for a picnic
under the shade of a magnolia and several redwood trees. ■TIP→ You
can reserve a boxed lunch two days ahead through the winery, a time-
saver on busy weekends. ⊠ *3770 Lambert Bridge Rd., off Dry Creek
Rd.* ☏ *707/433–1000, 800/864–9463* ⊕ *www.drycreekvineyard.com*
🍷 *Tastings $15–$50, tour $30.*

■ QUICK
BITES

Flying Goat Coffee. Healdsburg locals are as obsessive about coffee as
they are about wine. One hot stop for a cup of joe is FGC, where the town-
favorite Optimist Blend is made from all-organic beans. ⊠ *324 Center St.,
near Plaza St.* ☏ *707/433–3599* ⊕ *www.flyinggoatcoffee.com.*

Gary Farrell Vineyards & Winery. Pass through an impressive metal gate
and wind your way up a steep hill to reach Gary Farrell, a spot with
knockout views over the rolling hills and vineyards below. Although its
Zinfandels and Chardonnays often excel, the winery is best known for
its Russian River Valley Pinot Noirs, many from top nearby vineyards.

The ivy-covered château at Jordan Vineyard looks older than its four-plus decades.

Weather permitting, the best place to taste is out on the terrace, where you can sample several current-release single-vineyard wines by Theresa Heredia. Another option is a private indoor tasting that includes older vintages for comparison. All tastings are by appointment, preferably made two days ahead, although during the week, especially in winter, same-day reservations are usually possible. ■ TIP→ The Pinots from the Hallberg and Rochioli vineyards are worth checking out. ⊠ *10701 Westside Rd.* ☎ *707/473–2909* ⊕ *www.garyfarrellwinery.com* ✉ *Tastings $35–$65, tour $45.*

Fodor's Choice ★
Jordan Vineyard and Winery. A visit to this sprawling property north of Healdsburg revolves around an impressive estate built in the early 1970s to replicate a French château. A seated one-hour Library Tasting of current Cabernet Sauvignon and Chardonnay releases takes place in the château itself, accompanied by small bites prepared by executive chef Todd Knoll. The tasting concludes with an older vintage Cabernet Sauvignon paired with cheese. The 90-minute Winery Tour & Tasting includes the above, plus a walk through part of the château. All visits are by appointment only. ■ TIP→ For a truly memorable experience, splurge on the three-hour Estate Tour & Tasting, whose pièce de résistance is the Cabernet segment, which unfolds at a 360-degree vista point overlooking 1,200 acres of vines, olive trees, and countryside. ⊠ *1474 Alexander Valley Rd., 1½ miles east of Healdsburg Ave.* ☎ *800/654–1213, 707/431–5250* ⊕ *www.jordanwinery.com* ✉ *Library tasting $30, winery tour and tasting $40, estate tour and tasting $120* ☺ *Closed Sun. Dec.–Mar.*

Lambert Bridge Winery. Especially in spring, when its front-porch wisteria arbor blooms a nostalgia-inducing light purple, the twin-dormered Lambert Bridge winery building looks far older than its four decades. The weathered structure has matured early and well, not unlike the powerful yet polished artisanal wines produced inside. The flagship offering, the silky and supple Limited Selection Cabernet Sauvignon, is blended from winery's best lots of Dry Creek and Alexander Valley grapes. Lambert Bridge has won praise for this and other reds—among them Cabernet Franc, Petit Verdot, Petite Sirah, and Zinfandel—but also makes fine whites. All can be sampled at the main tasting bar, hewn from a single, intricately patterned old-growth curly redwood, and in the adjacent candlelit barrel room. Some tastings are by appointment only. ■TIP➜ **Top local chefs participate in the once-a-month Chef's Table Series of food and wine pairings.** ✉ *4085 West Dry Creek Rd., ½ mile south of Lambert Bridge Rd.* ☎ *707/431–4675* ⊕ *www.lambertbridge.com* 🍷 *Tastings $25–$60.*

Fodor'sChoice **Limerick Lane Cellars.** The rocky, clay soils of this winery's northeastern
★ sliver of the Russian River Valley combine with foggy mornings and evenings and hot, sunny afternoons to create the swoon-worthy Zinfandels that have been produced here for the past half decade. The coveted 1910 Block Zinfandel comes from old-style head-trained vines planted more than a century ago. Fruit from this block adds richness and depth to the flagship Russian River Estate Zinfandel, whose grapes also come from two sets of nearby vines—one planted a decade ago, the other in the 1970s. Limerick Lane's Syrah and a Petite Sirah can be tasted along with its Zins in a restored stone farm building with views of the vineyards and the Mayacamas Mountains. ■TIP➜ **Walk-ins are welcome, but it's best to make a reservation, especially on weekends.** ✉ *1023 Limerick La., 1 mile east of Old Redwood Hwy.* ☎ *707/433–9211* ⊕ *www.limericklanewines.com* 🍷 *Tasting $15.*

Fodor'sChoice **Mauritson Wines.** Winemaker Clay Mauritson's Swedish ancestors planted
★ grapes in what is now the Rockpile appellation in the 1880s, but it wasn't until his generation, the sixth, that wines bearing the family name first appeared. Much of the original homestead lies submerged under manmade Lake Sonoma, but the remaining acres produce the distinctive Zinfandels for which Mauritson is best known. Cabernet Sauvignon, other red Bordeaux grapes, Syrah, and Petite Sirah grow here as well, but the Zinfandels in particular illustrate how Rockpile's varied climate and hillside soils produce vastly different wines—from the soft, almost Pinot-like Westphall Ridge to the more structured and tannic Cemetery Ridge. The Mauritsons also grow grapes in Dry Creek Valley, where the winery and tasting room are located (good picnic area), and Alexander Valley. ✉ *2859 Dry Creek Rd., at Lytton Springs Rd.* ☎ *707/431–0804* ⊕ *www.mauritsonwines.com* 🍷 *Tastings $20–$25, tours $40.*

Fodor'sChoice **Ridge Vineyards.** Ridge stands tall among California wineries, and not
★ merely because its 1971 Monte Bello Cab placed first in a 2006 Judgment of Paris rematch. The winery built its reputation on Cabernet Sauvignons, Zinfandels, and Chardonnays of unusual depth and complexity, but you'll also find blends of Rhône varietals. Ridge makes wines using grapes from several California locales—including the Dry

Creek Valley, Sonoma Valley, Napa Valley, and Paso Robles—but the focus is on single-vineyard estate wines, such as the exquisitely textured Lytton Springs Zinfandel blend from grapes grown near the tasting room. In good weather you can taste outside, taking in views of rolling vineyard hills while you sip. ■TIP➔ **The $20 tasting option includes a pour of the top-of-the-line Monte Bello Cabernet Sauvignon blend from grapes grown in the Santa Cruz Mountains.** ⊠ *650 Lytton Springs Rd., off U.S. 101* ☎ *408/867–3233* ⊕ *www.ridgewine.com/visit/lytton-springs* 🖾 *Tastings $5–$20, tours $30–$40.*

Fodor'sChoice
★
Rochioli Vineyards and Winery. Claiming one of the prettiest picnic sites in the area, with tables overlooking the vineyards, this winery has an airy little tasting room with a romantic view. Production is small and fans on the winery's mailing list snap up most of the bottles, but the winery is still worth a stop to sample the estate Chardonnay and Pinot Noir and, when available, the Sauvignon Blanc. Because of the cool growing conditions in the Russian River Valley, the flavors of the Chardonnay and Sauvignon Blanc are intense and complex, and the Pinot Noir, which helped cement the Russian River's status as a Pinot powerhouse, is consistently excellent. Tastings are by appointment only on Tuesday and Wednesday. ⊠ *6192 Westside Rd.* ☎ *707/433–2305* ⊕ *www.rochioliwinery.com* 🖾 *Tasting $20.*

Seghesio Family Vineyards. In 1895, the ancestors of the current winemaker, Ted Seghesio, planted some of the Alexander Valley's earliest Zinfandel vines, some of which supply grapes for the winery's highly rated Home Ranch Zinfandel. Seghesio crafts most of his wines—including other old-vine Zins and the Venom Sangiovese, from North America's oldest Sangiovese vineyard—using estate-grown fruit from the Alexander, Dry Creek, and Russian River valleys. The whites, from the relatively uncommon varietals Arneis and Vermentino, are special, too. You can learn about the winery's history and farming philosophy at tastings and food-wine pairings, on tours, and a few times a year on hikes of Home Ranch. The Family Tables Tasting is available from Friday through Sunday by appointment only. ■TIP➔ **When the weather's right, the tree-shaded picnic area fronting the tasting room is a sweet place to linger over wines purchased by the glass or bottle.** ⊠ *700 Grove St., off W. Grant St.* ☎ *707/433–3579* ⊕ *www.seghesio.com* 🖾 *Tastings $15–$75.*

Fodor'sChoice
★
Siduri Wine Lounge. Founded by two Texans with a yen for Pinot Noir, Siduri became a darling of the fruit-forward set in the mid-1990s and never looked back. The winery, named for the Babylonian goddess of wine, showcases its 20-Pinot (and counting) lineup in a casual lounge steps south of Healdsburg Plaza. Collectively, the wines—all of them good—reveal their varietal's diversity, but watch in particular for bottlings from the Sontera (Sonoma Coast), Lingenfelder (Russian River Valley), Pisoni (Santa Lucia Highlands), and Clos Pepe (Sta. Rita Hills) vineyards. The folks behind Backyard restaurant in Forestville prepare salumi, buttermilk fried chicken sliders, and other small bites to pair with the wines. Who knew fried chicken and Pinot—the Pisoni works best—could be this compatible? ⊠ *241 Healdsburg Ave., near Matheson St.* ☎ *707/433–6000* ⊕ *www.siduri.com* 🖾 *Tastings $20–$45.*

5

The focus at Ridge Vineyards is on single-vineyard estate wines.

Thumbprint Cellars Tasting Lounge & Art Gallery. With its exposed-brick walls and contemporary art exhibits, this stylish tasting room on Healdsburg Plaza's southern edge has the feel of a hip San Francisco loft. Owner-winemaker Scott Lindstrom-Drake, who believes in selecting good fruit and applying minimal manipulation during fermentation and aging—all his wines are unfined and unfiltered—specializes in single-vineyard Cabernet Franc, Cabernet Sauvignon, Pinot Noir, and Zinfandel. He also makes white, rosé, and red blends with alluring names such as Arousal, Four Play, and Three Some. The grapes come primarily from the Russian River, Dry Creek, and Alexander valleys. ■TIP→ A welcoming space during the day, the lounge often hosts comedy and other events in the evening. ✉ *102 Matheson St., at Healdsburg Ave.* ☎ *707/433–2393* ⊕ *www.thumbprintcellars.com* 🍷 *Tastings from $10.*

Truett Hurst Winery. When the weather's fine, few experiences rate more sublime ("pure magic," is the common refrain from visitors here) than sitting on Truett Hurst's sandy, tree-shaded Dry Creek shoreline, sipping a Pinot Noir or a Zinfandel rosé, chatting with friends, and watching the water flow by. A few of Truett Hurst's half dozen Zinfandels are always poured in the high-ceilinged tasting room. Other wines to look for include Petite Sirah, Cabernet Sauvignon, and the Dark Horse GPS (Grenache, Syrah, Mourvèdre, and Petite Sirah). Picnickers are welcome creek-side or on the outdoor patio; meats, smoked fish, cheeses, and spreads are available for sale on-site. ■TIP→ Bands—sometimes local, sometimes from beyond—liven things up in the tasting room on weekend afternoons. ✉ *5610 Dry Creek Rd., 2 miles south of Canyon Rd.* ☎ *707/433–9545* ⊕ *www.truetthurst.com* 🍷 *Tasting $10.*

Twomey Cellars. The draws at the Sonoma County location of this winery founded by the owners of Silver Oak include six world-class Pinot Noirs, a Merlot crafted using a centuries-old French technique, and vineyard and Mayacamas Mountains views from the glass-walled tasting room. The Pinot Noirs, from grapes grown in prime California locales, are made by Erin Miller, also responsible for the Sauvignon Blanc. The extremely supple Merlot is made at Twomey's Calistoga winery employing the *soutirage traditionnel* method of transferring the wine from oak barrel to oak barrel multiple times during aging to soften the tannins and intensify the aromas. ■ TIP→ **If the weather's nice, you can taste on the patio and enjoy its splendid views.** ✉ *3000 Westside Rd., ¼ mile south of Felta Rd.* ☎ *707/942–7026* ⊕ *www.twomey.com* ⌨ *Tastings $15–$30, tour $15 (includes tasting).*

WORTH NOTING

Alexander Valley Vineyards. The 1840s homestead of Cyrus Alexander, for whom the valley is named, is the site of this winery known for Chardonnay, Cabernet Sauvignon, and a trio of Zinfandels, most notably the widely distributed Sin Zin. The standard tasting is free, but consider opting for the Private Reserve Tour and Tasting ($15) to sample the single-vineyard Cabernet Sauvignon and the Bordeaux blend called Cyrus; a $25 wine and cheese pairing is also available. Tours, one of them free, take in the winery and wine caves dug deep into a nearby hillside. Weather permitting, you can take an invigorating vineyard hike. ■ TIP→ **The winery welcomes picnickers.** ✉ *8644 Hwy. 128, at Sonnikson Rd.* ☎ *707/433–7209* ⊕ *www. avvwine.com* ⌨ *Tastings free–$25, tours free–$15, vineyard hike $50.*

Alley 6 Craft Distillery. Krystle and Jason Jorgensen make small-batch rye and single malt whiskey, plus gin and candy-cap bitters, at the couple's industrial-park distillery 2 miles north of Healdsburg Plaza. The rye derives its overlapping flavors from its "mash bill" of rye and malted barley aged in heavily charred American oak barrels that add further layers of spice and complexity. The Jorgensens pride themselves on crafting their spirits entirely on-site, from grain milling through bottling, a process they describe with enthusiasm at their apothecarylike tasting room, open on weekends (weekdays by appointment only). ■ TIP→ **Visit the website to learn how to volunteer for the bottling process, which takes place every four to six weeks.** ✉ *1401 Grove St., Unit D, north of Dry Creek Rd.* ☎ *707/484–3593* ⊕ *www.alley6.com* ⌨ *Tasting $10.*

Christopher Creek Winery. Petite Sirah and Syrah made this winery's reputation, but since the current owners took over in 2011, Pinot Noir and Rhône whites are also an emphasis. The varied portfolio lends itself to three separate experiences, two of which are best enjoyed basking in the outdoor patio's views of vineyards, and, beyond them, Mt. Fitch. One tasting surveys the estate-grown whites and reds, the other the "legacy" reds, including the reserve Petite Sirah. The third experience takes place in the barrel room, where guests sample Pinots right from the barrel— ask for the Love and Anderson Valley editions—and place orders for "futures" available after bottle aging. ■ TIP→ **On a sunny day, you may find the impulse to while away the afternoon on the patio irresistible.** ✉ *641 Limerick La., ¼ mile east of Los Amigos Rd.* ☎ *707/433–2001* ⊕ *www.christophercreek.com* ⌨ *Tastings $15–$40.*

5

Ferrari-Carano Winery. Known for its over-the-top Italian villa and manicured gardens—not a stray blade of grass anywhere here—this winery produces mostly Chardonnays, Fumé Blancs, Zinfandels, and Cabernet Sauvignons. Although whites have traditionally been the specialty, the reds also garner attention—in particular the Bordeaux-style blend called Trésor—and some guests come just for the dessert wines. Tours cover the wine-making facilities, underground cellar, and the gardens, where you can see a cork oak tree and learn about how cork is harvested. The tour is by appointment only. ■ TIP→ For a more leisurely experience than the main tasting room, head downstairs to the reserve tasting room. ⊠ *8761 Dry Creek Rd., at Yoakim Bridge Rd.* ☎ *707/433–6700, 800/831–0381* ⊕ *www.ferrari-carano.com* ✉ *Tastings $10–$50, tour free.*

Healdsburg Museum and Historical Society. For a short break from wine tasting, visit the Healdsburg Museum and its collection of local historical objects, including baskets and artifacts from native tribes. Other exhibits cover the Mexican Rancho period, the founding and growth of Healdsburg in the 1850s, and the history of local agriculture. ⊠ *221 Matheson St., at Fitch St.* ☎ *707/431–3325* ⊕ *www.healdsburgmuseum. org* ✉ *Free* ☉ *Closed Mon. and Tues.*

Fodor's Choice ★

Hudson Street Wineries. This under-the-radar joint tasting room of five family-run wineries provides a vivid snapshot of northern Sonoma small-lot production. Reds to look for include the Kaufman Sunnyslope Vineyard Pinot Noir from Willowbrook Cellars, the Enriquez Pinot Noir lineup plus Tempranillo, the Kelley & Young Malbec, the Shippey Petite Sirahs and Zinfandels, and the Owl Ridge Dry Creek Valley Zinfandel and Alexander Valley Cabernet Sauvignon. The Kelley & Young Sauvignon Blanc and Shippey Rosé of Petite Sirah stand out among the lighter wines. Locals, who appreciate the unfussy atmosphere and generous pours, often bring their out-of-town guests to this barnlike space about half a mile southeast of Healdsburg Plaza. ■ TIP→ With most bottles costing between $20 and $30, the prices are beyond reasonable for wines of this quality. ⊠ *428 Hudson St., near Front St.* ☎ *707/433–2364* ⊕ *www.hudsonstreetwineries.com* ✉ *Tasting $10* ☉ *Closed Tues. and Wed.*

J Vineyards & Winery. A top sparkling-wine maker, J also receives high marks for its Pinot Gris, Chardonnay, Pinot Noir, and other still wines. A contemporary metal-and-glass wall sculpture installed by Napa artist Gordon Huether provides visual entertainment at the stand-up Signature Bar. For a more personalized experience, indulge yourself in the Bubble Room (reservations recommended), where wines are paired with small bites by executive chef Carl Shelton, whose previous stops include Spoonbar in Healdsburg and The Restaurant at Meadowood in the Napa Valley. Winery tours, a little more than an hour long, take place twice daily. ■ TIP→ From mid-spring through mid-fall, tastings are also held on a creek-side terrace. ⊠ *11447 Old Redwood Hwy., at Eastside Rd.* ☎ *707/431–3646* ⊕ *www.jwine.com* ✉ *Tastings $20–$110, tour $30.*

Medlock Ames Tasting Room. Owners Chris James and Ames Morison converted a century-old country store and bar into a contemporary showcase for the small-lot wines Ames makes from organically farmed grapes

The Russian River Valley AVA extends from Healdsburg west to Guerneville.

grown at their nearby Bell Mountain estate ranch. In good weather, many guests sip their wine in a garden that supplies the berries and other edibles that supplement pairings of wine and artisanal cheeses. The winery, known for Bordeaux-style reds and Cabernet Sauvignon, also produces Sauvignon Blanc, Chardonnay, rosé, and Pinot Noir. When the tasting room closes, the attached Alexander Valley Bar, snazzed up but still reminiscent of days gone by, opens for the evening (except on Wednesday). ■ TIP→ To learn more about the Medlock Ames wine-growing philosophy, schedule a tour of the ranch and winery. ✉ 3487 Alexander Valley Rd., at Hwy. 128 ☎ 707/431–8845 ⊕ www.medlock-ames.com ✉ Tastings $15–$20, ranch tour $40 (includes tasting).

Moshin Vineyards. If you've ever wondered how your college math professor might fare as a winemaker, slip over to this winery known for small-lot, single-vineyard Pinot Noirs. Rick Moshin, formerly of San Jose State University's math department, started out small in 1989, but by the mid-2000s demand for his Pinots supported construction of a four-tier, gravity-flow winery on his hillside property across Westside Road from the Russian River. Tours (by appointment only) focus on the winery's layout and Moshin's penchant for picking grapes earlier than most of his neighbors to preserve acidity, which he believes helps his wines pair well with food. In the tasting room, which always has a curated art exhibit, guests sip Pinot Noirs along with Chardonnay, Merlot, Sauvignon Blanc, Zinfandel, and other wines. ✉ 10295 West-side Rd., off Wohler Rd. ☎ 707/433–5499, 888/466–7446 ⊕ moshin-vineyards.com ✉ Tasting $15, tour $30.

CLOSE UP

Dry Creek Valley AVA

If you drive north along Healdsburg Avenue and turn left onto Dry Creek Road, you'll soon feel as though you've slipped back in time. Healdsburg looks totally urban in comparison with the unspoiled countryside of Dry Creek Valley. The valley's well-drained, gravelly floor is planted with Chardonnay grapes to the south, where an occasional sea fog creeps in from the Russian River and cools the vineyards. Sauvignon Blanc is planted in the warmer north. The red decomposed soils of the benchlands bring out the best in Zinfandel—the grape for which Dry Creek has become famous—but they also produce great Cabernet Sauvignon and Petite Sirah. And these soils seem well suited to such white Rhône varietals as Viognier, Roussanne, and Marsanne, along with Grenache, Syrah, and Mourvèdre reds. Wineries within this AVA include Dry Creek, Preston, Lambert Bridge, Mauritson, and Ridge.

QUICK BITES

Moustache Baked Goods. This shop specializes in sweets incorporating local, organic ingredients: cupcakes, brownies, snickerdoodles, whoopie pies, and macarons, to name a few. **Known for:** The Outlaw (chocolate, caramel, sea salt) and The Butcher (maple-spice frosting, bacon) cupcakes; ice-cream sandwiches; Moustache O's (Oreo-style cookies). ⊠ *381 Healdsburg Ave., at North St.* ☎ *707/395–4111* ⊕ *moustachebakedgoods.com.*

Papapietro Perry. The mood is almost always upbeat at the copper-topped tasting bar as regulars and first-timers sip some of the 10 Pinot Noirs—eight from Russian River Valley grapes and one each from Sonoma Coast and Mendocino County fruit. A Russian River Valley Chardonnay and a Dry Creek Zinfandel also grace the lineup. The house style with all the wines is to pick early and shoot for elegance rather than the "overexpression" that can result from using riper fruit. Wine and cheese pairings (by appointment only) take place on the vineyard-view patio. ⊠ *4791 Dry Creek Rd., at Timber Crest Farms* ☎ *707/433–0422, 877/467–4668* ⊕ *www.papapietro-perry.com* 🍷 *Tastings $15–$45.*

Porter Creek Vineyards. About as down-home as you can get—there's just a small redwood-beam tasting room amid a modest family farm—Porter Creek makes notably good wines, some from estate biodynamically grown Chardonnay and Pinot Noir grapes. Its vineyards climb up steep hillsides of volcanic soil that is said to impart a slight mineral note to the Chardonnay; cover crops planted between the vines provide erosion control in addition to nutrients. Winemaker Alex Davis—son of George Davis, who founded the winery—also makes two distinctive wines from old-vine grapes, Carignane from Mendocino County and Zinfandel from Sonoma County, and his lineup includes Viognier and Syrah. ■TIP→ Look closely for the winery's sign; the driveway is at a sharp bend in Westside Road. ⊠ *8735 Westside Rd.* ☎ *707/433–6321* ⊕ *www.portercreekvineyards.com* 🍷 *Tasting $15.*

FAMILY **Preston of Dry Creek.** The long driveway at homespun Preston, flanked by vineyards and punctuated by the occasional olive tree, winds down to farmhouses encircling a large shady yard. Year-round, organic produce grown in the winery's gardens is sold at a small shop near the tasting room; house-made bread and olive oil are also available. Owners Lou and Susan Preston are committed to organic growing techniques and use only estate-grown grapes in their wines, which include a perky Sauvignon Blanc, Barbera, Petite Sirah, Syrah, Viognier, and Zinfandel. Tours, on Thursday and Friday only, are by appointment. ■TIP→ With several outdoor areas set up with tables (there's also a boccie court), Preston is a terrific place for a weekday picnic; weekends, though also good, can be crowded, and there's no boccie. ⊠ *9282 W. Dry Creek Rd., at Hartsock Rd. No. 1* ☏ *707/433–3372* ⊕ *www.prestonvineyards. com* ⌣ *Tasting $10, tour $25.*

Quivira Vineyards and Winery. Solar panels top the modern wooden barn at Quivira, which produces Sauvignon Blanc, Zinfandel, Grenache, Syrah, and other wines using organic and biodynamic agricultural practices. The emphasis is on "growing wine"—farming grapes so meticulously that little manipulation is required in the winery. That said, winemaker Hugh Chappelle's mastery of technique is in evidence in wines such as the flagship Fig Tree Sauvignon Blanc, whose zesty yet refined characteristics derive from the combination of stainless steel and oak and acacia barrels used during fermentation. Guided tours (by appointment only) cover the farming and wine-making philosophies and offer a glimpse of the property's garden and animals. ■TIP→ In a separate salon, you can taste ($20) the Pinot Noirs and Chardonnays of La Follette Wines, which shares ownership with Quivira. Sourced from prime vineyards, they're worth investigating. ⊠ *4900 W. Dry Creek Rd., near Wine Creek Rd.* ☏ *707/431–8333, 800/292–8339* ⊕ *www. quivirawine.com* ⌣ *Tastings $15–$25, tour $40.*

Rodney Strong Vineyards. The late Rodney Strong was among the first winemakers to plant Pinot Noir grapes in the Russian River Valley; his namesake winery still makes Pinot Noirs, but it's known more for Cabernet Sauvignon–based wines. The headliners include the Bordeaux-style blend Symmetry and three single-vineyard Alexander Valley Cabernets: Alexander's Crown, Rockaway, and Brothers Ridge. You can sample Cabs and Pinots—along with Sauvignon Blanc, Chardonnay, Malbec, Zinfandel, and other wines—in the octagonal tasting room and, in good weather, on an umbrella-shaded terrace. A self-guided tour provides a good view of the fermentation tanks and machinery; guided tours also take place. ■TIP→ The winery hosts popular outdoor rock concerts (including Huey Lewis, the B-52s, and Smokey Robinson in recent years) during summer. ⊠ *11455 Old Redwood Hwy., north of Eastside Rd.* ☏ *707/431–1533, 800/678–4763* ⊕ *www.rodneystrong. com* ⌣ *Tastings $10–$30, tour free.*

Stonestreet. From the broad patio that fronts the Stonestreet Alexander Mountain Estate's stablelike building you can see some of the steep, rugged terrain where grapes for the winery's full-bodied Chardonnays and wild-as-a-stallion Cabernet Sauvignons are grown. At 5,100 acres (900 planted), this is among the world's largest mountain vineyards. Farming

The Russian River Valley's hot summer days and cool nights create ideal conditions for growing Chardonnay and Pinot Noir.

these steep hills is difficult and labor-intensive, but the hard-won output finds its way into top boutique wines in addition to Stonestreet's. You can taste a flight of whites, reds, or a combination; for stunning views and to experience the vineyards close up, take the mountain tour (by appointment only), which includes lunch. ■ TIP→ **Stonestreet also has a tasting room in downtown Healdsburg.** ⊠ *7111 Hwy. 128, off W. Sausal La.* ☎ *800/355–8008* ⊕ *www.stonestreetwines.com* ☖ *Tastings $30–$50, mountain tour $125–$150.*

Stuhlmuller Vineyards. Zinfandels and Cabernet Sauvignons from estate-grown grapes are the specialty of this off-the-beaten-path winery inside a distinctive stained-redwood building. Standout wines include the Rogers Schoolhouse Estate Zinfandel, crafted from small lots of old-vine grapes, and two estate Cabernets from specific grape blocks that grow side by side. Two Chardonnays and a Russian River Valley Pinot Noir from the noteworthy Starr Ridge Vineyard are also made here, and there's a rich dessert wine made from estate Cabernet fortified with brandy. Tastings take place in a room adjoining the aging cellar, and in good weather you can sip outdoors on a gravel patio near the vineyards. ■ TIP→ **Picnickers are welcome here.** ⊠ *4951 W. Soda Rock La., off Alexander Valley Rd.* ☎ *707/431–7745* ⊕ *www.stuhlmullervineyards. com* ☖ *Tastings $20–$29.*

Unti Vineyards. There's a reason why Unti, known for Zinfandel and wines made from sometimes obscure Rhône and Italian varietals, often bustles even when business is slow elsewhere in Dry Creek: this is a fun, casual place. You'll often find the sociable cofounder, Mick Unti, who manages the winery, chatting up guests and pouring wine in the rustic-not-trying-to-be-chic tasting room. Tastings often begin with Cuvée Blanc, a blend of Vermentino, Grenache Blanc, and Picpoul grapes, followed by another white and then Barbera, Sangiovese, and Syrah. The Segromigno blend showcases the estate-grown Sangiovese and Montepulciano grapes. ■ TIP→ **Visits here require appointments, but it's usually possible to get one on short notice.** ✉ *4202 Dry Creek Rd., ¾ north of Lambert Bridge Rd.* ☎ *707/433–5590* 🌐 *www.untivineyards.com* 🎫 *Tasting $10.*

Viszlay Vineyards. In 2010, Chicagoan John Viszlay purchased 10 acres along Limerick Lane, where the climate, terrain, and sun exposure are so variable the owner-winemaker has won awards for wines as diverse as prosecco and a Cabernet-based Bordeaux-style blend—all of whose grapes grow within rows of each other. There's also a laudable Eastside Hills Pinot Noir. Tastings take place indoors amid looming stacks of oak aging barrels or on a concrete patio in view of the grapevines. Although it's possible to taste at this small operation without an appointment, it's best to call ahead. ■ TIP→ **Visiting Viszlay plus neighboring Limerick Lane Cellars and Christopher Creek Winery makes for an engaging, easy-to-navigate afternoon of tasting.** ✉ *929 Limerick La., ½ mile east of Los Amigos Rd.* ☎ *707/481–1514* 🌐 *www.viszlayvineyards.com* 🎫 *Tasting $10–$30.*

5

Fodor's Choice ★ **Zichichi Family Vineyard.** Most winery owners would love to be in Steve Zichichi's shoes: his wines are largely sold out before they're bottled, and in one case while the grapes are still on the vine. As a result, customers of this northern Dry Creek Valley operation taste out of the barrel and purchase "futures"—wines available for shipping or pickup after aging is complete. The highlight, not always available for tasting, is the Old Vine Zinfandel, some of whose vines were planted in the 1920s during Prohibition, when many vineyard owners switched over to other crops. Zichichi makes another estate Zinfandel and an estate Petite Sirah, and a 100% Cabernet from the Chalk Hill appellation. ■ TIP→ **Cabernet bottles are usually still available for purchase at the time of a visit.** ✉ *8626 W. Dry Creek Rd., at Yoakim Bridge Rd.* ☎ *707/433–4410* 🌐 *www.zichichifamilyvineyard.com* 🎫 *Tasting $10.*

WHERE TO EAT

$$$ ITALIAN 🍴 **Baci Café & Wine Bar.** Tourists keep this neighborhood trattoria bustling during high season, but after things die down locals continue dropping by for pizza, one of the many pastas, and osso buco, saltimbocca, and other stick-to-your ribs Italian standards. The Iranian-born chef, Shari Sarabi, applies a pan-Mediterranean sensibility to area sourced, mostly organic ingredients, and his dishes satisfy without being overly showy. **Known for:** wine selection; enthusiastic owners; many gluten-free dishes. [$] *Average main: $25* ✉ *336 Healdsburg Ave., at North St.* ☎ *707/433–8111* 🌐 *www.bacicafeandwinebar.com* 🕒 *Closed Tues. and Wed. No lunch.*

$$$$ AMERICAN Fodor's Choice ★ 🍴 **Barndiva.** Electronic music plays quietly in the background while servers ferry the inventive seasonal cocktails of this restaurant that abandons the homey vibe of many Wine Country spots for a more urban feel. Make a light meal out of yellowtail hamachi crudo or baby-kale salad, or settle in for the evening with California sea bass with caviar crème

fraîche or roasted chicken with chanterelles and ricotta-and-egg-yolk ravioli. **Known for:** cool cocktails; stylish cuisine; open-air patio. [$] *Average main: $34* ✉ *231 Center St., at Matheson St.* ☎ *707/431–0100* 🌐 *www.barndiva.com* ⏲ *Closed Mon. and Tues.*

$$$ SPANISH Fodor's Choice ★ 🍴 **Bravas Bar de Tapas.** Spanish-style tapas and an outdoor patio in perpetual party mode make this restaurant, headquartered in a restored 1920s bungalow, a popular downtown perch. Contemporary Spanish mosaics set a perky tone inside, but unless something's amiss with the weather, nearly everyone heads out back for flavorful croquettes, paella, jamón, *pan tomate* (tomato toast), duck egg with chorizo, pork-cheek sliders, skirt steak, and crispy fried chicken. **Known for:** casual small plates; specialty cocktails, sangrias, and beer; sherry flights. [$] *Average main: $26* ✉ *420 Center St., near North St.* ☎ *707/433–7700* 🌐 *www.barbravas.com.*

$$$ PORTUGUESE 🍴 **Café Lucia.** Healdsburg native Lucia Azevedo Fincher runs this Portuguese restaurant where diners go the all-tapas route—fried goat cheese and fried spicy pig's ear are two staples—or sample a few small plates before moving on to a full entrée. Tops among the latter are the Portuguese variation on paella and *feijoada completa,* the Brazilian national dish, a thick mass of stewed beef, pork, smoked sausage, and black beans. **Known for:** sedate ambience; caldo verde (potato-thickened beef consommé with sausage). [$] *Average main: $25* ✉ *235 Healdsburg Ave., near Matheson St.* ☎ *707/431–1113* 🌐 *www.cafelucia.net.*

$$ ITALIAN Fodor's Choice ★ 🍴 **Campo Fina.** Chef Ari Rosen closed popular Scopa restaurant in 2017 but still showcases his contemporary-rustic Italian cuisine at this converted storefront that once housed a bar notorious for boozin' and brawlin'. Sandblasted red brick, satin-smooth walnut tables, and old-school lighting fixtures strike a retro note for a menu built around pizzas and Scopa gems such as Rosen's variation on his grandmother's tomato-braised chicken with creamy-soft polenta. **Known for:** outdoor patio and boccie court out of an Italian movie set; memorable lunch sandwiches. [$] *Average main: $19* ✉ *330 Healdsburg Ave., near North St.* ☎ *707/395–4640* 🌐 *www.campofina.com.*

$$ MODERN AMERICAN Fodor's Choice ★ 🍴 **Chalkboard.** Unvarnished oak flooring, wrought-iron accents, and a vaulted white ceiling create a polished yet rustic ambience for executive chef Shane McAnelly's playfully ambitious small-plate cuisine. Starters such as pork-belly biscuits might seem frivolous, but the silky flavor blend—maple glaze, pickled onions, and chipotle mayo playing off feathery biscuit halves—signals a supremely capable tactician at work. **Known for:** chef's four-course tasting menu; pasta "flights" (choose three or six styles); The Candy Bar dessert. [$] *Average main: $19* ✉ *Hotel Les Mars, 29 North St., west of Healdsburg Ave.* ☎ *707/473–8030* 🌐 *www.chalkboardhealdsburg.com.*

$ FRENCH 🍴 **Costeaux.** Breakfast, served all day at this bright-yellow French-style bakery and café, includes the signature omelet (sun-dried tomatoes, applewood-smoked bacon, spinach, and Brie) and French toast made from thick slabs of cinnamon-walnut bread. Croques, salads, smoked duck sandwiches, and an au courant Monte Cristo (turkey, ham, and Jarlsberg cheese) on that addictive cinnamon-walnut bread are among the lunch favorites. **Known for:** breads, croissants, and fancy pastries; quiche and omelets; front patio (arrive early on weekends). [$] *Average* *main: $14 ⊠ 417 Healdsburg Ave., at North St.* ☎ *707/433–1913* ⊕ *www.costeaux.com* ◔ *No dinner.*

$ ✕ **Downtown Bakery & Creamery.** To catch the Healdsburg spirit, hit the

BAKERY plaza in the early morning for a cup of coffee and a fragrant sticky bun or a too-darlin' *canelé*, a French-style pastry with a soft custard center surrounded by a dense caramel crust. Until 2 pm from Friday through Monday you can also go the full breakfast route: pancakes, granola, poached farm eggs on polenta, or perhaps the dandy bacon-and-egg pizza. **Known for:** morning coffee and pastries; lunchtime pizzas and calzones. $ *Average main: $8 ⊠ 308A Center St., at North St.* ☎ *707/431–2719* ⊕ *www.downtownbakery.net* ◔ *No dinner.*

$$$$ ✕ **Dry Creek Kitchen.** Chef Charlie Palmer's ultramodern restaurant

MODERN enchants diners with clever combinations of flavors and textures in

AMERICAN dishes based on seasonal, often local ingredients. A favorite among the starters is the risotto with Parmesan broth, foam, and "snow" (the cheese finely grated), with a similar level of complexity achieved in main courses that might include Sonoma lamb loin with crispy lamb *bisteeya* (lamb in a flaky pastry). **Known for:** sophisticated cuisine and atmosphere; no corkage fee on Sonoma County wines. $ *Average main: $34 ⊠ Hotel Healdsburg, 317 Healdsburg Ave., near Matheson St.* ☎ *707/431–0330* ⊕ *www.drycreekkitchen.com* ◔ *No lunch.*

$$$ ✕ **Guiso Latin Fusion.** Three years after graduating from Santa Rosa Junior

LATIN AMERICAN College's culinary arts program, chef Carlos Mojica opened this small Latin American and Caribbean restaurant next to the Raven theater. Fish tacos, *pescado con coco* (fish sautéed in sweet coconut), *pupusas* (corn tortillas stuffed with crab, pork, or vegetables and cheese), and intriguing *elotitos* (oven-roasted slices of sweet corn on the cob with Jamaican jerk spice, butter, and garlic) are among the dishes regulars return for. **Known for:** attentive service; intimate space; neighborhood feel. $ *Average main: $26 ⊠ 117 North St., near Center St.* ☎ *707/431–1302* ◔ *Closed Mon. No lunch Sun.–Thurs.*

$ ✕ **KINSmoke.** Beef brisket and St. Louis ribs are the hits at this saloon-

BARBECUE like, order-at-the-counter joint whose house-made sauces include espresso barbecue, North Carolina mustard, and the sweet-and-sourish KIN blend. Along with the expected sides of potato salad, corn bread, and baked beans (the latter bourbon infused), the spiced sweet-potato tater tots and Granny Smith–and-horseradish slaw stand out. **Known for:** upbeat crew; chicken with Alabama white sauce; beer selection and sensibly priced local wines. $ *Average main: $14 ⊠ 304 Center St., at Matheson St.* ☎ *707/473–8440* ⊕ *www.kinsmoke.com.*

$ ✕ **Noble Folk Ice Cream and Pie Bar.** Customers exiting this pie palace

BAKERY beloved for seasonal pies including blood-orange custard with graham-

Fodor'sChoice cracker crust always seem to have smiles on their faces. The bakers use

★ heritage grains like buckwheat and farro in the crusts, filling them with local fruits and other ingredients, and, if desired, topping the ensemble with ice cream in flavors from Swiss chocolate and vanilla bean to root beer, almond-cardamom, cornflake-maple, and other obscurities. **Known for:** seasonal pies; house-made waffle cones; sarsaparilla floats. $ *Average main: $7 ⊠ 116 Matheson St., near Center St.* ☎ *707/395–4426* ⊕ *www.thenoblefolk.com.*

$$$ MODERN AMERICAN 🍴 **Shed Café.** With previous stints at top Wine Country restaurants, culinary director Perry Hoffman added farm-to-table sophistication to this combination café, coffee bar, and "fermentation bar" serving house-made kombucha, kefir water, and vinegar-based "shrub" sodas. A recent fall dish, Liberty Farms duck leg served with baba ganoush, black lentils, fairytale eggplant, and pistachio *dukkah* (an Egyptian-style seed-nut mixture) hints at Hoffman's level of artistry. **Known for:** heirloom-grain Belgian waffles, Doug's eggs at breakfast; small lunch and dinner plates; four-course dinner option. [$] *Average main: $25* ✉ *25 North St., near Healdsburg Ave.* ☎ *707/431–7433* 🌐 *healdsburgshed.com/eat.*

$$$$ ECLECTIC Fodor's Choice ★ 🍴 **SingleThread Farms Restaurant.** The seasonally oriented, multicourse Japanese dinners known as *kaiseki* inspired the prix-fixe vegetarian, meat, and seafood menus at this restaurant from the internationally renowned culinary artists Katina and Kyle Connaughton (she farms, he cooks), which debuted in late 2016. As Katina describes the endeavor, the 72 microseasons of their farm, 5 acres at a nearby vineyard plus SingleThread's rooftop garden of fruit trees and microgreens, dictates Kyle's rarefied fare. **Known for:** culinary precision; spare, elegant setting; impeccable wine pairings. [$] *Average main: $294* ✉ *131 North St., at Center St.* 🌐 *www.singlethreadfarms.com* 🕓 *Closed Mon. No lunch.*

$ AMERICAN 🍴 **Sonoma Cider Taproom and Restaurant.** The organic-apple-based craft ciders (nearly two dozen) at this spiffy space south of Healdsburg Plaza really cleanse the palate after a day of wine tasting. Enjoy them straight, or use them to wash down bar food—think pickled vegetables, deviled duck eggs, raw seafood, cheeses, and the like—and dinner entrées like chicken Normandy, crepes, and baby back ribs. **Known for:** light lunch or dinner; outdoor patio; cidery tours (Friday and Saturday 11–2). [$] *Average main: $14* ✉ *44F Mill St., at Healdsburg Ave.* ☎ *707/723–7018* 🌐 *sonomacider.com.*

$$$ MODERN AMERICAN 🍴 **Spoonbar.** Midcentury modern furnishings, concrete walls, and an acacia-wood communal table create an urbane setting for the h2hotel restaurant's contemporary American fare. The seasonally changing selections might include slowly braised lamb shank and crab-and-scallop agnolotti, one of several house-made pasta dishes. **Known for:** creative seasonal and historical cocktails; happy hour; three-course meals on Wine and Dine Wednesday (a true deal). [$] *Average main: $23* ✉ *h2hotel, 219 Healdsburg Ave., at Vine St.* ☎ *707/433–7222* 🌐 *www.h2hotel.com/spoonbar* 🕓 *No lunch.*

$$$$ MODERN AMERICAN Fodor's Choice ★ 🍴 **Valette.** Northern Sonoma native Dustin Valette opened this gorgeously appointed homage to the area's artisanal agricultural bounty with his brother, who runs a tight front-of-house ship. Charcuterie is an emphasis, but also consider the cocoa nib–crusted Liberty duck breast and day-boat scallops *en croûte* (in a pastry crust), a signature dish at Healdsburg's Dry Creek Kitchen when Valette served as its executive chef. **Known for:** intricate cuisine; "Trust me" (the chef) tasting menu; well-chosen mostly Northern California wines. [$] *Average main: $31* ✉ *344 Center St., at North St.* ☎ *707/473–0946* 🌐 *www.valettehealdsburg.com.*

$$$ SEAFOOD 🍴 **Willi's Seafood & Raw Bar.** The crowd at Willi's likes to enjoy specialty cocktails at the full bar before sitting down to a dinner of small, mostly seafood-oriented plates. The warm Maine lobster roll with garlic butter and fennel remains a hit, and the ceviches, barbecued bacon-wrapped scallops, and "kale Caesar!" with toasted capers count among its worthy rivals: **Known for:** gluten-, dairy-, nut-, and seed-free options; Key lime cheesecake; caramelized banana split, and other desserts. [$] *Average main: $25* ✉ *403 Healdsburg Ave., at North St.* ☎ *707/433–9191* 🌐 *www.willisseafood.net* ☞ *Reservations not accepted Fri.–Sun.*

WHERE TO STAY

$ HOTEL 🏨 **Best Western Dry Creek Inn.** Easy access to downtown restaurants, tasting rooms, and shopping, as well as outlying wineries and bicycle trails makes this California Mission–style motel near U.S. 101 a good budget option. **Pros:** laundry facilities; some pet-friendly rooms; frequent Internet discounts. **Cons:** thin walls; highway noise audible in many rooms. [$] *Rooms from: $172* ✉ *198 Dry Creek Rd.* ☎ *707/433–0300, 800/222–5784* 🌐 *www.drycreekinn.com* 🛏 *163 rooms* 🍽 *Breakfast.*

$$ B&B/INN 🏨 **Camellia Inn.** In a well-preserved Italianate Victorian completed in 1871, this colorful bed-and-breakfast sits on a quiet residential street a block from Healdsburg Plaza. **Pros:** decent rates; family-friendly atmosphere; within easy walking distance of restaurants. **Cons:** a few rooms have a shower but no bath; all rooms lack TVs. [$] *Rooms from: $235* ✉ *211 North St.* ☎ *707/433–8182, 800/727–8182* 🌐 *www.camelliainn.com* 🛏 *9 rooms* 🍽 *Breakfast.*

$$ B&B/INN 🏨 **Healdsburg Inn on the Plaza.** A genteel antidote to Healdsburg's mania for tech-chic accommodations, this inn occupies a 19th-century office building whose former tenants include a Wells, Fargo & Co. Express office and stagecoach stop. **Pros:** central location; competent service. **Cons:** garish room lighting; so-so beds; slightly impersonal feel for this type of inn; street noise audible in plaza-facing rooms. [$] *Rooms from: $295* ✉ *112 Matheson St.* ☎ *800/431–8663* 🌐 *www.healdsburginn.com* 🛏 *12 rooms* 🍽 *Breakfast.*

$$$ B&B/INN Fodor's Choice ★ 🏨 **The Honor Mansion.** An 1883 Italianate Victorian houses this photogenic hotel; guest rooms in the main home preserve a sense of the building's heritage, whereas the larger suites are comparatively understated. **Pros:** homemade sweets available at all hours; spa pavilions by pool available for massages in fair weather. **Cons:** almost a mile from Healdsburg Plaza; walls can seem thin. [$] *Rooms from: $325* ✉ *891 Grove St.* ☎ *707/433–4277, 800/554–4667* 🌐 *www.honormansion.com* 🕒 *Closed 2 wks at Christmas* 🛏 *13 rooms* 🍽 *Breakfast.*

$$$$ RESORT 🏨 **Hotel Healdsburg.** Across the street from the tidy town plaza, this spare, sophisticated hotel caters to travelers with an urban sensibility. **Pros:** several rooms overlook the town plaza; comfortable lobby with a small attached bar; extremely comfortable beds. **Cons:** exterior rooms get some street noise; rooms could use better lighting. [$] *Rooms from: $445* ✉ *25 Matheson St.* ☎ *707/431–2800, 800/889–7188* 🌐 *www.hotelhealdsburg.com* 🛏 *49 rooms, 6 suites* 🍽 *Breakfast.*

5

$$$$ HOTEL Fodor's Choice ★ 🏨 **Hôtel Les Mars.** This Relais & Châteaux property takes the prize for opulence with guest rooms spacious and elegant enough for French nobility, 18th- and 19th-century antiques and reproductions, canopy beds dressed in luxe linens, and gas-burning fireplaces. **Pros:** large rooms; just off Healdsburg's plaza; fancy bath products; room service by Chalkboard restaurant. **Cons:** very expensive. [$] *Rooms from: $540* ✉ *27 North St.* ☎ *707/433–4211* 🌐 *www.hotellesmars.com* 🛏 *16 rooms* 🍴 *Breakfast.*

$$$ HOTEL 🏨 **h2hotel.** Eco-friendly touches abound at this hotel, from the plant-covered "green roof" to wooden decks made from salvaged lumber. **Pros:** stylish modern design; complimentary bikes; sister property H3 GuestHouse opens a few doors away by early 2018. **Cons:** least expensive rooms lack bathtubs; no fitness facilities. [$] *Rooms from: $322* ✉ *219 Healdsburg Ave.* ☎ *707/922–5251* 🌐 *www.h2hotel.com* 🛏 *36 rooms* 🍴 *Breakfast.*

$$$ B&B/INN Fodor's Choice ★ 🏨 **Madrona Manor.** This Victorian mansion dating to 1881 is surrounded by 8 acres of wooded and landscaped grounds. **Pros:** old-fashioned and romantic (especially Rooms 203 and 204); pretty veranda perfect for a cocktail; destination restaurant. **Cons:** pool heated from May through October only. [$] *Rooms from: $305* ✉ *1001 Westside Rd.* ☎ *707/433–4231, 800/258–4003* 🌐 *www.madronamanor.com* 🛏 *22 rooms* 🍴 *Breakfast.*

$$$$ B&B/INN Fodor's Choice ★ 🏨 **SingleThread Farms Inn.** Although the physical elements, from the custom bedding and furnishings down to the trays on which breakfast is delivered, speak to husband-and-wife team Kyle and Katina Connaughton's phenomenal attention to detail, in the end it's the spirit of this rare place that astounds the most—that someone would *care* this much about the intricacies of understated service and comfort away from home and pull it off so flawlessly. **Pros:** high style; in-room amenities from restaurant; rooftop garden; multicourse breakfast. **Cons:** one must eventually check out. [$] *Rooms from: $900* ✉ *131 North St., at Center St.* 🌐 *www.singlethreadfarms.com* 🛏 *5 rooms* 🍴 *Breakfast.*

NIGHTLIFE AND PERFORMING ARTS

Healdsburg has always been hospitable to craft beer and cocktail drinkers. In addition to Bear Republic (beer), Bergamot Alley (beers on tap, international wines), and Duke's (artisanal cocktails), downtown restaurants such as Spoonbar, Chalkboard, and Campo Fina *(see above)*, all have talented mixologists. For cocktails farther afield, check out the Alexander Valley Bar north of town. The Raven arts center presents local theater and other performances.

ARTS CENTER

Raven Performing Arts Theater. The Raven Players theater group is the resident company of this venue that also presents comedy and, in June, Healdsburg Jazz Festival performances. ✉ *115 North St., at Center St.* ☎ *707/433–6335* 🌐 *www.raventheater.org.*

BARS AND PUBS

Fodor's Choice ★ **Alexander Valley Bar.** When the Medlock Ames winery opened its tasting room in a former country store, the deal included the adjoining bar, which after remodeling gained the feel of a postmodern speakeasy.

The artisanal cocktails at this spot, whose other pluses include its vineyard-view outdoor patio, often incorporate fruit and herbs from the on-site organic garden. ⊠ *3487 Alexander Valley Rd., at W. Sausal La.* ☎ *707/431–1904* ⊕ *www.medlockames.com/alexander-valley-bar* ☞ *Closed Wed.*

Bear Republic Brewing Company. Lovers of the brew make pilgrimages to Bear Republic to sample the flagship Racer 5 IPA, the Hop Rod Rye, the mighty Big Bear Black Stout, and many other offerings at this craft-brew pioneer. The brewery's spacious pub is an okay stop for a casual lunch or dinner—all kinds of burgers (beef, portobello, veggie, and more), chili, pastas, and artisanal-cheese and charcuterie plates. ■TIP➔ **In warm weather there's often a wait for the seats outdoors, but there's usually room inside.** ⊠ *345 Healdsburg Ave., at North St.* ☎ *707/433–2337* ⊕ *www.bearrepublic.com.*

Duke's Spirited Cocktails. Fruity and savory "farm-to-bar" cocktails, many powered by local artisanal spirits and organically farmed ingredients, are among the specialties of this bar on Healdsburg Plaza's northern periphery. The old-school-in-a-fresh-setting vibe suits the inventive libations, but the owner-mixologists who opened this happenin' hangout in mid-2016 fashion the classics with equal aplomb. ⊠ *111 Plaza St., near Healdsburg Ave.* ☎ *707/431–1060* ⊕ *www.drinkatdukes.com.*

SHOPPING

Healdsburg is the Wine Country's most pleasant spot for an afternoon of window-shopping, with dozens of art galleries, boutiques, and high-end design shops clustered on or around Healdsburg Plaza. Should you weary of shopping, countless cafés and tasting rooms hold the key to revival.

ART GALLERIES

Christopher Hill Gallery. In a town with many worthy galleries, Christopher Hill's brick-walled space stands out for both the quality of the art and his willingness to exhibit edgier styles and subject matter than most of his counterparts. ⊠ *326 Healdsburg Ave., at Plaza St.* ☎ *707/395–4646* ⊕ *www.chgallery.com* ☽ *Closed Tues.*

Fodor's Choice ★ **Gallery Lulo.** A collaboration between a local artist and jewelry maker and a Danish-born curator, this gallery presents changing exhibits of jewelry, sculpture, and objets d'art. ⊠ *303 Center St., at Plaza St.* ☎ *707/433–7533* ⊕ *www.gallerylulo.com.*

BOOKS

Copperfield's Books. In addition to magazines and best-selling books, this store, part of a local indie chain, stocks a wide selection of discounted and remaindered titles, including many cookbooks. ⊠ *106 Matheson St., near Healdsburg Ave.* ☎ *707/433–9270* ⊕ *www.copperfieldsbooks.com/healdsburg.*

CLOTHING

Looking Glass Luxe. Sip sparkling wine from Sonoma and beyond while perusing this exposed-brick shop's cool couture from Rag & Bone, Love Shack Fancy, Tom Ford, and other top women's clothing designers. ⊠ *332 Healdsburg Ave., near North St.* ☎ *707/433–7033* ⊕ *www.lookingglassluxe.com.*

5

CRAFTS

Fodor'sChoice **One World Fair Trade.** Independent artisans in developing countries create
★ the clothing, household items, jewelry, gifts, and toys sold in this bright,
well-designed shop whose owners have a shrewd eye for fine craftsmanship. ⊠ *104 Matheson St., near Healdsburg Ave.* ☎ *707/473–0880*
⊕ *www.oneworldfairtrade.net.*

FOOD AND WINE

Big John's Market. If the sandwich line is too long at Healdsburg's fancier
markets, head north of the plaza 11 blocks and save time and money
at Big John's, a full-service grocery that sells excellent gourmet sandwiches, sushi made on the spot, artisanal cheeses, and bread from Costeaux and other local bakers. ⊠ *1345 Healdsburg Ave., at Dry Creek
Rd.* ☎ *707/433–7151* ⊕ *www.bigjohnsmarket.com.*

Dry Creek General Store. The Dry Creek Valley is so picture-perfect, it
would be a shame to pass up the opportunity to picnic at one of the
wineries. For breakfasts, sandwiches, bread, cheeses, and picnic supplies, stop by the general store, established in 1881 and still a popular
spot for locals to hang out on the porch or in the bar. ⊠ *3495 Dry
Creek Rd., at Lambert Bridge Rd.* ☎ *707/433–4171* ⊕ *www.drycreek-
generalstore1881.com.*

Fodor'sChoice **Healdsburg Farmers' Market.** The long-running market, held from late
★ spring into the fall, showcases locally produced cheeses, breads, herbs,
meats, and oils, in addition to the usual (ultratasty) fruits and vegetables. The flavors and smells arouse the senses, and the passion of
the participating artisans warms the heart. ⊠ *North and Vine Sts., 1
block west of Healdsburg Plaza* ☎ *707/431–1956* ⊕ *www.healdsburg-
farmersmarket.org.*

Fodor'sChoice **Jimtown Store.** The Alexander Valley's best picnic-packing stop has great
★ espresso and a good selection of deli items, including the Classic Ham
& Brie sandwich. While you're here, take a few minutes to browse the
gifts, which include housewares and old-fashioned toys like sock mon-
keys. ⊠ *6706 Hwy. 128, near W. Sausal La.* ☎ *707/433–1212* ⊕ *www.
jimtown.com* ☺ *Closed Tues.*

Oakville Grocery. The Healdsburg branch of this Napa-based store is
filled with wine, condiments, and deli items, and sells sandwiches and
other picnic fixings. A terrace with ample seating makes a good place
for an impromptu meal, but you might want to lunch early or late to
avoid the crowds. ⊠ *124 Matheson St., at Center St.* ☎ *707/433–3200*
⊕ *www.oakvillegrocery.com.*

Fodor'sChoice **The Shed.** Inside a glass-front, steel-clad variation on a traditional grange
★ hall, this shop-cum-eatery celebrates local agriculture. It stocks specialty
foods, seeds and plants, gardening and farming implements, cookware,
and everything a smart pantry should hold. ⊠ *25 North St., west of
Healdsburg Ave.* ☎ *707/431–7433* ⊕ *healdsburgshed.com.*

HOUSEHOLD ITEMS AND FURNITURE

Saint Dizier Home. With its selection of furniture and contemporary items
for the home, this shop reminds mere mortals why the universe provides
us with decorators and designers—they really do know best. ⊠ *259
Center St., at Matheson St.* ☎ *707/473–0980* ⊕ *www.saintdhome.com.*

Fodor's Choice
★

Urban Lumber Company. Master woodworker Seth San Filippo creates contemporary, designer-quality furniture out of reclaimed, salvaged, and sustainably harvested hardwoods. The one-of-a-kind pieces include tables, cabinets, chairs, counters, and bar tops. ✉ *328 Healdsburg Ave., at Plaza St.* ☎ *707/756–5044* ⊕ *www.urbanlumber.co.*

SPAS

Fodor's Choice
★

Spa Dolce. Owner Ines von Majthenyi Scherrer has a good local rep, having run a popular nearby spa before opening this stylish facility just off Healdsburg Plaza. Spa Dolce specializes in skin and body care for men and women, and waxing and facials for women. Curved white walls and fresh-cut floral arrangements set a subdued tone for such treatments as the exfoliating Hauschka body scrub, which combines organic brown sugar with scented oil. There's a romantic room for couples to enjoy massages for two. ■ TIP→ **Many guests come just for the facials, which range from a straightforward cleansing to an anti-aging peel.** ✉ *250 Center St., at Matheson St.* ☎ *707/433–0177* ⊕ *www.spadolce. com* 🗺 *Treatments $50–$225.*

The Spa Hotel Healdsburg. Taking a page from its restaurant's farm-to-table approach, the Hotel Healdsburg's spa also sources many of its treatments' ingredients from area farms. The plush robes for patrons, an outdoor Jacuzzi, and soothing minimalist decor make this a tranquil choice for massages, body wraps, facials, and hand and foot treatments. The most popular ones include the Meyer lemon body polishes, herbal wraps, and massages and the lavender-and-peppermint restorative massage, all of which leave the skin tingling and rejuvenated. The hotel's signature Swedish-style massage involves aromatic oils, hot stones, and, as necessary, acupressure. ✉ *327 Healdsburg Ave., at Matheson St.* ☎ *707/433–4747* ⊕ *www.hotelhealdsburg.com/spa* 🗺 *Treatments $45–$240.*

SPORTS AND THE OUTDOORS

BICYCLING

Fodor's Choice
★

Wine Country Bikes. This shop several blocks southeast of Healdsburg Plaza is perfectly located for single or multiday treks into the Dry Creek and Russian River valleys. Bikes, including tandems, rent for $39–$145 per day. One-day tours start at $149. ■ TIP→ **The owner and staff can help with bicycling itineraries, including a mostly gentle loop, which takes in Westside Road and Eastside Road wineries and a rusting trestle bridge, as well as a more challenging excursion to Lake Sonoma.** ✉ *61 Front St., at Hudson St.* ☎ *707/473–0610, 866/922–4537* ⊕ *www.winecountrybikes.com.*

BOATING

Russian River Adventures. This outfit rents inflatable canoes for self-guided, full- and half-day trips down the Russian River. Pack a swimsuit and a picnic lunch and shove off. You'll likely see wildlife on the shore and can stop at fun swimming holes and even swing on a rope above the water. The fee includes a shuttle ride back to your car. The full-day trip is dog-friendly. ✉ *20 Healdsburg Ave., at S. University St.* ☎ *707/433–5599, 800/280–7627* ⊕ *www.russianriveradventures. com* 🗺 *From $45.*

5

A Great Drive in Northern Sonoma County

Cover three AVAs in one day on a scenic loop drive that begins in downtown Healdsburg. Before departing, break your fast at **Flying Goat Coffee** or **Downtown Bakery & Creamery,** then pick up everything you need for a picnic at nearby **Oakville Grocery.** Thus prepared, hop in the car and head south on Healdsburg Avenue.

RUSSIAN RIVER VALLEY AVA
A few blocks south of Healdsburg Plaza, stay left to avoid U.S. 101. About ½ mile past the bridge over the Russian River, Healdsburg Avenue becomes Old Redwood Highway. Just past the driveway for the J and Rodney Strong wineries—by all means stop at one of them if you're eager to start tasting—make a right onto Eastside Road and continue past Copain Wines to Wohler Road and turn right. Before long you'll cross the rusting, highly photogenic Wohler Bridge. At Westside Road, turn north to reach **Arista Winery.** After tasting there head north on Westside Road about 6 miles past Arista.

DRY CREEK VALLEY AVA
Turn northwest at the intersection of Westside and West Dry Creek Roads—**Madrona Manor,** worth a peek for its well-tended estate garden, borders them both—and continue on West Dry Creek for about 9 miles to **Preston of Dry Creek.** Sample some wines and perhaps pick up a bottle—the peppy

Sauvignon Blanc is a natural pick on a hot summer day, and the Barbera is a good red—to enjoy while picnicking on the property.

From Preston, head southeast on West Dry Creek Road and east on Yoakim Bridge Road. If it's summer and the **Dry Creek Peach & Produce** stand is open, stop to sample the fruit; otherwise continue directly to Dry Creek Road and turn south, heading east after about ¼ mile onto Canyon Road. After 2 miles, just after you pass under U.S. 101, turn south (right) on Highway 128 east, also signed as Geyserville Avenue.

ALEXANDER VALLEY AVA
Let your mood determine your stop in the Alexander Valley. Taste flights of wines from small producers at the **Locals Tasting Room** or, for Cab, Zin, and a Zin-based blend, continue east on Highway 128, turning left on River Road to **Zialena.** If Hollywood glitz is more your speed, head south on Geyserville Avenue to U.S. 101, hop on the freeway for 1 mile, and take the Independence Lane exit. Follow signs west from the exit to **Francis Ford Coppola Winery.**

After your Alexander Valley stop, enjoy dinner at **Diavola Pizzeria & Salumeria** or **Catelli's** in Geyserville, or head back to Healdsburg, south on Geyserville Avenue, briefly east (left) onto Lytton Springs Road, and south on Healdsburg Avenue.

GEYSERVILLE

8 miles north of Healdsburg.

Several high-profile Alexander Valley AVA wineries, including the splashy Francis Ford Coppola Winery, can be found in the town of Geyserville, a small part of which stretches west of U.S. 101 into northern Dry Creek. Not long ago this was a dusty farm town, and downtown Geyserville retains its rural character, but the restaurants, shops, and tasting rooms along the short main drag hint at Geyserville's growing sophistication.

GETTING HERE AND AROUND

From Healdsburg, the quickest route to downtown Geyserville is north on U.S. 101 to the Highway 128/Geyserville exit. Turn right at the stop sign onto Geyserville Avenue and follow the road north to the small downtown. For a more scenic drive, head north from Healdsburg Plaza along Healdsburg Avenue. About 3 miles north, jog west (left) for a few hundred feet onto Lytton Springs Road, then turn north (right) onto Geyserville Avenue. In town, the avenue merges with Highway 128. Sonoma County Transit Bus 60 serves Geyserville from downtown Healdsburg.

VISITOR INFORMATION

Geyserville Chamber of Commerce. ⊠ *Geyserville* ☎ *707/276–6067* ⊕ *www.geyservillecc.com.*

EXPLORING

TOP ATTRACTIONS

David Coffaro Estate Vineyard. Easily one of the Dry Creek Valley's least pretentious wineries, David Coffaro specializes in red blends and single-varietal wines from grapes grown on a 20-acre estate. Zinfandel and Petite Sirah are strong suits, but Coffaro and his team also make wines using Lagrein, Aglianico, and other less familiar grapes, which also find their way into his unique blends, including the Rhône-style Terra Melange, with Peloursin and Carignane added to the usual Grenache, Syrah, and Mourvèdre mix. The tour is by appointment only. ⊠ *7485 Dry Creek Rd., near Yoakim Bridge Rd.* ☎ *707/433–9715* ⊕ *www. coffaro.com* ✉ *Tasting $5, tour free.*

Fodor'sChoice **Locals Tasting Room.** If you're serious about wine, Carolyn Lewis's tast-★ ing room alone is worth a trek 8 miles north of Healdsburg Plaza to downtown Geyserville. Connoisseurs who appreciate Lewis's ability to spot up-and-comers head here regularly to sample the output of a dozen or so small wineries, most without tasting rooms of their own. There's no fee for tasting—extraordinary for wines of this quality—and the extremely knowledgeable staff are happy to pour you a flight of several wines so you can compare, say, different Cabernet Sauvignons. ⊠ *21023A Geyserville Ave., at Hwy. 128* ☎ *707/857–4900* ⊕ *www. tastelocalwines.com* ✉ *Tasting free.*

Fodor'sChoice **Robert Young Estate Winery.** The whitewashed colonial-style residence ★ and barnlike winery building at Robert Young lend an appropriate air of permanence to this longtime grower whose Chardonnays and Cabernet Sauvignons wine critics routinely applaud. The first Youngs began farming this land in the mid-1800s, but it was the late Robert Young, of the third generation, who planted two Chardonnay clones now named for him. Those grapes go into the Area 27 Chardonnay, noteworthy for the quality of its fruit and craftsmanship. The reds shine even brighter: if poured, don't miss the Petit Verdot, Cabernet Franc, and Cabernet Sauvignons. The tour and a wine and cheese pairing are by appointment only. ■ TIP→ Tables for picnickers are set up outside the two entrances to the winery's caves. ⊠ *4960 Red Winery Rd., off Hwy. 128* ☎ *707/431–4811* ⊕ *www.ryew.com* ☜ *Tastings $10–$30, tour $35.*

Fodor's Choice
★
Silver Oak. The Sonoma County operation of the same-named Napa Valley winery produces just one wine each year: a robust, well-balanced Alexander Valley Cabernet Sauvignon. Unlike many Wine Country Cabernets, this one is aged in American rather than French oak barrels (half new, half once-used) for 24 months. One tasting includes the current Alexander Valley Cabernet and Napa Valley Bordeaux blend plus two older vintages, and another showcases Silver Oak wines and ones (Sauvignon Blanc, Pinot Noir, Merlot) of sister winery Twomey Cellars. The Silver Oak–Twomey tasting and the tour are by appointment only. Note: By early 2018 the Geyserville tasting room will likely have closed in favor of a new one at Silver Oak's state-of-the-art facility at 7370 Highway 128 in Healdsburg on the former Sausal Winery site. ⊠ *24625 Chianti Rd., off Canyon Rd.* ☎ *707/942–7082* ⊕ *www.silveroak.com/visit-us/alexander* ☜ *Tastings $20–$30, tour and tasting $25.*

Fodor's Choice
★
Trattore Farms. The tectonic shifts that created the Dry Creek Valley are in full evidence at this winery atop one of several abruptly rolling hills tamed only partially by grapevines and olive trees. All tastings include selections of olive oils milled on-site, but the main events are the valley views and the lineup of Rhône-style whites, among them an exotic Marsanne-Roussanne blend, and reds that range from the dazzling Laughlin Ranch Vineyard Pinot Noir and estate Grenache and Zinfandel to two rich blends. Kerry Damskey, a respected winemaker and international consultant, crafts the wines. The Napa Valley Stagecoach Vineyard Cabernet Sauvignon isn't always on the list, but if you like Cabs, ask if a taste is possible. The tour is by appointment only. ■ TIP→ For a real treat on a fair-weather weekend, book a seated outdoor tasting. ⊠ *7878 Dry Creek Rd., ¾ mile north of Yoakim Bridge Rd.* ☎ *707/431–7200* ⊕ *www.trattorefarms.com* ☜ *Tastings $20–$35, tour $70 (vineyard, orchard, olive mill).*

Virginia Dare Winery. Leave it to vintner-filmmaker Francis Ford Coppola to fashion a playful excursion out of the interlocking tales of the New World's first European child—Virginia Dare of the ill-fated 16th-century Roanoke Colony—and the once-prominent 20th-century wine brand named for her. Cheery staffers fill in the story while pouring modestly priced wines with labels reflecting these themes. Notable reds include The Lost Colony—a recent vintage comprising Syrah, Malbec, Petite Sirah, Cabernet Franc, and Petit Verdot—and the equally adventurous Manteo. The Virginia Dare Russian River Chardonnay also impresses. The winery's restaurant, Werowocomoco, emphasizes "American native" dishes such as bison ribs. ■ TIP→ Stars of Hollywood's golden

CLOSE UP

Alexander Valley AVA

The Alexander Valley extends north-east of Healdsburg through Geyserville all the way to Mendocino County. Driving through the rolling hills along Highway 128, you're as likely to have to slow down for tandem bicyclists as for other drivers. And you might find a handful of visitors at most in the tasting rooms of some of the small, family-owned wineries.

The Alexander Valley AVA got a boost in 2006, when director and winemaker Francis Ford Coppola bought the old Chateau Souverain winery and opened a tasting room, but some combination of distance from San Francisco (a drive here takes a little under two hours in light traffic) and hairpin switchback roads seems to have preserved the region's unpretentious, rustic nature. This remains a spot to enjoy life in the slow lane.

As recently as the 1980s the Alexander Valley was mostly planted to walnuts, pears, plums, and bulk grapes, but these days grapes for premium wines, particularly Cabernet Sauvignon, but also Sauvignon Blanc, Merlot, and Zinfandel, have largely replaced them. Rhône varietals such as Grenache and Syrah, along with Sangiovese, Barbera, and other Italian grapes, also make great wines here.

age tout Virginia Dare wines of yore in amusing magazine ads adorning the elevator ("'Vintage Schmintage,' says Bert Lahr," aka the Cowardly Lion). ⊠ 22281 Chianti Rd., at Canyon Rd. ☎ 707/735–3500 ⊕ www.virginiadarewinery.com ⊠ Tasting $15.

Fodor'sChoice ★ **Zialena.** Sister-and-brother team Lisa and Mark Mazzoni (she runs the business, he makes the wines) debuted their small winery's first vintage in 2014, but their Italian-American family's Alexander Valley winemaking heritage stretches back more than a century. Mark—whose on-the-job teachers included the late Mike Lee of Kenwood Winery and Philippe Melka, a premier international consultant—specializes in smooth Zinfandel and nuanced Cabernet Sauvignon. Most of the grapes come from the 120-acre estate vineyard farmed by Lisa and Mark's father, Mike, who sells to Jordan and other big-name wineries. Other Zialena wines include a Dry Creek Valley Sauvignon Blanc and Cappella, a Zin-based blend Lisa describes as "Mark's fun wine." A contemporary stone, wood, and glass tasting room amid the family's vineyards opened in 2017. Tours, one focusing on production, the other on the vineyards, are by appointment only. ⊠ 21112 River Rd., off Hwy. 128 ☎ 707/955–5992 ⊕ www.zialena.com ⊠ Tastings $15–$25, tours $50–$75.

WORTH NOTING

FAMILY **Francis Ford Coppola Winery.** The fun at what the film director calls his "wine wonderland" is all in the excess. You may find it hard to resist having your photo snapped standing next to Don Corleone's desk from *The Godfather* or beside other memorabilia from Coppola films (including some directed by his daughter, Sofia). A bandstand reminiscent of one in *The Godfather Part II* is the centerpiece of a large pool area where you can rent a changing room, complete with shower, and spend the afternoon lounging poolside, perhaps ordering food from the adjacent café. A more elaborate restaurant, Rustic, overlooks the vineyards. As for the wines, the excess continues in the cellar, where more than 40 varietal wines and blends are produced. ✉ *300 Via Archimedes, off U.S. 101* ☎ *707/857–1400* 🌐 *www.franciscoppolawinery.com* 🎟 *Tastings free–$25, tours $20–$75, pool pass $35.*

Trentadue Winery. Sangiovese, Zinfandel, and La Storia Cuvée 32 (a Super Tuscan–style blend of Sangiovese, Merlot, and other grapes) are among the strong suits of this Alexander Valley stalwart established in 1959 by the late Leo and Evelyn Trentadue. Tastings ($10 for the Trentadue Family wines, $25 for La Storia reserve selections) take place inside an ivy-covered villa. The diverse lineup includes a sparkler from French Colombard grapes, along with Sauvignon Blanc, a Sangiovese rosé, Merlot, Cabernet Sauvignon, Petite Sirah, Zinfandel, and dessert wines, all moderately priced. The tour and some tastings are by appointment only. ✉ *19170 Geyserville Ave., off U.S. 101* ☎ *707/433–3104* 🌐 *www.trentadue.com* 🎟 *Tastings $10–$25, tour and tasting $25.*

WHERE TO EAT AND STAY

$$ ITALIANITALIAN Fodor's Choice ★

🍴 **Catelli's.** Cookbook author and *Iron Chef* judge Domenica Catelli teamed up with her brother Nicholas to revive their family's American-Italian restaurant, a Geyserville fixture. Contemporary abstracts, reclaimed-wood furnishings, and muted gray and chocolate-brown walls signal the changing times, but you'll find good-lovin' echoes of traditional cuisine in the sturdy meat sauce that accompanies the signature lasagna dish's paper-thin noodles and ricotta-and-herb-cheese filling. **Known for:** three-meat ravioli and other pastas; festive back patio; organic gardens. [$] *Average main: $20* ✉ *21047 Geyserville Ave., at Hwy. 128* ☎ *707/857–3471* 🌐 *www.mycatellis.com* 🕒 *Closed Mon.*

$$ ITALIAN Fodor's Choice ★

🍴 **Diavola Pizzeria & Salumeria.** A dining area with hardwood floors, a pressed-tin ceiling, and exposed-brick walls provides a fitting setting for the rustic cuisine at this Geyserville mainstay. Chef Dino Bugica studied with several artisans in Italy before opening this restaurant that specializes in pizzas pulled from a wood-burning oven and several types of house-cured meats, with a few salads and meaty main courses rounding out the menu. **Known for:** wood-fired pizzas; smoked pork belly, pancetta, and spicy Calabrese sausage. [$] *Average main: $19* ✉ *21021 Geyserville Ave., at Hwy. 128* ☎ *707/814–0111* 🌐 *www.diavolapizzeria.com.*

$ HOTEL

🏨 **Geyserville Inn.** Clever travelers give the Healdsburg hubbub and prices the heave-ho but still have easy access to outstanding Dry Creek and Alexander Valley wineries from this modest, family-run inn. **Pros:** pool; second-floor rooms in back have vineyard views; picnic area. **Cons:** occasional noise bleed-through from corporate and other events. [$] *Rooms from: $149* ✉ *21714 Geyserville Ave.* ☎ *707/857–4343, 877/857–4343* 🌐 *www.geyservilleinn.com* 🛏 *41 rooms* 🍽 *No meals.*

NIGHTLIFE

BARS AND PUBS

Geyserville Gun Club Bar & Lounge. Next door to the great Diavola pizzeria (same ownership), this long, skinny bar in Geyserville's Odd Fellows Building wows locals and tourists with Sazeracs, Gibsons, and other classic cocktails and a bar menu centered around pickles, chicken wings, and fish crudos. Hardwood floors, exposed brick, taxidermied animals, and contempo lighting set the mood at this cool spot. Closed Tuesday and Wednesday. ✉ *21025 Geyserville Ave., at Hwy. 128* ☎ *707/814–0036* ⊕ *www.geyservillegunclub.com.*

WEST COUNTY

The portion of Sonoma County west of Healdsburg and Santa Rosa goes by the name West County. The towns in this area, many of them along or near the Russian River, include Forestville, Guerneville, Occidental, Sebastopol, and Graton. Redwoods tower over much of the region, which since the 1980s has seen grapes supplant apples and other crops on its many farms. Long before that, West County was a getaway for city and suburban dwellers, but despite the increased attention brought by wine making, West County remains generally unfussy and resolutely rural, especially the farther west you head.

FORESTVILLE

13 miles southwest of Healdsburg.

To experience the Russian River AVA's climate and rusticity, follow the river's westward course to the town of Forestville, home to a highly regarded restaurant and inn and a few wineries producing Pinot Noir from the Russian River Valley and well beyond.

GETTING HERE AND AROUND

To reach Forestville from U.S. 101, drive west from the River Road exit north of Santa Rosa. From Healdsburg, follow Westside Road west to River Road and then continue west. Sonoma County Transit Bus 20 serves Forestville.

EXPLORING

Hartford Family Winery. Pinot Noir lovers appreciate the subtle differences in the wines Hartford's Jeff Stewart crafts from grapes grown in four Sonoma County AVAs, along with fruit from nearby Marin and Mendocino counties and Oregon. Stewart also makes highly rated Chardonnays and old-vine Zinfandels. If the weather's good and you've made a reservation, you can enjoy a flight of five or six wines on the patio outside the opulent main winery building. Indoors, at seated private library tastings, guests sip current and older vintages. ■TIP→ **Hartford also has a tasting room in downtown Healdsburg.** ✉ *8075 Martinelli Rd., off Hwy. 116 or River Rd.* ☎ *707/887–8030, 800/588–0234* ⊕ *www.hartfordwines.com* 🍷 *Tastings $15–$45.*

Joseph Jewell Wines. A decade ago, Micah Joseph Wirth and Adrian Jewell Manspeaker—still in their twenties—started this winery whose name combines their middle ones. Pinot Noirs from the Russian River Valley and Humboldt County to the north are the strong suit. Wirth, who worked for seven years for vintner Gary Farrell, credits his interactions with Farrell's Russian River growers, among them the owners of Bucher Vineyard and Hallberg Ranch, with easing the winery's access to prestigious fruit. Manspeaker, a Humboldt native, spearheaded the foray into Pinot Noir grown among coastal redwoods. Joseph Jewell's playfully rustic storefront tasting room in downtown Forestville provides the opportunity to experience what's unique about the varietal's next Northern California frontier. The bonuses: a Zinfandel from 1970s vines and two Chardonnays. ⊠ *6542 Front St.* ☎ *707/820–1621* ⊕ *www.josephjewell.com* ⊠ *Tastings $10–$30, tours $95–$500 per couple (the $500 tour is in a helicopter).*

Fodor'sChoice
★
Russian River Vineyards Restaurant, Farm, Tasting Lounge. The lengthy moniker of this operation specializing in single-vineyard Russian River Valley Pinot Noirs hints at the bustle taking place: dining indoors, farming outdoors, and wine tasting in the courtyard under pergolas, shade trees, and umbrellas. Woodpeckers pilfer acorns from nearby oaks, punctuating the quiet as they cache their booty in the redwood roof of the hop-barn-style structure out back. The rustic setting has been known to induce "couch lock," causing patrons to while away hours sipping wine and nibbling on cheese, charcuterie, and other snackables, even settling in with a book. Tours of the farm, which include tasting, are by appointment only. ■TIP→ The tasting lounge stays open late, making this a good last stop of the day. Musicians perform on weekends from noon and weekdays after 6. ⊠ *5700 Hwy. 116 N, ¾ mile south of town* ☎ *707/887–2300* ⊕ *www.russianrivervineyards.com* ⊠ *Tastings from $15, farm tour and tasting $65.*

WHERE TO EAT AND STAY

$$$
MODERN
AMERICAN
✕ **The Backyard.** The folks behind this casually rustic modern American restaurant regard Sonoma County's farms and gardens as their "backyard" and proudly list their purveyors on the menu. Dinner entrées, which change seasonally, might include herb tagliatelle with lamb meatballs or maitake mushroom cassoulet with roasted fennel, spiced squash, and other vegetables. **Known for:** buttermilk fried chicken with buttermilk biscuits; poplar-shaded outdoor front patio in good weather. ⓢ *Average main: $24* ⊠ *6566 Front St./Hwy. 116, at 1st St.* ☎ *707/820–8445* ⊕ *backyardforestville.com* ⊘ *Closed Tues.*

$$$$
FRENCH
Fodor'sChoice
★
✕ **The Farmhouse Inn.** From the sommelier who assists you with wine choices to the servers who describe the provenance of the black truffles shaved over the intricate pasta dishes, the staff matches the quality of this restaurant's French-inspired prix-fixe meals. The signature dish, "Rabbit Rabbit Rabbit," a trio of confit of leg, rabbit loin wrapped in applewood-smoked bacon, and roasted rack of rabbit, is typical of preparations that are both rustic and refined. **Known for:** upscale accommodations with full-service spa; sophisticated cuisine; romantic dining. ⓢ *Average main: $95* ⊠ *7871 River Rd., at Wohler Rd.* ☎ *707/887–3300, 800/464–6642* ⊕ *www.farmhouseinn.com* ⊘ *Closed Tues. and Wed. No lunch.*

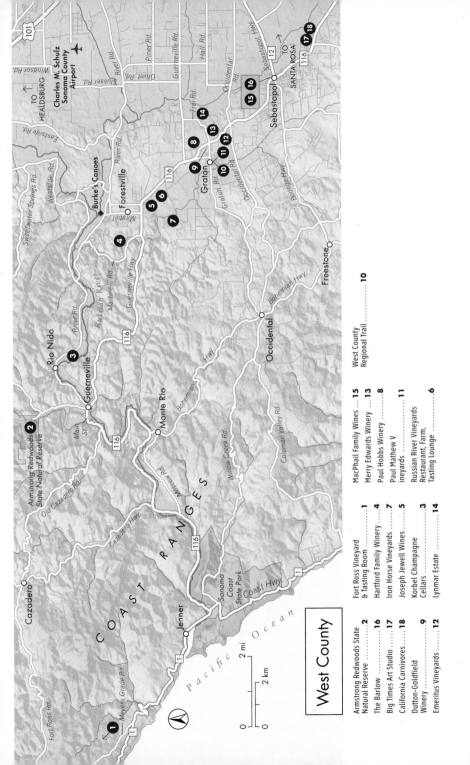

West County

Armstrong Redwoods State
Natural Reserve **2**
The Barlow **16**
Big Times Art Studio **17**
California Carnivores **18**
Dutton-Goldfield
Winery **9**
Emeritus Vineyards **12**

Fort Ross Vineyard
& Tasting Room **1**
Hartford Family Winery ... **4**
Iron Horse Vineyards **7**
Joseph Jewell Wines **5**
Korbel Champagne
Cellars **3**
Lynmar Estate **14**

MacPhail Family Wines ... **15**
Merry Edwards Winery ... **13**
Paul Hobbs Winery **8**
Paul Mathew
Vineyards **11**
Russian River Vineyards
Restaurant, Farm,
Tasting Lounge **6**

West County
Regional Trail **10**

CLOSE UP

Russian River Valley AVA

As the Russian River winds its way from Mendocino to the Pacific Ocean, it carves out a valley that's a near-perfect environment for growing certain grape varietals. Because of its low elevation, sea fog pushes far inland to cool the soil, yet in summer it burns off, giving the grapes enough sun to ripen properly. Fog-loving Pinot Noir and Chardonnay grapes are king and queen in the Russian River Valley AVA, which extends from Healdsburg west to the town Guerneville. The namesake river does its part by slowly carving its way downward through many layers of rock, depositing a deep layer of gravel that in parts of the valley measures 60 or 70 feet. This gravel forces the roots of grapevines to go deep in search of water and nutrients. In the process, the plants absorb trace minerals that add complexity to the flavor of the grapes.

$ × **Twist.** A perky lunch-only spot on Forestville's blink-and-you'll-
AMERICAN miss-it main drag, Twist serves sandwiches like moms of yore made, only better: Cajun meat loaf, pulled pork with house-made barbecue sauce, and a local-favorite BLT when tomatoes are in season. The option with grilled yams, eggplant, red peppers, and other seasonal ingredients on a focaccia roll with sun-dried tomatoes and goat cheese wows the no-meat-for-me set. **Known for:** gluten-free soups; down-home cooking with flair; good beers, wines, and soft drinks; all-day egg scrambles. $ *Average main: $12* ✉ *6536 Front St., near Railroad Ave.* ☎ *707/820–8443* ⊕ *www.twisteatery.com* ⊘ *Closed Sun. and Mon. No dinner.*

SPORTS AND THE OUTDOORS

Burke's Canoe Trips. You'll get a real feel for the Russian River's flora and fauna on a leisurely 10-mile paddle downstream from Burke's to Guerneville. A shuttle bus returns you to your car at the end of the journey, which is best taken from late May through mid-October and, in summer, on a weekday—summer weekends can be crowded and raucous. ✉ *8600 River Rd., at Mirabel Rd.* ☎ *707/887–1222* ⊕ *www. burkescanoetrips.com* ✉ *$70 per canoe.*

GUERNEVILLE

7 miles northwest of Forestville; 15 miles southwest of Healdsburg.

Guerneville's tourist demographic has evolved over the years—Bay Area families in the 1950s, lesbians and gays starting in the 1970s, and these days a mix of both groups, plus techies and outdoorsy types—with coast redwoods and the Russian River always central to the town's appeal. The area's most famous winery is Korbel Champagne Cellars, established nearly a century and a half ago. Even older are the stands of trees that except on the coldest winter days make Armstrong Redwoods State Natural Reserve such a perfect respite from wine tasting.

On a hot summer day the shady paths of Armstrong Redwoods State Natural Reserve provide cool comfort.

GETTING HERE AND AROUND

To get to Guerneville from Healdsburg, follow Westside Road south to River Road and turn west. From Forestville, head west on Highway 116; alternatively, you can head north on Mirabel Road to River Road and then head west. Sonoma County Transit Bus 20 serves Guerneville.

VISITOR INFORMATION

Guerneville Visitor Center. ⊠ *16209 1st St, at Armstrong Woods Rd.* ☎ *707/869–9000* ⊕ *www.russianriver.com.*

EXPLORING

FAMILY
Fodor's Choice
★

Armstrong Redwoods State Natural Reserve. Here's your best opportunity in the western Wine Country to wander amid *Sequoia sempervirens*, also known as coast redwood trees. The oldest example in this 805-acre state park, the Colonel Armstrong Tree, is thought to be more than 1,400 years old. A half mile from the parking lot, the tree is easily accessible, and you can hike a long way into the forest before things get too hilly. ■TIP→ **During hot summer days, Armstrong Redwoods's tall trees help the park keep its cool.** ⊠ *17000 Armstrong Woods Rd., off River Rd.* ☎ *707/869–2958 for visitor center, 707/869–2015 for park headquarters* ⊕ *www.parks.ca.gov* ⤳ *$8 per vehicle, free to pedestrians and bicyclists.*

OFF THE
BEATEN
PATH

Fort Ross Vineyard & Tasting Room. The Russian River and Highway 116 snake west from Guerneville through redwood groves to the coast, where Highway 1 twists north past rocky cliffs to this windswept ridgetop winery. Until recently many experts deemed the weather this far west too chilly even for cool-climate varietals, but Fort Ross

Vineyard and other Fort Ross–Seaview AVA wineries are proving that Chardonnay and Pinot Noir can thrive above the fog line. The sea air and rocky soils here produce wines generally less fruit-forward than their Russian River Valley counterparts but equally sophisticated and no less vibrant. Many coastal wineries are appointment-only or closed to the public; with its rustic-chic, barnlike tasting room and wide outdoor patio overlooking the Pacific, Fort Ross provides an appealing introduction to this up-and-coming region's wines. ✉ *15725 Meyers Grade Rd., off Hwy. 1, Jenner ✢ From Guerneville, take Hwy. 116 west 12 miles, then Hwy. 1 north 6 miles to Meyers Grade Rd.* ☎ *707/847–3460* ⊕ *www.fortrossvineyard.com* 🍷 *Tasting $25.*

Korbel Champagne Cellars. The three brothers Korbel (Joseph, Francis, and Anton) planted Pinot Noir grapes in the Russian River Valley in the 1870s, pioneering efforts that are duly noted on 50-minute tours of the well-known brand's Guerneville facility. Tours include a clear explanation of the *méthode champenoise* used to make the company's sparkling wines, a walk through ivy-covered 19th-century buildings, and tastings of Korbel's bubblies and still wines. You can also taste without touring. ■**TIP**➜ **If you have the time, stroll through the rose garden, home to more than 250 varieties.** ✉ *13250 River Rd., west of Rio Nido* ☎ *707/824–7000* ⊕ *www.korbel.com/winery* 🍷 *Tasting and tour free* ⊙ *No garden tours mid-Oct.–mid-Apr.*

WHERE TO EAT

$ | ✕ **Big Bottom Market.** Foodies love this culinary pit stop and grocery for
MODERN | its breakfast biscuits, clever sandwiches, and savory salads to go or eat
AMERICAN | here. Everything from butter and jam and mascarpone and honey to barbecue pulled pork with pickles and slaw accompanies the biscuits, whose mix made Oprah's Favorite Things 2016 list, and the stellar sandwiches include the Colonel Armstrong (curried chicken salad with currants and cashews on a brioche). **Known for:** biscuits and heartier breakfast fare; sandwiches and salads for lunch. $ *Average main: $11* ✉ *16228 Main St., near Church St.* ☎ *707/604–7295* ⊕ *www.bigbottommarket.com* ⊙ *Closed Tues. No dinner.*

$$$ | ✕ **boon eat+drink.** A casual storefront restaurant on Guerneville's main
MODERN | drag, boon eat+drink has a menu built around small, "green" (salads
AMERICAN | and cooked vegetables), and main plates assembled for the most part
Fodor'sChoice | from locally produced organic ingredients. Polenta lasagna, a beguil-
★ | ingly creamy mix of ricotta salata cheese and polenta served on greens sautéed in garlic, all of it floating upon a spicy marinara sauce, is among the signature dishes. **Known for:** adventurous culinary sensibility; all wines from Russian River Valley. $ *Average main: $24* ✉ *16248 Main St., at Church St.* ☎ *707/869–0780* ⊕ *eatatboon.com* ⊙ *Closed Wed. Nov.–late May. No lunch Wed. late May–Oct.*

$$ | ✕ **Dick Blomster's Korean Diner.** The KFC at this local favorite stands for
KOREAN FUSION | "Korean Fried Crack"—fried chicken whose addictive components include its tangy barbecue sauce and vanilla slaw—but the inventive plays on comfort food don't stop there: even iceberg lettuce with blue cheese dressing gets jazzed up, in this case with the chili-laced sweet paste *gochujang*. Noodle and rice bowls, kimchi pancakes, and hand-cut Seoul fries with Korean chilies are among the other popular items.

Known for: retro diner decor; full bar; attractive preparations. Ⓢ *Average main: $16* ✉ *16236 Main St., near Church St.* ☎ *707/869–8006* ⊕ *www.dickblomsters.com* ⊗ *Closed Tues. in winter.*

WHERE TO STAY

$$

B&B/INN

FAMILY

Fodor's Choice

★

⬚ **AutoCamp Russian River.** Guests at this spot along the Russian River that debuted in 2016 camp (well, sort of) in luxury under the redwoods in cute-as-a-button Airstream trailers decked out with top-notch oh-so-contemporary beds, linens, and bath products. **Pros:** hip, retro feel; comfortable down beds; campfire and barbecue pit for each trailer. **Cons:** lacks room service and other hotel amenities; fee for housekeeping; two-guest maximum (including children) for tents. Ⓢ *Rooms from: $275* ✉ *14120 Old Cazadero Rd.* ☎ *888/405–7553* ⊕ *autocamp.com/location/russian-river* ⬑ *24 rooms* ⦿ *No meals* ⌁ *Tents (late spring–mid-fall) from $175.*

$

HOTEL

Fodor's Choice

★

⬚ **boon hotel+spa.** Redwoods, Douglas firs, and palms supply shade and seclusion at this lushly landscaped resort ¾ mile north of downtown Guerneville. **Pros:** memorable breakfasts; lush landscaping; on-site spa. **Cons:** lacks amenities of larger properties. Ⓢ *Rooms from: $155* ✉ *14711 Armstrong Woods Rd.* ☎ *707/869–2721* ⊕ *boonhotels.com* ⬑ *14 rooms* ⦿ *Breakfast.*

$

B&B/INN

FAMILY

⬚ **Cottages on River Road.** Redwoods on a steep slope tower above this tidy roadside complex of single and duplex cottages separated by a grassy lawn. **Pros:** family business run with care; affordable rates; 5 two-bedroom cottages good for families and groups. **Cons:** books up far in advance in summer; lacks upscale amenities; some road noise audible (ask for a cottage under the trees). Ⓢ *Rooms from: $99* ✉ *14880 River Rd., 1¼ miles east of town* ☎ *707/869–3848* ⊕ *www.cottagesonriverroad.com* ⬑ *19 rooms* ⦿ *Breakfast.*

NIGHTLIFE

El Barrio. Mescal and classic tequila margaritas are the mainstays of this bar—a festive spot to begin or end the evening or to park yourself while waiting for a table at owner Crista Luedtke's nearby boon eat + drink. The Barrio Frances (top-shelf rye, cognac, vermouth, Bénédictine, and bitters) and more fanciful creations also await at this serape-chic watering hole. ✉ *16230 Main St., near Church St.* ☎ *707/604–7601* ⊕ *www.elbarriobar.com* ⌁ *Closed Tues.*

OCCIDENTAL

11 miles south of Guerneville.

A village surrounded by redwood forests, orchards, and vineyards, Occidental is a former logging hub with a bohemian vibe. The small downtown, which contains several handsome Victorian-era structures, has a whimsically decorated bed-and-breakfast inn, two good restaurants, and a handful of art galleries and shops worth poking around.

GETTING HERE AND AROUND

From Guerneville, head west on Highway 116 for 4 miles to the town of Monte Rio, then turn south on Church Street and travel past the old Rio Theater and over the bridge spanning the Russian River. At this point the road is signed as the Bohemian Highway, which takes you into town, where the road's name changes to Main Street. Public transit is not a convenient way to travel here.

WHERE TO EAT AND STAY

$$ MODERN AMERICAN Fodor's Choice ★ 🍴 **Hazel.** Pizza and pastries are the specialty of this tiny restaurant whose owner-chefs, Jim and Michele Wimborough, forsook their fancy big-city gigs for the pleasures of small-town living. Jim's mushroom pizza, adorned with Brie and truffle oil, and the pie with sausage and egg are among the headliners, with Michele's sundae with salted caramel and hot fudge among the enticements for dessert. **Known for:** flavorful seasonal cuisine; roasted chicken with lemon vinaigrette entrée; Sunday brunch (try the beignets). [$] *Average main: $21* ✉ *3782 Bohemian Hwy., at Occidental Rd.* ☎ *707/874–6003* 🌐 *www.restauranthazel.com* 🕒 *Closed Mon. No lunch Tues.–Sat.*

$ AMERICAN 🍴 **Howard Station Cafe.** The mile-long list of morning fare at Occidental's neo-hippie go-to breakfast and weekend brunch spot includes biscuits and gravy, huevos rancheros, omelets, eggs Benedict, waffles, pancakes, French toast, and "healthy alternatives" such as tofu rancheros, oatmeal, and house-made granola. Soups, salads, burgers, and monstrous sandwiches are on the menu for lunch. **Known for:** mostly organic ingredients; juice bar; vegetarian and gluten-free items. [$] *Average main: $11* ✉ *3611 Main St./Bohemian Hwy., at 2nd St.* ☎ *707/874–2838* 🌐 *www.howardstationcafe.com* 💳 *No credit cards* 🕒 *No dinner.*

$ BAKERY 🍴 **Wild Flour Bread.** The sticky buns at jovial Jed Wallach's Wild Flour are legendary in western Sonoma—on weekends they're often all gone by the early afternoon—as are the rye breads and sock-it-to-me scones in flavors like double chocolate, espresso, and hazelnut. There's a long table inside, but most patrons enjoy their baked goods on the benches outside. **Known for:** pastry lineup; fougasse (Provençal flatbread), rye, and other breads; cookies and biscotti. [$] *Average main: $5* ✉ *140 Bohemian Hwy., at El Camino Bodega, 4 miles south of Occidental, Freestone* ☎ *707/874–2938* 🌐 *www.wildflourbread.com* 💳 *No credit cards* 🕒 *Closed Tues.–Thurs. No dinner.*

$$ B&B/INN 🏨 **The Inn at Occidental.** Quilts, folk art, and original paintings and photographs fill this colorful and friendly inn. **Pros:** whimsical decor; most rooms have private decks and jetted tubs. **Cons:** not for those with minimalist tastes; not for kids. [$] *Rooms from: $259* ✉ *3657 Church St.* ☎ *707/874–1047, 800/522–6324* 🌐 *www.innatoccidental.com* 🛏 *17 rooms* 🍽 *Breakfast.*

SPORTS AND THE OUTDOORS

Sonoma Canopy Tours. Zip through the trees with the greatest of ease—at speeds up to 25 mph—at this ziplining center 2½ miles north of Occidental. Friendly guides prepare guests well for their 2½-hour natural high. ■ **TIP→ Participants must be at least 10 years old and weigh between 70 and 250 pounds.** ✉ *6250 Bohemian Hwy.* ☎ *888/494–7868* 🌐 *www.sonomacanopytours.com* 🎟 *From $99.*

CLOSE UP

Crush Camp in Sonoma County

Harvest in late summer and early fall is a prime time to connect with the beauty of sprawling Sonoma County, the rhythms of agricultural life, and the passionate professionalism of its grape farmers and winemakers.

IMMERSE YOURSELF
To go behind the scenes and meet the people who make the wine, consider attending a "crush camp" like the **Sonoma County Grape Camp,** 3½ days of immersion in grape harvesting, wine production, and food and wine pairing. You'll see the inner workings of the wineries and even pick your own grapes. And yes, you'll taste wine: dozens of Pinot Noirs, Chardonnays, Zinfandels, Cabernets, Sauvignon Blancs, and other varietals.

UNIQUE EXPERIENCE
Such access to wine professionals and outstanding food comes at a premium: $3,000-plus per person, including accommodations, food and wine, and transportation during the trip. As for your fellow attendees, you can expect wine lovers enthusiastic about learning, not wine snobs. After this unique communal experience—celebrated on the final day at a lavish dinner—you'll never drink a glass of wine the same way. For information visit the website of the Sonoma County Winegrape Commission (⊕ *www.sonomagrapecamp.com*).

SHOPPING

Laurence Glass Works. A true find, this glass-arts gallery displays the works of its Parisian-born namesake owner, who creates bowls, plates, and other items from recycled, recast glass. Laurence achieves her imaginative colors and shapes in part by etching the glass while it's in the kiln. Works by other artists are also sold here. ⊠ *72 Main St./Bohemian Hwy., at 1st. St.* ☎ *707/874–3465.*

SEBASTOPOL

6 miles east of Occidental; 7 miles southwest of Santa Rosa.

A stroll through downtown Sebastopol—a town formerly known more for Gravenstein apples than for grapes but these days a burgeoning wine hub—reveals glimpses of the distant and recent past and perhaps the future, too. Before entering the district of browsable, if mostly modest, shops, you may notice a sign declaring Sebastopol a "Nuclear Free Zone." Many hippies settled here in the 1960s and 70s and, as the old Crosby, Stills, Nash & Young song goes, they taught their children well: the town remains steadfastly, if not entirely, countercultural. (Those hankering for a 1960s flashback can truck on over to Main Street's Grateful Bagel, complete with Grateful Dead logo.)

Sebastopol has long had good, if somewhat low-profile, wineries, among them Iron Horse, Lynmar Estate, and Merry Edwards. With the replacement in 2016 of the town's beloved Fosters Freeze location with a vaguely industrial-chic venue for California coastal cuisine and the continuing evolution of the cluster of artisanal producers at the Barlow, the site of a former apple-processing plant, the town may be poised for a Healdsburg-style transformation. Then again, maybe not—stay tuned (in, not out).

GETTING HERE AND AROUND

Sebastopol can be reached from Occidental by taking Graton Road east to Highway 116 and turning south. From Santa Rosa, head west on Highway 12. Sonoma County Transit Buses 20, 22, 24, and 26 serve Sebastopol.

VISITOR INFORMATION

Sebastopol Visitor Center. ✉ *265 S. Main St., at Willow St.* ☎ *707/823–3032* ⊕ *www.sebastopol.org.*

EXPLORING

TOP ATTRACTIONS

The Barlow. A multibuilding complex on the site of a former apple cannery, The Barlow celebrates Sonoma County's "maker" culture with tenants who produce or sell wine, beer, spirits, crafts, clothing, art, and artisanal food and herbs. Only club members can visit the anchor wine tenant, Kosta Browne, but MacPhail, Wind Gap, and Marimar Estate have tasting rooms open to the public. Crooked Goat Brewing and Woodfour Brewing Company make and sell ales, and you can have a nip of vodka, gin, sloe gin, or wheat and rye whiskey at Spirit Works Distillery. In 2018, an artist using traditional methods should be completing his five-year project to create the world's largest *thangka* (Tibetan painting). ∎TIP➔ **During summer and early fall, the complex hosts a Thursday-night street fair, with live music and more vendors.** ✉ *6770 McKinley St., at Morris St., off Hwy. 12* ☎ *707/824–5600* ⊕ *www.thebarlow.net* ✉ *Complex free; tasting fees at wineries, breweries, distillery.*

Dutton-Goldfield Winery. An avid cyclist whose previous credits include developing the wine-making program at Hartford Court, Dan Goldfield teamed up with fifth-generation farmer Steve Dutton to establish this small operation devoted to cool-climate wines. Goldfield modestly strives to take Dutton's meticulously farmed fruit and "make the winemaker unnoticeable," but what impresses the most about these wines, which include Pinot Blanc, Chardonnay, Pinot Noir, and Zinfandel, is their sheer artistry. Among the ones to seek out are the Angel Camp Pinot Noir, from Anderson Valley (Mendocino County) grapes, and the Morelli Lane Zinfandel, from grapes grown on the remaining 1.8 acres of an 1880s vineyard Goldfield helped revive. Tastings often begin with Pinot Blanc, a white-wine variant of Pinot Noir, proceed through the reds, and end with a palate-cleansing Chardonnay. ✉ *3100 Gravenstein Hwy. N/Hwy. 116, at Graton Rd.* ☎ *707/827–3600* ⊕ *www. duttongoldfield.com* ✉ *Tastings $20–$40.*

Fodor'sChoice ★

Emeritus Vineyards. Old-timers recall the superb apples grown at Hallberg Ranch, but since a 2000 replanting this dry-farmed property has evolved into an elite Pinot Noir vineyard. Owner Brice Jones coveted this land for its temperate climate and layer of Goldridge sandy loam soil atop a bed of Sebastopol clay loam, a combination that forces vine roots to work hard to obtain water, which in turn produces berries concentrated with flavor. Some grapes are sold to other wineries, with the remainder used to craft the flagship Emeritus Hallberg Ranch Pinot Noir. The winery also makes a sometimes even more acclaimed wine from its nearby Pinot Hill vineyard. You can taste both in a cleverly designed structure whose floor-to-ceiling windows are retracted in good weather to create an extended open-air space. The tour is by appointment only; tasting reservations are recommended, especially on good-weather weekends. ✉ *2500 Gravenstein Hwy. N, at Peachland Ave.* ☎ *707/823–9463* ⊕ *www.emeritusvineyards.com* 🍷 *Tasting $20, tour and tasting $30.*

Fodor'sChoice **Iron Horse Vineyards.** A meandering one-lane road leads to this winery
★ known for its sparkling wines and estate Chardonnays and Pinot Noirs. The sparklers have made history: Ronald Reagan served them at his summit meetings with Mikhail Gorbachev; George H.W. Bush took some along to Moscow for treaty talks; and Barack Obama included them at official state dinners. Despite Iron Horse's brushes with fame, a casual rusticity prevails at its outdoor tasting area (large heaters keep things comfortable on chilly days), which gazes out on acres of rolling, vine-covered hills. Regular tours take place on weekdays at 10 am. Tastings and tours are by appointment only. ■TIP➜ When his schedule permits, winemaker David Munksgard leads a private tour by truck at 10 am on Monday. ✉ *9786 Ross Station Rd., off Hwy. 116* ☎ *707/887–1507* ⊕ *www.ironhorsevineyards.com* 🍷 *Tasting $25, tours $30–$50 (includes tasting).*

NEED A
BREAK

Screaming Mimi's. Sebastopol's hands-down favorite for ice cream and sorbet often appears in feature stories listing the nation's best shops. Mimi's Mud (espresso-ice-cream cookies, chocolate, and homemade fudge) and strawberry made from local fruit are among the popular ice creams, with passion fruit, lemon, and raspberry among the top palate-cleansing sorbets. **Known for:** Mimi's Mud; New York–style egg creams; seasonal blackberry fudge; "affagato" (ice cream with a double espresso shot). ✉ *6902 Sebastopol Ave./Hwy. 12, at Petaluma Ave./Hwy. 116* ☎ *707/823–5902* ⊕ *www.screaminmimisicecream.com.*

Fodor'sChoice **Merry Edwards Winery.** Winemaker Merry Edwards describes the Russian
★ River Valley as "the epicenter of great Pinot Noir," and she produces wines that express the unique characteristics of the soils, climates, and grape clones from which they derive. (Edwards's research into Pinot Noir clones is so extensive that one is named after her.) The valley's warmer-than-average daytime temperatures, says Edwards, encourage more intense fruit, and evening fogs mitigate the extra heat's potential negative effects. Group tastings of single-vineyard and blended Pinots take place throughout the day, and there are five sit-down appointment slots. Edwards also makes a Sauvignon Blanc that's lightly aged in old oak. Tastings end, rather than begin, with this singular white wine so as not to distract guests' palates from the Pinot Noirs. ✉ *2959 Gravenstein Hwy. N/Hwy. 116, near Oak Grove Ave.* ☎ *707/823–7466, 888/388–9050* ⊕ *www.merryedwards.com* 🍷 *Call winery for tasting fee.*

WORTH NOTING

Big Times Art Studio. The whimsical sculptures of local junk artist Patrick Amiot and his wife, Brigitte Laurent (he creates them, she paints them), can be seen all over Sonoma County, but their studio and gallery along Highway 116 south of Sebastopol is one of two good places to see many works up close. The other is on **Florence Avenue**, north of Bodega Avenue (Highway 12), three blocks west of Main Street. Amiot reclaims old car parts, abandoned appliances, and the like, refashioning them into everything from pigs, dogs, and people to mermaids and Godzilla. ✉ *2371 Gravenstein Hwy. S/Hwy. 116, 2½ miles south of downtown* ☎ *707/824–9388* ⊕ *www.patrickamiot.com* 💰 *Free* ⊙ *Closed Sun. and Mon.*

California Carnivores. Its cool collection of carnivorous plants, said to be the world's largest, makes this nursery a diverting stop. The colors are sublime, and the mechanics of the plants are fascinating. Venus flytraps and several insect-nabbing relatives are on display and for sale; shipping is easily arranged. Even more effective than the Venus plants are the American pitchers, whose flashy leaves take down flies but also wasps. Drop by and see what catches your eye (sorry, couldn't resist). ■TIP→ The nursery is less than a mile from the Big Times Art Studio of junk artist Patrick Amiot, another fun stop. ✉ *2833 Old Gravenstein Hwy., near Fredericks Rd.* ☎ *707/824–0433* ⊕ *www.californiacarnivores.com* 💰 *Free* ⊙ *Closed Tues. and Wed.*

Lynmar Estate. *Elegant* and *balanced* describe Lynmar's landscaping and contemporary architecture, but the terms also apply to the winemaking philosophy. Expect handcrafted Chardonnays and Pinot Noirs with long, luxurious finishes, especially on the Pinots. The attention to refinement and detail extends to the tasting room, where well-informed pourers serve patrons enjoying garden and vineyard views through two-story windows. The consistent winner is the Quail Hill Pinot Noir, a blend of some or all of the 14 Pinot Noir clones grown in the vineyard outside, but the Russian River Pinot Noir and the Summit Pinot Noir are also exceptional. Most of the wines can be bought only by belonging to the allocation list or at the winery, which offers seasonal food and wine pairings. Tastings are by appointment only. ✉ *3909 Frei Rd., off Hwy. 116* ☎ *707/829–3374* ⊕ *www.lynmarestate.com* 💰 *Tastings $35–$90* ⊙ *Closed Tues.*

MacPhail Family Wines. A two-story cascade of crumpled ruby-red Radio Flyer wagons meant to mimic wine pouring out of a bottle grabs immediate attention inside this swank industrial space. Consulting winemaker Matt Courtney, who also makes the wines at Arista, crafts the lineup of bright, classy Pinots, no two tasting alike. The grapes come from vineyards that include Mendocino County's Anderson Valley and several prime Sonoma County appellations. The winery also makes Chardonnay and rosé (of Pinot Noir, of course). ✉ *The Barlow, 6761 McKinley St., off Morris St.* ☎ *707/824–8400* ⊕ *macphailwine.com* 💰 *Tastings $20–$30.*

Paul Hobbs Winery. Major wine critics routinely bestow high-90s scores on the Chardonnays, Pinot Noirs, Cabernet Sauvignons, and a Syrah produced at this appointment-only winery set amid gently

The views, wine, and architecture make a visit to Paul Hobbs Winery special.

rolling vineyards in northwestern Sebastopol. Owner-winemaker Paul Hobbs's university thesis investigated the flavors that result from various oak-barrel toasting levels, and he continued his education—in both vineyard management and wine making—at the Robert Mondavi Winery, Opus One, and other storied establishments before striking out on his own in 1991. Tastings take place in a space designed by winery specialist Howard Backen's architectural firm. Guests on a Signature Tasting visit the winery and sip several wines; the Vineyard Designate Experience includes the tour plus small bites paired with limited-edition single-vineyard wines. ⊠ *3355 Gravenstein Hwy. N, near Holt Rd.* ☎ *707/824–9879* ⊕ *www.paulhobbswinery.com* ⊠ *Tastings $65–$135* ⊘ *Closed weekends and holidays.*

WHERE TO EAT

$$ ✕ **Fork Roadhouse.** Pork belly fried-egg tacos, polenta bowls with
AMERICAN   chèvre, greens, and a poached egg, and thick French toast served with seasonal fruit, whipped cream, and maple syrup draw the breakfast crowd to this low-slung haven 3 miles west of downtown Sebastopol. Salads, grass-fed burgers, and BLTs are among the lunchtime lures, with barbecued pork chops, chicken paillard, and petrale sole piccata typical dinner fare. **Known for:** many organic ingredients; alfresco dining on tree-shaded creek-side outdoor patio. $ *Average main: $21* ⊠ *9890 Bodega Hwy./Hwy. 12, near Montgomery Rd.* ☎ *707/634–7575* ⊕ *www.forkcatering.com/the-roadhouse* ⊘ *Closed Mon.–Wed.*

$
MODERN
AMERICAN
FAMILY
Fodor's Choice
★

✕ **Handline Coastal California.** Lowell Sheldon, who runs a fine-dining establishment (Peter Lowell's) a mile away, teamed up with farmer-partner Natalie Goble to convert Sebastopol's former Foster's Freeze location into a perky paean to coastal California cuisine. The lineup includes oysters raw and grilled, fish tacos, ceviches, tostadas, three burgers (beef, vegan, and fish), and, honoring the location's previous incarnation, chocolate and vanilla soft-serve ice cream for dessert. **Known for:** upscale comfort food; 21st-century roadside decor; light-hearted atmosphere. $ *Average main: $12* ✉ *935 Gravenstein Hwy. S, near Hutchins Ave.* ☎ *707/827–3744* ⊕ *www.handline.com.*

$
CAFÉ
Fodor's Choice
★

✕ **Pascaline Gourmet Shop.** Delicate pastries and quiches, croques mon-sieur, and other bistro bites have made locals as passionate about this Highway 116 café as its owners are about their cuisine and hospital-ity. Though it seemed to emerge out of nowhere in 2015, the execu-tive and pastry chefs have several decades of experience between them at prestigious establishments in Paris, San Francisco, and elsewhere. **Known for:** kouign amann (a Breton pastry); French-style coffee; joy-ous atmosphere. $ *Average main: $8* ✉ *4550 Gravenstein Hwy. N, almost to Forestville* ☎ *707/521–9348* ⊕ *www.pascalinefinecatering. com/gourmet-shop* ⊙ *Closed Jan., and Mon. and Tues. No dinner.*

$$
PIZZA

✕ **Vignette.** Helming a cobalt-blue-tile, igloo-shape Neapolitan pizza oven that burns almond wood at 850°F–900°F, chef Mark Hopper turns out thin-crust pies in less than two minutes. Formerly of Thomas Keller's The French Laundry and Bouchon, Hopper serves a straightfor-ward menu of antipasti, salads, and pizza faves that include the mush-room Alfredo (garlic cream, roasted mushrooms, stracciatella cheese, and tomatoes) and a pie topped with meatballs, tomatoes, Parmesan, and mozzarella. **Known for:** pizza dough made fresh daily; wine and beer selection. $ *Average main: $17* ✉ *The Barlow, 6750 McKinley St., off Morris St.* ☎ *707/861–3897* ⊕ *www.vignettepizzeria.com* ⊙ *Closed Wed., and Tues. mid-Sept.–late May.*

$$$
MODERN
AMERICAN

✕ **Zazu Kitchen + Farm.** The raised gardens on Zazu's patio supply pro-duce and spices for executive chef Duskie Estes's pig-centric cuisine, which incorporates salumi by her husband and co-owner, John Stew-art. Small plates such as miso-and–Aleppo pepper chicken wings can add up to a meal, or you can sample a few appetizers before moving on to a bacon burger or porcini-noodle-and-mushroom stroganoff. $ *Average main: $23* ✉ *The Barlow, 6770 McKinley St., No. 150, off Morris St.* ☎ *707/523–4814* ⊕ *www.zazukitchen.com* ⊙ *Closed Tues. No lunch Mon.*

WHERE TO STAY

$$$
B&B/INN
Fodor's Choice
★

▥ **Avalon Bed & Breakfast.** Set amid redwoods and impeccably fur-nished, the Tudor-style Avalon provides romance, luxury, and seclu-sion in a creek-side setting. **Pros:** lavish breakfasts; woodsy, romantic setting; fireplaces in all rooms. **Cons:** two-person maximum occu-pancy; two-night minimum for some stays; atmosphere may be too low-key for some. $ *Rooms from: $299* ✉ *11910 Graton Rd.* ☎ *877/328–2566, 707/824–0880* ⊕ *avalonluxuryinn.com* ⇲ *3 rooms* ❮○❯ *Breakfast.*

$ HOTEL **Fairfield Inn & Suites Santa Rosa Sebastopol.** A safe West County bet that often has availability when other inns and hotels are full, the three-story Fairfield, a fairly new property a bit south of Sebastopol's core, is a competently run chain hotel. **Pros:** convenient to West County wineries and Santa Rosa; good-size outdoor pool and spa; frequent Internet specials. **Cons:** hardly a unique Wine Country experience; occasional service letdowns. [$] *Rooms from: $149* ✉ *1101 Gravenstein Hwy. S* ☎ *707/829–6677* 🌐 *www.marriott.com* 🛏 *82 rooms* 🍴 *Breakfast.*

GRATON

½ mile west of Sebastopol.

Mere steps from Sebastopol and not far from Occidental, the tiny hamlet of Graton has a one-block main drag one can stroll in two minutes—although it's possible to while away a few hours at the block's artist-run gallery, nostalgia-inducing antiques shop, a small winery's tasting room (open from Thursday through Sunday), and three notably fine restaurants. For more strolling, you can hit the local hiking trail.

GETTING HERE AND AROUND

To reach Graton from Sebastopol, head west from Highway 116 a half-mile on Graton Road. Sonoma County Transit Bus 20 passes through Graton.

EXPLORING

Paul Mathew Vineyards. With experience that includes stints as a winery tour guide, cellar rat, sales rep, vineyard developer, and finally winemaker, owner Mat Gustafson of Paul Mathew Vineyards knows how to make and market his single-vineyard Pinot Noirs and other wines. Gustafson specializes in spare, low-alcohol, food-friendly Russian River Valley Pinots and makes Chardonnay, a surprisingly light Cabernet Franc, a Syrah, and a sparkling brut rosé. On a hot summer day his rosé of Pinot Noir makes for delightful sipping in the picnic area behind the tasting room, which occupies a century-old Edwardian storefront along Graton's short main drag. ✉ *9060 Graton Rd., at Ross Rd.* ☎ *707/861–9729* 🌐 *www.paulmathewvineyards.com* 🎫 *Tasting $15* 🕒 *Closed Mon.–Wed. (appointments sometimes possible).*

West County Regional Trail. Oaks, poplars, and other trees shade this trail that winds north from Graton through land once used by the local railway line. In summer you'll see plenty of blackberries (and sometimes local pickers) along the 3-mile stretch between Graton and Forestville. The path is so quiet it's hard to believe that nearby in 1905 the Battle of Sebastopol Road raged between crews of two rival rail lines. **TIP→ There's free trailhead parking behind the old Graton Fire Station.** ✉ *Entrance off Graton just west of Ross Rd.* ☎ *707/565–2041* 🌐 *parks.sonomacounty.ca.gov* 🎫 *Free.*

5

WHERE TO EAT

$$$ MODERN AMERICAN Fodor's Choice ★ 🍴 **Underwood Bar & Bistro.** Run by the same people who operate the Willow Wood Market Cafe across the street, this restaurant with a sophisticated Continental ambience has a seasonal menu based on smaller and larger dishes. The petite offerings might include anything from glazed ribs and ahi tuna crudo to Chinese broccoli; depending on the season, osso buco, mushroom-leek ravioli, or Catalan fish stew might be among the entrées. [$] *Average main: $25* ✉ *9113 Graton Rd., about ½ mile west of Hwy. 116* ☎ *707/823–7023* 🌐 *www.underwoodgraton.com* 🕒 *Closed Mon. No lunch Sun.*

$$ MODERN AMERICAN 🍴 **Willow Wood Market Cafe.** This café across the street from the Underwood Bar & Bistro serves simple, tasty soups, salads, and sandwiches. Brunch is amazing, but even breakfast—specialties include hot, creamy polenta and house-made granola—is modern-American down-home solid. **Known for:** casual setting; outdoor back patio; ragouts on polenta. [$] *Average main: $17* ✉ *9020 Graton Rd., about ½ mile west of Hwy. 116* ☎ *707/823–0233* 🌐 *willowwoodgraton.com* 🕒 *No dinner Sun.*

$ EASTERN EUROPEAN 🍴 **Zosia Café and Kitchen.** Cabbage borscht, roasted beet salad, pierogi, traditional Polish and Siberian dumplings, kielbasa, savory crepes, and sandwiches from burgers to grilled cheese satisfy patrons of this Graton newcomer fronted by an arbored beer and wine garden. At breakfast the chefs prepare egg dishes with Eastern European accents, along with sweet crepes, pancakes, and muesli and steel-cut oatmeal. **Known for:** comfort food; Eastern European specialties; beer and wine garden. [$] *Average main: $10* ✉ *9010 Graton Rd., at Edison St.* ☎ *707/861–9241* 🌐 *www.zosiacafe.com.*

SHOPPING

Graton Gallery. The West County hills are alive with talented fine-arts painters, sculptors, and photographers, and this artist-run gallery in downtown Graton displays their works and those of their counterparts nearby and beyond. ✉ *9048 Graton Rd., at Ross Rd.* ☎ *707/829–8912* 🌐 *www.gratongallery.net* 🕒 *Closed Mon.*

Fodor's Choice ★ **Mr. Ryder & Company.** Named for its impresario's deceased pooch, this co-op of a baker's dozen antiques dealers distinguishes itself with its pleasing layout and tastefully offbeat selections of a century-plus of mostly Americana. Even *Martha Stewart Living* has taken note. ✉ *9040 Graton Rd., near Ross Rd.* ☎ *707/824–8221* 🌐 *www.mrryderantiques.com.*

SANTA ROSA

6 miles east of Sebastopol; 55 miles north of San Francisco.

Urban Santa Rosa isn't as popular with tourists as many Wine Country destinations—which isn't surprising, seeing as there are more office parks than wineries within its limits. However, this hardworking town is home to a couple of interesting cultural offerings and a few noteworthy restaurants and vineyards. The city's chain motels and hotels can be handy if you're finding that everything else is booked up, especially since

Matanzas Creek Winery is a star of the tiny Bennett Valley AVA.

Santa Rosa is roughly equidistant from Sonoma, Healdsburg, and the western Russian River Valley, three of Sonoma County's most popular wine-tasting destinations.

GETTING HERE AND AROUND

To get to Santa Rosa from Sebastopol, drive east on Highway 12. From San Francisco, cross the Golden Gate Bridge and continue north on U.S. 101. Santa Rosa's hotels, restaurants, and wineries are spread over a wide area; factor in extra time when driving around the city, especially during morning and evening rush hour. To get here from downtown San Francisco take Golden Gate Transit Bus 101. Several Sonoma County Transit buses serve the city and surrounding area.

VISITOR INFORMATION

Visit Santa Rosa. ⊠ *9 4th St., at Wilson St.* ☎ *800/404–7673* ⊕ *www. visitsantarosa.com.*

EXPLORING

TOP ATTRACTIONS

Fodor'sChoice
★
Balletto Vineyards. A few decades ago Balletto was known for quality produce more than for grapes, but the new millennium saw vineyards emerge as the core business. About 90% of the fruit from the family's 650-plus acres goes to other wineries, with the remainder destined for Balletto's estate wines. The house style is light on the oak, high in acidity, and low in alcohol content, a combination that yields exceptionally food-friendly wines. On a hot summer day, sipping a Pinot Gris, rosé of Pinot Noir, or brut rosé sparkler on the outdoor patio can feel

transcendent, but the superstars are the Chardonnays and Pinot Noirs. ■TIP→ **Look for the unoaked and Cider Ridge Chardonnays and the Burnside, Sexton Hill, and Winery Block Pinots, but all the wines are exemplary—and, like the tastings, reasonably priced.** ⊠ *5700 Occidental Rd., 2½ miles west of Hwy. 12* ☎ *707/568–2455* ⊕ *www.ballettovineyards.com* ⌦ *Tasting $10.*

Carol Shelton Wines. It's winemaker Carol Shelton's motto that great wines start in the vineyard, but you won't see any grapevines outside her winery—it's in an industrial park 4 miles north of downtown Santa Rosa. What you will find, and experience, are well-priced Zinfandels from grapes grown in vineyards Shelton, ever the viticultural sleuth, locates from Mendocino to Southern California's Cucamonga Valley. With coastal, hillside, valley, inland, and desert's-edge fruit the Zins collectively reveal the range and complexity of this varietal that so arouses Shelton's passion. Although Zinfandel gets all the attention, Shelton also makes Cabernet Sauvignon, Carignane, and Petite Sirah reds, and whites that include Chardonnay, Viognier, and the Rhône-style Coquille Blanc blend. ■TIP→ **Shelton picks fruit on the early side, leaving her Zins lean with low alcohol rather than heavy and jammy.** ⊠ *3354-B Coffey La., off Piner Rd.* ☎ *707/575–3441* ⊕ *www.carolshelton.com* ⌦ *Tasting free.*

La Crema at Saralee's Vineyard. The high-profile brand's multistory tasting space occupies a restored early-1900s redwood barn used over the years for hops, hay storage, and as a stable. With its relatively cool Russian River Valley maritime climate, the celebrated Saralee's Vineyard, named for a former owner, fits the preferred La Crema profile for growing Chardonnay and Pinot Noir. You can sample wines from set flights, or staffers will customize one based on your preferences. Seated private Nine Barrel tastings of the best wines require reservations, as does the golf cart tour of the property and its vines, lake, and wildlife. ■TIP→ **On sunny days the barn's decks and patio and the nearby Richard's Grove, with its broad lawn and diverse foliage, attract much attention.** ⊠ *3575 Slusser Rd., ¾ mile north of River Rd., Windsor* ☎ *707/525–6200* ⊕ *www.lacrema.com* ⌦ *Tastings $15–$40, tour $65.*

Fodor'sChoice ★ **Martinelli Winery.** In a century-old hop barn with the telltale triple towers, Martinelli has the feel of a traditional country store, but the sophisticated wines made here are anything but old-fashioned. The winery's reputation rests on its complex Pinot Noirs, Syrahs, and Zinfandels, including the Jackass Hill Vineyard Zin, made with grapes from 130-year-old vines. Noted winemaker Helen Turley set the Martinelli style—fruit-forward, easy on the oak, reined-in tannins—in the 1990s, and her successor, Bryan Kvamme, continues this approach. You can sample current releases at a Classic Tasting, but a better choice (which also doesn't require a reservation) is the Terroir Tasting, which focuses on how soil and other vineyard characteristics influence wines. Rarer and top-rated vintages are poured at appointment-only sessions. ⊠ *3360 River Rd., east of Olivet Rd., Windsor* ☎ *707/525–0570, 800/346–1627* ⊕ *www.martinelliwinery.com* ⌦ *Tastings $12–$75.*

Fodor's Choice ★ **Matanzas Creek Winery.** The visitor center at Matanzas Creek sets itself apart with an understated Japanese aesthetic, extending to a tranquil fountain, a koi pond, and a vast field of lavender. The winery makes Sauvignon Blanc, Chardonnay, Merlot, Pinot Noir, and Cabernet Sauvignon under the Matanzas Creek name, and three equally well-regarded wines— a Bordeaux red blend, a Chardonnay, and a Sauvignon Blanc—bearing the Journey label. No reservation is required for the pairing of small-lot wines and local artisanal cheeses, offered in the tasting room. The winery encourages guests to bring a picnic, buy a bottle, and enjoy the meal on the property. ■ TIP→ **An ideal time to visit is in May and June, when lavender perfumes the air.** ⊠ *6097 Bennett Valley Rd.* ☎ *707/528–6464, 800/590–6464* ⊕ *www.matanzascreek.com* 🍷 *Tastings $15–$25.*

FAMILY **Safari West.** An unexpected bit of wilderness in the Wine Country, this African wildlife preserve covers 400 acres. Begin your visit with a stroll around enclosures housing lemurs, cheetahs, giraffes, and rare birds like the brightly colored scarlet ibis. Next, climb with your guide onto open-air vehicles that spend about two hours combing the expansive property, where more than 80 species—including gazelles, cape buffalo, antelope, wildebeests, and zebras—inhabit the hillsides. If you'd like to extend your stay, lodging in well-equipped tent cabins is available. ⊠ *3115 Porter Creek Rd., off Mark West Springs Rd.* ☎ *707/579–2551, 800/616– 2695* ⊕ *www.safariwest.com* 🍷 *98–$115 ($45–$50 ages 4–12).*

WORTH NOTING

FAMILY **Charles M. Schulz Museum.** Fans of Snoopy and Charlie Brown will love this museum dedicated to the late Charles M. Schulz, who lived his last three decades in Santa Rosa. Permanent installations include a re-creation of the cartoonist's studio, and temporary exhibits often focus on a particular theme in his work. ■ TIP→ **Children and adults can take a stab at creating cartoons in the Education Room.** ⊠ *2301 Hardies La., at W. Steele La.* ☎ *707/579–4452* ⊕ *www.schulzmuseum.org* 🍷 *$12 ($5 age 4–18).*

DeLoach Vineyards. Best known for its Russian River Valley Pinot Noirs, DeLoach also produces Chardonnays, old-vine Zinfandels, and a few other wines. Some of the reds are made using open-top wood fermentation vats that have been used in France for centuries to intensify a wine's flavor. Tours focus on these and other wine-making techniques and include a stroll through organic gardens and vineyards. You can also take a wine-blending seminar, compare California and French Chardonnays and Pinot Noirs, or (depending on the time of year) taste Pinots by a fireplace or enjoy a gourmet picnic. Tours are by appointment only; tastings are by appointment from Monday through Thursday. ■ TIP→ **The sparklers and still wines of the JCB label, whose letters match the initials of its dapper creator, DeLoach's Burgundy-born owner, Jean-Charles Boisset, are poured in a separate tasting room.** ⊠ *1791 Olivet Rd., off Guerneville Rd.* ☎ *707/526–9111* ⊕ *www. deloachvineyards.com* 🍷 *Tastings $30–$75, tour and tasting $50.*

Inman Family Wines. "The winemaker is in," reads a driveway sign when owner Kathleen Inman, who crafts her winery's Chardonnay, Pinot Noir, and other western Russian River Valley wines, is present. She's often around, and it's an extra treat to learn directly from the source about her

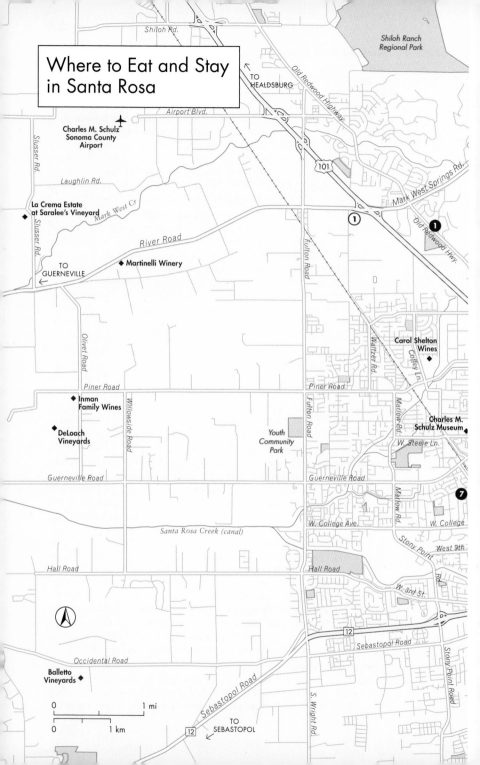

Where to Eat and Stay in Santa Rosa

Shiloh Rd.

Shiloh Ranch Regional Park

Old Redwood Highway

TO HEALDSBURG

Airport Blvd.

Charles M. Schulz Sonoma County Airport

101

Laughlin Rd.

Mark West Springs Rd.

La Crema Estate at Saralee's Vineyard

Slusser Rd.

Mark West Cr.

River Road

Old Redwood Hwy.

1

1

Fulton Road

TO GUERNEVILLE

Martinelli Winery

Waltzer Rd.

Carol Shelton Wines

Coffey Ln.

Olivet Road

Piner Road

Piner Road

Fulton Road

Inman Family Wines

Willowside Road

Youth Community Park

Marlow Rd.

Charles M. Schulz Museum

W. Steele Ln.

DeLoach Vineyards

Guerneville Road

Guerneville Road

Marlow Rd.

7

W. College Ave.

W. College

Santa Rosa Creek (canal)

Stony Point

West 9th

Hall Road

Hall Road

W. 3rd St.

12

Sebastopol Road

Stony Point Road

Occidental Road

Balletto Vineyards

Sebastopol Road

0   1 mi

0   1 km

S. Wright Rd.

12

TO SEBASTOPOL

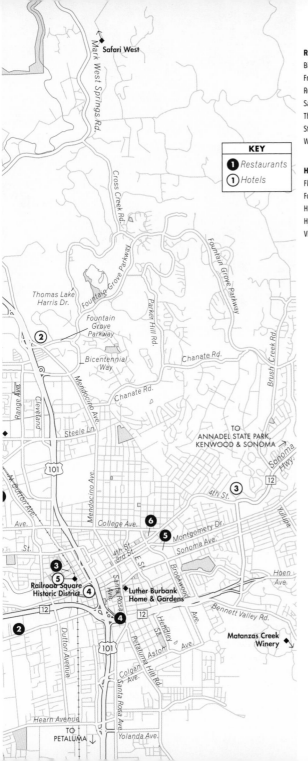

A familiar-looking hat provides shade at the Charles M. Schulz Museum.

farming, fermenting, and aging methods. Her restrained, balanced wines complement sophisticated cuisine so well that top-tier restaurants include them on their menus. Inman shows equal finesse with rosé of Pinot Noir, two sparkling wines, and a Pinot Gris. Her zeal to recycle is in evidence everywhere, most conspicuously in the tasting room, where redwood reclaimed from an on-site barn was incorporated into the design, and crushed wine-bottle glass was fashioned into the bar. Tastings are by appointment only. ✉ *3900 Piner Rd., at Olivet Rd.* ☎ *707/293–9576* ⊕ *www.inmanfamilywines.com* 🖥 *Tastings $20–$35.*

Luther Burbank Home & Gardens. Renowned horticulturist Luther Burbank lived and worked on these grounds and made great advances using the modern techniques of selection and hybridization. The 1.6-acre garden and greenhouse showcase the results of some of Burbank's experiments to develop spineless cactus and such flowers as the Shasta daisy. ■TIP→ **Use your cell phone on a free self-guided garden tour, or from April through October take a docent-led tour (required to see the house).** ✉ *204 Santa Rosa Ave., at Sonoma Ave.* ☎ *707/524–5445* ⊕ *www.lutherburbank.org* 🖥 *Gardens free, tour $10.*

Railroad Square Historic District. The location of Santa Rosa's former Northwestern Pacific Railroad depot—built in 1903 by Italian stonemasons and immortalized in Alfred Hitchcock's coolly sinister 1943 film *Shadow of a Doubt*—provides the name for this revitalized neighborhood west of U.S. 101. The depot is now a visitor center, and Fourth Street between Wilson and Davis Streets contains restaurants, bars, and antiques and thrift shops worth checking out, as do nearby lanes. ✉ *Depot visitor center, 9 4th St., at Wilson St.* ☎ *707/577–8674* ⊕ *railroadsquare.net.*

WHERE TO EAT

$$$ ✕ **Bird & The Bottle.** The owners of Willi's Wine Bar, Bravas Bar de Tapas,
ECLECTIC and other Sonoma County favorites operate this "modern tavern" serving global bar bites and comfort food. Shrimp wontons, chicken-skin cracklings, fried cheddar-cheese curds, matzo-ball soup, grilled romaine Cobb salad, pastrami pork riblets, and skirt steak all go well with the astute "Booze" menu of cocktails, wines, and artisanal beers, ciders, and spirits. **Known for:** small bites, full meals; happy hour (Sunday–Thursday); nostalgic yet contemporary design. $ *Average main: $24* ⊠ *1055 4th St., near College Ave.* ☎ *707/568–4000* ⊕ *birdandthebottle.com.*

$$ ✕ **Franchetti's.** Despite its location in a business park near an urgent-care
AMERICAN facility, Franchetti's attracts locals and clever tourists for its beautifully realized brunch items, pastas, soups, sandwiches, and wood-fired pizzas and entrées. Even the lemonade is prepared with precision at this concrete-floored hangout whose denlike corner with a wide-screen TV and a Ping-Pong table contributes to the home-away-from-home feel. **Known for:** brunch until early afternoon; succulent fried and roasted chicken; calamari fritti; exotic-mushroom pizza; wines, beers, and ciders. $ *Average main: $18* ⊠ *1229 N. Dutton Ave., near W. College Ave.* ☎ *707/526–1229* ⊕ *www.franchettis.com* ☾ *No dinner Mon. and Tues.*

$$ ✕ **Rosso Pizzeria & Wine Bar.** Ask local wine pourers where to get the best
PIZZA pizza, and they'll often recommend lively Rosso, also acclaimed for
Fodor's Choice its diverse wine selection and crispy double-fried chicken. Two peren-
★ nial Neapolitan-style pizza favorites are the Moto Guzzi, with house-smoked mozzarella and spicy Caggiano sausage, and the Funghi di Limone, with oven-roasted mixed mushrooms and Taleggio and fontina cheese. **Known for:** pizza and California wines; fried chicken's pancetta bits and sweet-and-sour sauce; salads and gluten-free dishes. $ *Average main: $18* ⊠ *Creekside Center, 53 Montgomery Dr., at Brookwood Ave.* ☎ *707/544–3221* ⊕ *www.rossopizzeria.com.*

$$$ ✕ **Sazon Peruvian Cuisine.** Join Peruvian locals enjoying a taste of back
PERUVIAN home at this strip-mall restaurant whose name means "flavor" or "sea-
Fodor's Choice soning." Several ceviche appetizers—including one with ponzu sauce
★ for a Japanese twist—show the range of tastes the lead chef and co-owner, José Navarro, conjures up, as does the *arroz con mariscos*, a velvety, turmeric-laced seafood paella. **Known for:** skillfully spiced Peruvian food; small and large plates to share family-style; welcoming atmosphere. $ *Average main: $24* ⊠ *1129 Sebastopol Rd., at Roseland Ave.* ☎ *707/523–4346* ⊕ *www.sazonsr.com.*

$$$ ✕ **The Spinster Sisters.** Modern, well-sourced variations on eggs Benedict
MODERN and other standards are served at this concrete-and-glass hot spot's
AMERICAN weekday breakfast and weekend brunch. Dinner consists of shareable bites and small and large plates—think kimchi-and-bacon deviled eggs, sweet-corn-and-coconut fritters, and grilled hanger steak. **Known for:** stellar local and international wines; happy hour (daily 4–6); horseshoe-shape bar, a good perch for dining single and drinking in wine-world gossip. $ *Average main: $25* ⊠ *401 S. A St., at Sebastopol Ave.* ☎ *707/528–7100* ⊕ *thespinstersisters.com.*

$$$$ ✕ **Stark's Steak & Seafood.** The low lighting, well-spaced tables, and
STEAKHOUSE gas fireplaces at Stark's create a congenial setting for dining on steak,

5

Luther Burbank Home and Gardens showcases the results of its namesake's many botanical experiments.

seafood from the raw bar, and sustainable fish. With entrées that include a 20-ounce, dry-aged rib eye and a 32-ounce porterhouse for two, there's not a chance that meat eaters will depart unsated, and nonsteak options such as tamarind barbecue prawns and halibut with cherry-tomato confit surpass those at your average temple to beef. **Known for:** thick steaks; high-quality seafood. $ *Average main: $35* ✉ *521 Adams St., at 7th St.* ☎ *707/546–5100* ⊕ *www.starkssteak-house.com* 🕙 *No lunch weekends.*

$$$
ECLECTIC
Fodor'sChoice
★

✕ **Willi's Wine Bar.** Although this restaurant's name suggests a sedate spot serving wine and precious nibbles, boisterous crowds fill the warren of cozy enclaves here, snapping up small plates from the globe-trotting menu. Dishes such as the pork-belly pot stickers represent Asia, and Tunisian roasted local carrots and Moroccan-style lamb chops are among the Mediterranean-inspired foods. **Known for:** small plates; inspired wine selection; 2-ounce pours so you can pair a new wine with each dish; California-sourced cheese and charcuterie; covered patio. $ *Average main: $29* ✉ *4404 Old Redwood Hwy., at Ursuline Rd.* ☎ *707/526–3096* ⊕ *williswinebar.net* 🕙 *No lunch Sun. and Mon.*

WHERE TO STAY

$
HOTEL

🏨 **Flamingo Conference Resort & Spa.** If Don Draper from *Mad Men* popped into Santa Rosa, he'd feel right at home in this 1950s-style resort just beyond downtown. **Pros:** cool pool; retro vibe; good value. **Cons:** 30-minute walk to downtown; small bathrooms in some rooms. $ *Rooms from: $169* ✉ *2777 4th St.* ☎ *707/545–8530, 800/848–8300* ⊕ *www.flamingoresort.com* 🍽 *170 rooms* ⦿ *No meals.*

$$ 🛏 **Fountaingrove Inn.** Low-slung and handsomely clad in stone and
HOTEL wood, the Fountaingrove has rooms that often cost half the price of
their equivalents in Healdsburg, yet the town's plaza is only a 15-minute
drive away. **Pros:** frequent Internet specials; amenities for business trav-
elers; room service. **Cons:** small pool; some public areas look tattered;
uneven housekeeping; corporate events can detract from vacationers'
experiences. ⓢ *Rooms from: $209* ✉ *101 Fountaingrove Pkwy., at Men-
docino Ave.* ☎ *800/222–6101* ⊕ *www.fountaingroveinn.com* 🛏 *124
rooms* ⏐🍽️⏐ *No meals.*

$ 🛏 **Hotel La Rose.** The obvious choice for travelers seeking historic atmo-
HOTEL sphere and proximity to Railroad Square restaurants, nightlife, and
shopping, Hotel La Rose delivers a comfortable stay, if one lacking the
boutique-hotel style and polished service the grand stone exterior might
imply. **Pros:** convenient to Railroad Square; historic atmosphere. **Cons:**
inconsistent hospitality; some rooms feel cramped; no pool or fitness
center; street noise heard in some rooms; some travelers find the neigh-
borhood scruffy. ⓢ *Rooms from: $159* ✉ *308 Wilson St.* ☎ *707/579–
3200, 707/527–6738* ⊕ *hotellarose.com* 🛏 *48 rooms* ⏐🍽️⏐ *No meals.*

$$ 🛏 **Hyatt Vineyard Creek Hotel and Spa.** Relentlessly corporate but easy
HOTEL on the eyes, the Hyatt wins points for its convenient downtown loca-
tion, decent-size pool, courteous staff, and arbor-lined sculpture garden.
Pros: well-maintained property; pool and garden; convenient to Railroad
Square dining and shopping; frequent online specials. **Cons:** the many
events booked here detract from the leisure-traveler experience; not
worth full price; disruption from renovations and expansion may carry
into 2018. ⓢ *Rooms from: $282* ✉ *170 Railroad St.* ☎ *707/284–1234*
⊕ *vineyardcreek.hyatt.com* 🛏 *139 rooms, 16 suites* ⏐🍽️⏐ *No meals.*

$$ 🛏 **Vintners Inn.** The owners of Ferrari-Carano Vineyards operate this
HOTEL oasis set amid 92 acres of vineyards that's known for its comfortable
lodgings. **Pros:** spacious rooms with comfortable beds; jogging path
through the vineyards; online deals pop up year-round. **Cons:** occa-
sional noise from adjacent events center. ⓢ *Rooms from: $265* ✉ *4350
Barnes Rd.* ☎ *707/575–7350, 800/421–2584* ⊕ *www.vintnersinn.com*
🛏 *38 rooms, 6 suites* ⏐🍽️⏐ *No meals.*

NIGHTLIFE AND PERFORMING ARTS

NIGHTLIFE
BREWPUBS
Fodor's Choice **Russian River Brewing Company.** It's all about Belgian-style ales, "aggres-
★ sively hopped California ales," and barrel-aged beers at this popular
brewery's large pub. The legendary lineup includes Pliny the Elder
(and Younger, but only in February), Blind Pig I.P.A., Mortification
(nuances of clove, toffee, and roasted malts), and so many more.
■TIP→ Happy hour (from 4 to 6:30 on weekdays and all day on Sun-
day) is a jolly time to visit. ✉ *725 4th St., near D St.* ☎ *707/545–2337*
⊕ *www.russianriverbrewing.com.*

CASINO

Graton Resort & Casino. Slots predominate at this spiffy casino. Blackjack, baccarat, and a few other table games are also available. Dining options include Chinese and pizza restaurants and a pricey food court. The casino's glam hotel opened in late 2016. ⊠ *288 Golf Course Dr. W, west off U.S. 101, Rohnert Park* ☎ *707/588–7100* ⊕ *www.gratonresortcasino.com.*

PERFORMING ARTS

ARTS CENTERS

Joan and Sanford I. Weill Hall. The acoustically sophisticated hall, which debuted in 2012, hosts classical (the San Francisco and Santa Rosa symphonies), jazz (Jazz at Lincoln Center with Wynton Marsalis), pop (Gispy Kings), and other ensembles, as well as performers from Audra McDonald and Laurie Anderson to Ice-T and Emanuel Ax. During summer, the hall's back wall opens out to include a terraced lawn. ■TIP→ If driving, park in Lots L through O. ⊠ *Sonoma State University, Rohnert Park Expwy. and Petaluma Hill Blvd., east off U.S. 101, Rohnert Park* ☎ *866/955–6040* ⊕ *www.gmc.sonoma.edu/events.*

Luther Burbank Center for the Arts. This cultural hub, configured theater style or open floor depending on the performance, books acts and ensembles as varied as Neko Case, Donnie and Marie (Osmond), Tracy Morgan, and the risk-taking local theater group Left Edge. ⊠ *50 Mark West Springs Rd., east off U.S. 101* ☎ *707/546–3600* ⊕ *www.lutherburbankcenter.org.*

SPORTS AND THE OUTDOORS

Annadel State Park. More than 40 miles of hiking, mountain biking, and equestrian trails lace this day-use park that swarms with locals in April and May when the wildflowers bloom around Lake Ilsanjo. The rest of the year you can take to the trails or fish for black bass or bluegill (state fishing license required). ⊠ *6201 Channel Dr., off Montgomery Dr.* ☎ *707/539–3911* ⊕ *www.parks.ca.gov/?page_id=480* ⊠ *$8 per vehicle.*

Up & Away Ballooning. Being so close to the coast means that if the balloon you're in gets high enough, you'll have ocean views on a sunny day. You'll also take in plenty of vineyard vistas. Journeys begin with coffee and pastries at Healdsburg's The Shed and conclude there with breakfast and a sparkling-wine toast. ⊠ *Healdsburg* ☎ *707/836–0171* ⊕ *www.up-away.com* ⊠ *$239 per person.*

SHOPPING

Hot Couture Vintage Fashion. Patrons love Hot Couture for its knowledgeable owner, Marta, and eclectic vintage fashions and accessories from the 1900s to the 1980s. ⊠ *101 3rd St., at Wilson St.* ☎ *707/528–7247* ⊕ *hotcouturevintage.com.*

Whistlestop Antiques. The "granny's attic" ambience of this mélange of antiques, art, and bric-a-brac makes for a nostalgic shopping experience. The prices aren't bad, either. ⊠ *140 4th St., at Davis St.* ☎ *707/542–9474* ⊕ *whistlestop-antiques.com.*

TRAVEL SMART
NAPA AND
SONOMA

GETTING HERE AND AROUND

Most travelers to the Wine Country start their trip in San Francisco. Getting to southern Napa or Sonoma takes less than an hour in normal traffic. Using public transportation can be time-consuming. If you base yourself the Napa Valley towns of Napa, Yountville, or St. Helena, or in Sonoma or Healdsburg in Sonoma County, you'll be able to visit numerous tasting rooms and nearby wineries on foot.

The 511 SF Bay website (⊕ *511.org*) can help you plan trips to and within the Wine Country. *See the Planning sections at the front of each chapter for more public transit information.*

Contact 511 SF Bay. ⊕ *511.org.*

▌ AIR TRAVEL

Nonstop flights from New York to San Francisco take about 6½ hours, and with the three-hour time change, it's possible to leave JFK by 8 am and be in San Francisco before noon. Some flights require changing planes midway, making the total excursion between 8 and 9½ hours.

More than three dozen airlines serve San Francisco's airport, and a few of the same airlines also serve the airports in Oakland and Sacramento. Fares to San Francisco are often the cheapest, but the two smaller airports can sometimes be more convenient, especially if your destination is southern Napa. Alaska, American, Delta, jetBlue, and Southwest serve all three airports. United serves San Francisco and Sacramento. Frontier and Virgin America serve San Francisco. Allegiant serves Oakland. Allegiant, Alaska's subsidiary Horizon Air, American, and United serve Santa Rosa's Charles M. Schulz Sonoma County Airport. Horizon also serves Sacramento.

Airline Contacts Alaska Airlines. ☎ *800/252-7522* ⊕ *www.alaskaair.com.* **Allegiant.** ☎ *702/505-8888* ⊕ *www.allegiant-air.com.* **American Airlines.** ☎ *800/433-7300*

⊕ *www.aa.com.* **Delta Airlines.** ☎ *800/221-1212* ⊕ *www.delta.com.* **Frontier Airlines.** ☎ *801/401-9000* ⊕ *www.flyfrontier.com.* **jetBlue.** ☎ *800/538-2583* ⊕ *www.jetblue.com.* **Southwest Airlines.** ☎ *800/435-9792* ⊕ *www.southwest.com.* **United Airlines.** ☎ *800/864-8331* ⊕ *www.united.com.* **Virgin America.** ☎ *877/359-8474* ⊕ *www.virginamerica.com.*

AIRPORTS

The major gateway to the Wine Country is San Francisco International Airport (SFO), 60 miles from the city of Napa. Oakland International Airport (OAK), almost directly across San Francisco Bay, is actually closer to Napa, which is 50 miles away. Most visitors choose SFO, though, because it has more daily flights. Another option is to fly into Sacramento International Airport (SMF), about 68 miles from Napa and 76 miles from Sonoma. Wine Country regulars often fly into Santa Rosa's Charles M. Schulz Sonoma County Airport (STS), which receives daily nonstop flights from San Diego, Las Vegas, Los Angeles, Phoenix, Portland, and Seattle. The airport is 15 miles from Healdsburg. Avis, Budget, Enterprise, Hertz, and National rent cars here. ▌TIP→ Alaska allows passengers flying out of STS to check up to one case of wine for free.

Airport Information Charles M. Schulz Sonoma County Airport (*STS*). ✉ *2290 Airport Blvd., 1½ miles west of U.S. 101* ☎ *707/565-7243* ⊕ *www.sonomacountyairport.org.* **Oakland International Airport** (*OAK*). ✉ *1 Airport Dr., 2 miles west of I-880, Oakland* ☎ *510/563-3300* ⊕ *www.flyoakland.com.* **Sacramento International Airport** (*SMF*). ✉ *6900 Airport Blvd., off I-5* ☎ *916/929-5411* ⊕ *www.sacramento.aero/smf.* **San Francisco International Airport** (*SFO*). ✉ *McDonnell and Link Rds., San Francisco* ☎ *800/435-9736, 650/821-8211* ⊕ *www.flysfo.com.*

GROUND TRANSPORTATION

To the Wine Country: Two shuttle services serve Napa and Sonoma from both San Francisco International Airport and Oakland International Airport. Evans Airport Service, affiliated with California Wine Tours, is an option for travelers without cars staying in Napa or Yountville. The service, which costs $40 per person, drops you off at any hotel. If you're heading elsewhere, the company will arrange for taxi service from its drop-off point. The Sonoma County Airport Express shuttles passengers between the airports and the cities of Santa Rosa, Rohnert Park, and Petaluma for $34. Ask the driver to call ahead so that a taxi is waiting for you when you arrive.

If you'll be staying in the town of Napa, it's possible to take BART from SFO or OAK to the El Cerrito Del Norte station and then board VINE Bus 29. If you're headed to the town of Sonoma, transfer in Napa to Bus 25. Private limousine service costs up to $300, depending on your destination. SF Limo Express charges $50 an hour with a three-hour minimum for up to four people.

Charles M. Schulz Sonoma County Airport is just off U.S. 101 in Santa Rosa. Healdsburg is north of the airport via U.S. 101. For the town of Sonoma, drive south to Highway 12 and head east.

To San Francisco: If you're headed to downtown San Francisco, a taxi ride from San Francisco International Airport costs $50–$55. More economical are GO Lorrie's Airport Shuttle and SuperShuttle, both of which take you anywhere within the city limits for $18 per person. Both pick up passengers outside the airport's lower level near baggage claim. SF Limo Express charges $70 for a town car ride. Rates for ride-sharing services Uber and Lyft vary depending on the type of vehicle and the travel time. The smallest Uber or Lyft vehicle costs $97–$126 to Sonoma, $91–$116 to Napa, and $109–$141 to Santa Rosa.

Bay Area Rapid Transit (BART) commuter trains take you directly to downtown San Francisco. The trip takes about 30 minutes and costs $8.95. BAR the international ter minutes, depending Two SamTrans bu inexpensive option $2.25) and the K only one small can Board SamTrans buses on the

A taxi from Oakland International Airport to downtown San Francisco costs $41–$46.

The best public-transit option is BART. Follow signs in the terminal to the driverless BART shuttle train, which operates between the airport and the Coliseum station. After exiting the shuttle, you can purchase a ticket whose price covers the cost of shuttle and the train to your destination. The fare to San Francisco is $10.20.

Limos, Shuttles, and Ride Services

Evans Airport Service. ✉ *Napa Office and Airporter Terminal, 4075 Solano Ave., Napa* ☎ *707/255–1559* ⊕ *www.evanstransportation.com.* **GO Lorrie's Airport Shuttle.** ☎ *415/334–9000* ⊕ *www.gosfovan.com.* **Lyft.** ⊕ *www.lyft.com.* **SF Limo Express.** ☎ *415/990–6364* ⊕ *www.sflimoexpress. net.* **Sonoma County Airport Express.** ☎ *707/837–8700* ⊕ *www.airportexpressinc. com.* **SuperShuttle.** ☎ *800/258–3826* ⊕ *www. supershuttle.com.* **Uber.** ⊕ *www.uber.com.*

Public Transit
Bay Area Rapid Transit (BART). ☎ *415/989–2278* ⊕ *www.bart.gov.* **SamTrans.** ☎ *800/660–4287* ⊕ *www.samtrans.com.*

■ BUS AND COMMUTER TRAIN TRAVEL

The knee-jerk local reaction to the notion of getting to tasting rooms—or the Wine Country—via public transit is that it's impossible or will take forever, but it's definitely possible. The two easiest towns to visit are Napa and Sonoma (trips to either take about three hours), and both have numerous tasting rooms, restaurants, and lodgings in their downtown areas.

m San Francisco or Oakland, ake a BART train to the Cer- Norte station and then pick up Express Bus 29, which stops at the col Gateway Transit Center in down- own Napa. Once in Napa you can connect with VINE buses that travel up the entire valley to Calistoga. VINE Bus 25 connects the towns of Napa and Sonoma.

To Santa Rosa: Golden Gate Transit Bus 101 serves Santa Rosa, from whose Transit Mall you can transfer to buses serving Healdsburg, Sebastopol, and other Sonoma County destinations. Greyhound serves Santa Rosa from Oakland.

Bus Lines Golden Gate Transit.
☏ 415/455–2000 ⊕ www.goldengatetransit. org. **Greyhound.** ☏ 800/231–2222 ⊕ www. greyhound.com. **Sonoma County Transit.** ☏ 707/576–7433, 800/345–7433 ⊕ www. sctransit.com. **VINE.** ✉ Soscol Gateway Transit Center, 625 Burnell St., Napa ☏ 707/251–2800, 800/696–6443 ⊕ www.ridethevine.com.

■ CAR TRAVEL

A car is the most logical and convenient way to navigate Napa and Sonoma. Although some thoroughfares can get congested, especially during rush hour and on summer weekends, there are plenty of less trafficked routes. Parking is generally not a problem.

To drive to the Wine Country from San Francisco International, follow signs north out of the airport to Interstate 380, which leads to Interstate 280. As you approach San Francisco, follow signs for the Golden Gate Bridge. By the time you begin crossing the bridge, you're on U.S. 101. Head north for northern Sonoma County. For southern Sonoma County and the Napa Valley, head east on Highway 37 at the town of Novato, then follow Highway 121 into southern Sonoma. At Highway 12, turn north to reach the town of Sonoma. For the Napa Valley, continue east on Highway 121 to Highway 29 and head north.

From Oakland International, the best way to get to Sonoma County is via Interstate 880 north. Follow signs for Interstate 80 East/Interstate 580 West, which takes you across the Richmond–San Rafael Bridge. After you cross the bridge, follow the signs to U.S. 101 North. From here, continue north for northern Sonoma County or head east of Highway 37 for southern Sonoma County and the Napa Valley. A quicker option if you're heading to the Napa Valley is to stay on Interstate 80 to Highway 37 in Vallejo. Head west on Highway 37 and north on Highway 29, following the signs for Napa.

If you fly into Sacramento International, take Interstate 5 South to Interstate 80 West. Exit onto Highway 12 and continue west to Highway 29 north for the city of Napa. For the town of Sonoma continue west on Highway 121 and north on Highway 12.

From Sonoma's airport, take U.S. 101 south to Santa Rosa and then east and south on Highway 12 to reach Kenwood, Glen Ellen, and Sonoma; head north on U.S. 101 for Healdsburg; and head south on Laughlin Road and west on River Road for Guerneville, Forestville, Sebastopol, and other Russian River Valley towns. To reach the Napa Valley, take U.S. 101 south to the River Road exit and head east on Mark Springs West Road, Porter Creek Road, and Petrified Forest to Calistoga.

CAR RENTALS

If you're flying into the area, it's almost always easiest to pick up a car at the airport. You'll also find rental companies in major Wine Country towns. The beautiful landscapes make it a popular place for renting specialty vehicles, especially convertibles. Exotic Car Collection by Enterprise or the locally based City Rent-a-Car rent such vehicles. ■TIP➔ **When renting a specialty car, ask about mileage limits. Some companies stick you with per-mile charges if you exceed 100 or 150 miles a day.**

Most rental companies require you to be at least 20 years old to rent a car, but some agencies won't rent to those under 25; check when you book. Super Cheap Car Rentals, near San Francisco International, has competitive prices and, unlike many agencies, rents to drivers between 21 and 24 for no extra charge.

Car-rental costs in the area vary seasonally, but in San Francisco generally begin at $50 per day and $275 per week for an economy car with unlimited mileage. Rates can be slightly higher in Oakland and substantially higher in Sacramento, often offsetting any airfare savings. This doesn't include car-rental taxes and other surcharges and fees, which can add another 20% to the per-day rate.

Rental agencies in California aren't required to include liability insurance in the price of the rental. If you cause an accident, you may be liable. When in doubt about your own policy's coverage, take the liability coverage the agency offers.

Automobile Associations American Automobile Association (AAA). ☎ 800/222-4357 ⊕ www.aaa.com. **National Automobile Club.** ☎ 800/622-2136 ⊕ www.thenac.com.

Local Agencies City Rent-a-Car. ✉ 1433 Bush St., near Van Ness Ave., Polk Gulch ☎ 415/359-1331 ⊕ www.cityrentacar.com. **Super Cheap Car Rental.** ✉ 10 Rollins Rd., at Millbrae Ave., Millbrae ☎ 650/777-9993 ⊕ www.supercheapcar.com.

Major Agencies Alamo. ☎ 800/462-5266 ⊕ www.alamo.com. **Avis.** ☎ 800/633-3469 ⊕ www.avis.com. **Budget.** ☎ 800/218-7992 ⊕ www.budget.com. **Exotic Car Collection by Enterprise.** ☎ 415/292-2150, 866/458-9227 ⊕ exoticcars.enterprise.com/sanfrancisco. **Hertz.** ☎ 800/654-3131 ⊕ www.hertz.com. **National Car Rental.** ☎ 877/222-9058 ⊕ www.nationalcar.com.

GASOLINE

Gas is readily available on all but the most remote back roads. Expect to pay 10%–20% more than you would back home.

PARKING

Parking is rarely a problem in the Wine Country, as wineries and hotels have ample free parking. In some communities, street parking is limited to two or three hours during the day. There are often reasonably priced municipal lots downtown; signs will generally point you in the right direction.

ROAD CONDITIONS

Roads in the Wine Country are generally well maintained. Traffic jams do occur, though the biggest tie-ups you'll experience will likely be in and around San Francisco. Trying to negotiate morning and afternoon rush hours will add considerable time to your trip. On Sunday evening you'll encounter lots of traffic as you head back to San Francisco, but it's nothing compared with the crush of cars trying to leave town on a Friday afternoon. Traffic can be equally bad heading north from Oakland to Napa along Interstate 80, especially during the afternoon rush hour. For real-time traffic info, visit ⊕ 511.org or tune your radio to 740 AM and 106.9 FM, which broadcast traffic news every 10 minutes.

Once you've reached the Wine Country, the roads become less crowded and more scenic. Expect heavier traffic during rush hours, generally between 7 and 9 am and 4 and 6 pm. Things can also get congested on Friday and Sunday afternoons, when weekenders add to the mix. Highway 29, which runs the length of Napa Valley, can be slow going in summer, especially on weekends, and it can slow to a crawl around the town of St. Helena.

ROADSIDE EMERGENCIES

Dial 911 to report accidents on the road and to reach police, the highway patrol, or the fire department. The American Automobile Association (to members) and the National Automobile Club provide roadside assistance.

RULES OF THE ROAD

Carpool lanes. To encourage carpooling during rush hour, some freeways have special lanes for so-called high-occupancy vehicles (HOVs)—cars carrying more than one or two passengers. Look for the white diamond in the middle of the lane. Signs next to or above the lane indicate the hours that carpooling is in effect. If you get stopped for not having enough passengers, expect a fine of nearly $500.

Seatbelts. Seatbelts are required. Children must ride in child car seats in the backseat until they are eight years old or 4 feet 9 inches tall. Children under the age of two must ride in a rear-facing car seat.

Smartphone usage. State law bans drivers from using smartphones for any purpose, including mapping applications unless the device is mounted to a car's windshield or dashboard and can be activated with a single swipe or finger tap.

Speed limit, turns. The speed limit on city streets is 25 mph unless otherwise posted. A right turn after stopping at a red light is legal unless posted otherwise.

■TIP→ If you're wine tasting, either select a designated driver or be careful of your wine intake—the police keep an eye out for tipsy drivers.

▌ FERRY TRAVEL

The San Francisco Bay Ferry sails from the Ferry Building and Pier 41 in San Francisco to Vallejo ($13.80), where you can board VINE Bus 11 to the town of Napa. Buses sometimes fill in for the ferries.

Contact **San Francisco Bay Ferry.**
☏ *707/643–3779, 800/643–3779*
⊕ *sanfranciscobayferry.com.*

▌ TAXI TRAVEL

Taxis aren't common in the Wine Country, and choices in some areas are limited. Still, you might want to take a cab to and from dinner, especially if you want to indulge in a cocktail or a few glasses of wine. All cabs are metered: expect to pay $3 upon pickup and another $2.50–$3 per mile thereafter, depending on the city you're in. Taxi drivers usually expect a 15%–20% tip for good service. Cabs must be called rather than hailed.

Yellow Cab of Napa Valley serves the entire valley. Over in Sonoma County, Vern's Taxi serves the Sonoma Valley (Sonoma, Glen Ellen, Kenwood, Santa Rosa). Healdsburg Pedicab is a convenient option weekdays until midafternoon and until 10 pm on weekends.

Taxi Companies **Healdsburg Pedicab.**
☏ *707/696–2453* ⊕ *www.healdsburgpedicab. com.* **Vern's Taxi.** ☏ *707/938–8885* ⊕ *www. vernstaxi.com.* **Yellow Cab of Napa Valley.**
☏ *707/226–3731* ⊕ *www.yellowcabnapa.com.*

ESSENTIALS

▌ ACCOMMODATIONS

Wine Country inns and hotels range from low-key to sumptuous, and generally maintain high standards. Many inns are in historic Victorian buildings, and when rates include breakfast the preparations often involve fresh, local produce. Newer hotels tend to have a more modern, streamlined aesthetic and elaborate, spalike bathrooms, and many have excellent restaurants on-site. The towns of Napa and Santa Rosa have the widest selection of moderately priced rooms.

INFORMATION AND RESERVATIONS

BedandBreakfast.com has details about member inns in the Napa and Sonoma County. The Napa Valley Hotels & Resorts page on the Visit Napa Valley website lists hotels, inns, and other accommodations throughout Napa County. The Sonoma Hotels & Lodging page on the Visit Sonoma site has similarly comprehensive listings for Sonoma County. The members of the Sonoma Valley Bed & Breakfast Association operate noteworthy small inns and vacation-rental properties throughout the valley; Wine Country Inns represents 20 small lodgings throughout Sonoma County. You can check availability at its members' inns on the website, which can save you time. The various innkeepers share phone duties, so the level of assistance offered varies depending on whose turn it is.

Reservations are a good idea, especially from late spring through the fall harvest season and on many weekends. Two- or even three-night minimum stays are commonly required, especially at smaller lodgings; if you'd prefer to stay a single night, innkeepers are more flexible in winter. Some lodgings aren't suitable for kids, so ask before you make a reservation.

Contacts BedandBreakfast.com. ☎ 844/271-6829, 512/322-2710 ⊕ www. bedandbreakfast.com. **Napa Valley Hotels & Resorts.** ☎ 707/251-9188, 855/333-6272 ⊕ www.visitnapavalley.com/hotels. **Sonoma Hotels & Lodging.** ⊕ www.sonomacounty. com/hotels-lodging. **Wine Country Inns.** ☎ 800/946-3268 ⊕ www.winecountryinns.com.

FACILITIES

When pricing accommodations, always ask what's included. Some small inns may not have air-conditioning, so be sure to ask if you're visiting in July or August, when temperatures can reach 90°F. Most hotels have Wi-Fi, although it's not always free. Most large properties have pools and fitness rooms; those without usually have arrangements with nearby gyms, sometimes for a fee.

PRICES

Wine Country lodging prices, which on average exceed those even in high-end San Francisco, may come as an unpleasant surprise. Even the humblest accommodations start at nearly $200 a night in high season. Rates are often lower on weeknights, and generally about 20% lower in winter. If you're having difficulty finding something in your price range, remember that Napa and Santa Rosa have the widest selection of moderately priced rooms. Rates vary widely; call the property directly, but also check its website and online booking agencies.

Our local writers vet every hotel to recommend the best overnights in each price category, from budget to expensive. Unless otherwise specified, you can expect private bath, phone, and TV in your room. *Prices in the reviews are the lowest cost of a standard double room in high season. For expanded reviews, visit Fodors.com.*

▌ EATING OUT

Excellent meals can be found in all the major Wine Country towns, and tiny Yountville has become a culinary crossroads under the influence of chef Thomas Keller. In St. Helena the elegant

Restaurant at Meadowood, helmed by chef Christopher Kostow, has achieved almost as much critical acclaim as Keller's The French Laundry, yet is somewhat easier to get into. And the buzzed-about restaurants in Sonoma County, including Kyle and Katina Connaughton's Single-Thread and the Farmhouse Inn, offer equally intricate cuisine.

The Wine Country's top restaurants tend to serve what is often called "California cuisine," which incorporates elements of French and Italian cooking and emphasizes the use of fresh, local products. If the restaurant scene here has a weakness, it's the absence of a greater variety of cuisines. However, the number of immigrants from Latin America ensures that in almost any town you'll find good, inexpensive spots selling tacos, fajitas, and similar fare.

Vegetarians shouldn't have any trouble finding excellent choices on Wine Country menus. The region's fresh produce and California's general friendliness toward vegetarians mean that restaurants are usually willing to go out of their way to accommodate them.

The Wine Country's restaurants, though excellent, can really dent your wallet. If you're on a budget, many high-end delis prepare superb picnic fare. Stopping for lunch or brunch can be a cost-effective strategy at pricey restaurants, as can sitting at the bar and ordering appetizers instead of having a full meal. It also doesn't hurt to ask about a restaurant's corkage policy: some restaurants eliminate their corkage fee one night a week, or even every night, hoping to attract locals in the wine industry who would rather drink bottles from their own cellar than the restaurant's.

Except as noted in individual restaurant listings, dress is informal. Where reservations are indicated as essential, book a week or more ahead in summer and early fall. *Prices in the reviews are the average cost of a main course at dinner or, if dinner is not served, at lunch.*

MEALS AND MEALTIMES

Lunch is typically served from 11:30 to 2:30 or 3, and dinner service in most restaurants starts at 5 or 5:30 and ends around 9 or 10. The Wine Country is short on late-night dining, so don't put off eating until any later than 10. Most hotels and inns offer breakfast service—anything from a basic continental breakfast to a lavish buffet to an individually prepared feast—but if yours doesn't, you'll find a good bakery in just about every Wine Country town.

Some restaurants close for a day or two a week, most often on Tuesday or Wednesday, when the number of visitors is fewest, so be sure to check in advance if you're planning on dining midweek. Unless otherwise noted, the restaurants listed here are open daily for lunch and dinner.

PAYING

Almost all restaurants in the Wine Country accept credit cards. On occasion, you might find a bakery or a casual café that takes cash only. *For guidelines on tipping see Tipping, below.*

RESERVATIONS AND DRESS

The sheer number of Wine Country restaurants means you can always find an empty table somewhere, but it pays to make a reservation, even if only a day or two before you visit. In reviews we mention reservations only when essential (i.e., there's no other way you'll ever get a table) or when they are not accepted. For popular restaurants, book as far ahead as you can, and reconfirm as soon as you arrive. If your party is large, it's wise to call ahead to check the reservations policy. Tables at many Wine Country restaurants can be reserved through OpenTable and Urbanspoon.

Customs regarding attire tend to be fairly relaxed in Sonoma except in the most expensive restaurants. Matters are slightly more formal in the Napa Valley, where you're less likely to see jeans or shorts at dinner except at casual restaurants. In both counties, jackets are rarely required for men, though they're necessary for both lunch and dinner at The

French Laundry and would certainly be appropriate at top-tier restaurants such as The Restaurant at Meadowood and SingleThread Farms Restaurant. We mention dress only when men are required to wear a jacket or a jacket and tie.

Contacts Open Table. ⊕ *www.opentable.com.* **Urbanspoon.** ⊕ *www.urbanspoon.com.*

WINES, BEER, AND SPIRITS

Nowhere in the United States are you more likely to see someone enjoying a glass or two of wine not only with dinner, but with lunch as well. Only the smallest dives and most casual cafés lack a wine menu; lists here are usually strongest in local bottles, with other West Coast wines and perhaps some French and Italian wines as well. Upscale restaurants generally have full bars. Although it's legal to serve alcohol as late as 2 am in California, most restaurants close down by 10 pm or so.

▮ HOURS OF OPERATION

Winery tasting rooms are generally open from 10 or 11 am to 4:30 or 5 pm. Larger wineries are usually open every day, but some of the smaller ones may open only on weekends or for three or four days. Tuesday and Wednesday are the quietest days of the week for wine touring. If you have a particular winery in mind, check its hours before you visit, and keep in mind that many wineries are open by appointment only.

▮ MONEY

The sweet life costs a pretty penny in most Wine Country areas, where even a basic hotel tends to cost around $200 per night. That said, it is possible to stick to a lower budget if you're willing to stay in a fairly basic motel, eat at some of the less expensive restaurants, and take advantage of the many picnicking opportunities.

Prices for attractions and activities are given for adults. Reduced fees are almost always available for children, students, and senior citizens.

▮ SAFETY

The Wine Country is generally a safe place for travelers who observe all normal precautions. Most visitors will feel safe walking at night in all the smaller towns and in the downtown area of towns like Sonoma. Still, the largest towns, such as Napa and Santa Rosa, have a few rougher areas (typically far from the tourist spots), so you should check with a local before you go wandering in unknown neighborhoods. Car break-ins are not particularly common here, although it's always best to remove valuables from your car, or at least keep them out of sight.

The main danger you face in the Wine Country is the threat of drunk drivers. Keep an eye out for drivers who may have had one too many glasses of wine, as well as for bikers who might be hidden around the next bend in the road.

▮ SHIPPING

Because alcoholic beverages are regulated by individual states, shipping wine back home can be easy or complicated, depending on where you live. Some states (e.g., Alabama and Utah) prohibit direct shipments from wineries. Others allow the shipment of limited quantities—a certain number of gallons or cases per year—if a winery has purchased a permit to do so. The penalties for noncompliance can be steep: it's a felony, for instance, to ship wines to Utah (this includes shipping the wines yourself). Since selling wine is their business, wineries are well versed in the regulations.

If you decide to send wines back home, keep in mind that most states require that someone 21 or older sign for the delivery. The Wine Institute, which represents California wineries, has up-to-date information about shipping within the United States and abroad.

Information Wine Institute. ⊕ *www.winein- stitute.org/initiatives/stateshippinglaws.*

▪ SPECIAL-INTEREST TOURS AND EDUCATION

BIKING, HIKING, KAYAKING

Biking, hiking, and kayaking tours of the Wine Country range from one-hour and one-day excursions to weeklong vacations with lavish picnic lunches, leisurely dinners, and stays at luxury inns. You might pay less than $100 for a half- or full-day trip; multiday excursions can cost $250–$500 per person per day.

Backroads. This Berkeley-based outfit conducts several premium multiday guided tours of various levels of difficulty. A typical Sonoma County tour might start in the Russian River Valley and take in Dry Creek Valley and Alexander Valley wineries as well. Some Napa Valley tours cover out-of-the-way wineries and the greatest hits. Overnight stays are at top hotels, luggage transfers and other logistics are taken care of, and support vans are stocked with all the comforts and necessities riders need. ☎ *800/462–2848* ⊕ *www.backroads.com* 🖃 *From $1,998.*

Napa & Sonoma Valley Bike Tours. Afternoon and all-day guided and self-guided tours of wineries, vineyards, and other sights are this company's specialty. The pace is leisurely, and all-day tours include a picnic lunch at a winery. One combination tour starts with an early-morning balloon ride. ☎ *707/251–8687 for Napa trips*, *707/996–2453 for Sonoma trips* ⊕ *www.napavalleybiketours.com* 🖃 *From $108.*

Wine Country Bikes. This family-owned Healdsburg outfitter rents bikes by the day and organizes single- and multi-day trips throughout Sonoma County. ☎ *707/473–0610, 800/922–4537* ⊕ *www.winecountry-bikes.com* 🖃 *From $149 for all-day trips.*

Wine Country Trekking. This well-regarded company has multiday self-guided "luxury on foot" experiences. Participants hike through vineyards, meadows, and mountains, stopping at wineries along the way and staying in stylish small inns and hotels. The excursions include hiking and running Sonoma Valley treks and a

Napa Valley hike. ✉ *Glen Ellen* ☎ *707/935–4497* ⊕ *winecountrytrekking.com* 🖃 *From $1,000.*

CULINARY TOURS AND CLASSES

Tours usually include one or more of the following: cooking classes, festive dinners at fine restaurants, excursions to local markets, and the opportunity to meet some of the area's top chefs. Tours can last from a few days to a week and start at around $500 per day, accommodations included.

Culinary Institute of America at Copia. In late 2016 the institute reopened the long-dormant Copia food and wine facility adjacent to the Oxbow Public Market in Napa and began offering daily classes and demonstrations. Among the topics covered are sparkling wines, sauces, honey, ancient grains, cheeses, food-wine pairing, preserving foods, and making hors d'oeuvres that wow guests. Some classes are family-oriented. Weekend classes are also held at the institute's Greystone campus in St. Helena. ✉ *500 1st St., near McKinstry St., Napa* ☎ *707/967–2500* ⊕ *enthusiasts.ciachef.edu/cia-at-copia* 🖃 *From $15.*

Culinary Institute of America at Greystone. The chef-instructors at the institute's Greystone campus present live one-hour cooking demonstrations on most weekends. Attendees taste the dish made, accompanied by a glass of wine. Hands-on cooking classes cover topics such as baking, grilling, making sauces, and pairing food and wine. ✉ *2555 Main St., St. Helena* ☎ *707/967–1100* ⊕ *enthusiasts.ciachef.edu/ca-cooking-demonstrations-and-tours* 🖃 *From $25.*

Food and Wine Trails. Providing its clients with insights into more than just Napa and Sonoma wines and wine making is the goal of this company that folds spa and restaurant trips and non-wine activities into its custom itineraries. ☎ *800/367–5348* ⊕ *www.foodandwinetrails.com* 🖃 *Varies depending on itinerary and time of year.*

Ramekins Culinary School. Locals and visitors attend the wine-and-food events and hands-on and demonstration cooking classes at Ramekins. The topics range from soups, game, and the cuisine of Peru to the flavors of fall and how to shop at a farmers' market; current and former Wine Country restaurant chefs teach some of the courses. Winemaker dinners often introduce up-and-coming talents. ✉ *450 W. Spain St., Sonoma* ☎ *707/933–0450* ⊕ *www.ramekins.com* ✉ *From $65.*

WINERY TOURS

With several million visitors to the Wine Country every year, dozens of tour companies have sprung up to provide tours. Many of these companies are well organized and will chauffeur you to places you might not otherwise find on your own. Whether you're content to tour the Wine Country in a full-size bus with dozens of other passengers or you want to spring for your own private limo to take you to your favorite wineries, there are plenty of operators who can accommodate you. If you know the wineries, regions, or even the grape varietals that interest you, these operators can help you develop a satisfying itinerary.

Most tours last from five to seven hours, with stops at four or five wineries. Rates vary widely, from $80 per person for a day of touring to $250 or more, depending on the type of vehicle and whether the tour includes other guests. Some rates include tasting fees, but others do not. You can also book a car and driver by the hour for shorter trips. Rates for a limo generally run $50–$85 per hour, and there's usually a two- or three-hour minimum.

Perata Luxury Tours & Car Services. Perata's customized private tours, led by well-trained, knowledgeable drivers, are tailored to its patrons' interests; you can create your own itinerary or have your guide craft one for you. Tours, in luxury SUVs, cover Napa and Sonoma. The options include exclusive, appointment-only boutique wineries. ☎ *707/227–8271* ⊕ *www.perataluxurycarservices.com* ✉ *From $85 per hr for 2 guests (includes tax, fuel, and 15% gratuity but not tasting fees).*

Platypus Wine Tours. The emphasis at Platypus is on "fun" experiences at off-the-beaten-path wineries. Expect intimate winery experiences with jolly, well-informed guides. You can join an existing tour with other guests or book a private one. ☎ *707/253–2723* ⊕ *www.platypustours.com* ✉ *From $110 (excludes tasting fees).*

Segway of Healdsburg. There's nothing quite like watching the vineyards zip by from the vantage of a Segway. After a 20-minute safety and training session, the solicitous guides at Shira Steiger's company conduct tours to two boutique Russian River Valley wineries (the lineup varies) for a total of two hours. There's also a tour through Armstrong Redwoods State Natural Reserve in Guerneville. Look for off-season deals through Groupon and similar websites. ✉ *Healdsburg* ☎ *707/953–3477* ⊕ *segwayofhealdsburg.com* ✉ *From $99.*

Valley Wine Tours. Historic, family-owned wineries are the specialty of this Sonoma-based company that provides a gourmet picnic lunch—on china with cloth napkins, no less. ☎ *707/975–6462* ⊕ *www.valleywinetours.com* ✉ *From $135 (includes tasting fees).*

Woody's Wine Tours. The amiable, well-informed Woody Guderian favors small wineries but will customize a tour to suit your taste and budget. In addition to winery tours in both Napa and Sonoma, Woody and his guides also conduct tours of craft breweries. ☎ *707/396–8235* ⊕ *www.woodyswinetours.com* ✉ *From $80 per hr (excludes tasting fees).*

▌ TAXES

Sales tax is 8% in Napa County and 8¼%–9¼% in Sonoma County. The tax on hotel rooms adds 9%–14% to your bill in Sonoma County and 14% in Napa County.

▌ TIME

California is on Pacific Time. Chicago is two hours ahead of the West Coast, and New York is three hours ahead. Depending on whether daylight saving time is in effect, London is either 8 or 9 hours ahead and Sydney is 17 or 18 hours ahead.

▌ TIPPING

TIPPING GUIDELINES FOR NAPA AND SONOMA	
Bartender	About 15%, starting at $1 per drink at casual places
Bellhop	$2–$5 per bag, depending on the level of the hotel
Hotel concierge	$5 or more, if he or she performs a service for you
Hotel doorman, room service, or valet	$3–$5
Hotel maid	$3–$5 a day (either daily or at the end of your stay, in cash)
Taxi Driver	15%–20%, but round up the fare to the next dollar amount
Tour Guide	10%–15% of the cost of the tour
Waiter	18%–22%, with 20% being the minimum at high-end restaurants; nothing additional if a service charge is added to the bill

▌ VISITOR INFORMATION

Visitor Centers California Welcome Center. ✉ 9 4th St., at Wilson St., Santa Rosa ☎ 800/404-7673 ⊕ visitcalifornia.com/attraction/california-welcome-center-santa-rosa. **Napa Valley Welcome Center.** ✉ 600 Main St., at 5th St., Napa ☎ 707/251-5895 ⊕ www.visitnapavalley.com/welcome_centers.htm. **Sonoma Valley Visitors Center.** ✉ 453 1st St. E, east side of Sonoma Plaza, Sonoma ☎ 707/996-1090, 866/996-1090 ⊕ www.sonomavalley.com.

Visitor Information Sonoma Valley Visitors Bureau. ☎ 707/996-1090, 866/996-1090 ⊕ www.sonomavalley.com. **Visit Napa Valley.** ☎ 707/251-5895, 855/847-6272 ⊕ www.visitnapavalley.com. **Visit Sonoma.** ☎ 707/522-5800, 800/576-6662 ⊕ www.sonomacounty.com.

Websites and Apps CellarPass. ☎ 707/255-4390 ⊕ www.cellarpass.com. **VinoVisit.** ☎ 888/252-8990 ⊕ www.vinovisit.com. **Wine Country.** ⊕ www.winecountry.com/regions. **Winery Finder.** ⊕ www.econcierges.com.

Wines and Wineries Alexander Valley Winegrowers. ☎ 888/289-4637 ⊕ www.alexandervalley.org. **Carneros Wine Alliance.** ☎ 707/996-4140 ⊕ www.carneros.com. **Heart of Sonoma Valley Winery Association.** ☎ 707/431-1137 ⊕ www.heartofsonomavalley.com. **Napa Valley Vintners Association.** ☎ 707/963-3388 ⊕ www.napavintners.com. **Russian River Wine Road.** ☎ 707/433-4335, 800/723-6336 ⊕ www.wineroad.com. **Sonoma County Vintners.** ☎ 707/522-5828 ⊕ www.sonomawine.com. **Sonoma Valley Vintners & Growers Alliance.** ☎ 707/935-0803 ⊕ www.sonomavalleywine.com. **West Sonoma Coast Vintners.** ⊕ www.westsonomacoast.com. **Winegrowers of Dry Creek Valley.** ☎ 707/433-3031 ⊕ www.drycreekvalley.org.

INDEX

PHOTO CREDITS

Front cover: Walter Bibikow / AWL Images Ltd [Description: Napa Valley, California]. 1, Ljupco Smokovski/Shutterstock. 2, Rebecca Gosselin Photography. 6, Robert Holmes. **Chapter 1: Experience Napa and Sonoma:** 8-9, Robert Holmes. 14 (left), Terry Joanis/Frog's Leap. 14 (top right), Round Pond Estate. 14 (bottom right), French Laundry. 15 (top left), Vincent Thompson, Fodors.com member. 15 (right), Napa Valley Bike Tours. 15 (bottom left), The Culinary Institute of America. 16 (left), Far Niente+Dolce+Nickel & Nickel. 16 (top right), Artesa Vineyards and Winery. 16 (bottom right), Rocco Ceselin. 17 (top left), Eric Risberg/Schramsberg Vineyards. 17 (right), The Hess Collection. 17 (bottom left), M. J. Wickham. 18 (left). Merry Edwards Winery. 18 (top right), Laurence G. Sterling/ Iron Horse Vineyards. 18 (bottom right), Copain Wines. 19 (top left), Robert Holmes. 19 (right), Matanzas Creek. 19 (bottom left), Rocco Ceselin/Ram's Gate Winery. **Chapter 2: Visiting Wineries and Tasting Rooms:** 29, 30, and 38, Robert Holmes. 42, Warren H. White. **Chapter 3: Napa Valley:** 53, Robert Holmes. 55 (top), Megan Reeves Photography. 55 (bottom), Courtesy of Napa Valley Balloons, Inc.. 56, Andy Dean Photography / Shutterstock. 60, Napa Valley Wine Train. 65, Avis Mandel. 67, Robert Holmes. 77, di Rosa. 80, Teodora George | Dreamstime.com. 84, OPENKITCH-ENPhotography. 95, Far Niente+Dolce+Nickel & Nickel. 96, Opus One. 100, Olaf Beckman. 107, The Culinary Institute of America. 113, Avis Mandel. 114, Scott Chebagia. 123, Smcfeeters | Dreamstime.com. 131, Calistoga Ranch. **Chapter 4: Sonoma Valley:** 135, ivanastar/iStockphoto. 136, James Fanucchi. 137 (bottom), Stevan Nordstrom. 138, Robert Holmes Photography. 145, Rocco Ceselin/Ram's Gate Winery. 149, Nigel Wilson/Flickr. 155, 2012 LeoGong. 162, Benziger Family Winery. **Chapter 5: Northern Sonoma, Russian River and West Country:** 171, Eric Wolfinger/Single Thread. 172, Sonoma County Tourism. 173 (left), Martinelli Winery. 173 (right), Copain Wines. 174, Helio San Miguel. 185, Matt Armendariz. 188, Robert Holmes. 191 and 194, Warren H. White. 213, Sonoma County Tourism. 221, Mitch Tobias, courtesy of Paul Hobbs Winery. 225, Matanzas Creek. 230, Joe Shlabotnik/Flickr. 232, Jeffrey M. Frank/Shutterstock. **Back cover, from left to right:** Lee Jorgensen; Glen Ellen Star; Napa Valley Wine Train. **Spine:** Sonoma County Tourism. **About Our Writer:** Daniel Mangin, courtesy of J. Rodby.

ABOUT OUR WRITER

 Daniel Mangin returned to California, where he's maintained a home for three decades, after two stints at the Fodor's editorial offices in New York City, the second one as the Editorial Director of Fodors.com and the Compass American Guides. While at Compass he was the series editor for the *California Wine Country* guide and commissioned the *Oregon Wine Country* and *Washington Wine Country* guides. A wine lover whose earliest visits to Napa and Sonoma predate the Wine Country lifestyle, Daniel is delighted by the evolution in wines, wine making, and hospitality. With several dozen wineries less than a half-hour's drive from home, he often finds himself transported as if by magic to a tasting room bar, communing with a sophisticated Cabernet or savoring the finish of a smooth Pinot Noir.